FILTERS AND FILTRATION HANDBOOK

GULF PUBLISHING COMPANY
Book Division
Houston, London, Paris, Tokyo

FILTERS AND FILTRATION HANDBOOK

This edition published 1981
by Gulf Publishing Company
Houston, Texas

Simultaneously published in 1981
by The Trade & Technical Press Ltd,
Crown House, Morden, Surrey SM4 5EW, England.
Copyright© 1981 by The Trade & Technical Press Ltd.

ISBN 0–87201–283–2

Library of Congress Catalog Card No. 81–84307

PREFACE

The basic elements of our Earth, air, water and soil, have all been subject to contamination by natural suspended impurities since time began, and nature, taking its own time and course, has evolved a means of purifying most of these natural contaminants, ready for recycling, in order to maintain the balance and keep this "great big world" turning. Modern man has introduced countless artificial impurities into an industrial society, posing problems of contamination for which there is no natural progress of recyclement and no time to spare. The matter is urgent. The problem enormous and still growing. The solution? There is no one solution. The problems are so varied, complicated, changing, and the possible solutions so numerous that the Publishers have produced this 1st Edition, FILTERS AND FILTRATION HANDBOOK for the very purpose of providing most, if not all, the practical answers to contamination in industry as faced by the engineer. The work is comprehensive; incorporating principles, types, media, construction, application, selection, data and purchasing information, with means of easy reference and an adequate subject index. It contrives to combine in one volume, all essential and much useful information and data on filters and filtration.

The Publishers

CONTENTS

SECTION 1

Basics

Filters and Separators

A FILTER is basically a device for separating one substance from another — hence filtration is basically a process of *separation*. Immediately this expands the scope of filtration beyond the use of *filters,* as such. It must equally well include *separating* devices which work on other than pure filtering mechanics.

Two immediate problems then arise. Where to stop — and how to group and classify the various types of filters and separators. There is no complete answer to either, except that the various methods and processes of filtration and/or separation fall broadly into four categories:-

   i) Solids-gas separation

  ii) Solids-liquids separation

 iii) Liquids-liquids separation

 iv) Solids-solids separation.

The broad field of solids-gas separation is mainly represented by air filters and air filtration services, but also includes industrial gas processing, *etc.* The former uses mainly filters; the latter mainly separators, precipitators and scrubbers; plus filters as necessary.

Five Lakos in-line model separators (installed in common manifold), act as a prefilter to a deep-bed sand media ultrafiltration system, reducing the necessary backflushing of the deep-bed system from once an hour to once a day.

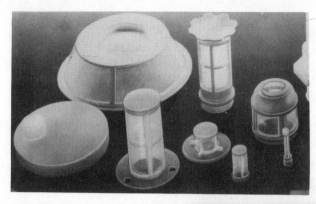

Moulded nylon filters and strainers.
(Plastic Engineers (New Milton) Ltd).

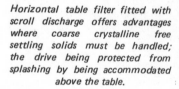

Horizontal table filter fitted with
scroll discharge offers advantages
where coarse crystalline free
settling solids must be handled;
the drive being protected from
splashing by being accommodated
above the table.

Solids-liquids separation is also an obvious field for mechanical filtration as such, but varying widely in volume requirements. Equally, it is a practical field for the application of inertial separation, particularly for process industries, and other methods which can readily be automated or semi-automated.

Liquids-liquids and solids-solids separation are more restrictive in the types of filters or separators which can be used successfully, and economically. These categories, therefore, represent more specialized fields of filtration/separation. Yet they are particularly significant in many industrial processes, although the process involved may be marginal or beyond representative coverage of filtration/separation. A *basic* method of liquids-liquids separation, for example, is distillation or thermal splitting — not a process to be elaborated on in a book covering filtration. Similarly, the *simplest* form of solids-solids separation where the solids involved are of different physical size is by *sieving*. Here the process is too obvious to require more than passing comment on sieve, mesh or screen sizes. Between these two extremes there are, however, specific processes which demand individual coverage for liquids-liquids separation in particular — inertial separators, precipitators, coalescers, *etc,* right up to the fringe subject of homogenization.

This, in fact, has been the main problem in the compilation of this Handbook — coverage of all filter types, related to process applications. Ideally, too, one would like to be positive in stating which type of filter is best for a particular job (or why type A is better than type B), but that is not a completely realistic question. Certain types of filters, or separators, are more or less standard choice for certain applications; but in other cases there are several possible alternatives to consider, offering comparable performance.

The main problems to be answered, in fact, are what you *want* to do, resolved as what you *need* to do, and the efficiency and cost-effectiveness of the possible solutions. There can be a danger in over-simplifying such answers. For example, Fig 1 presents a picture of the range of contaminant

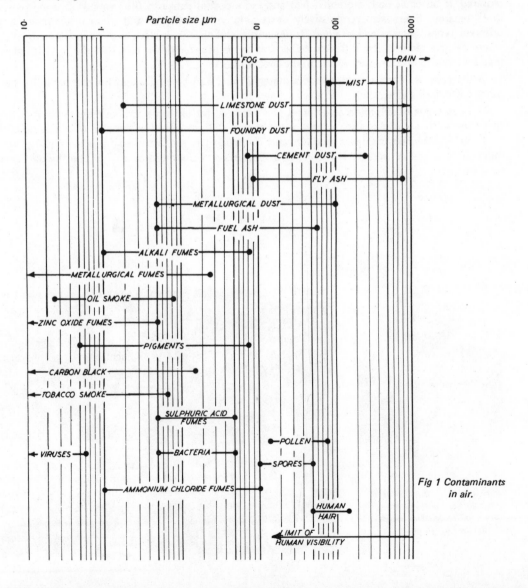

Fig 1 Contaminants in air.

particles which may be present in air. (These are further delineated in more specific detail in the chapter on *Contaminants*). The type of contaminants present, and their concentration, will obviously depend on the environment. A fabric dust collector is capable of filtering out contaminants ranging from the largest size down to about 0.1 μm — or the complete range illustrated, but would only be justified in particular circumstances (*eg* treating a heavily contaminated industrial atmosphere). Simple panel filters would be more than adequate for most other applications.

The filtering *range* of a particular type of filter or separator can also be misleading in terms of both efficiency and cost-effectiveness. The finer the filter the more readily it becomes clogged in the presence of coarser contaminants. In many cases, therefore, where fine or ultra-fine filtering is required, it becomes both more efficient and more cost-effective to filter in stages, using two or more separate filters with progressively decreasing cut-off ratings. And these filters may be of different types. Screens and strainers, for example, still have their place as primary filters in an era where particle removal (by filtration or separation) is possible down to 0.001 μm (*eg* with membrane filters and possibly with electrostatic precipitators).

In the case of filters, too, the media material must also be considered for compatibility (and other possible side effects).

The size range of sulphuric acid fumes and bacteria, for example, is about the same. An ultra-fine filter with a cut-off rating of the order of 0.2—0.3 μm would be capable of removing both from air — provided the filter medium and its housing is not attacked by acid. Equally, it is improbable that the need for removing both bacteria *and* sulphuric acid would be the particular requirement.

'Mistkop' filter drum as used for dust extraction from precision tap girders (right). (Belisle Filtration Ltd).

These give rise to reasonably closely defined groups of separating devices — *eg* centrifuges, cyclones, *etc* working on inertial principles; and others often described by purpose, although they may be essentially basic filter or separator types adapted for a specific purpose. *Clarifiers,* for example, specifically remove solid impurities from a single liquid phase. This solids-liquids separation duty may be performed by basic mechanical filters, precoat filters, filter presses, or specific types of centrifuges, depending on the media, volume and specific requirements involved. A *purifier,* on the other hand, is more restrictive by definition. It separates a denser liquid from a lighter liquid, *ie* is a liquids-liquids separator. In the same theme a *classifier* is, or should be, a solids-solids separator, but the description is not always used this way. Also progressive development has greatly extended the competitiveness and scope of application of specific types of filters and separators.

The centrifuge, for example — and particularly the decanter centrifuge — has to some considerable extent outstripped the filter press and other types of filters for applications in the process and chemical industries, as well as finding new applications. This trend could now reverse with continual improvements in filter press mechanization and automation; and improvements in other process filter types and the appearance of more 'packaged' equipment.

Equally, 'standard' types of filters for general or specific use outside the process industries now cover virtually all possible requirements, defined broadly by type and application. Chapter subjects have been arranged in groups on this basis, cross referenced where thought desirable or necessary.

New filtration problems continue to arise, many calling for advanced techniques. Particularly critical applications are in filtration for nuclear power plant at one extreme, to the removal of bacteria and micro-emboli in biomedicine at the other. Equally, too, sterile air is a basic requirement in the manufacture of pharmaceuticals. Brewers, winemakers and soft drink manufacturers also need to remove unwanted yeasts and micro-organisms from their products.

Bank of hermetic desludgers for champagne clarification, Germany. (Westfalia Separators)

The range of filter *performance* required is thus vast. From removal of micro-organisms down to 0.2 μm in size (the smallest bacteria) or better (the size of the polio virus is only 0.025 μm) — particles only visible under an electron microscope; up to abrasive particles of the order of 50 μm size acceptable without harm by some machines. Challenging, competitive fields for mechanical filters, precipitators and separators.

Materials, too, have been a subject of much development and change. Many of the traditional materials for mechanical filters retain competitive performance with cost effectiveness. New materials have mainly added to the choice and scope of filter media in the range from about 5 μm up. Below that level of contaminant size the newer materials and techniques have provided protection hitherto unrealized, except possibly by asbestos fibres. But here the considerable health hazards held to be present to people working with asbestos has meant that virtually all filter manufacturers have worked towards the complete elimination of asbestos, particularly as there are now equally efficient and cost-effective materials capable of performing similar duties, usually with greatly reduced bulk.

A word on units might also be appropriate. Despite 'metrication' the UK has never *fully* adopted SI units to the exclusion of English units. Some industries have; others have started to and then reverted to English units or a mixture of both. The subject of filtration and separation covers a whole range of industries and commercial applications which in their 'working' language are not uniform in the units they continue to employ. This confusion is not of engineers' and designers' making.

The basis adopted in this book is to employ SI units where more or less universally recognized — *eg* μm or micrometres (originally microns) for particle size, and for such UK industries which have fully adopted metric units (*eg* the compressed air industry). The bulk of quantitative figures quoted remain in English units followed by metric equivalents.

TABLE I — MICROMETRES (MICRONS) TO MICROINCHES

Micro-metres	Micrometres (Microns)									
	0	0.1	0.2	0.3	0.4	0.5	0.6	0.7	0.8	0.9
0	—	4	8	12	16	20	24	28	32	36
1	40	43	47	51	55	59	63	67	71	75
2	79	83	87	91	94	98	102	106	110	114
3	118	122	126	130	134	138	142	146	150	154
4	157	161	165	169	173	177	181	185	189	193
5	197	201	205	209	213	217	220	224	228	232
6	236	240	244	248	252	256	260	264	268	272
7	276	280	283	287	291	295	299	303	307	311
8	315	319	323	327	331	335	339	343	346	350
9	354	358	362	366	370	374	378	382	386	390
10	394	—	—	—	—	—	—	—	—	—

Contaminants

CONTAMINANTS ARE normally present in all fluids, *ie* gases and liquids. Where contamination is significant it becomes necessary (or obligatory) to separate contaminants from the basic fluid so as to reduce contamination to acceptable levels. Contaminants may be solids or semi-solids, in which case they can normally be removed by filtration. Fluid contaminants in fluids normally need more specialized separation treatment.

Filtration and separation are, in fact, synonymous processes in that both involve separation of products, although the techniques involved may differ considerably. There is also the fact that filtration and separation are not restricted to pollution control (*ie* removal of contaminants). Separation of one product from another is also an important part of many production processes (*eg* grinding, drying, dehydration, pneumatic conveying, *etc*); or recovery of separate products from a mixture. In the latter case in particular there can be a complete absence of contaminants as such.

Filtering involves, basically, the screening or mechanical separation of solids from fluids. Except for process industries the fluid is usually the working medium and such solids as may be present are contaminants. Removal of such contaminants is then a desirable, and often necessary, feature to ensure proper functioning of the machine with which the working medium is associated. In process industries involving a mixture of solids and fluid, one or other may be a contaminant or a carrier, although it is more usual that the fluid is the carrier. Separation of solids and fluid may be an essential part of processing involving filtering, but the cleaned fluid or filtrate may only be of secondary value, or indeed a waste product. The need for separation in such cases is specific, and obvious. When dealing with working fluids, however, filtering is essentially a protective process and an appreciation of the contaminants involved is necessary in order to arrive at a satisfactory degree of protection.

The critical factor in the case of solid contaminants in a fluid is the particle size. Theoretically, at least, solid particles will settle out of a still fluid under the action of gravity with a vertical velocity or settling rate proportional to the particle density and the square of its diameter, and inversely proportional to the viscosity of the fluid —

$$\text{Velocity} \propto \frac{(\text{particle diameter})^2}{\text{fluid viscosity}} \times \text{density of particle}$$

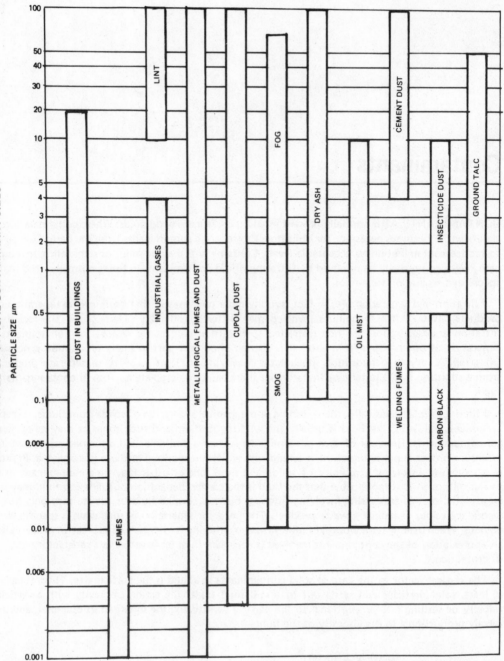

TABLE IA – RANGE OF TYPICAL CONTAMINANT SIZES

PARTICLE SIZE μm

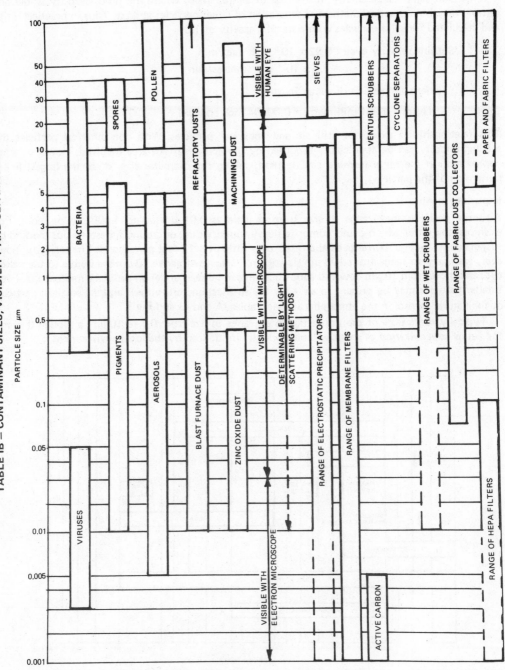

TABLE IB — CONTAMINANT SIZES, VISIBILITY AND SEPARATION

This is of significance chiefly in the case of air (or gases) where the fluid viscosity is low and *settling* may be a practical method of separation of larger particles at least. Thus in practical units, and calculated for solid particles with a specific gravity of 1.0

$$\text{Settling velocity in air} = 5.92 \times 10^{-5} \times d^2 \text{ feet/min}$$
$$= 1.8 \times 10^{-5} \times d^2 \text{ metres/min}$$

where d = particle diameter in μm

(1 μm = 0.001 millimetre = 0.00004 inch approx)

This relationship is exact for still air and spherical particles. With non-spherical particles the settling velocity can be appreciably modified by the actual surface area involved. However, as an approximation the same formula can be used, taking the diameter size 'd' as the largest linear dimension of the particle.

Impurities in Air

Airborne particles may range in size from as little as 0.01 μm up to 1 000 μm or more. For example, the latter which could comprise heavy foundry dust or ground limestone dust, would be suspended in thermal currents of the order of a little over 12 feet per second. The majority, however, are likely to range from 100 μm size down. Particles of above 10 μm are visible to the naked eye; and those from 10 μm down to about 0.2 μm can be seen under an ordinary microscope. Even smaller particles may be present in air — *eg* the smallest bacteria viruses and the smallest particles of the natural aerosol in the atmosphere — see Tables IA and IB and Fig 1.

Typically some 90% of the impurities in air range in size from 0.1 to 10 μm, although this and the actual *concentration* of solids will be markedly influenced by the local environment.

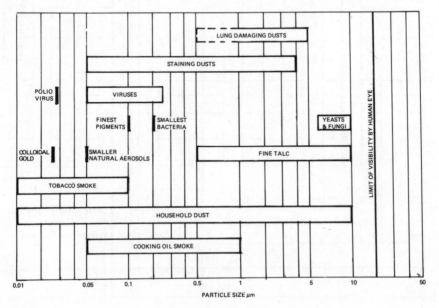

Fig 1 Impurities in air.

TABLE II — APPROXIMATE SETTLING VELOCITIES IN STILL AIR
(Nominally spherical particles of sg = 1)

Particle size μm	Settling Velocity	
	ft/min	m/min
1000	800	245
600	600	183
500	500	150
400	450	137
300	400	122
200	250	75
100	60	18
90	48	14.5
80	38	11.5
70	29	9.0
60	21	6.5
50	15	4.5
40	9.5	3.0
30	5.35	1.6
20	2.33	0.7
10	0.60	0.2
5	0.15	0.045
1	0.006	0.0018
0.1	0.00006	0.000018

Typical settling velocities generally applicable to atmospheric impurities are given in Table II. With very small particles the settling velocity is so low that these particles are effectively permanently suspended. This effect is further enhanced by Brownian movement of the molecules in the carrier fluid. Thus for all practical purposes particles of 1 μm size and smaller are permanently suspended in still air.

If the air is in motion very much larger particles may remain in suspension, particularly if the flow is turbulent. Thus considering air again as the carrier fluid, particles of up to 10 μm size are readily suspended by relatively gentle air movement, whilst particles as large as 100 μm may be suspended when strong vertical air velocities are involved, for example, 1 foot per second or more, (such as might be present in flue gases).

Effect on Humans

The average person breathes about 440 ft^3 (12.5 m^3) or 35 lb (16 kg) of air each day. Normal atmospheric air is usually far from clean, but the actual concentration of dust particles may be less than 1 grain per 1 000 cubic feet. This may well rise to between 3 and 5 grains per 1 000 cubic feet in industrial atmospheres or very much higher in heavily contaminated atmospheres, such as cement works, quarries, foundries, and heavy industrial installations.

Breathing contaminated air, which may well contain particularly aggressive substances, is a common cause of ill health contributing to the common cold, emphysema, headaches, eye irritation, coughing, dizziness and the build up of poisons in the bloodstream.

Impurities enter the body through the mouth and nose and gradually become deposited on the bronchial mucous membrane. At the initial stage of deposition, the bronchial membrane itself is able to provide excretory counteractions in the form of sputum and coughing. The physical adjustment becomes impossible during the repeated influence of contaminating deposits over an extended period of time. As a result, the functions of the bronchi become abnormal. In the lungs, congestion of alveoli and fibrinous changes occur also affecting pulmonary circulation and leading to diseases such as pulmonary emphysema and so on. Functional deterioration of the lungs even affects the heart adversely, causing diseases such as cor pulmonale, and other functional deteriorations.

The aforementioned specifically states the case for 'clean air' quite apart from any legislation involved (*eg* The Health & Safety at Work Act), *etc.*

TABLE III — WEIGHT OF ATMOSPHERIC DUST INDUCTED BY TYPICAL MACHINES

Environment	Dust Concentration grains per $10^3 ft^3$	i/c Engine oz per $10^6 ft^3$ inducted	Larger Air Compressor lb per $10^6 ft^3$ inducted
Clean air	less than 0.1		
Country or seaside air	less than 1		
	1	4.8	1.5
Town air	2	9.6	3.0
Town with light industry	3	14.4	4.5
Industrial towns	4	19.2	6.0
	5	24.0	7.5
	6	28.8	9.0
Heavy industrial areas	7	33.6	10.5
	8	38.4	12.0
	9	43.2	13.5
	10	48.0	15.0
Heavily contaminated	20	96.0	30.0
industrial atmospheres	30	144.0	45.0

Effect on Machines

In air-breathing machines a major factor is the actual *weight* of solids which are inducted (see also Table III). The automobile engine inducts something like 1 500 cubic feet of air for every gallon of petrol burnt inside the cylinders, so that the average motor car may 'breathe' between 1 and 2 million cubic feet of air per year. Without the air being filtered this could mean that a pound or more of solid particles, many of which may be highly abrasive, has been sucked into the engine. In the case of larger machines the position can be even worse. Thus a large air compressor may induct 10 pounds or more of solid particles *per week,* unless protected by a filter on the intake side.

Inducted solids will tend to accumulate as deposits on pistons, cylinder heads, valves, and other internal components of machines, with the strong possibility of their being bonded in place by the oil film normally present on such surfaces. The oil film, in fact, tends to collect an abrasive content. Further fine particles coming into contact with oil mist or oil spray will be washed out of the air and collect in the lubricant, to be circulated through the machine with possible blocking and abrasive effects.

The purpose of a filter is to screen off and prevent the induction of such airborne solids which are held, or known, to be definitely harmful. This must involve a certain degree of compromise, based on what is a suitable cut-off. Excessively fine filtering would only involve unnecessary cost, greater restriction to inducted airflow (or an excessive size of filter) and more rapid clogging. On the other hand, cut-off must be related to minimum internal clearances or orifice diameters involved in the machine in order to ensure that no particles large enough to jam and score, or clog, are passed by the filter.

With most machines the majority of harmful contaminants will be of 20 μm diameter or above. Thus filtering to this order should provide fair protection. However, particles of the order of 10—20 μm can be damaging where reasonably fine clearances are involved and it is generally preferable to provide protection down to this lower figure, particularly as this can be met by the improved forms of simple filter elements commonly employed for air filters.

The requirements for filtering atmospheric air are specific to the application and the operating conditions involved. A small machine operating in country air may well dispense with an air filter, whereas that same machine used in a heavy industrial area would most definitely need protection. But where the machine is mass produced and used under widely differing circumstances a compromise filter performance may be accepted as standard.

Internally Generated Contaminants

Virtually all machines and actuator systems generate internal contaminants which can be harmful if not removed. Wear products, for example, are at their highest concentration when a machine is new and being run-in or bedded down. During this period there is also a considerable possibility of other contaminants, such as foundry sand, also being present.

Protection at this stage can be provided by conventional filters, sometimes with the addition of magnetic plugs or magnetic filters for the separate collection of ferrous metal particles. The incidence of wear products should then decrease, with corrosion or erosion-corrosion products becoming predominant, together with degradation products of the carrier fluid (oil) itself. The latter is largely a factor of the chemical stability of the carrier fluid.

Filtration requirements to deal with internally generated contaminants are essentially specific to the type of machine — eg i/c engine, hydraulic system, etc, and to the working clearances involved.

Process Industries

In process industries, requirements are usually even more specific — viz the removal of unwanted products from a mixture by liquid/solid separation either by suitable filters or separating devices. These cannot be dealt with generally, but are covered in separate chapters.

Liquid Contaminants in Air

Water vapour is always present in air although not generally significant as a contaminant except in compressed air systems and certain process plant.

Compressed air, as derived from a compressor, is normally heavily contaminated with water vapour (from the inducted air) and oil (from the compressor). The chances of the latter being deposited in the distribution system and machines or equipment fed by the compressor are high because of the cooling of the air as it expands and the consequent condensation of water vapour.

Atmospheric air inducted into the compressor will contain a certain weight of water per unit volume, depending on the relative humidity — Table IV. During compression the air temperature will rise (increasing its capacity to carry water in vapour form), but its actual volume is substantially reduced. The result is that the compressed air leaving the compressor will inevitably be nearly or fully saturated with water. The amount of water this represents is quite substantial — Table V.

TABLE IV — WEIGHT OF WATER PER CUBIC FOOT OF AIR AT ATMOSPHERIC PRESSURE
(Weight in grains)

Temp. °F	RELATIVE HUMIDITY OR PERCENTAGE SATURATION									
	10	20	30	40	50	60	70	80	90	100
32	0.211	0.422	0.634	0.845	1.056	1.268	1.479	1.690	1.902	2.113
40	0.285	0.570	0.855	1.140	1.424	1.709	1.994	2.279	2.564	2.849
50	0.408	0.815	1.223	1.630	2.038	2.446	2.853	3.261	3.668	4.076
60	0.574	1.149	1.724	2.298	2.872	3.447	4.022	4.596	5.170	5.745
70	0.798	1.596	2.394	3.192	3.990	4.788	5.586	6.384	7.182	7.980
80	1.093	2.187	3.280	4.374	5.467	6.560	7.654	8.747	9.841	10.934
90	1.479	2.958	4.437	5.916	7.395	8.874	10.353	11.832	13.311	14.780
100	1.977	3.953	5.930	7.906	9.883	11.860	13.836	15.813	17.789	19.766

TABLE V — FLUID OUNCES OF WATER VAPOUR PER 1 000 ft^3 OF SATURATED COMPRESSED AIR

Air Temp °F	AIR PRESSURE — $lb/in^2 g$												
	0	30	40	50	60	70	80	90	100	110	120	130	150
32	4.34	1.43	1.16	0.98	0.85	0.75	0.67	0.61	0.55	0.51	0.47	0.44	0.38
40	6.00	1.98	1.60	1.36	1.16	1.03	0.91	0.89	0.77	0.70	0.65	0.60	0.52
50	8.69	2.87	2.35	2.06	1.70	1.92	1.43	1.23	1.12	1.02	0.95	0.89	0.79
60	12.41	4.10	3.32	2.80	2.35	2.13	1.90	1.77	1.58	1.46	1.35	1.26	1.10
70	17.85	5.90	5.05	4.08	3.52	3.10	2.66	2.52	2.28	2.10	1.95	1.82	1.59
80	24.97	8.25	6.80	5.70	4.87	4.38	3.88	3.52	3.20	2.93	2.78	2.53	2.23
90	30.81	10.20	9.33	7.90	6.78	6.00	5.33	4.90	4.42	4.06	3.76	3.50	3.13
100	43.40	14.30	12.70	10.80	9.28	8.25	7.32	6.93	6.03	5.57	5.15	4.80	4.20
110	64.50	21.30	18.80	14.60	12.60	11.10	9.85	8.98	8.12	7.46	6.93	6.45	5.66
120	97.00	28.70	23.20	19.70	16.80	14.80	13.30	11.60	10.90	10.10	9.30	8.67	7.56

The amount of moisture which will separate out as condensed water in the system can be estimated directly from this Table. Thus if the compressed air leaves the compressor at 120 lb/in² (8.4 bar) and a temperature of 100°F it will be saturated with 5.15 fluid ounces of water per 1 000 cubic feet (28 m³) of air. If that volume of air is now cooled to, say, 60°F at the same pressure it can only retain 1.35 fluid ounces in saturation. The difference (5.15 − 1.35 = 3.8 fluid ounces) will be deposited out as water in the system. Thus each 1 000 cubic feet (28 m³) of compressed air passing through the system will leave behind 3.8 fluid ounces of water.

Removal of water may be attempted in stages — for example, by aftercooling and separation following the air compressor, and subsequently by in-line filters. Separation and filtering may also be effective in removing oil vapour, although the presence of oil in compressed air is often desirable, rather than undesirable. Basically, however, the presence of fluid contaminants in air (or other gases) represents a quite different aspect of filtering or separation requirements.

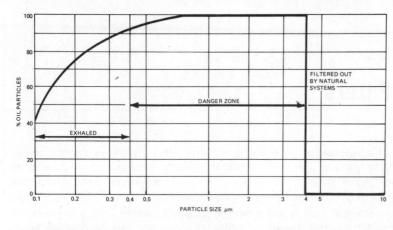

Fig 2 Oil particle size μm.

Oil Mist in Air

Compressed air normally contains oil, except when generated by an oil-free compressor or where the delivery line is fitted with a filter for removing oil. Oil mist particles can range in size from 0.2 to 5 μm, and can represent some hazard to human health if breathed in with air. Particles over 3.5 μm in size will normally be filtered out naturally and particles below 0.3 μm in size are thought to be exhaled. The potential hazard thus lies in the presence of oil particles in the 0.4 — 3 μm range. (Fig 2).

See also chapters on *Bulk Air Filters, Air Filter Services* and *Dust and Fume Respirators.*

Mechanical Filters

THE BASIS of working of a 'mechanical' filter is that the filter element works as a porous screen, removing and retaining solid particles too large to pass through the openings which provide the porosity, but allowing the 'carrier' fluid to pass. Specifically, the filter provides *direct interception* of such solids although there may in fact be other physical phenomena present.

The simplest type of mechanical filter is one providing *surface retention* — *eg* a simple screen which is generally satisfactory for simple straining and filtering duties, and can also have the advantage of being readily cleanable. Dirt retention is directly related to surface area, so surface filter media are commonly fabricated in pleated form for extended area. Pleating can also considerably increase the strength of the filter, especially with paper filters.

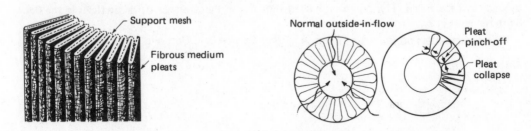

Support mesh

Fibrous medium pleats

Normal outside-in-flow

Pleat pinch-off

Pleat collapse

Typical pleated paper element. A support mesh may be incorporated to prevent pinch-off or pleat collapse.

Surface Filtration

Surface filtration works largely by direct interception. Particles larger than the pore size of the medium are stopped at the upstream surface of the filter; their size prevents them from entering and/or passing through the pores or openings. Adsorptive forces, though present, are small in magnitude; surface type media are not perfectly smooth on their upstream surfaces, nor are their pores perfectly uniform in shape or direction. Thus some depth filtration can take place and can have a profound effect on the filtration characteristics and life of a surface filter.

When most surface-type filters are exposed to the flow of contaminated fluid, two effects start to take place almost immediately:

(i)   A gradual reduction in the effective pore size of the medium as some of the pores become partially blocked by particles, so the filter starts to become 'finer', *ie* more efficient in removing fine particles. This can be caused by the retention of extremely small particles within the pores by adsorptive forces. (Fig 1a).

It can also occur due to the partial intrusion of soft, deformable particles into the pores, acting under the forces generated by fluid flow, so that those pores are effectively reduced in size. Deformable particles have the ability to conform more closely to the shape of flow-passages, thus blocking them to a greater degree than do hard particles. They can form a slime or gel that can completely clog a filter.

(ii)   A 'cake' or bed of trapped particles starts to build on the surface of the medium, itself forming a filter which, by the same clogging mechanism noted previously, becomes progressively finer as operating time continues. (Fig 1b).

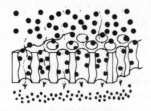

(a) Blocking action of
fine particles retained
by surface filter

Fig 1

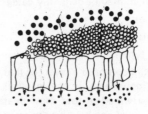

(b) Cake build-up on
surface type filter

The other basic type of mechanical filter employs an element with a significant amount of thickness providing *filtering in depth*. The mechanism of filtering then becomes much more complex. The path through the filter is much longer and random, providing greater possibility for both direct interception and dirt retention. In general larger particles will tend to be trapped in the surface layers with the finer particles trapped by succeeding layers. If necessary the structure of the filter can be density graded. This has a particular advantage where the particle sizes of the contaminant are widely distributed; less so if they are of more or less uniform size where a surface filter may be equally effective. Also, of course, filtering in depth will give a higher pressure drop than a surface filter.

The overall performance of a *depth-type* filter, however, can be better than that given by its purely mechanical action of direct interception. The inertia of particles impinging directly onto the filter medium may generate absorptive surface forces, and Brownian movement effects may be present with fine particles, again developing absorptive retention. As a result the depth filter may trap and retain particles finer than that provided by pure mechanical filtration alone.

Brownian movement applies only to particles of about 1 μm in size or less, causing such particles to diffuse through the filter medium regardless of fluid flow, where they are likely to be retained by adsorptive forces. This phenomenon is most marked where the fluid carrier is a dry gas (the dryer the gas the more powerful the electrostatic adsorptive forces); and least marked with higher viscosity liquids.

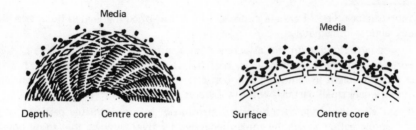

Fig 2 Graded depth type filter compared with surface filter.

Depth-Type Media

The ideal depth-type filter medium has increasingly dense layers from the outside (upstream) to the inside (downstream) side — Fig 2. Such a graded structure provides increasing chance of finer particles being trapped on their passage through the filter. Practical depth-type filters are made from media which may be generally categorized as:-

(i)   Fibrous

(ii)   Porous

(iii)   Cake-type

Fibrous media comprise a layer, or mat, of numerous very fine fibres, of diameters ranging from 0.5 to 30 μm, depending on the material. These fibres are randomly oriented to each other, intermixed and intertwined so that they create numerous tortuous flow-passages or pores in which the particles are trapped and held by the mechanisms described previously.

The fibrous materials most commonly used are:

Cellulose   Cotton   Micro glass fibre   Synthetics (*eg* rayon, polypropylene)

Relative efficiencies of these media types are a function of fibre diameter; the more narrow the fibres, the closer they can be compacted. The result is that smaller diameter fibres have smaller flow paths. Micro glassfibre is smaller in diameter than cellulose and has, therefore, a better filtration efficiency.

Typically the layer is 0.010 to 0.080 in (0.25 to 2 mm) thick and is impregnated with resin (phenolic, epoxy or acrylic) to bind it together to ensure structural strength and stability. The maintenance of stable structure, including pore size, and therefore of stable filtration characteristics throughout the medium's service life, commonly referred to as *filter integrity,* is a function of the fibre-binding system.

Porous media are similar in that they have flow pores presenting a capillary-type passage. This differs from a fibrous medium in that its parent material is solid or in the form of randomly-shaped particles of roughly spherical proportions.

There are three major forms of porous media:

(i)   Particles of the parent materials are cast to shape, then baked or sintered to bond them together into a self-supporting structure. Typical materials are metals, ceramics and stone.

(ii)   A sheet of parent plastic material is cast, then pores are formed by solvent evaporation, leaching, stretching, piercing or nuclear bombardment.

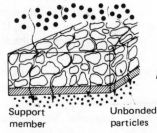

Fig 3 Cake type filter medium.

Support member   Unbonded particles

(iii)   Porous media are formed by the foaming of plastic materials, typically poly-
        urethanes.

Cake-type media are more limited in application and generally employed in bed-type filtration
for removal of solids in significant bulk. (Fig 3).

They comprise a layer or bed of separate, loose, discrete particles formed into a 'cake' on a
supporting screen or mesh, usually by the action of fluid flow. The voids between the particles
form the pores and flow-passages required for filtration. Binding materials are not used to bond
the particles to each other.

Typical materials used to form the cake are:-

        Diatomaceous earth   Sand   Clays   Wood fibres   Cotton fibres

This loose bed construction makes them generally unsuitable for fluid power applications,
where stability, compactness and resistance to vibration are of prime importance. The characteristic of recirculating some of the discrete particles through the system until the cake is formed is a
definite deterrent to use in fluid power systems.

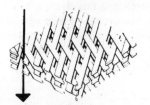

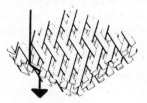

*Examples of different flow paths pro-
vided by flat wire mesh filter elements.*

Straight-through (For
75 μm up). Two
layers of straight-
through POROLOY T
as wound.

Zig-Zag (For 2–75
μm filtration).
Two layers of zig-zag
POROLOY T as
wound.

Surface Filtration Media

Surface filtration media are of three broad types:

1) **Screen:** a thin, essentially two-dimensional, structure with a series of uniform pores through it.
Generally made of metal or plastic, screens are of the following forms:

(i)   *Woven fibre* — only woven-screen types over approximately 25 micrometres
      pore-size can reasonably be cleaned; other types cannot be cleaned or require
      expensive equipment and considerable time and labour.

A significant characteristic of a woven medium is the degree of its ability to retain its original configuration — as woven — during the subsequent manufacturing processes and service life, especially under high loads. If the fibres shift, larger than planned pores may be created, thus degrading the filtration rating on the medium.

Some manufacturers sinter this type of medium with the aim of stabilizing it by fusing the strands together at their interstices. The necessity for this added processing has not been completely proven.

(ii)   *Etched sheet,*   in which the pores are produced by chemical or electrolytic processes.

(iii) *Sintered powder,* thin membrane-like versions of porous media described earlier.

(iv)   *Cast membrane,* a film of cast polymeric plastic in which pores are produced by chemical leaching, photo-etching or atomic bombardment.

Cast membranes are normally used only when true micro-filtration is required. High clean pressure drop and cost, plus low dirt-capacity of membrane filters generally discourage their use in fluid power applications. (See also chapter on *Membrane Filters).*

2) Edge-Type Filters

Edge-type filters also involve the use of cartridge type elements with flow directed from the outside inwards, but the element is composed of a stack of discs or washers of paper, felt, plastic or metal clamped together in compression. Flow takes place from the edge inwards between the discs, which may be in intimate contact in the case of non-rigid disc materials; or through the controlled clearance space between individual discs provided by spacing washers.

Such a construction has the advantage that the collected contaminant can be scraped from the upstream surface more easily and completely than it can be from a screen and this cleaning can be performed during operation of the unit. In addition, this type can be manufactured with inherent self-cleaning properties, so that cake build-up on the upstream surface can be virtually eliminated.

Paper ribbon edge-type filter.

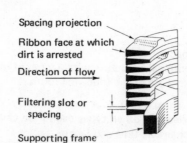

Spacing projection

Ribbon face at which dirt is arrested

Direction of flow

Metal edge-type filters.

Filtering slot or spacing

Supporting frame

Tapered flow paths in a metal-edge element prevent clogging. Particles that fail to pass through may fall off or can be scraped off the surface.

Wedging action as particles jam in screen

Every particle that can enter will pass through

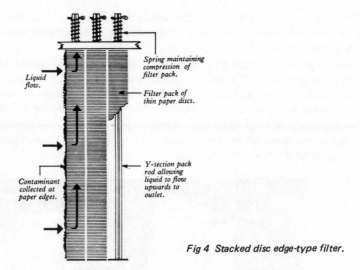

Liquid flow.

Spring maintaining compression of filter pack.

Filter pack of thin paper discs.

Y-section pack rod allowing liquid to flow upwards to outlet.

Contaminant collected at paper edges.

Fig 4 Stacked disc edge-type filter.

An edge filter element employing stacked paper discs is shown in Fig 4. The pack is held under compression by springs at the top of the assembly, so that the liquid undergoing filtration can only pass through the minute interstices between the discs in layers of near molecular thickness. Virtually all solid impurities are, in fact, left on the edge of the discs since such an element can be capable of yielding an absolute cut-off of 1 μm or less.

A further property of such an edge filter employing unimpregnated paper discs is that it can trap and retain finely dispersed water in fuels, oils, or similar fluids. It is even possible to remove dissolved water by the provision of moderate heat and vacuum. The presence of water will, however, substantially increase the back pressure of the filter due to the swelling of the discs, further restricting the clearance space available for flow. This can, if necessary, be used to operate a warning device that water is present in the fluid being filtered.

It will also be appreciated that whilst the performance of such a paper element is considerably better than that of a pleated paper element its normal resistance, and thus back pressure, is very much higher, or, size for size, its capacity is appreciably less. On the other hand it is one of the best types of filters for removing very fine solids from liquids — even colloidal graphite from oils — it is virtually immune to the effects of shock pressure, and element life is long with a minimum of maintenance requirements. Cleaning can usually be accomplished quickly and efficiently by a reverse flow of compressed air. The ultra-fine filtering properties may inhibit its use for particular applications due to the build-up of ultra-fine solids restricting flow where very frequent cleaning is impractical. A particular example is its unsuitability for use as a bypass filter for engine lubricating oil systems employing detergent oils.

3) Stacked Disc Filters

A stacked disc filter employs individual discs which are stacked over a perforated inner tube, with intermediate spacing washers. Flow is between, and subsequently through, the filter discs and into the inner tube. The discs are typically of composite construction, *eg* the face of the disc formed by a fine metal wire screen with a further back-up screen to provide effective use of the full filtration area. In the centre of the pack is a fitted separator to provide radial passageways for flow into the central perforated tube. The complete disc assembly is then held together by inner and outer binding rings.

Performance is nominally that of the mesh elements or filter screen apertures, typical standard openings being from 0.01 down to 0.001 inch (0.25 to 0.025 mm) equivalent to ratings of approximately 250 μm and 25 μm, respectively. With this form of construction, however, performance materially improves as dirt collects in the screen providing increasingly finer filtration.

This particular form of filter is an aperture rather than an edge type with the depth of filtering restricted to the depth of the face screen and back-up screen. It provides a large surface area in a compact volume and low pressure drop.

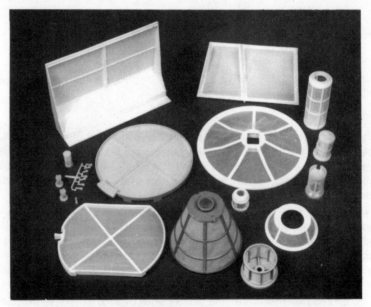

Selection of 'Strylon' filters currently incorporated into O.E.M. equipment in the domestic appliance, hydraulic, pneumatic, automotive, computer, power tools and dairy industries.
(Plastic Engineers (New Milton) Ltd.)

Filter Ratings

FILTERS ARE rated on their ability to remove particles of a specific size from a fluid, but various different methods are applied to specifying performance in this way. Quantitative figures are only valid for specific operating or test conditions.

Absolute Rating

The *absolute rating*, or cut-off point of a filter refers to the diameter of the largest particle, normally expressed in micrometres (μm), which will pass through the filter. It therefore represents the pore opening size of the filter medium. Filter media with an exact and consistent pore size or opening thus, theoretically at least, have an exact absolute rating.

This does not usually apply in practice, as pore size is not necessarily consistent with the actual open areas, and is further modified by the form of the filter element. Also tests to establish ratings employ spherical glass beads as the artificial contaminant in the fluid (or a mixture of glass beads and carbonyl iron E for 5 μm absolute measurement). In a practical filter system the actual form of the contaminants are not necessarily spherical, in which case the nominal diameter is generally taken as the largest of the linear dimensions. The actual shape of the particle, however, may be such that its two other linear dimensions are very much smaller than the nominal diameter, permitting it to pass through a very much smaller hole. As a typical example, consider the edge type filter where the open space is a slot with the rating fixed by the dimension of the slot — Fig 1. A disc-shaped particle with a thickness less than the slot opening will readily pass through the slot, although the nominal particle size, established by the disc diameter, is very much larger than the filter rating. Having passed the filter this particle could well cause scoring by jamming at a different attitude in a clearance space less than the particle diameter — a very strong possibility since the particle is more likely to be irregular than smooth.

The passage of 'oversize' particles in this manner depends very largely on the size and shape of he opening, and also the depth over which filtering is provided. With elements filtering in depth,

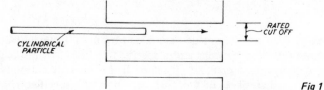

CYLINDRICAL
PARTICLE

RATED
CUT OFF

Fig 1

the chance of such asymmetric particle shapes being trapped increases. This also depends on the physical arrangement of the element. Thus a random arrangement of pores in successive but interconnecting layers would eliminate the possibility of a direct through passage via individual pores in line.

There is also the fact that the majority of filters do, to a large extent, generate a filter bed. That is to say, contaminants collecting on the surface impart a blocking action decreasing the permeability of the element and improving filter efficiency. Efficiency can go on improving, up to the point where the blocking is so severe that the pressure drop is excessive, seriously decreasing the flow rate through the filter. This explains why the performance of a filter can often exceed its given rating (based on the performance of a clean element); and also why test figures for identical elements can differ widely with different conditions of test. The former description explains why particles larger than the cut-off figure may also be found downstream of the filter.

Certain types of filter media, such as papers, felts and cloths have a variable pore size and thus no absolute rating at all. The effective cut-off is largely determined by the random arrangement involved and the depth of the filter. Performance may then be described in terms of nominal cut-off or nominal rating.

Although widely used for types of filters which cannot be rated on an absolute basis, a nominal cut-off rating is largely meaningless, and often misleading, since cut-off is seldom, if ever, complete at this rating. Thus a block felt element with, say, a typical nominal rating of 30 μm may well pass 20 to 40% of particles of this size. At the same time it may well stop a high proportion of much smaller particles. A proportion of particles smaller than the cut-off rating will always be stopped, the actual amount depending on the design and type and also the specific flow velocity through the element.

It may be argued that the term 'absolute rating' is not in most cases a realistic description. Strictly speaking an absolute rating is absolute – no particle larger than that rating can pass through the filter. This limits the type of media which can have an absolute rating to those of consistent pore size where they show 100% retention of particles, although this does not preclude the possibility of individual larger particles actually penetrating the filter in service. This rating, also, would tend to be so much higher than a mean or nominal rating that it could give the impression that the filter was very 'coarse', which would not necessarily be true.

On the other hand, even with consistent pore sizes or openings, an absolute rating is not realistic if based on the smallest dimension in the case of non-circular openings (such as squares, triangles and rectangles).

Considerable difference between actual performance and quoted ratings may also occur due to the differences between actual service and test conditions. Practical tests to establish ratings are normally conducted with high concentrations of contaminant which will tend to yield a higher filter efficiency because of the 'bed' effect. Many tests, in fact, may be conducted under near-clogged conditions of the filter. In service, the filter may be operating with relatively clean fluids over a long period, when the efficiency of the filter will be that much lower. The only performance figure which holds good under such extremes is a true absolute rating.

Nominal Rating

A *nominal filter rating* is an arbitrary value determined by the filter manufacturer and expressed in terms of percentage retention by weight of a specified contaminant (usually glass beads again) of given size. It also represents a *nominal* efficiency figure, or more correctly a degree of filtration. Figures normally used are 90%, 95% or 98% retention of a specified contaminant size. The only standards relating are MIL-E5504A and MIL-F5504B, where Version A defines a 10 micrometre filter as being capable of removing 98% by weight of test dust larger than 10 μm at a certain high concentration; and Version B defines a 10 micrometre filter as being able to remove 95% of 10—20 μm glass beads at a high concentration.

Many filter manufacturers use similar tests, but due to lack of uniformity and reproducibility of the basic method the use of nominal filter ratings has fallen into disfavour.

Mean Filter Rating

A *mean filter rating* is a measurement of the mean pore size of a filter element. It is far more meaningful than a nominal rating, and in the case of filter elements with varying pore size, more realistic than an absolute rating. It establishes the particle size above which the filter starts to be effective. This is relatively easy to establish by the bubble test (see chapter on *Filter Test*).

Beta (β) Ratio

The Beta ratio is a comparatively new rating system introduced with the object of giving both filter manufacturer and user an accurate and representative comparison amongst filter media. It is determined by a Multi-Pass Test which establishes the ratio of the number of upstream particles larger than a specific size to the number of downstream particles larger than a specified size, *ie*

$$\beta x = \frac{Nu}{Nd}$$

where

βx = beta rating (or beta ratio) for contaminants larger than Xμm

Nu = number of particles larger than Xμm per unit of volume upstream

Nd = number of particles larger than the Xμm per unit volume downstream

It follows that the higher the β ratio the more particles are retained by the filter, and hence the greater the efficiency of the filter. Efficiency for a given particle size (Ex) can be derived directly from the β ratio by the following equation

$$Ex = \frac{\beta x - 1}{\beta x} \times 100$$

Alternatively, as a guide to efficiency:

β ratio	efficiency
1	0
2	50%
10	90%
20	95%
50	98%
100	99%
1 000	99.9%
10 000	99.99%

Example: If a filter has a β5 rating of 100 this would mean that the filter is capable of removing 99% of all particles of greater size than 5 μm.

Filter Efficiency

As noted previously the nominal rating is expressed in terms of an efficiency figure. Efficiency can also be derived directly from the beta ratio as this is constant with the basic definition of filter efficiency, which is:-

$$1 - \frac{\text{number of emergent particles}}{\text{number of incident particles}} \times 100 \ (\%)$$

This applies over the range of particle sizes considered, down to the absolute cut-off. At this point the number of emergent particles will be nil and the efficiency 100%. At any particle size level smaller than the absolute cut-off the efficiency must necessarily be less than 100%.

The classic method of measuring filter efficiency (and absolute rating) is by the glass bead test. In modern practice efficiencies are now normally quoted in beta ratios — eg $\beta x > 75$ specifies an efficiency of 98.6% or better relative to a particle size of x μm.

Filter Permeability

Permeability is the reciprocal expression of the resistance to flow offered by a filter. Thus high permeability represents low resistance, and low permeability high resistance. It is normally expressed in terms of a *permeability coefficient* (α) related to pressure drop (ΔP) at a given flow rate (Q), viz:-

$$\alpha = \frac{Q \nu t}{Ad \, \Delta P}$$

where

ν = fluid viscosity

t = filter thickness

A = filter area

d = fluid density at inlet pressure

Any consistent series of units can be employed, the permeability coefficient then being expressed in a unit of length.

In practice, such a formula is cumbersome and unnecessary. Permeability is far better expressed directly in terms of pressure drop against flow rate. Such curves are then specific to the individual filter, but individual curves will be generated with respect to—

(i)   filter size

(ii)   fluid temperature

(iii) time or degree of contamination

Typical size curves are shown in Fig 2. For a given flow rate an increase in filter size will reduce pressure drop by virtue of the fact that the quantity flowing through unit area will be reduced (ΔP being inversely proportional to A). This is a standard method of 'sizing' a filter, the flow rate required associated with the acceptable pressure drop figure determining an optimum size. Note, however, that this refers to the initial pressure drop and the actual figure will rise with time.

If the filter is varied in size and thickness a different series of curves will be produced since the effect of thickness is to increase pressure drop (ΔP being directly proportional to t). Each particular filter element, therefore, will have its specific pressure drop/flow rate curve, depending on area and thickness and the permeability of the material.

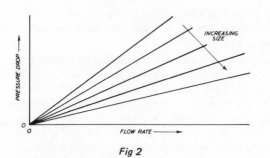

Fig 2

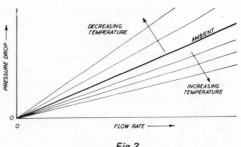

Fig 3

Temperature will affect the pressure drop/flow rate characteristics by altering the viscosity of the fluid. Since pressure drop is directly proportional to viscosity, any decrease in fluid temperature will increase pressure drop for the same flow rate, and an increase in temperature will decrease pressure drop. A series of temperature curves thus establishes the characteristics of a single filter over that working temperature range — for example see Fig 3. This is more significant for liquids than for gases.

Secondary temperature effects may also be present. Thus at low temperatures water in the fluid may freeze, producing blockage or partial blockage of the element and an abnormal rise in pressure drop. Similarly, waxes in the fluid may thicken or solidify out with a similar effect. These effects are often noticeable on aircraft fuel feeds at altitudes where ambient temperatures are very low.

The effect of time is to produce a cumulative build-up of contaminants on the filter element, reducing permeability in direct proportion to the degree of contamination — Fig 4. Again such a series of curves is specific to an individual filter. Characteristics expressed in this manner, however, are largely unrealistic since the filter will already have been 'sized' for flow rate and the latter is really a fixed working figure. It is thus more informative to plot pressure drop directly against time to yield a single curve — Fig 5. Equally, percentage contamination could be used instead of time, although the two are essentially the same thing in terms of practical working. In other words, it is the increase in pressure drop after a period (time) of working which is significant. The fact that it is caused by 'x' per cent build up of contaminants is only a cause and not an effect.

The amount or weight of contaminant retained by a filter can be significant, as this may affect choice of both types and size of a suitable element.

Pressure drop-time curves generally show a linear rise after a fairly sharp initial rise, eventually rounding into a much steeper rise. The 'knee' represents the point (time) at which the element has

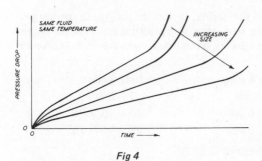

Fig 4

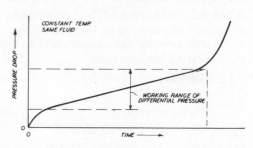

Fig 5

become too clogged for further efficient working. Note that 'efficient' here refers to the excessive pressure drop which would arise from continued working, not the efficiency of the filter itself at this stage. Filter efficiency increases with increasing pressure drop.

'Squaring' the knee can indicate a suitable element life and the corresponding differential pressure. Once the latter level is reached this can be employed to operate an indicator to draw attention to a clogged filter, or a relief valve to bypass fluid flow to avoid further restriction to flow. This is ideal analysis, but not necessarily practical. The rise in differential pressure, however, is always significant as this remains unchanged regardless of the rate of contamination. Thus a suitable cut-out or bypass pressure differential holds good for a single filter operated under any conditions. The time base, however, may vary widely for the same filter depending on the working conditions and degree of contamination present. Yet it is more usual to rate filter element life in terms of 'time' since this is the simplest unit to employ.

Effect of Pulsating Flow

The effect of pulsating flow is to agitate the filter 'bed' loosening fine particles which would otherwise be retained and allowing them to pass downstream. This effect is illustrated graphically in Fig 6. This is another instance of where filter performance in a practical system can depart markedly from the performance achieved with the same filter under laboratory test conditions. Since it is mainly the finer particles which are affected this can affect the initial choice of filter rating — *eg* demand the use of a finer filter than originally anticipated (or which would be satisfactory under steady flow conditions) in order to achieve the required filter efficiency.

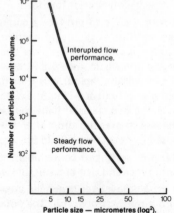

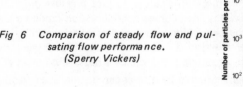

Fig 6   Comparison of steady flow and pulsating flow performance.
(Sperry Vickers)

Silt Control/Chip Removal

A practical classification of filter performance is on the ability, or lack of ability, to remove fine particles or *silt,* taken to be particles in the 3–5 μm size range. In a practical situation the degree of filtration provided will normally fall into three categories, given below, together with equivalent absolute ratings and beta ratios.

Category	Absolute Rating	Beta Ratio*
Silt control	3 – 5 μm	3 – 5 > 75
Partial silt control	10 – 15 μm	10 – 15 > 75
Chip control (no silt control)	25 – 40 μm	25 – 40 > 75

*Note: these are representative of a filter with an efficiency > 98.6%.

Absorbent and Adsorbent Filters

AN *ABSORBENT* medium is a material akin to a sponge in that it can draw in fluid and retain it within its structure. In this sense it can act as a filter to remove (absorb) and retain fluid. For example, an untreated paper, being an absorbent material, could filter out water particles from air. However, its usefulness as a practical filter in such a case would be very limited — both as regards retention (soon achieving maximum possible absorption); and mechanical strength (being weakened by the water content, which may also act as a solvent for the binder).

Wet strength may be imparted to papers by impregnating with such substances as neoprene or phenol formaldehyde and other synthetic resins. The choice of impregnant will also govern its compatibility with other fluids which would normally attack untreated papers. Thus special papers can be made resistant to oils, acids, and other chemical solutions, while still retaining the porous nature of the basic medium. At the same time impregnation can increase the mechanical strength of the paper.

Natural fibres, and to a lesser extent, natural felts are other absorbent media, as are cellular materials with interconnected pores. However the use of absorbent media purely as absorbent

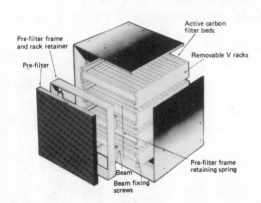

Activated carbon filters are an effective means of odour control because of their ability to remove gases and vapours. AAF activated carbon filters are offered in four sizes from 0.24 m^3/s to 0.94 m^3/s (500 cfm to 2 000 cfm) and with various options.

filters is very limited. They are normally employed as mechanical filters where any absorbent properties are of secondary or even negligible significance. In fact papers especially may be specifically treated to render them non-absorbent to provide maximum mechanical strength and resistance to solvent action when used as liquid filters.

Adsorbent Filters

Adsorption is the attraction and/or retention of particles by molecular attraction or electrostatic forces present between the particles and a filter medium. This phenomenon may be present to some extent in mechanical filters but is generally minimal. Specific types of media, normally in the form of finely divided granular solids can, however, exhibit high adsorptive properties in contact with vapours and non-solid contaminants present in fluids.

Provided such particles can be suitably contained in a bed or column they can also form a very effective mechanical filter for trapping solid particles in tiny random paths between adjacent granules. The effective surface area of such a bed or filter pack can, in fact, be vast. Provided the pack is reasonably compacted and restrained it can also withstand moderate flow rates and working pressures, although, of course, the possibility of element migration is higher than with rigid screen materials.

The chief adsorptive media used for filters are activated charcoal and similar forms of carbon (*eg* bone black); and Fuller's earth and other active clays. These are all in granular form. A more rigid form of adsorbent filter can be produced by chemical treatment of papers with an adsorbent medium. One of the latest materials available here is *charcoal cloth.*

Adsorbent media are widely used for the removal of odours, smoke, fumes, *etc*, in a wide range of applications from domestic (*eg* kitchen cooker hood filters), through air-conditioning plant to industrial fume removal. Activated charcoal is also the filter medium normally used for water purifying/clarifying on small scale applications (*eg* drinking water supplied in caravans or boats). Industrially adsorbent filters are used for the removal of odours from oils, odours and tastes from foodstuffs, *etc*. The adsorbent property of the media means that they remove dissolved as well as undissolved contaminants, the medium being chosen accordingly. At the same time, adsorbent media set definite limits to their application. They cannot, for example, be used to filter additives. Typical examples of the unsuitability of adsorbent filters are for use with crankcase lubricating oils (other than straight mineral oils) and hydraulic fluids. They are also generally unsuitable for the filtering of aqueous solutions, synthetic fluids, and the majority of mild chemical solutions (including acids and alkalis).

See also chapter on *Media.*

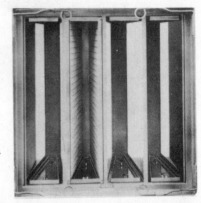

Carbon pack adsorbent filters.

Membrane Filters

MODERN MEMBRANE filters are produced in the form of thin sheets of plastic materials with a microporous structure. Pore sizes may range from 12 μm down to 0.005 μm with a capability of micro-, macro- and ultra-filtration. They are pure surface retention filters although the section in thickness is spongelike with broken, interconnected pores equivalent in effect to staggered sieve layers. Particular characteristics are that the separated substance is always deposited on the surface; and high flow rates are possible because of the high porosity. In a typical membrane only 15—35% by volume is solid material, the remainder is pore space.

The pore size determines the degree of separation in the case of liquids. With dust-laden gases retention is increased considerably by inertial forces and adsorption through electrostatic forces generated. Effective separation of particles down to about five times smaller than the mean pore diameter of the membrane may be achieved in such cases — eg yeasts and moulds in air may be removed by a membrane filter with a pore size of 8 μm, and viruses in air by a membrane filter with a pore size of 0.2 μm.

Materials used for membrane filters range from gelatin and alginates to cellulose, nylon, PVC, PTFE and other fluorocarbons. Typically these are produced in the form of thin sheets with a high

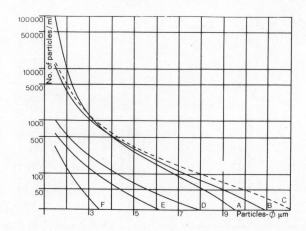

Particle count in 0.9% Na C1 intravenous solution. (Recommended purity, not more than 50 particles larger than 5 μm per ml).
A — unfiltered
B—D — filtration through various depth-type filters.
E—F — filtration through membrane filters of different pore size.

TABLE I – EXAMPLES OF TYPES AND APPLICATIONS OF MEMBRANE FILTERS

Duty	Material	Applications	Average pore size μm	Thickness μm	Flow rate for water ml/min per cm²	Flow rate for air l/min per cm²	Bubble point in bar
Clarification and sterile filtration of low molecular weight alcohols and of aqueous solutions	Cellulose acetate	Sterile filtration of gases; Particle removal from hot gases; Clarification of oils and low molecular weight alcohols; CSF cell diagnosis; Cytology.	0.9 0.8	140 130	225 150	1.25 0.65	1.3 1.7
		Residue analysis of oils and fuels; Liquid-scintillation measurements; Insulin-radioimmuno-assay; Phosphate determination in drinking water.	0.6	120	65	0.4	2.7
		Sterile filtration of pharmaceutical, cosmetic and biological solutions, and of heat-sensitive solutions, eg raw materials for ointments, benzyl benzoate, propylene glycol and arachis oil.	0.3	120	25	0.22	3.7
Separation of coarse dispersed, suspended substances	Cellulose nitrate	Particulate contamination in refined sugar, in motors, oilpumps and other parts; Gravimetric determination of industrial dust; Tank ventilation (for the separation of yeasts and moulds); Chemotaxis investigations	5	140	1100	7	0.4
		Determination of the amount of precipitation of wort in breweries; Cerebrospinal fluid diagnosis; Chemotaxis investigations (Boyden technique); Particle removal from ion exchange water; Removing particles from pharmaceutical solutions directly in front of filling needles; Cytology.	2	140	440	2.7	0.6
		Quantitative plankton separation; Cerebrospinal fluid diagnosis; Tissue transplantation; Gravimetric dust analysis; Separation of cell particles; Cytology	1	140	300	1.5	0.9
Separation of fine dispersed and colloidal particles	Cellulose nitrate	Sterile filtration of gases; Cold stabilization of beverages; Clarification of infusion solutions and other biological liquids; Quantitative separation of radioactive aerosols; Quality control of precious metal galvanizing baths	0.9	140	225	1.25	1.3
		Gravimetric determination of impurities in oils and fuels; Separation of fine analytical precipitates	0.8	130	150	0.65	1.7
		Ultracleaning of deionized water; Colour determination of white sugar, according to European Common Market regulations; Hybridity tests (study of replication procedures); Ferric hydroxide determination in boiler water; Cleaning of electrolyte solutions for blood counters; Clarification of fuels; Part removal (approx. 90%) of micro-organisms from liquids	0.6	130	65	0.4	2.7

Application	Material	Description	0.4	130	35	0.3	3.5
Clarification and sterile filtration of aqueous solutions	Cellulose nitrate	Sterile filtration under certain conditions, *eg* when micro-organisms smaller than 0.3 μm are absent.					
		Sterile filtration of pharmaceutical, biological, heat sensitive solutions; Water for specific pathogen free animal breeding; Sterile filtration of water for the urological endoscopy; Sterility testing of pharmaceutical and cosmetic products; Quantitative determination of viruses in air; Ultracleaning in the electronic industry.	0.3	130	25	0.22	3.7
Separation of submicroscopic particles	Cellulose nitrate	Production of ultraclean reagents and other liquids, *eg* for light scattering measurements; Separation of colloidal analytical precipitates; Physiological membrane models	0.27 / 0.2	100 / 100	14 / 4.5	0.13 / 0.08	4.8 / 6.0
		Separation of phages and larger viruses (100–250 μm); Separation of coarse goldsol; Free passage of proteins with a molecular weight of < 1 million.	0.15 / 0.1	80 / 80	1.6 / 0.6	0.06 / 0.03	– / –
Clarification and sterile filtration of non-aqueous liquids	Regenerated cellulose	Photo resists and lacquer thinner. Ultracleaning of solvents; Cytology	0.9 / 0.8 / 0.6 / 0.3	90 / 90 / 90 / 90	225 / 150 / 65 / 25	1.25 / 0.65 / 0.4 / 0.22	– / 0.5 / 1 / 2
Clarification of strongly alkaline media	Polyamid (nylon)	For particle-free filtration of all photoresists. Photo resist-developer; Residue determination in alkaline media	5 / 2 / 1 / 0.9 / 0.8	200 / 200 / 200 / 200 / 200	1100 / 440 / 300 / 225 / 150	7 / 2.7 / 1.5 / 1.25 / 0.65	– / – / – / – / –
Clarification and sterile filtration of strongly alkaline and acidic media	Gelatin	Photo resist-developer; Residue determination in alkaline and acid liquids; Diaphragm for galvanic plants; Removing particles from acids (*eg* hydrofluoric acid) and bases or from strongly alkaline or acidic chemicals	5 / 0.9 / 0.6 / 0.3	165 / 130 / 130 / 130	1100 / 225 / 65 / 25	7 / 1.25 / 0.4 / 0.22	0.4 / 1.3 / 2.7 / 3.7

proportion of filler, subsequently treated to remove the filler and render the sheet in microporous form with a predetermined pore size. Particular materials and applications are:-

Cellulose nitrate — a widely used membrane material with good flexibility and easy handling and almost negligible extractable content.

Cellulose acetate — resistant to aqueous solutions, alcohols, glycols, *etc*. Readily capable of sterilization with hot air at 180°C (or autoclaving).

Regenerated cellulose — resistant to organic solvents. Widely used for clarification and sterile filtration of non-aqueous media.

Nylon (polyamid) — good chemical resistance and particularly suitable for use with ketones, esters, photo-resists, *etc*. The material is weldable.

PVC — slightly hydrophobic and needs wetting with ethanol before being used to filter aqueous solutions. Good chemical resistance, particularly suitable for filtering acids and alkalies.

Polystyrene — particularly effective for filtering dust from air, or for dust sampling, due to the high electrostatic forces generated on this material. The material absorbs no moisture, can be burned leaving practically no residue, and is soluble in organic solvents.

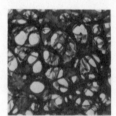 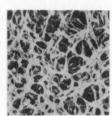

Electron microscope photographs of cellulose nitrate membrane filter structures
(Sartorius-Membrane Filters)

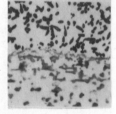

Separation of Bac.subtlis on a membrane filter.

Membrane Filters in Use

For filtration through membrane filters either a vacuum or pressure source is required. These are commonly produced as complete systems incorporating filter holders, pressure tanks, pumps and pipework for vacuums and pressures up to 10 bar. In process filtration prefilters are normally employed for initial clarification, either mounted directly on the membrane filter or at some suitable upstream point. Glassfibre prefilters are commonly used. In particularly difficult conditions serial filtration may be employed through a stack of membrane filters with gradually diminishing pore sizes.

Flow rates are normally specified for proprietary membrane filters, but besides being related to filter type and size they are also influenced by pressure, fluid viscosity and temperature, type and concentration of contaminant present and application. In general operating pressure should be as large as possible (within any limits given for the membrane). It is significant that operating pressure does not affect filter efficiency as it does with depth-type filters.

Filter life handling liquids is limited only by clogging, as evident from the decrease in flow rate. Particles of the same size as the pores tend to clog a membrane filter far more rapidly than larger particles. Fibrous, slimy and colloidal particles also cause rapid clogging of membrane filters. When filtering air or gases clogging is far less apparent and may even be negligible.

Examples of types and applications of membrane filters are given in Table I.

Electrostatic Precipitators

ELECTROSTATIC PRECIPITATION is an extremely effective method of removing dust, smoke and other small particles from air or gases over a particle size range from about 10 μm down to 0.01 μm, or even 0.001 μm. The principle involved is that of passing the air through an ionizer screen where electrons colliding with air molecules generate positive ions which adhere to dust and other small particles present giving them a positive charge. (Positive ionization is preferred since it eliminates over-production of ozone in air purification systems). The charged dust particles then enter a region filled with closely spaced parallel metal plates alternately charged with positive and negative voltages of the order of 6 000 volts d.c. above ground. Positive plates repel the charged particles which are attracted by and retained on the negative plates by electrostatic forces, further supplemented by intermolecular forces, causing the dust to agglomerate.

Application of 'Smog-Eater' units for removal of oil mist, machining smoke, welding fumes, soldering fumes, air borne dust, fumes, bacteria, pollen, dirt, printing ink mist, smoke from EDM machines, etc.
(Horizon Mechanical Services(International) Ltd.)

'Armiga' electrostatic mobile air filter. An integral mobile electrostatic air filter fitted with intake adaptor, elbow, swivel joint and a 2m self-supporting cantilever arm. The electrostatic filter unit comprizes mechanical pre-filters, heavy duty collector cells and a centrifugal fan and motor, all contained in a robust casing.
(Environmental Pollution Control Devices & Services Ltd.)

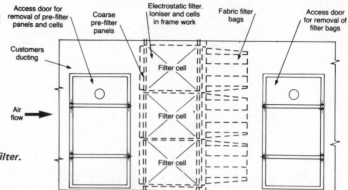

Access door for removal of pre-filter panels and cells

Coarse pre-filter panels

Electrostatic filter. Ioniser and cells in frame work

Fabric filter bags

Access door for removal of filter bags

Customers ducting

Air flow

Filter cell

Filter cell

Filter cell

Agglomerator type electrostatic filter.
(Myson International Ltd.)

'Electro Pak' agglomerator type electro-
static air cleaner.
(AAF Ltd.)

Air entering side

Air leaving side

Each collecting plate is rapped by individual hammers, sequenced to eliminate reentrainment of collected dust.

Each row of discharge electrodes is individually rapped eliminating over- or under-rapping.

'Rollotron' combined agglomerator type
electrostatic precipitator and roll type
(disposable) filter.
(AAF Ltd.)

'Rapping' system in heavy duty electro-
static precipitator.
(AAF Ltd.)

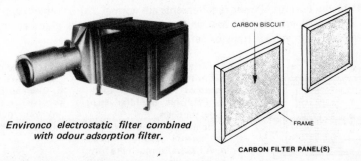

Environco electrostatic filter combined with odour adsorption filter.

CARBON BISCUIT

FRAME

CARBON FILTER PANEL(S)

Further treatment then depends on the system and application. Some plate sections are designed with relatively large spacing to cope with a large contaminant load before they need cleaning, *eg* by 'rapping' or vibrating and gravity release, or washing. This is usually the preferred method for a continuous straight through air filter. In others the agglomerate may be allowed to build up until the layer breaks down or flakes and is carried downstream by the airflow where it is collected in a filter bag (or similar dust-holding device). This type of dry cleaning can be initiated at any stage by a separate purge air flow. Filter bags are then changed as necessary.

Other alternatives include the use of a prefilter to remove larger particles before the ionizer section, and the inclusion of an absorbent element (*eg* activated charcoal) downstream of the plates to remove odours.

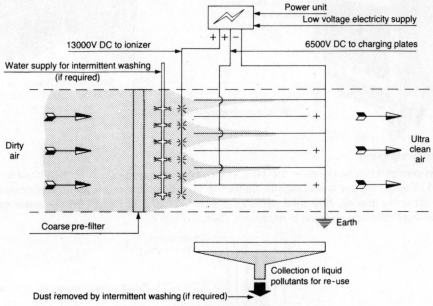

Fig 1   Two stage electrostatic filter.
(Myson International Ltd.)

An example of a straightforward two-stage electrostatic air filter is shown in Fig 1. This employs a prefilter with the facility for intermittent washing if required. Dust and other solid contaminants remain on the plates until removed by washing. Liquid contaminants collected on the plates drain off to the bottom. Power requirements are normal mains voltage supply, the required d.c. potentials of 13 000 volts for the ionizer and 6 500 volts for the plates being generated by a power unit based on a high voltage transformer and a doubler circuit.

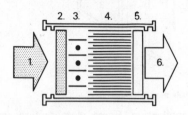

Working principle of electrostatic room air filter.
(Myson International Ltd.)

1. Dirty air is drawn into the electrostatic air filter from the occupied room.
2. Washable pre-filter traps larger particles.
3. Ionizing section gives dust an intense positive charge.
4. Air passes through the bank of dust collecting plates which are charged alternatively positive and earth. The dust is attracted to the plates and is held on the surface until removed by washing.

5. Activated carbon after-filter traps odours.
6. Clean air is returned to the occupied area virtually free from dust, pollen, bacteria and tobacco smoke.

Very heavy duty cell for low capacity airflows. Used in commercial and defence gearbox ventilation applications.

Examples of cell construction.
(Myson International Ltd.)

Medium duty Micronair range of cells. Note the separate ionizer and prefilter.

Oil Mist Precipitators

Oil mist precipitators working on the same principle employ vertical rather than horizontal plates — Fig 2. Vapour flow is then upwards, collecting oil mist on the plates where it agglomerates and drains off under gravity. Any solid particles present will tend to remain on the plates calling for periodic inspection and cleaning as necessary. (See also Fig 3).

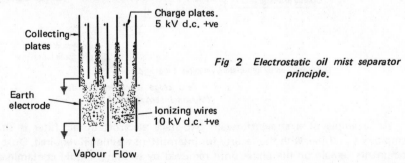

Collecting plates

Charge plates. 5 kV d.c. +ve

Earth electrode

Ionizing wires 10 kV d.c. +ve

Vapour Flow

Fig 2   Electrostatic oil mist separator principle.

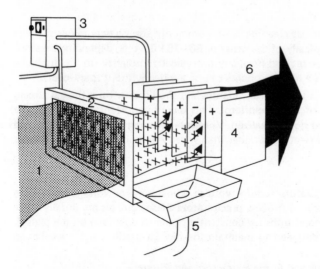

*Fig 3 Working principle of Myson electrostatic
oil mist and fog precipitator.*

(a) Oil mist, smoke and dirt are first drawn through a mechanical pre-filter which removes any large particles. (b) The contaminated air (1) then passes through the Ionizing section (2) where the particles receive a positive charge delivered at high voltage from the power unit (3).

(c) The Ionized or positively charged particles are then attracted and collected by the negatively charged aluminium collecting plates (4). This collection is achieved by the magnetic law of like poles repelling and unlike poles attracting. The collecting plates are alternatively charged positively and negatively so that the negative plate will attract the positively charged particle (+), whilst the positive (+) plate simultaneously exerts a repelling action because of its (+) polarity.

(d) The collected oil particles then run down the plates and are returned to source for re-use via a small pipe (5). (This draining action also cleans the plates).

(e) The cleaned air (6) is drawn by a fan from the filter and is re-circulated into the premises or discharged to atmosphere as required.

'Elex' large-scale process gas precipitator.

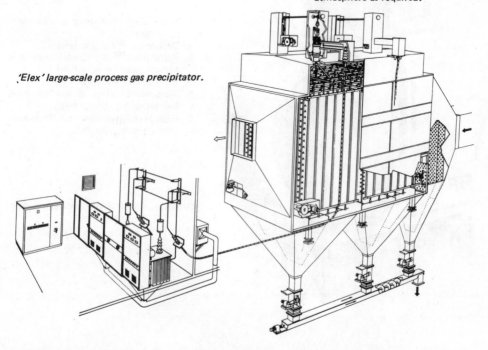

Process Gas Precipitators

Large size electrostatic precipitators for gas cleaning again commonly use vertical plates of large area and require higher d.c. voltages (typically of the order of 30—75 kilovolts, depending on size). Such voltages are provided by a rectifier set and normally give negative polarity on the discharge electrodes since the corona is smoother (*ie* higher voltages can be applied without spark-over).

With increasing size gas inlet design is a significant feature and should distribute the gas stream uniformly over the entire cross-section of the precipitator. This is very important as otherwise the full effect of the electrostatic field would not be realized. Vibratory cleaning is commonly adopted for such units, with heavily constructed electrodes rather than wire-type ionizer screens for greater rigidity and reduced risk of breakage.

Voltage Controls

All types of electrostatic filters/precipitators require voltage adjustment or voltage control to adapt for different or variable conditions. In process precipitators these controls are usually automatic to self-adjust to variable process conditions (*eg* constantly changing dust load on the plates). Automatic controls are (or should be) designed to maintain the highest usable voltage level at an acceptable spark rate.

See also chapters on *Air Filter Services* and *Fume Extractors and Filters*.

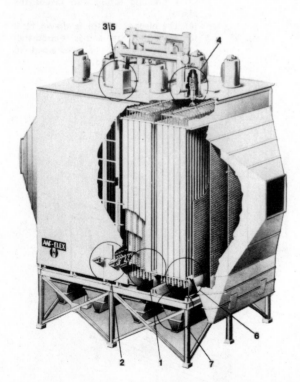

1. Heavy duty roll-formed tubular electrode assembly.
2. Sectionalized rapping system.
3. Automated voltage control maintains highest usable voltage level.
4. Fully protected support insulators.
5. Automated voltage control maintains highest usable voltage level.
6. Rigid, stabilized discharge electrodes.
7. Dust collecting hopper.

Cut-away view of AAF-Elex electrostatic precipitator.

Magnetic Filters

MAGNETIC FILTERS are, in effect, simple magnets or magnet assemblies which when suitably located in a fluid system can attract and retain ferrous metal, nickel and cobalt particles which may be present; and also composite particles in which a ferromagnetic material is entrained. Their main uses are for the trapping and retention of ferrous metal wear products in lubrication oil systems and hydraulic systems (particularly while running-in a new system); removal of ferrous particles from ceramic slip in the pottery industry; removal of ferrous particles from process feed lines and pneumatic conveyors; and the separation and retention of swarf, *etc*, from machine tool coolants.

Elements employed in such cases are invariably permanent magnets. Until the appearance of high energy permanent magnet materials the efficiency of magnetic filters was somewhat limited. With modern alloys offering a remanence in excess of 10 000 gauss and a BH_{max} of the order of 4×10^6 gauss-oersteds, the efficiency of a permanent magnet can be extremely high.

In its simplest form a magnetic filter may comprise a plug, replacing the conventional drain plug in a crankcase — Fig 1. Ferrous metal particles flowing into the magnetic field generated by the plug are attracted to the plug, where they adhere and remain trapped. The plug can then be cleaned by scraping off when it is removed, for example, at each oil change. Plugs of this type are particularly useful for trapping initial wear products generated during the running-in period of internal combustion engines, gearboxes, gear pumps, and similar machines. A more efficient form of magnetic drain plug is shown in Fig 2 where, instead of relying purely on magnetic attraction, the ferrous contaminants are trapped between a number of magnetized rings or magnets encircling the plug core.

For other applications the magnetic element can be designed to suit the flow conditions involved. Basically any such assembly of magnets should be designed so that fluid is caused to flow over or through those parts of the elements at which the magnetic field is strongest, and preferably

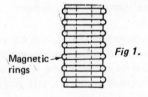

Magnetic rings

Fig 1.

Fig 2

Magnetic filter.
(Neldco Processes Ltd.)

Frantz in-line magnetic filter for high
pressure systems.

this flow should be free from turbulence. It is also desirable, whenever possible, to arrange that the majority or all of the particles are retained outside the main stream of flow, so that accumulation of contaminant cannot impede the flow. For maximum efficiency it is further desirable that the direction of flow of the fluid is the same as that of the magnetic field. The particles are then more readily diverted to the magnetic elements and withdrawn from the main flow. The normal arrangement is a series of magnets of cylindrical or quadrant shape retained in position by a non-ferrous metal cage or cylinder and clamped between two mild steel pole pieces at the top and bottom of the assembly. The external field passes between the pole pieces via a mild steel cage which has a series of gaps across which a strong flux is maintained. These gaps provide a concentration of the field and thus ensure a strong field gradient for effective removal of ferrous contaminants. A magnetic assembly of this type is shown in Fig 3.

Fig 3   Typical magnetic assembly.
(Philips)

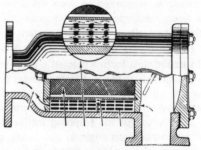

Fig 4 Magnetic pipeline filter.
(Philips)

Pipeline Filters

Special forms of magnetic filters have been developed specifically for installation in pipelines. An example is shown in Fig 4. Here the central core of the filter element comprises a permanent magnet enclosed in a non-magnetic cover. Surrounding this cover are a number of mild steel or iron segments connected by brass strips so as to leave a small gap between each segment in which ferrous contaminant is trapped.

The purpose of the non-magnetic cover around the magnet is to ensure that it does not become contaminated with particles. Thus the majority of the contaminants are collected between the segments, with some on the end pieces. The cages are split for ease of removal, and once removed from the magnet assembly are no longer magnetized, so that cleaning is simple and straightforward.

Line filters of this type can be made in virtually any size — for example, standard productions cover flow rates from 100 gallons per hour or less up to 4 000 gallons per hour. In the larger sizes two or more banks of rings may be provided in the cages to increase the number of air gaps, and thus the particle retention capacity of the filter — otherwise the design follows similar lines. Similar elements may also be incorporated in in-line housings rather than 'L' housings.

As an alternative to removing the cages for cleaning, the central magnet itself may be withdrawn to de-energize the rings, when the contaminant can be flushed out of the housing. A filter of this type is shown in Fig 5, again following essentially the same construction. In this case, however, the top cover of the filter body can be removed, or swung out of the way, and the magnet withdrawn to de-energize the cages for flushing clean. To avoid flushing contaminant into the normal outlet a further port is provided at the bottom of the casing for flushing direct into a separate draining bucket or receptacle.

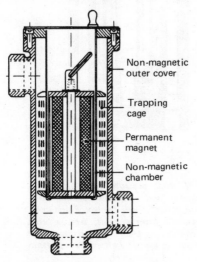

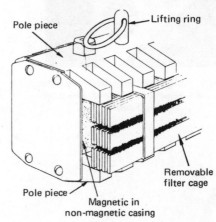

Fig 6   Magnetic filter for tanks or troughs.

Fig 5 Easy-clean magnetic filter.
(Philips)

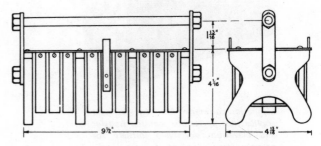

Fig 7   Magnetic filter for troughs.

Trough Filters

A design of permanent magnet filter suitable for use in troughs or settling tanks is shown in Fig 6. A number of core magnets are arranged side by side in a non-magnetic housing and effectively connected in parallel by the special pole pieces. The filter cage then consists of a series of strips on either side of the magnets, located between the pole pieces. The filter is placed in the trough in the line of flow. A complete assembly is shown in Fig 7.

Magnetic elements may also be fitted into the feed pipes of troughs or funnels, the funnel filter being widely used in the pottery and paint industries — Fig 8. In other cases, magnetic filter elements may be combined with mechanical filter elements in a single housing to remove both ferrous and non-ferrous contaminants in a single pass through the filter. More simply, the same effect may be provided by inserting a magnetic plug in the main flow channel of a standard mechanical filter.

Fig 8   Magnetic filter funnel as used by the ceramic and paint industries. (Philips)

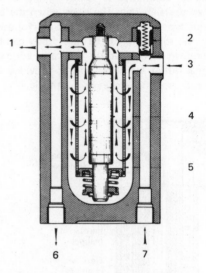

Fig 9   High pressure micro-filter with magnetic and mechanical elements. 1-side outlet. 2-relief-valve. 3-side inlet. 4-magnetic filter element. 5-replaceable micro-filter element. 6-alternative bottom outlet. 7-alternative bottom inlet.
(Pratt Precision Hydraulics Ltd.)

Magnetic conveyor for dry or wet applications of ferrous material transfer and elevation, developed initially for primary separation of ferrous solids. (Belisle Filtration Ltd.)

Magnetic/Mechanical Filters

Magnetic filter elements may be combined with mechanical filter elements in a common casing to provide protection against both magnetic and non-magnetic particles. A typical example of a high duty filter of this type is shown in Fig 9.

Combined fabric and magnetic filter,
the magnetic drum being used for first
stage removal of ferrous solids.
(Belisle Filtration Ltd.)

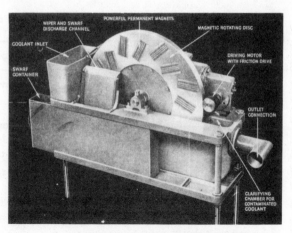

Fig 10 Magnetic clarifier.

Magnetic Clarifiers

Another application of the magnetic filter is the use of a rotating magnetic disc as the filter element. This is adopted in magnetic clarifiers, particularly for the treatment of machine tool coolants, the disc unit being so designed that it can be mounted at any height alongside a grinding wheel or honing machine, Fig 10. Coolant from the machine is fed direct to a clarifying chamber containing the rotating magnetic disc where ferrous swarf and grindings are removed from the coolant and also collected off the wheel into swarf containers which are withdrawn periodically for emptying.

Essentially the entry to the clarifier comprises a narrow channel into which the coolant leaving the machine is fed under gravity. It then flows past a slowly rotating aluminium disc turning in an opposing direction, inset into the periphery of which are a series of permanent magnets or magnet assemblies. These collect any ferrous contaminants present in the fluid and lift them clear of the tank where the magnets are scraped clean by wiper blades, sweeping the contaminants into separate containers.

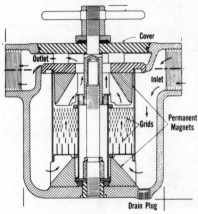

Frantz 'Ferrofilter' (magnetic separator)
employs grids (detailed right) magnetized by permanent magnets.
(Belisle Filtration Ltd.)

SUMMARY OF MAGNETIC FILTER TYPES AND APPLICATIONS

Type	Application(s)	Typical Size Range	Remarks
Sump plugs	Engine crankcase sumps, gearboxes, bearings	Wide range	
Cartridge	Engine lubrication systems Smaller pipelines	Wide range up to 20 000 gal/h	In-line filters Single or twin
Pipeline	Fluid pipelines	up to 30 000 gal/h	Single or twin
Combined	Fluid pipelines	up to 100 000 gal/h	Combined mechanical and magnetic filters
Pneumatic line	Pneumatic pipelines	2½ in to 10 in bore	
Drum	Batch filtering	up to 10 000 gal/h	Generally known as clarifiers
Pressurized clarifier	Finishing processes and coolants	up to 4 000 gal/h	
Vacuum clarifier	Finishing processes and coolants	up to 2 000 gal/h	Commonly used with machine tools
Chip conveyor	Waste removal from cutting tools	Various	
Dry separator	Removing ferrous particles from dry solids (eg foundry work etc)	Various	Incorporates vibrating conveyor
Magnetic funnels	Removal of ferrous particles from slurries etc.	up to 2 000 gal/h	Mainly used by ceramic and paint industries
Trough traps	Tanks filters	Various	Used in settling tanks, troughs, etc.
Skimmers	Removal of ferrous particles from liquids in settling tanks	up to 24 ins	

Frantz magnetic separator. These units are designed for high volume swarf separation and with flows of up to 200 gal/min combined with a compact small design available in two forms, one for direct gravity feeding and the second for secondary force fed systems required when being used in elevated locations. The systems are designed to operate on both soluble and neat cutting oils.

Squeegie-action

Sludge
discharge

Dirty
coolant

Clean
coolant

Permanent Alcomax magnets 8 lbs
for every 4 gals capacity

*Fig 11   Magnetic coolant separator.
(Gaston E. Marbaix)*

Magnetic Separators

Magnetic separators work on the same principle as magnetic filters, attracting and retaining ferromagnetic solids contained in a product being treated. Particular, and quite different, major spheres
of application are for the removal of harmful metallic particles and sludges from coolants in re-
moulding machine tool systems; and for mineral processing.

An example of a rotary magnetic separator for continuous cutting fluid filtration is shown in
Fig 11, in this case employing Alcomax magnets in the proportion of 2 lb magnet weight for each
gallon of fluid capacity — an empirical figure determined as providing optimum filtration performance. A further feature of this design is that accumulated sludge is carried round on the outside of
the rotor and discharged continuously into a sludge pan.

A similar form of magnetic separator working on a conveyor belt principle may be used for
mineral processing. Others work on filtration through an expanded metal mesh or wire matrix
forms of carbon steel or (magnetic) stainless steel energized by strong permanent magnets or
electromagnets. The use of electromagnets provides control of the magnetic field strength and the
possibility of separating diamagnetic and paramagnetic particles differentially (also dependent on
the carrier fluid used).

Contaminant Levels

THE USE of a filter with a specific rating consistent with the requirements of the system does not necessarily imply satisfactory performance. Apart from the fact that the filter will be less than 100% efficient under working conditions, particularly if pulsating flow is present, contaminant particles may be dislodged from the pores of the filter element allowing more fine particles to pass through. In critical or sensitive systems, therefore, monitoring of the contaminant level can be desirable.

The object of this is twofold. First, to check that contaminant accumulation does not exceed an acceptable level; and also possibly from this to establish what is an acceptable contaminant level in the absence of available guidelines. Second, to check that the initial filter specification is adequate for the system in practical use. Here it should be mentioned that it is not necessarily just the filter which is involved.

The system pressure and duty cycle, and the location of the filter(s) are additional parameters which can influence contaminant level. Intelligent attention must also be given to the point(s) in the system from which fluid samples are drawn for analysis when measuring contaminant levels; and the method of extracting the fluid samples. Thus the system should have been operated for at least 30 minutes to distribute contaminants uniformly before sampling, and if the sample is drawn from a valve, a flushing flow should be drawn off first before taking the actual sample. Alternative sampling points are a sampling tank fitted with a 'clean' valve (eg ball valve with PTFE seat), or possibly the reservoir in the case of hydraulic systems. In all cases, samples should only be taken under the cleanest conditions possible.

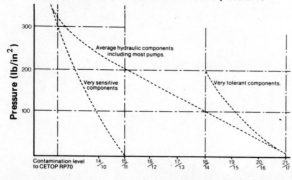

Suggested contaminant levels for
hydraulic systems.
(Sperry Vickers)

Treatment of Samples

To analyze the contaminants in a fluid sample the fluid is filtered through a laboratory-standard membrane. Particles retained on the membrane are then sized and counted. This can be done by microscope methods (*eg* ARD-598A), or by automatic particle counters. The latter eliminate the tedium of misroscope counting and the variations between the results of individual operations due to human error. Modern automatic counting machines employ scanning computers and TV screens, with the count displayed as numbers. It is also possible to programme the computer to provide specific digital information.

In general particle count methods are only suitable for particles larger than 5 μm, but they do also give some indication of the type of contaminant. Light-interception counters can handle smaller (as well as larger) particles, but only record the equivalent circular area size. Also they do not differentiate between solid particles and air or gas bubbles. They have the distinct advantage, however, of adjustable (pre-set) thresholds whereby individual channels can be selected to count particles by particular size ranges.

Even light-interception counters do not give entirely satisfactory results for particle sizes smaller than 5 μm and at the present state of the art, non-quantitative methods are normally used for lower ranges. Probably the most used is the *Silt Index* which is the ratio of the rate of flow of clean fluid through a membrane to that of the sample fluid at the same pressure. This, too, has its limitations in that any immissible fluid present (*eg* water in oil) can clog the membrane and artificially increase the Silt Index Number.

CETOP RP70 System

The CETOP RP70 code is a method of expressing contaminant particle counts in a standard manner by *range numbers*, viz:

Number of particles per 100 millilitres	RP70 Range Number
1 – 2	1
2 – 4	2
4 – 8	3
8 – 16	4
16 – 32	5
32 – 64	6
64 – 130	7
130 – 250	8
250 – 500	9
500 – 1 000	10
1 000 – 2 000	11
2 000 – 4 000	12
4 000 – 8 000	13
8 000 – 16 000	14
16 000 – 32 000	15
32 000 – 64 000	16
64 000 – 130 000	17
130 000 – 250 000	18
250 000 – 500 000	19
500 000 – 1 000 000	20
1 000 000 – 2 000 000	21
2 000 000 – 4 000 000	22
4 000 000 – 8 000 000	23
8 000 000 – 16 000 000	24

Particles are grouped according to size, when the count for each size group can be specified by range number. In practice only two parameters are normally used (although this may vary when applied to specific systems);

(i)   Total count of all particles above 5 μm.

(ii)   Total count of all particles above 15 μm.

Each count is then allocated a range number and the contaminant level expressed as these two numbers separated by an oblique, *eg*

16/10

This would represent a count of between 32 000 and 64 000 for all particles above 5 μm size in a 100 ml sample; together with a count of between 500 and 1 000 particles above 15 μm in size in the same 100 ml sample. Table I is a useful reference for converting code numbers into actual particle counts over the range likely to be encountered in practice.

The CETOP RP70 standard is merely a method of expressing sample particle counts in terms of a simple code. It does not specify the method of sampling or making the count, nor does it indicate the type or geometry of the contaminants.

TABLE I – NUMBER OF PARTICLES PER 100 ML OF SAMPLE FLUID

Code	Larger than 5 μm	Larger than 15 μm
10/8	500 – 1 000	130 – 250
11/8	1 000 – 2 000	130 – 250
12/8	2 000 – 4 000	130 – 250
12/9	2 000 – 4 000	250 – 500
13/8	4 000 – 8 000	130 – 250
13/9	4 000 – 8 000	250 – 500
13/10	4 000 – 8 000	500 – 1 000
14/8	8 000 – 16 000	130 – 250
14/9	8 000 – 16 000	250 – 500
14/10	8 000 – 16 000	500 – 1 000
14/11	8 000 – 16 000	1 000 – 2 000
15/9	16 000 – 32 000	250 – 500
15/10	16 000 – 32 000	500 – 1 000
15/11	16 000 – 32 000	1 000 – 2 000
15/12	16 000 – 32 000	2 000 – 4 000
16/10	32 000 – 64 000	500 – 1 000
16/11	32 000 – 64 000	1 000 – 2 000
16/12	32 000 – 64 000	2 000 - 4 000
16/13	32 000 – 64 000	4 000 – 8 000
17/11	64 000 – 130 000	1 000 – 2 000
17/12	64 000 – 130 000	2 000 – 4 000
17/13	64 000 – 130 000	4 000 – 8 000
17/14	64 000 – 130 000	8 000 – 16 000
18/12	130 000 – 250 000	2 000 – 4 000
18/13	130 000 – 250 000	4 000 – 8 000
18/14	130 000 – 250 000	8 000 – 16 000
18/15	130 000 – 250 000	16 000 – 32 000
19/12	250 000 – 500 000	2 000 – 4 000
19/13	250 000 – 500 000	4 000 – 8 000
19/14	250 000 – 500 000	8 000 – 16 000
19/15	250 000 – 500 000	16 000 – 32 000
19/16	250 000 – 500 000	32 000 – 64 000
20/13	500 000 – 1 000 000	4 000 – 8 000
20/14	500 000 – 1 000 000	8 000 – 16 000
20/15	500 000 – 1 000 000	16 000 – 32 000
20/16	500 000 – 1 000 000	32 000 – 64 000
20/17	500 000 – 1 000 000	64 000 – 130 000

Filter Tests

THE CLASSIC method of determining the absolute rating of a filter and/or its efficiency is by the *glass bead test*. Glass beads of varying but known diameter sizes are introduced into the fluid as a contaminant in measured quantities and the fluid filtered through the element. The filtrate is then searched for the beads which have been passed and analyzed in the following ways:-

(i)   The filtrate is searched for the largest bead which has been passed. This establishes absolute cut-off rating for the filter.

(ii) The glass beads are pre-counted. The filtrate is then segregated and counted. The count can then be expressed in the form of a graph such as Fig 1 establishing the filter characteristics. From this a nominal rating can be established — for example, at the bead size at which x% or less than this size is passed (100-x% efficiency at nominal rating). The value of 'x' adopted may be anything between 10 and 2 per cent.

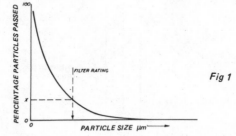

Fig 1

The true efficiency equation for calculating the efficiency of a filter on a 'count' test is

$$\% \text{ removal} = \frac{A - (B - C)}{A} \times 100$$

where
A = number of contaminants added at the test filter housing outlet with no filter element installed.

B = count of contaminant passing through the filter.

C = system blank value with test filter element installed and no contaminant added

This ensures that the actual number of contaminants incident on the filter are measured and introduced as a blank value to correct for any (uncounted) contaminants already in the system. The latter is particularly important where incident contaminant and filtrate contaminant are measured by weighing rather than counting.

The glass bead test has considerable practical limitations where micron sized particles have to be counted. Whilst the initial dosage can be counted by weighing, segregation and counting of the filtrate can be most exacting and time consuming, as well as being subject to limitations such as the determination of accurate depth of focus and limited field of view imposed by optical instruments.

In addition to glass beads, various other forms of contaminants are employed for particle 'counts'. Available bead sizes are seldom smaller than 10 to 20 micrometres, giving a useful size range of between 12 and 24 μm for evaluation. Finer particles are required for finer counts. These include—

Sand — particle size range from about 0.25 μm to 60 μm

Iron oxide — particle size range from about 0.5 μm to 5 μm

Test dusts (usually sands or silica sand) — particle size range from 1 to 100 μm

Dioctyl Phthalate — particle size range 0.3 μm (normally used for the evaluation of air filters only).

Cotton linters may also be used for coarse filtering and straining tests.

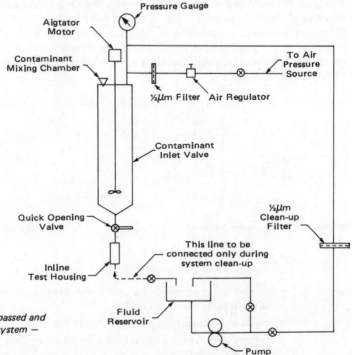

Fig 2 Maximum particle passed and
degree of filtration test system —
schematic.
(Purolator)

Mean Particle Passed Test

This test is used to determine the size of the largest hard spherical particle which will pass through a filter, using a test system of the form shown in Fig 2. Fluid is first circulated through a 'clean-up' filter until sampling shows a cleanliness level of 0.0004 gm/100 ml by gravimetric analysis. A measured quantity of artificial contaminant in graded sizes (usually glass beads from 2 to 80 μm diameter) is then introduced into the mixing chamber. After agitation a measured volume of fluid with contaminant is passed through the test unit and delivered to a beaker. It is then passed through a very fine membrane filter which removes the contaminant present and the diameter of the largest bead found in the filtrate is measured with a high powered microscope. This value (diameter size in μm) gives the *absolute rating* of the filter.

Degree of Filtration Test

The apparatus used for this test is similar to that for the mean particle passed test except that the weight of contaminant added is measured and also the weight of contaminant representing the filtrate (*ie* retained by the final membrane filter). The *degree of filtration* is then calculated as

$$\frac{W1 - W2}{W1} \times 100 \ (\%)$$

where

W1 = weight of added contaminant

W2 = weight of filtrate (on membrane)

This figure also establishes a *nominal rating* for the filter, relative to the specified contaminant.

Multi-Pass Test

This is used specifically to establish the *beta ratio* of a filter, using a test system of the form shown in Fig 3. The fluid is circulated with contaminant in the form of AC Fine Test Dust fed continuously into the system so that the same contaminant level is maintained in the fluid. In other words, make-up contaminant is added to replace that trapped by the filter under test.

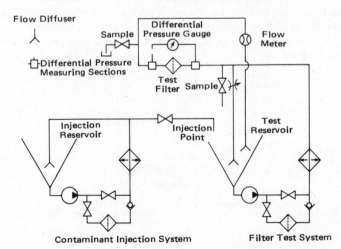

Fig 3 Multi pass test — schematic.
(Purolator)

Samples of the test fluid are drawn simultaneously upstream and downstream of the element under test at predetermined levels of differential pressure across the filter and analyzed with an automatic particle counter. The cumulative particle size distribution per millilitre of fluid is then determined, usually at particle sizes of 5, 10, 20, 30 and 40 μm. The beta ratio can then be calculated for each, or any, particle size, viz

βx = number of particles greater than X μm in size per millilitre in upstream flow
divided by number of particles greater than X μm in size per millilitre in downstream flow

A corresponding efficiency rating (Ex) follows as:

$$Ex = \frac{\beta x - 1}{\beta x} \times 100 \text{ (\%)} \quad or \quad Ex = 100 - \frac{100}{\beta x} \text{ (\%)}$$

Bubble Point Test

The bubble point test is based on the fact that for a given fluid and pore size, with constant wetting, the pressure required to force an air bubble through the pore is in inverse proportion to the size of the hole. In practice, this means that the pore size of a filter element can be established by wetting the element with the fluid and measuring the pressure at which the first stream of bubbles is emitted from the upper surface of the element when air pressure is applied from the underside.

The point from which the first stream of bubbles emerges is the largest hole. A further increase in pressure will then produce bubbling from the second largest hole, then the third, and so on. Eventually a point is reached where air bubbles appear over the entire surface of the element. This is known as the open bubble point or 'boil' point. The corresponding pressure at which this occurs is an accurate measure of the mean pore size of the element.

Apparatus for a bubble point test is shown in Fig 4. Two distinct measurements may be made, as outlined previously. The initial bubble test pressure determines the size (and location) of the largest hole. The open bubble point pressure determines the mean pore size of the element. The latter can be affected by flow velocity as well as pressure, so comparative tests on different types of elements to determine the mean pore size should be conducted at the same flow rate. Airflow velocity has no effect on the initial bubble point.

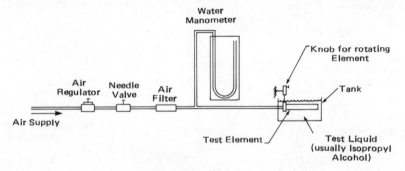

Fig 4 Bubble point test — schematic.

The theoretical relationship between bubble point pressure and pore diameter is given by Poiseuille's law for capillary tubes, viz:

$$P = \frac{4 \, \tau \cos \theta}{d}$$

where P = bubble point pressure
   τ = surface tension of wetting fluid
   θ = angle of contact of wetting fluid to the filter medium
   d = pore diameter

Since no pores in a practical filter element are likely to be shaped like capillary tubes it is necessary to introduce a shape correction factor (K) into the formula which then becomes

$$P = \frac{4 \, K \, \tau \cos \theta}{d}$$

Equally, since τ and θ are effectively constants the formula can be further simplified to

$$P = \frac{K_1}{d}$$

where K_1 is an empirical factor dependent on the filter material and form of the units employed

A particular advantage of the bubble test is that it is non-destructive (ie does not contaminate the filter) and so can be used to determine the integrity of a filter at any time, as well as for establishing an absolute rating. It can also be correlated to glass bead tests. Further, if the bubble point is measured prior to a Maximum Particle Passed Test, the value of K or K_1 can be established for other filter elements using the same medium.

Dirt Capacity Test

This test may be used to determine a life figure for a filter and/or assess its dirt-holding capacity. A typical test system is shown in Fig 5, providing continuous recirculating flow through the filter under test. Specified contaminant is added upstream at regular time intervals and the differential pressure across the filter recorded so that a plot can be made of contaminant added against differential pressure. The dirt capacity of the filter is then established by a limiting value of pressure drop (differential pressure) across the filter.

Pressure Drop Test

This uses the same (or similar) apparatus to Fig 5 except that no contaminant is added. Only clean fluid is circulated at measured flow rates and at a standard, controlled temperature. The differential pressure or pressure drop across the filter is then established for different flow rates.

Such tests may be conducted on the complete filter (in its housing), or on the filter element only. Sometimes housing and filter element are evaluated separately, but it does not necessarily follow that the pressure drop of the complete filter is the exact sum of these two separate pressure drops.

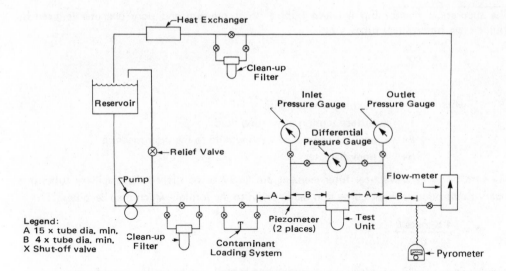

Fig 5   Clean pressure drop and dirt capacity tests (schematic).

Collapse Test

This is virtually a continuation of the pressure drop test, but using contaminated fluid and a flow rate equivalent to the rating of the filter. The test continues until the differential pressure becomes high enough to cause the filter element to fail or collapse.

Media Migration Test

The apparatus used for this test can be the same as or similar to, that employed for the Maximum Particle Passed Test. It is normally conducted with clean fluid so that the only contaminant present downstream is material which has migrated from the test filter. This is removed by a membrane filter and analyzed microscopically and gravimetrically.

Media Migration Tests may be modified to simulate actual service conditions including such other parameters as fluctuating flow, flow reversal, and mechanical vibration.

Fatigue Tests

The test circuit used for fatigue tests subjects the filter to stop-start cycles (for evaluating fatigue under steady flow conditions), or cycles of pressure fluctuation (for evaluating fatigue under pulsating flow conditions). A Bubble Test applied to the filter element before, and again after, the fatigue test determines the integrity of the filter.

Acceptable figures for cycle life can vary widely with different types of filter elements, but as a general guide are of the order of 10 000 cycles for steady flow condition and 100 000 to 1 250 000 cycles for pulsating flow applications.

Air Filter Tests

Contaminants used for air filter tests include mixtures of natural sand and quartz, aluminium oxide dusts and methylene blue. Sand/quartz mixture is specified for British Standard Test Code BS1701, intended for the valuation of air filters for internal combustion engines and compressors.

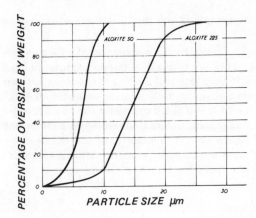

Fig 6

TABLE I – METHYLENE BLUE CLOUD PARTICLE DISTRIBUTION

Size μm	% Undersize by Number	% Undersize by Weight
0.011	16.5	0.006
0.032	36.0	0.08
0.065	56.5	1.17
0.130	81.0	8.66
0.216	92.5	19.7
0.305	96.8	31.0
0.390	98.2	41.5
0.475	99.0	53.2
0.610	99.5	74.2
0.785	99.8	91.7
1.13	99.9	97.5
1.30	100.0	100.0

Aluminium oxide dusts Aloxite 50 and Aloxite 225 are specified for British Standard Test Code BS2831 for ventilation applications. Particle sizes of these standard contaminants are shown in Fig 6.

Methylene blue dust is used primarily for the testing of low penetration filters. The particles are extremely fine, with a mesh size of 0.5 μm and no particles larger than 1.3 μm — see Table I. It would not be used for testing ordinary air conditioning filters as these would show relatively low efficiency with such a medium.

Test technique with methylene blue is to atomize a solution of the blue dye through a spray nozzle at a specified pressure, discharging the spray into a duct which houses the filter on test. Sampling points are located upstream and downstream in a straight section. The upstream section of the duct is of sufficient length to allow moisture to evaporate from the methylene blue, leaving a dust cloud of completely dispersed methylene blue particles. The performance of the filter is then assessed by comparing stain samples on the clean and dirty sides of the unit.

A more recent technique involves the use of salt solution contaminant and measurement of the cloud concentration passing through the filter by its yellowing effect on a hydrogen flame (BS 3928). This is a more accurate method than methylene blue for the testing of low penetration filters and can be completed in a matter of minutes, compared with the 30 minutes which may be necessary with the methylene blue test.

Apparatus used is shown in Fig 7. The test cloud is formed by the evaporation of a 2% common salt solution, particles formed having a mean size of 0.6 μm with a distribution as shown in Fig 8 and Table II. The test spray is directed through a sufficient length of ducting to dry it out (or over heaters if necessary), and thence to the test section containing the filter to be evaluated. A sampling point downstream then collects a sample of the filter test cloud and passes this to a hydrogen flame. The colour of this flame is observed by a photosensitive cell connected to a meter, the meter being calibrated to read the brightness of yellow light. The intensity of the yellow in the hydrogen flame is directly proportional to the amount of salt particles in the sampling volume of air. Thus the meter can, in fact, be calibrated to read directly the amount of salt present.

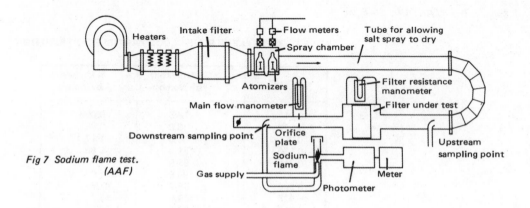

Fig 7 Sodium flame test.
(AAF)

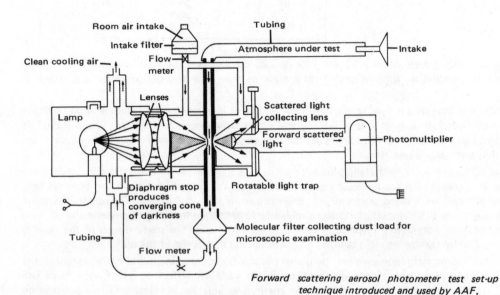

Forward scattering aerosol photometer test set-up — a technique introduced and used by AAF.

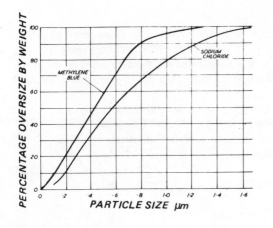

Fig 8

TABLE II – SODIUM CHLORIDE CLOUD PARTICLE DISTRIBUTION

Size μm	% Undersize
0.1	58.0
0.2	55.0
0.3	93.5
0.4	96.7
0.5	98.2
0.6	99.0
0.7	99.45
0.8	99.65
0.9	99.80
1.0	99.87
1.1	99.91
1.2	99.94
1.3	99.96
1.4	99.97
1.5	99.98
1.6	99.99
1.7	100.00

TABLE III – CONTAMINANTS USED FOR FILTER TESTS

Artificial Contaminant	Useful Size Range μm	Remarks
Glass Beads	10–20 and up	Common standard for fluid filters
Sand	40–100 mesh	Natural sand (MIL-E-5007B and BS1701)
Test Dust (Silica)	1 μm up or 1–100 mesh	Graded sand (MIL-E-5504A) Graded sand (MIL-E-5007B)
Iron Oxide	0.5–5	
Cotton Linters	up to 50 000	
Aluminium Oxide	5–10 (Aloxite 90) 10–20 (Aloxite 225)	(BS2831)
Methylene Blue	0.01 to 1.3	Low penetration air filters only (BS2831)
Sodium Chloride (Cloud)	0.58 mean	Low penetration air filters only (BS3928)
Dioctyl Phthalate	0.3 mean	Air filters only
Carbon Black	0.01 to 0.1	Used for compression type edge filters; also other types of sub-micron filters

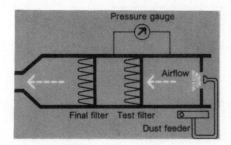

Test set-up for arrestance measurements

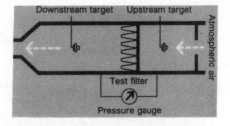

Fig 9

Test set-up for dust spot efficiency measurements

Air Filter Tests (ASHRAE)

The American Society of Heating, Refrigeration and Air-conditioning Engineers (ASHRAE) specifies a number of test procedures recognized worldwide by the filter industry and which also form the basis of 'Eurovent' standard 4/5. These tests determine resistance, dust spot efficiency and dust holding capacity, using a test rig to ASHRAE specification 52-76 — see Fig 9. Test procedures are:

(i)   By measuring the pressure drop across the filter under test, its initial arrestance is found for various airflows. The results are plotted as shown in.curve A, Fig 10. From this graph the initial resistance of the sample filter, at its rated airflow (100%) is 170 Pa. This is recorded on curve B.

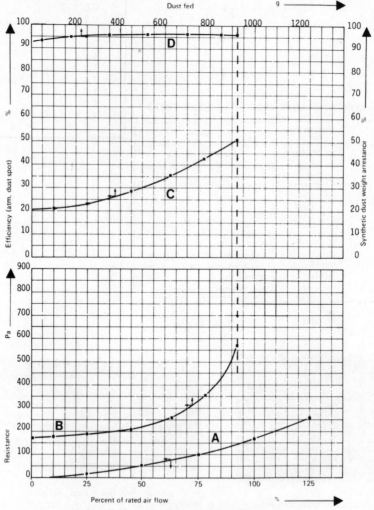

Fig 10 Typical ASHRAE test characteristics.

(ii)   Initial dust spot efficiency is measured by drawing atmospheric air through the filter under test. A separate vacuum pump draws air through samplers, each consisting of a small disc of high efficiency medium, located on either side of the filter. As the test proceeds, the samplers are darkened by the dirt collected. To make the final calculations easier, both samplers should be equally darkened at the end of the test. Because the upstream sampler darkens a lot more quickly than the downstream sampler, air is only drawn through it for a predetermined portion of the total test. When the test is completed, the samplers are removed, checked on an opacity meter to ensure that they have been equally darkened (difference not more than 20% of the highest value) and, if not, the test is repeated. Otherwise the dust spot efficiency can be calculated by

$$\epsilon \ = \ 100 \times (1 - \frac{Q_1}{Q_2} \quad \times \quad \frac{O_2}{O_1}) \ \%$$

and the result plotted on curve C.

Q_1 = total volume of air drawn through the upstream target,

Q_2 = total volume of air drawn through the downstream target,

O_1 = opacity of dust spot upstream target,

O_2 = opacity of dust spot downstream target.

The first arrestance measurement is then made. A final high efficiency filter of known weight is inserted downstream of the filter under test. A fixed weight of synthetic dust, composed according to ASHRAE 52-76 requirements, is injected into the airflow. At the end of the test the final filter is reweighed and thus the weight of dust captured by the sample filters is known. Arrestance is calculated by

$$A = 100 \times (1 - \frac{W_2}{W_1})\%$$

and the value plotted on curve D.

(W_1 = total weight of synthetic dust,

W_2 = weight of dust not captured by sample filter).

Dust spot efficiency is then measured again and the second point plotted on curve C. The resistance is also measured for inclusion on curve B.

Clean piece of high
efficiency filter paper

Staining effect of
unfiltered air

Staining effect of
filtered air

Dust spot efficiency is measure of the filter's ability to remove staining elements from an airstream.

Arrestance, dust spot efficiency and resistance measurements are repeated five times in all. Average values of these, together with the dust holding capacity, can then be determined. These results are assessed to ensure that filter performance is up to specification and consistently high from production run to production run.

Compressed Air Filter Tests

Various test methods for proving filter performance have been available for some time and whilst being useful all have some drawbacks. Typically particle counters using light scattering techniques are employed in the tests but they can only sample very small volumes of air, which must be dry, otherwise results would be greatly affected by condensate readings. Typical sample rates are 1-28 l/min. The DOP test, which is very popular, uses a cloud of liquid aerosol to challenge the filter under test, but as with the even more common sodium flame test, which uses solid particles, only the retentive capacity of a filter working in a dry and unloaded condition can be tested.

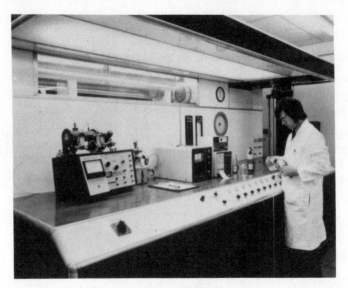

*Domnick Hunter integrity test rig for
sterile air filters.*

For a coalescing oil removal type filter the aforementioned tests can only be used as integrity tests, as of course oil removal filters do not operate in dry conditions at low flow rates. They operate in a saturated state often at high flow rates. From an initial low dry operating pressure drop, the pressure drop will rise quite quickly until the filter has reached its saturated, working pressure drop. It is important to consider the saturated pressure drop when allowing for the pressure drop in a system, as dry pressure drops most often quoted by filter manufacturers can be misleading. Likewise when testing the remaining oil content in the air after filtering, filters must be tested once the saturated pressure drop has been reached and when the coalescing action of the filter has started, *ie* oil is being separated from the air and dumped into the drainage area of the filter housing. Many tests give emphasis to the oil aerosol contained in the air, but apart from this there are other factors to consider, *eg* condensate, temperature, filter sizing and actual remaining oil content.

Condensate is present in most compressor systems due to the effects of pressure and heat losses after compression. Condensate will therefore add to the loading (pressure drop) across the filter. Even in systems using desiccant driers the filter will be fitted prior to the drier to remove oil aerosol and condensate, thus protecting the desiccant from pollution and excess condensate which would reduce the drier's effectiveness.

Temperature also has a significant effect on oil carryover and here again filter manufacturers and users need to be aware of this. Tests at ambient temperatures, (eg 21°C) are unrealistic except for terminal applications. A typical discharge temperature from an oil lubricated screw compressor with air blast aftercooler is 35°C. Tests have shown that at this temperature filters of similar DOP or sodium flame test efficiency, determined with small scale laboratory testing at ambient temperatures, can perform quite differently. Hence it is not good enough to rely on DOP or sodium flame tests alone in determining filter performance.

Filter sizing is also important. Overrating filter elements will increase pressure drop roughly proportionally to the increased flow whilst oil carryover can increase dramatically. The increased pressure drop costs a lot of money — much more than sizing the filter correctly to start with. Also filter element life is reduced.

It is still surprisingly common to see filter manufacturers claiming percentage efficiencies for oil removal filters based on DOP and sodium flame tests. In reality 99% efficiency is meaningless to the user and a more specific definition is required, eg remaining oil content after filter is X mg/m³, as recommended by Pneurop 14 on air quality standards.

A suitable filter test method needs to cover all the aforementioned requirements to be recognized as a meaningful and realistic test method. A simple check list can be drawn up for any test method as follows and only one which gives positive answers to all questions will ultimately be satisfactory.

1) Is the filter being tested under typical operating conditions?

2) Has the filter reached a working/saturated pressure drop?

3) Can filter performance be tested at various operating temperatures?

4) Is efficiency measured as remaining oil content in mg/m³ (rather than ppm)?

5) Can either the total air volume or most of it be actually sampled by the test method?

6) Can the test method operate under all conditions, eg with condensate, other gases, etc?

7) Is the test method sensitive enough to detect the very low oil carryover from the best high efficiency filters available, eg 0.01 mg/m³?

8) Has the test method been subject to ratification by an independent source?

9) Is the test method recognized by an international organization, eg Pneurop?

10) Is the test equipment portable for in situ testing?

PNEUROP Test System

A test method has been devised to meet all the laid down criteria and has now been adopted in the draft proposals of the Pneurop 14 Committee on compressed air quality.

Fig 11 shows a systematic layout of a typical Pneurop test system. Air in this case is being supplied by an oil lubricated screw compressor (1) and filters (2) are fitted close to the compressor and subjected to full flow conditions. The pressure drop across the filter is monitored (3) until a stable pressure drop is reached, meaning the filter has reached its operating or saturated pressure

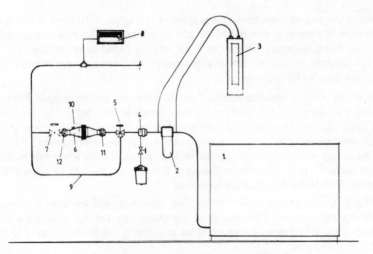

Fig 11 Pneurop test rig for compressed air filters.

drop; this time will, depending on oil/condensate loading, vary up to 24 hours. Air passes from the filter into the test apparatus. A wall flow separator (4) is used to collect any liquid on the walls of the pipe. Air then passes through a two way valve (5) then through a large diameter membrane holder (6) (capacity 420 m³/h) through a valve (7) and to the flow meter (8) before being discharged. Using valves (5) and (7) the air is diverted around the bypass leg (9) enabling the membrane holder to be depressurized using valve (10) and then removed using unions (11) and (12). Up to this point no membranes have been fitted in the holder. The holder is now cleaned and a membrane fitted before the holder is replaced in the system and air re-diverted through it.

Sample time will vary depending on the filter efficiency, but would typically be 2–5 minutes. Three samples would be taken as part of the procedure to ensure consistent results; the membranes are then analyzed using infra-red spectrophotometric techniques. The sampling procedure would be typically repeated every 24 hours and results plotted. The test would normally last 200 hours ensuring that consistent oil carryover figures are achieved.

SECTION 2

Types of Filters and Separators

Sub-section (a)

Strainers

STRAINERS OFFER a simple method of protection for pipeline systems for removal of debris such as dirt, swarf, weld sputter, scale *etc*. They fall broadly into two categories, temporary strainers and permanent strainers.

Temporary strainers are designed for short periods of application, *eg* fitted during the run-in period of a new system, or when restarting a system after shut-down and maintenance. They are intended to remove coarse debris particles present in the system. After a suitable period in use, they are removed (and can be cleaned and stored for future use).

Strainers of this type are normally designed with standard flange faces so that they can be fitted at a suitable flange joint in the pipeline. When removed they can be replaced by a spacer washer. They may take the form of a flat disc or a conical basket — Fig 1. Flat disc strainers are normally perforated plates. Basket strainers may be of perforated plate or supported wire mesh. They have a higher dirt capacity, normally have lower pressure drop and can provide finer filtering (*eg* typically down to 150 μm).

Fig 1 Examples of temporary strainers. (Filtration and Valves Ltd.)

Bath tub screen

Flat disc strainer

Conical basket strainer

Where fitting such strainers is difficult or impractical on a particular system, other types of temporary strainers are produced to match a blind T-junction fitting, into which they can readily be fitted and removed. These strainers are often of a trough shape, referred to as *bathtub* strainers.

Permanent strainers are conventionally complete fittings, most commonly of Y-configuration with a cylindrical strainer element — Fig 2. They can be used in both horizontal and vertical (downflow) lines. The element is retained by a plug end which may be plain or fitted with a valve which can be opened for 'blow-through' cleaning. In either case the element itself is removable and so this type can also be used as a temporary strainer. Typical data are summarized in Table I and Fig 3.

Fig 2 Y - type strainers.
(Filtration and Valves Ltd.)

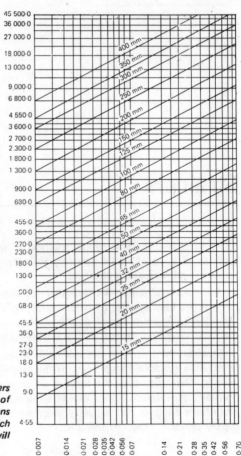

Flow Rate (Water) Litres/Min.

Pressure Drop lb/in^2

Fig 3 Estimation of pressure loss in typical Y - type strainers can be made from the chart which is based on water of specific gravity 1.0 and viscosity 32 secs Red No.1. Screens are clean and are 40 x 40 woven wire mesh. Liquids which are more viscous when used with finer weave meshes will create increased pressure drops.
(Filtration and Valves Ltd.)

TABLE I – TYPICAL PERFORATED CYLINDRICAL STRAINER DATA

Effective Screen Area				Suitable for Pipe Diameters	
1/16 in (1.5 mm) holes, 109 holes per in		0.021 in (0.5 mm) holes, 620 holes per in		in	mm
in^2	cm^2	in^2	cm^2		
0.76	4.9	0.52	3.3	¼–3/8	6–8
2.78	18.0	1.37	8.8	½	12.5
5.1	33	2.5	16	¾	19
9.6	62	4.7	30	1	25
12.4	80	6.1	40	1¼	31
15.7	101	7.7	50	1½	37.5
23.1	150	11.4	73.5	2	50
33.5	216	20.8	130	2½	67.5
33.5	216	20.0	130	3	75
38.0	245	24.0	155	3½	92.5

On larger pipelines *basket-type* strainers are often preferred; see Fig 4. These may be of in-line or off-line type. The principal advantages of basket strainers is that they can provide greater dirt-holding capacity and can have easier access for removal of the strainer for cleaning. They do, however, normally have a higher pressure drop than simple Y-type strainers.

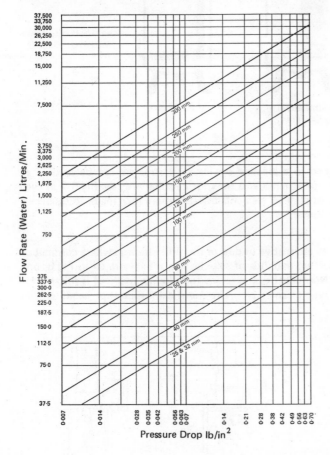

Fig 4   In-line basket-type strainer and typical pressure drop characteristics for basket with 3mm perforations. (Filtration and Valves Ltd.)

TABLE II – TYPICAL WIRE MESH Y-TYPE STRAINER DATA

Mesh Size	Rating μm
20 x 20	894
30 x 30	570
40 x 40	400
60 x 60	250
80 x 80	185
100 x 100	140

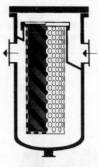
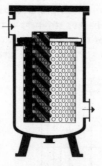

'Leitz' basket strainers.
(Seitz-Werk GmbH)

Single strainer   Double strainer   Multi-strainer
basket filter   basket filter   basket filter

Dual Strainers

Where continuous operation is required in a pipeline service, dual strainers can be used in an integral unit with provision to isolate one strainer at a time for cleaning — *eg* see Fig 5 — or even multiple strainers in one unit. Individual strainer elements or baskets are then made accessible via cover plates with static seals (usually O-rings).

Self-cleaning Strainers

Self-cleaning strainers may be used as an alternative to dual or multiple-strainers where continuous supply is critical in a process system. Two methods of self-cleaning are illustrated in Fig 6, one using a brush and the other a screen. Normally brush cleaning (or a similar method) is suitable for most applications. Screen- or scraper-type cleaners are more specifically suited for handling high viscosity products.

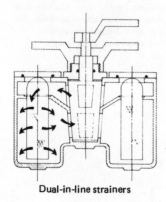

Dual-in-line strainers

Fig 5

Fig 6 Self-cleaning strainers.
(Alfa-Laval)

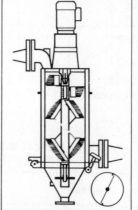

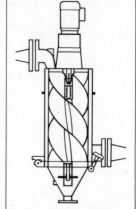

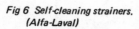

Brush model
Suitable for low viscosity products. A special feature is the two bars in the perforated cylinder for cleaning the brushes.

Screw model
Suitable for heavy viscosity products such as animal fat and wax and to enable cleaning-in-place (CIP).

Performance Range

Perforated plate strainers provide coarse filtration down to about 150 μm. For finer filtering wire mesh elements are normally used, in conjunction with perforated plate(s) or other forms of reinforcement if necessary for mechanical strength. Wire mesh strainers can provide filtration down to about 40 μm, but with reducing strength because of the increasingly finer wire which has to be used.

Strainer Sizing

Numerically the service life of a strainer (between cleaning times) can be expressed as the ratio of open area of the strainer to pipe cross section. Open area is determined by the choice of perforation or mesh, which would normally be of the order of 15–20%. Strainers are normally proportioned to provide a 3:1 area ratio for general service, although this may need to be doubled in the case of more viscous fluids.

See also chapters on *Perforated Metal Plates* and *Woven Wire Cloth*.

Screens

PLATE-TYPE screens are widely used for the removal of solids from water on large-scale water handling systems. Where water is pumped from rivers or lakes, screens are normally employed on the intake side to protect the pumps from debris in the water (although this does not necessarily eliminate the need for intake strainers or finer screens on the pump inlet itself). The problem of screening may also be specific to the locality involved, which can dictate the type of screen or protection necessary. Thus special protection may be needed to deal with weed or 'grass' in sea water which will pass through coarse screens, or readily clog fine screens. In other localities marine life inducted with the water may present a special clogging problem. These can demand highly individual solutions.

Screens are also used to remove large inorganic solids from sewage and industrial wastes. The principle involved is exactly the same. Solids are deposited on the screening surface and require removal at regular intervals to prevent clogging on the screen. This can be done by scraping or raking the screen, or employing moving screens.

A typical stationary screen consists of a grill of rectangular bars (a bar grill or bar rack) with spacings of 1 in or less. Two methods of cleaning are shown in Fig 1. In one example a rake extending the full width of the screen is mechanically operated to provide front cleaning by scraping the

Fig 1 Examples of raked bar screens.

surface of the grill and carrying solids up to the discharge point. In the second example, applicable to a wider screen, the trash rake traverses the width of the screen as well as being raised or lowered on a cable. The rake in this case is unguided to allow it to ride over any large obstructions in the water. Rake teeth are hydraulically operated to 'open' and 'closed' positions. All debris is picked up and then dumped over the top of the screen, not simply loosened and forced to the bottom of the channel.

A travelling screen is shown in Fig 2. Here the screening surface consists of a number of hinge-connected panels or 'baskets' which hang vertically, supported by guides, but are also elevated by a chain drive. Each screen is thus progressively raised to the head end, carrying debris with it, where it is cleaned by a spray of water. The cleaned screens are then returned vertically to the bottom and brought forward to repeat the cycle of operation, working on an 'endless belt' principle.

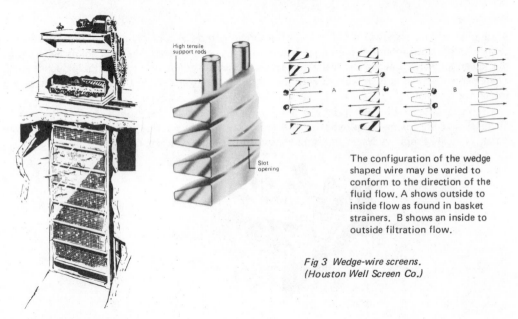

The configuration of the wedge shaped wire may be varied to conform to the direction of the fluid flow. A shows outside to inside flow as found in basket strainers. B shows an inside to outside filtration flow.

Fig 3 Wedge-wire screens.
(Houston Well Screen Co.)

Fig 2 Travelling water screen.
(Rex Chainbelt Inc.)

Profiled Screens

Profiled screens are made from bars of profiled shape or specially shaped wires, known generally as wedge wire. The resulting mesh structure can be used for flat screens or sieves or in such forms as troughs, curved or circular screens, discs, cylinders, etc. Wedge wire screens, in particular, are true edge filters and offer superior mechanical strength and finer apertures than it is possible to achieve with woven wire screens.

The typical form of wedge-shaped wire used is shown in Fig 3, with the configuration of the wedge arranged to conform to the direction of flow. External support rods welded to the wedge wires may or may not be necessary. Screening performance may be defined by slot opening, open area and apertures per linear dimension.

The wedge taper shape is most commonly employed with a flat top and is excellent for the dewatering of slurries. The top may be modified to a conical form for fine mesh screens for dewatering slurries. This shape is more likely to clog or 'blind' but reduces screen wear when abrasives are present in the slurry. However, a thickened and squared off top is normally preferred where high abrasive materials are handled as this allows for a considerable amount of wear to take place before the aperture opening is modified.

Screens of this type are widely used in the coal and coke industries for the removal of dust from fine coal, rinsing and dewatering processes and for suction filters. They are used by the sugar industry for drainage in tanks, in association with scrapers; by the chemical industries; for the dewatering of colloidal sludges; for scrim and knot catching in the pulp and paper making industries; as well as for filter bottoms and sieving for water and sewage treatment, water recovery and filtration.

Disc Screens

A rotating screen is shown in Fig 4. Here the screen comprises a revolving disc, normally in the form of wire cloth mounted on a rigid frame, rotating on a substantial shaft. Solids adhering to the screen are carried above the water surface, with heavier solids lifted by suitable bucket arms. The emergent screen is then washed with a spray of water, transferring the solids into a receiving trough for disposal.

Revolving disc screens of this type are normally limited in size from 6 feet to 14 feet in diameter and are mainly employed for the removal of relatively fine solids from fairly shallow water. They are simple in design and can be installed in simple concrete channels.

Fig 4 Revolving disc screen.

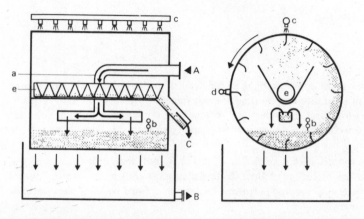

A - dirty liquid
B - clean liquid
C - solids
a - feed pipe
b - level monitor
c - blow-off device
d - flushing device
e - unloading screw

Fig 5 Drum screen.
(Alfa-Laval)

Drum Screens

A rotating drum screen is shown in Fig 5. This comprises a screen stretched around a drum with a blow-off device for cleaning the screen together with an unloading system for screened-off solids. The screen itself is wire mesh — *eg* in stainless steel or other metal according to the product being handled. Screens of this type may have a mesh opening from about 0.05 μm upwards, as required.

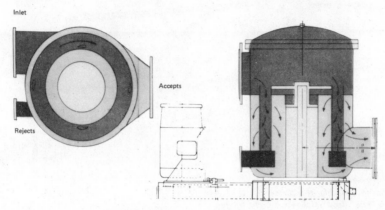

Fig 6 Bird 'Centriscreen' pressure screen

Pressure Screens

An example of a *pressure screen* is shown in Fig 6. Here the product being treated enters tangentially through the inlet into a trough which extends circumferentially around the screen casing. Flow from the inlet trough is inward and downward to the annular screening chamber which is bounded on the sides by two concentric, heavy duty screen cylinders and on the bottom by the reject gutter. The screen cylinders may be either conically-drilled or slotted.

Acceptable fibres pass through either the inner or outer perforated screen plate to the discharge outlet. The curved screen surfaces are kept constantly clean and open by the sweeping action of hydrofoils. These are the only rotating parts of the machine. They are suspended from the hub at the top and are driven by a motor from the base. The hydrofoils sweep through the screening chamber, aiding in breaking up incipient matting and assisting good fibres through the perforations.

Rejected material flows downward to the reject gutter and out of the screen. Flow is controlled to reduce passage of good fibre to a minimum and tailings maintained at a high level of

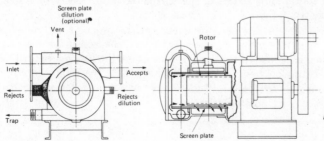

Beloit 'Centriscreen' pressure screen.

consistency. The long, narrow design of the annular chamber enables all of the stock to contact the screen plates so that very little of the clean stock reaches the reject gutter.

Screens of this type are widely used in the paper industry for stock preparation, accepting stock consistencies up to 4% or more and providing up to 97% screening efficiency.

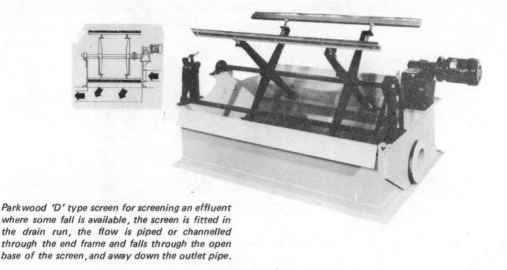

Parkwood 'D' type screen for screening an effluent where some fall is available, the screen is fitted in the drain run, the flow is piped or channelled through the end frame and falls through the open base of the screen, and away down the outlet pipe.

Bar-Lug   Slip-on   Bar-Lug Plus   Bar-Weld   Protecto-Screen
                       (Patent Pending)   (Patented)

Fig 7 Houston well screens.

Well Screens

Well screens are basically strainers fitted to the bottom of well pipes and may range from simple slotted pipes with or without a surrounding screen to specialized designs of sleeve-type screens. Some examples of the latter are shown in Fig 7.

The Bar-Lug screen is basically a wire wrap screen locating on vertical bars on a perforated pipe, facilitating free entry of fluid over the entire exposed surface of the screen to increase its efficiency. This principle is further extended in the Bar-Lug Plus where the bars are welded to the wedge-wire screen and the whole shrink fitted to the perforated pipe. The slip-on screen is of similar construction, but a slip-on fit. In the Bar-Weld screen the wedge wires are welded to vertical rods. The Protecto-Screen incorporates a perforated protective shell guard over the wedge-wire screen.

See also chapter on *Strainers*.

Perforated Metal Plates

PERFORATED METAL sheets are more rigid and can be made stronger than woven wire cloths and so find particular application for strainers,coarse filters and screens. Perforated metal strainers have a predictable and consistent performance since the size of the screen openings is controlled by manufacture. In their simplest form they can consist of a perforated metal sheet, the diameter of the holes providing an absolute cut-off rating and the number of holes per unit area governing the resistance to flow per unit area. A typical 'standard' screen of this type will have something like 100 1.55 mm (1/16 inch) diameter holes per square inch of metal surface; whilst a 'fine' screen may have 620 0.55 mm (0.021 inch) diameter holes per square inch. Perforations need not be circular. Various standard forms for perforated metal sheets are shown in Fig 1. Comparative open areas can be determined from Table I. (Standard sieves are detailed in Table II.)

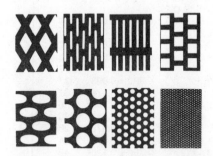

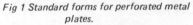

Fig 1 Standard forms for perforated metal plates.

Examples of expanded metal mesh. (The Expanded Metal Co.(Mfg.) Ltd.)

The effective screen area of such a strainer is defined as the total area of the holes only. For simple straining duties, for example, pipeline strainers, the screen area should exceed the cross sectional area of the pipe or entry it serves in order to avoid undue restriction of flow. In practice this means the finer the screen the less the effective screen area per unit of area and in consequence the greater the total surface area of strainer required. This can be realized by increasing the diameter of the strainer until the effective screen area is at least equal to that of the entry area; or equally by rendering the strainer in a can or cylindrical shape to achieve the required minimum effective screen area.

TABLE I — PERFORATED METAL DATA

Size of Hole		% Open Area	Size of Hole		% Open Area
mm	inch		mm	in	
ROUND HOLES			**ROUND END SLOTS (Alternate)**		
0.38	0.015	10	10.00 x 0.50	0.394 x 0.019	13
0.55	0.0215	26	10.00 x 1.00	0.394 x 0.039	23
0.70	0.0275	20	10.00 x 1.50	0.394 x 0.059	32
0.80	0.0315	32	20.00 x 1.50	0.787 x 0.059	34
1.09	0.043	25	10.00 x 2.00	0.394 x 0.079	30
1.40	0.049	25	20.00 x 2.00	0.787 x 0.079	30
1.50	0.055	32	13.00 x 2.50	0.511 x 0.098	28
1.5	0.059	37	20.00 x 2.50	0.787 x 0.098	31
1.64	0.065	36	12.00 x 3.00	0.472 x 0.118	38
1.75	0.069	39	20.00 x 3.00	0.787 x 0.118	47
2.16	0.085	33	25.00 x 3.50	0.984 x 0.137	38
2.45	0.097	36	**SQUARE END SLOTS (Parallel)**		
2.85	0.112	50	10.00 x 0.40	0.394 x 0.016	14
SQUARE HOLES (Parallel)			10.00 x 0.56	0.394 x 0.022	19
1.50	0.059	44	10.00 x 0.76	0.394 x 0.03	25
3.17	0.125	44	20.60 x 1.10	0.812 x 0.043	33
6.00	0.236	34	20.32 x 1.44	0.800 x 0.057	29
6.35	0.250	44	19.05 x 1.59	0.750 x 0.0625	27
7.00	0.275	41	13.00 x 2.50	0.511 x 0.098	37
9.52	0.375	44	20.00 x 3.25	0.787 x 0.128	41
11.00	0.437	49	19.84 x 3.96	0.781 x 0.156	42
12.70	0.500	44	19.05 x 4.75	0.750 x 0.187·	45
19.05	0.750	56	15.87 x 6.35	0.625 x 0.250	47
25.40	1.00	64	20.00 x 8.00	0.787 x 0.314	49
SQUARE HOLES (Alternate)			**DIAGONAL SLOTS**		
1.75	0.069	32	12.29 x 0.50	0.484 x 0.020	14
3.17	0.125	32	12.29 x 0.62	0.484 x 0.024	19
4.75	0.187	44	11.91 x 0.73	0.469 x 0.029	12
6.35	0.250	44	11.91 x 1.07	0.469 x 0.042	25
7.93	0.312	64	20.62 x 1.09	0.812 x 0.043	27
9.53	0.375	56	9.90 x 2.38	0.390 x 0.093	27
11.10	0.437	60	11.91 x 3.17	0.469 x 0.125	37
12.70	0.500	53	12.70 x 3.96	0.500 x 0.156	36
19.05	0.750	56	12.70 x 1.04	0.500 x 0.041	28
25.40	1.0	57	20.00 x 2.00	0.787 x 0.078	29
DIAMOND SQUARES			11.50 x 1.50	0.454 x 0.059	24
4.75	0.187	36	19.05 x 3.17	0.750 x 0.125	40
9.52	0.375	49	**TRIANGULAR HOLES**		
12.70	0.500	48	3.17	0.125	26
15.87	0.625	42	5.00	0.197	15
19.05	0.750	44	6.50	0.256	26
25.40	1.0	43	9.52 x 11.11	0.375 x 0.437	16
			OVAL HOLES		
			7.00 x 3.00	0.276 x 0.118	32
			9.00 x 4.25	0.354 x 0.167	38
			9.00 x 5.00	0.354 x 0.197	45
			14.00 x 6.00	0.551 x 0.236	46
			13.50 x 7.00	0.531 x 0.276	45

TABLE II — PERFORATED MESH SIEVES (BS410)

Nominal width of Aperture (side of square)		Plate Thickness	Aperture Tolerances			
			Average		Maximum	
mm	in	B.G.	per cent	units	per cent	units
101.60	4	10	0.20	80	0.50	200
88.90	3½	10	0.20	70	0.49	170
76.20	3	12	0.20	60	0.50	150
69.85	2¾	12	0.20	55	0.51	140
63.50	2½	14	0.20	50	0.52	130
57.15	2¼	14	0.20	45	0.53	120
50.80	2	16	0.20	40	0.50	100
47.63	1.7/8	16	0.21	40	0.53	100
44.45	1¾	16	0.20	35	0.51	90
41.28	1.5/8	16	0.21	35	0.55	90
38.10	1½	16	0.20	30	0.53	80
34.93	1.3/8	16	0.22	30	0.58	80
31.75	1¼	16	0.24	30	0.56	770
28.58	1.1/8	16	0.26	30	0.62	70
25.40	1	16	0.25	25	0.60	60
22.23	7/8	16	0.23	20	0.69	60
19.05	¾	16	0.27	20	0.80	60
15.88	5/8	16	0.32	20	0.80	50
12.70	½	16	0.40	20	1.00	50
9.53	3/8	18	0.53	20	1.06	40
7.94	5/16	18	0.58	18	1.16	36
6.35	¼	18	0.60	15	1.20	30
4.76	3/16	20	0.64	12	1.33	25

1 unit = 0.0001 in

Certain limitations are also imposed by materials. Thus whilst close-spaced 0.55 mm (0.210 inch) diameter holes are practical in brass, minimum hole size with aluminium or monel is normally 1.5 mm (1/16 inch). If finer straining is required with these materials then a mesh woven from metallic wire would have to be employed; or specially drilled plates.

Drilled Plates

With punched holes it is generally impractical (or uneconomic) to produce holes smaller in diameter than the thickness of the plate. This restriction is removed if holes are drilled, offering the possibility of reproducing small openings in plates whose thickness can be selected on strength requirements. Further, drilling can be applied to metals which are too hard to be punched. Also, to reduce flow resistance and eliminate clogging, conical or stepped holes can be drilled in thicker plate (Fig 2).

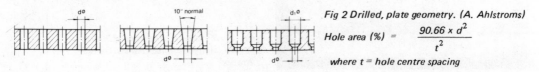

Fig 2 Drilled, plate geometry. (A. Ahlstroms)

$$\text{Hole area (\%)} = \frac{90.66 \times d^2}{t^2}$$

where t = hole centre spacing

Milled Plates

Where greater robustness is required, or where there are special requirements for handling the product, *slotted plates* are widely used. Again these may be punched (in thin plates), cast (in thick plates), or milled. Milling is particularly suitable for producing thin, clean slots, which may be further finished by electropolishing if required. Examples of slot types used on milled plates are given in Fig 3.

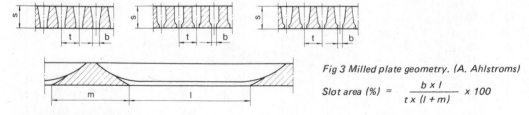

Fig 3 Milled plate geometry. (A. Ahlstroms)

$$Slot\ area\ (\%)\ =\ \frac{b \times l}{t \times (l + m)} \times 100$$

Expanded Metal Mesh

Expanded metal mesh is produced in a large variety of materials and forms with a wide range of applications both as filter elements and filter supports. The mesh is cut and stretched from metal sheet into the form of a jointless grille with no interweaving and no joints to loosen or part under stress — Fig 4. The mesh as originally formed may be further processed, *eg* rolled flat and smooth, corrugated, or with strands formed at an angle — Fig 5.

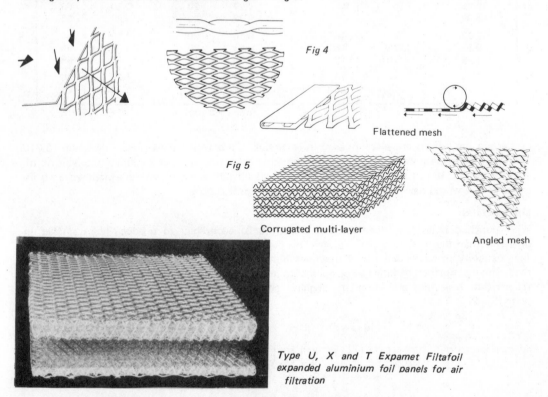

Fig 4

Flattened mesh

Fig 5

Corrugated multi-layer

Angled mesh

Type U, X and T Expamet Filtafoil expanded aluminium foil panels for air filtration

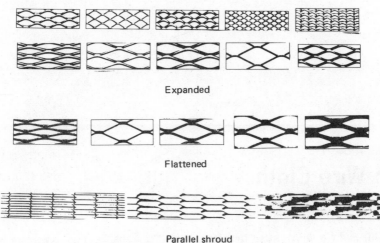

Expanded

Flattened

Parallel shroud

Fig 6 Examples of expanded metal mesh.
(The Expanded Metal Company Ltd).

Multiple layers of mesh may be used to provide filtration in depth, using plain or corrugated layers. Alternate mayers may be arranged at right angles — see also Fig 6.

Metals used include aluminium (particularly for air filters), brass, copper, steel, stainless steel, heat-resistant alloys, monel and titanium.

Expanded metal mesh is generally available in sheet form, cut-to-size mesh, and prefabricated panels layered to requirements.

Woven Wire Cloth

WOVEN WIRE cloth is widely used for filtration and is available in an extremely wide range of materials and mesh sizes. It can be woven from virtually any metal ductile enough to be drawn into wire form, preferred materials being phosphor bronze, stainless steel and monel. Other materials widely used include aluminium alloys (good strength with light weight and good corrosion resistance); copper (cheaper than bronze, but not suitable for corrosive conditions); brass (stronger than copper but more subject to corrosion); plain mild steel or coated mild steel (*eg* galvanized or tinned). Nickel, nickel-chrome alloys and titanium may be used for high temperature duties.

The minimum practical size of wire which can be used depends on the alloy, strength required, temperature and degree of abrasion likely to be experienced in service. Thus finer wire diameters in aluminium, brass, bronze or copper are not normally used for other than light duties. Stainless steel wire on the other hand is available and used down to 20 μm (0.02 mm or 50 swg equivalent).

Mesh is described by form of weave and mesh count. A square mesh is the usual form in a *plain* or *twilled* weave. The mesh count — normally called *mesh* — is effectively the number of openings per (25.4 mm) lineal inch measured from the centre of one wire to another 1 in from it. Specifically it is the number of pitches in 1 in, pitch being defined as (w + d) where w is the width of opening and d is the wire diameter.

These parameters also define the open area and strength of the cloth. Open area expressed as a percentage of the whole area is

$$\text{open area} = \frac{w^2}{(w + d)} \times 100$$

Thus variations in wire diameter (d) affect both the open area and strength.

Woven wire cloth is described nominally by a *mesh number* and *wire size, ie* N mesh M mm (or swg). Mesh numbers may range from 2 (2 wires per inch) up to 400. Fine mesh with more than 100 wires per lineal inch is called *gauze*. Mesh is described more specifically by aperture opening, *eg:-*

coarse — aperture opening 1 mm to 12 mm

medium — aperture opening 0.18 mm to 0.95 mm (180—950 μm)

fine — aperture opening 0.020 mm to 0.160 mm (20—160 μm)

Standards mainly applicable are BS481 Power 1, 1971 (see Table I) and ISO 3 — 1973, with the use of metric sizes now becoming increasingly common.

TABLE I – WOVEN ANNEALED WIRE CLOTH (BS481 : PART 1 : 1971)

Nominal aperture size		Light Class				Medium Class				Heavy Class			
		Nominal wire diameter	Nominal screening area	Meshes per		Nominal wire diameter	Nominal screening area	Meshes per		Nominal wire diameter	Nominal screening area	Meshes per	
R10	R20			centimetre (10 mm)	inch (25.4 mm)			centimetre (10 mm)	inch (25.4 mm)			centimetre (10 mm)	inch (25.4 mm)
mm	mm	mm	%			mm	%			mm	%		
16		1.80	81			2.24	77			3.15	70		
12.5		1.60	79			2.00	74			2.80	67		
10		1.40	77			1.80	72			2.50	64		
8		1.25	75			1.60	69			2.24	61		
6.3		1.00	74			1.40	67			2.00	58		
5		0.90	72			1.25	64			1.80	54		
4		0.71	72	2.1	5.4	1.00	64	2.0	5.1	1.40	55	1.9	4.7
3.15		0.56	72	2.7	6.8	0.80	64	2.5	6.4	1.12	54	2.3	5.9
2.5		0.50	69	3.3	8.5	0.71	61	3.1	7.9	1.00	51	2.9	7.3
2		0.40	69	4.2	10.6	0.56	61	3.9	9.9	0.90	48	3.4	8.8
1.6		0.355	67	5.1	13.0	0.50	58	4.8	12.1	0.71	48	4.3	11.0
1.25		0.315	64	6.4	16.2	0.40	57	6.1	15.4	0.56	48	5.5	14.0
1		0.28	61	8	20	0.355	54	7	19	0.50	44	7	17
0.8						0.315	51	9	23	0.45	41	8	20
0.63						0.28	48	11	28	0.40	37	10	25
0.5						0.25	44	13	34	0.315	38	12	31
0.4						0.224	41	16	41	*0.28	35	15	37
0.315						0.20	37	19	49	*0.25	31	18	45
0.25						0.16	37	24	62	0.20	31	22	56
0.2						0.125	38	31	78	0.16	31	28	71
	0.18					0.112	38	34	87	0.14	32	31	79
0.16						0.100	38	38	98	0.125	31	35	89
	0.14					0.090	37	43	110	0.112	31	40	101
0.125						0.080	37	49	124	0.100	31	44	113
	0.112					0.071	37	55	139	0.090	31	49	126
0.1						0.063	38	61	156	0.080	31	56	141
	0.09					0.056	38	68	174	0.071	31	62	158
0.08						0.050	38	77	195	0.063	31	70	178
	0.071					0.045	37	86	219	0.056	31	79	200
0.063						0.040	37	97	247	0.050	31	88	225
	0.056					*0.040	34	104	265				
0.05						*0.036	34	116	295				
0.04						*0.030	33	143	363				
0.032						*0.025	32	175	446				
0.025						*0.022	28	213	540				
1	2	3	4	5	6	7	8	9	10	11	12	13	14

*Normally supplied in twilled weave.

Note; Mesh counts are rounded off to the nearest whole number for apertures of 1 mm and smaller

Weaves

The weave adopted is usually one of five basic types. *Square mesh* has each shute wire passing alternately over and under each warp wire. The openings can be square or rectangular, and so this weave is more correctly referred to as plain weave or double crimped weave. It is generally satisfactory in strength from 10 to 60 mesh (wires per inch), but finer meshes demand the use of such smaller diameter wires that there is an appreciable loss of strength. The width of opening, it will be appreciated, is limited to the diameter of the wire and thus finer meshes can only be woven from finer wires. (Fig 1a).

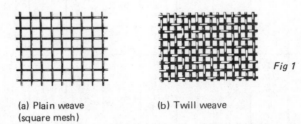

Fig 1

(a) Plain weave
(square mesh)

(b) Twill weave

Twilled weave (or plain twill) is the next strongest weave, each shute wire progressing one wire at a time and alternately crossing over two and then under two warp wires, producing a diagonal pattern. This allows the use of larger wire diameters for a given mesh and thus greater strength, but with proportionately smaller openings. This can be offset to some extent, if necessary, by reducing the number of shute wires yielding rectangular openings. (Fig 1b).

Plain Dutch single weave is a plain weave with the larger diameter wires in the warp and the weft wires crimped at each pass — Fig 2a. The range of cloths produced in this weave extend from 340 µm down to about 20 µm aperture size (*ie* coarse to medium). Openings are small in size, triangular in shape and not 'straight through'. The cloth itself is firm and compact with good strength.

(a) Plain Dutch weave

(b) Twilled Dutch weave

(c) Twilled Double Dutch weave

Fig 2 Types of Dutch weave.

Reverse plain Dutch weave is similar except that the thicker wire is in the weft and may also have more (thinner) wires in the warp. It is somewhat stronger but with lower porosity.

Twilled Dutch double weave has thicker warp wires with the thinner weft wires closely spaced and passing under and over two warp wires. The resultant pore openings are in the form of slots and triangles. It is particularly used for weaving finer cloths, together with a further variation known as *twilled Dutch single weave*. Here the weft wires are so closely spaced as to completely cover the warp wires, giving the appearance of a metal pole rather than a cloth.

Other types of weaves may be developed or adopted by individual manufacturers — *eg* basket weaves (multiplex), stranded weaves, and hybrids and mixtures — see also Tables II and III.

TABLE II — PRINCIPAL WEAVES FOR WIRE CLOTHS

Name	Characteristics	Absolute Rating Range μm	Remarks
Square Plain or twilled	Largest open area and lowest flow resistance. Aperture size is the same in both directions.	20—300+	Most common type of weave. Made in all grades from coarse to fine.
Plain Dutch single weave	Good contaminant retention properties with low flow resistance.	20—100	Openings are triangular.
Reverse plain Dutch weave	Very strong with good contaminant retention.	15—115	
Twilled Dutch double weave	Regular and consistent aperture size.	6—100	Used for fine and ultra-fine filtering.

TABLE III — EXAMPLES OF WIRE CLOTH GEOMETRY
(G. Bopp & Co Limited)

Rating	Aperture Size mm	Wire Diameter mm	Mesh	Free Area %
Coarse	1.00	0.63	16	38
	1.00	0.40	18	51
	1.00	0.37	19	58
	1.00	0.22	21	67
	2.00	1.00	8.5	44.4
	2.00	0.90	8.8	48
	2.00	0.63	10	57
	2.00	0.56	10	60
	2.00	0.32	11	74
	6.3	1.80	3.1	60
	6.3	1.40	3.3	67
	6.3	1.00	3.5	74
	μm	mm		%
Medium	250	0.20	56	31
	250	0.16	62	38
	250	0.10	74	51
	630	0.40	25	38
	630	0.28	28	48
	630	0.28	30	51
	630	0.16	32	64
Fine	50	0.040	280	31
	50	0.036	300	34
	50	0.030	325	39

Electroformed Mesh

Very finely perforated and uniform wire mesh can be produced by electroforming, yielding hole sizes from 0.031 inches down to 0.003 inches or even smaller, if necessary, in thicknesses varying between 0.015 inches and 0.0025 inches, depending on the count. Such a mesh is smooth and flat and can easily be punched, cut, bent and formed and jointed by soft soldering or spot or seam welding. Edges are free from fraying when cut, so edge binding is eliminated in the case of cut mesh shapes. Typical data are summarized in Table IV.

TABLE IV — EXAMPLES OF SOLID NICKEL MESH ELECTROFORMED

Count	Thickness		Hole Shape	Hole Size			Land Width		Open Area %
	mm	inch		mm	inch		mm	inch	
25 x 25	0.25	0.010	Square	0.40	0.016		0.60	0.024	16
	0.19	0.075	Square	0.525	0.021		0.475	0.019	27.5
	0.15	0.006	Square	0.575	0.023		0.425	0.017	33
	0.125	0.005	Square	0.625	0.025		0.375	0.015	39
40 x 10	0.25	0.010	Slot	0.06 x 1.55	0.0025 x 0.062		0.56 x 0.95	0.0225 x 0.038	6.5
	0.225	0.009	Slot	0.075 x 1.57	0.0003 x 0.063		0.55 x 0.93	0.022 x 0.037	7.5
	0.20	0.008	Slot	0.10 x 1.60	0.004 x 0.064		0.525 x 0.90	0.021 x 0.036	10
25 x 10	0.325	0.013	Slot	0.25 x 1.60	0.010 x 0.064		0.75 x 0.90	0.030 x 0.036	16
	0.30	0.012	Slot	0.30 x 1.65	0.012 x 0.066		0.70 x 0.85	0.028 x 0.034	20
	0.25	0.010	Slot	0.40 x 1.75	0.016 x 0.070		0.60 x 0.70	0.024 x 0.030	28

Test Sieves

Test sieves employ a mesh strictly in accordance with the specification for aperture size (*eg* BS410). The design of frame or holder is also important since it is essential that the sieve mesh be held flat and taut and, preferably, that there is a bevel entry to the mesh area to ensure that all the material is transferred to the sieve mesh when hand sieving at an angle of 30 degrees (recommended in BS1796).

Typical test sieve mesh data are summarized in Tables VA and VB.

TABLE VA — MEDIUM MESH SIEVES (BS410)

Nominal Width of Aperture		Nominal Diameter of Wire		Aperture Tolerances				
				Average		Maximum	
mm	in	mm	in	per cent	units	per cent	units
12.7	1/2	3.25	0.128	2.8	140	7	350
9.53	3/8	2.64	0.104	2.8	104	8	288
6.35	1/4	2.34	0.092	3.0	75	9	217
4.76	3/16	2.03	0.080	2.9	55	10	180
3.18	1/8	1.83	0.072	3.2	40	11	132
1.59	1/16	0.97	0.038	3.4,	21	12	76
0.79	1/32	0.53	0.021	4.8	15	14	45

1 unit = 0.0001 in

TABLE VB — HEAVY DUTY SIEVE PLATES (BS410)

Nominal and Maximum Size of Aperture (side of square)		Plate Thickness	Complete Apertures per side	Minimum Aperture Width	
				Average	Individual
m m	in	in		in	in
203.20	8	3/16			7.920
177.80	7	3/16			6.930
152.40	6	3/16			5.940
127.00	5	3/16	3	4.968	4.950
101.60	4	3/16	4	3.974	3.960
88.90	3.1/2	3/16	5	3.477	3.465
76.20	3	BG 10	6	2.980	2.970
63.50	2.1/2	10	7	2.484	2.475
50.80	2	10	9	1.987	1.980
38.10	1.1/2	10	12	1.490	1.485
25.40	1	10	18	0.993	0.990
12.70	1/2	10	30	0.493	0.490
6.35	1/4	16	60	0.243	0.240
3.18	1/8	16	88	0.118	0.115

Multi-Layer Cloths

Composite constructions consisting of multiple layers of woven cloth bonded together, are a recent development aimed at producing a high strength porous sheet of greater durability than single layer cloth. At the same time the layer construction provides filtering in depth, with increased dirt-holding capacity.

As a general rule different cloths are used for each layer, chosen and oriented to provide optimum strength with minimum of masking of pores in adjacent layers — Fig 3. Final bonding is then achieved by sintering, resulting in a porous one-piece material which is dimensionally stable with minimal possibility of delamination or migration. Fine or ultra-fine filtering can be provided by close-mesh layer(s), protected on either side by coarser back-up layers — *eg* nominal ratings for filters of this type can extend down to 5 μm.

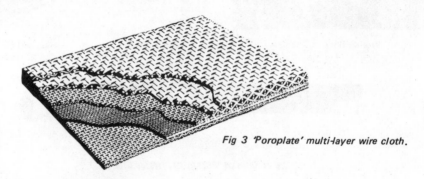

Fig 3 'Poroplate' multi-layer wire cloth.

Cartridge Filters

CARTRIDGE FILTERS are produced in a wide variety of configurations and materials of construction. Filter media include yarns, felts, papers, resin bonded fibres, woven wire cloths, sintered metallic and ceramic structures.

Some types of cartridges, such as those made from yarns or resin bonded fibres, normally have a structure that gradually increases in density toward the centre of the element. These 'depth-type' filters capture particles throughout the total thickness of the medium. Thin media, such as papers, felts, and woven wire cloths, are described as surface filters, because most of their particle capture occurs at or near the surface of the filter. The choice of a surface or depth type cartridge for a given application will depend upon a number of factors. Filtration performance obtained by cartridge filters may range from 500 μm down to 1 μm or even less.

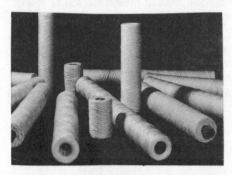

Wound fibre

Micro-cotton

Ceramic and metallic cleanable cartridges

Coalescing cartridge

High viscosity filter

Examples of 'Filterite' cartridge filters.

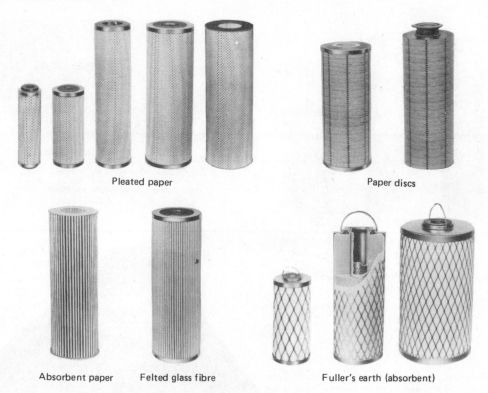

Pleated paper

Paper discs

Absorbent paper   Felted glass fibre

Fuller's earth (absorbent)

Examples of filter cartridges
(Williard Corporation)

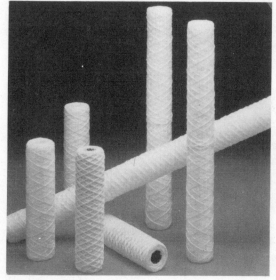

AMF Micro-Wind II filter cartridge employs media in blanket form retained in shape by a spiral wound matrix. Made in cotton media and matrix with stainless steel core and polypropylene media, matrix and core.

Horizontal larger-scale cartridge filter.
(Brunswick Technetics)

Perforated   Woven fibre   Metal edge-type
filter   media   filter

Examples of cleanable filter cartridges
(AAF)

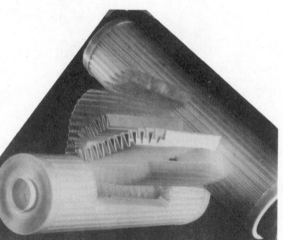

Sub-micronic polyolefin fibre cartridge filters for
services where glass fibre or asbestos fibre is not
permitted.
(Brunswick Technetics)

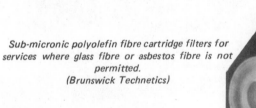

Stockdale cartridge filter —
detail photo right.

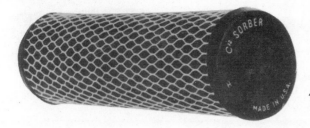

Activated carbon cartridge filter.
(Technical Fabricators Inc)

Microporous PTFE membrane bonded to
polyester support.
(Technical Fabricators Inc)

A continuously operating ultrafiltration plant with three
Alfa-Laval membrane cartridge filters. (35 m^2 membrane area
each) in series.

Micro-Klean — ratings 5, 10, 25, 50, 75 and 125 μm.

Micro-Wynd — ratings 1, 3, 5, 10, 25 and 50 μm.

Cuno-Cell (pleated paper) — ratings 5, 10 and 25 μm.

Activated carbon

Non-toxic biologically inert cartridge based on cellulose media and diatomaceous earth

Examples of disposable filter cartridges (AAF)

Extended area filter cartridge for coarse filtration (Technical Fabricators Inc)

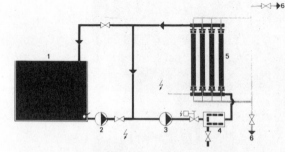

Batch mode filtration using cartridge filters. The soluble oil wastes are pumped from a batch tank and recirculated through the hollow fibre cartridges until the desired concentration is obtained. Pressures in the process manifolds are maintained at set levels by pressure-control valves. Permeate from each cartridge is collected in a permeate manifold and is sent to drain. When about 90% of the batch volume is drained off, ultrafiltration is stopped. The remaining concentrate, containing up to 40% oil, is drained from the system.
(Alfa-Laval)

1. Batch tank
2. Feed pump
3. Circulation pump
4. Strainer
5. Filter cartridges
6. Permeate.

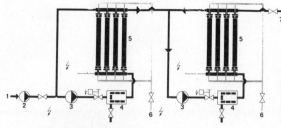

1. From batch tank
2. Feed pump
3. Circulation pump
4. Strainer
5. Filter cartridges
6. Permeate
7. End concentrate

Examples of application of large-scale membrane cartridge filters — one or more ultrafiltration units in series, operated continuously. The waste emulsion is continuously fed into the system and recirculated through the cartridges in each unit. The last unit delivers a concentrate with the required level of water removal.
(Alfa-Laval)

Remove end caps

Slip on screen

Replace caps

'Tiger' cartridges feature polypropylene or stainless steel element with removable end caps and a range of slip-on screws in nylon, polyester, polypropylene or stainless steel. (Stockdale Engineering Ltd).

The filter element (actual cartridge) of a cartridge filter is normally designed as a disposable component, to be replaced with a new cartridge when clogged. Some cartridge elements of robust construction may be specified as cleanable and re-usable.

Cartridge filters are compact, reliable, easy to operate and require less capital investment and operator training than most other types of filtration equipment.

In general, cartridge filtration is favoured in systems where the contaminant levels are less than 0.01% by weight (*ie* less than 100 ppm).

In very heavily contaminated systems, cartridge filters are most often used downstream of other types of filtration devices for final product clarification. However, there are some high contaminant load applications, particularly batch type operations, where only cartridge filters are specified simply because such factors as performance, reliability, safety and convenience outweigh any other considerations.

See also chapters on *Mechanical Filters* and *Filter Ratings*.

Precoat Filters

A DEFINITIVE *precoat filter* embodies a rigid, semi-flexible or flexible screen on which is deposited a filter medium. This medium, in fact, forms a filter bed on what is basically a strainer element, collecting much finer contaminants than would be arrested by the strainer. The 'bed' medium may also filter by absorption as well as mechanically. For cleaning purposes back-washing then removes the bed together with contaminants which have collected. The bed is then reformed, or the filter 're-coated' by running the bed medium through in a suitable carrier fluid. This fluid passes through the strainer element, leaving the coating material arrested and deposited on the surface to form a new bed. Coating materials used include diatomaceous earth, silica, perlite, pure asbestos fibres and other mineral wools.

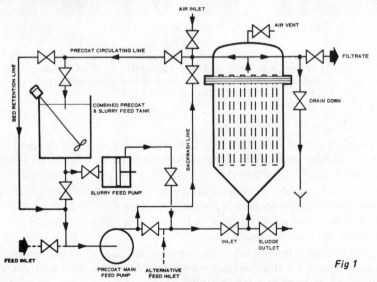

Fig 1

A typical precoat filter system is shown in Fig 1. The correct amount of filter medium is mixed with clean liquid and then pumped into the filter body where it is deposited uniformly over the filter elements. Coating is complete when all the original filter medium has been transferred to the filter itself. To obtain extremely fine filtration the process may be repeated with a further dose of finer medium to superimpose a second layer of this medium on the first.

This diagram also shows the connections for a slurry-feed. This may be employed when the substance being handled contains solids with a high clogging or binding nature which would rapidly reduce the porosity of the precoat by covering over the surface. In this case, instead of the normal precoating technique the precoating medium is mixed with the unfiltered fluid and fed together to the filter body. This results in a relatively porous cake or coating being built up on the filter elements, maintaining reasonable porosity and at the same time high filtering efficiency.

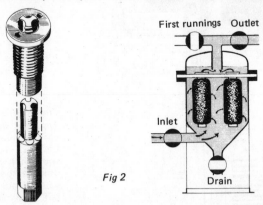

Fig 2

Instead of using cloth or similar elements, some types of precoat filter employ a rigid support to ensure maximum stability when subject to variations in pressure, temperature or flow. This is a feature of the ring pack elements shown in Fig 2, the support comprising a series of rings assembled on a fluted rod and tightened down. Each ring is flat on one side whilst the other is provided with scallops accurately raised above the general surface of the ring. These scallops are of such a size as just to touch the outer circumference tangentially. Assembly of the discs is flat side to scalloped side, tightening producing consistency of ring gap without distortion of the complete pack. The precoat is then deposited on the element in the usual manner, the total effective filtering area being the surface area over the precoat. Cake build-up is radial, which further increases the effective surface area. Compared with flat type supports, therefore, a radial support with radial cake build-up offers the advantage of reduced cake thickness and increased filtering area for any given total cake capacity per unit area of filter.

Precoat filters are an important type for handling chemical solutions, particularly for clarification. Diatomaceous earth is generally suitable for the clarification of almost every coarse suspension; and in selected finer grades will produce brilliant and clear filtrates with most solutions, inluding syrups, as well as being effective in the removal of colloids. The basic·media may also be modified or 'reinforced' by pretreatment to enhance specific properties. Typical examples are:-

(i)   reinforcement with hydrate of aluminium for the production of sparkling waters (*eg* mineral water production).

(ii)   incorporation of a dechlorinating agent to remove excess chlorine in the production of sterile or chlorine-free water.

(iii) incorporation of reagents to remove iron from water.

(iv)   surface treatment (*eg* silver coating) to inhibit the growth of bacteria on the filter element.

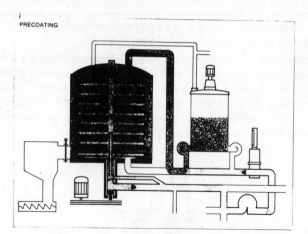

Precoating

The precoating mixtures are mixed in the unpressurized tank of the dosing unit. The agitator revolves slowly so that no air is stirred in. A separate precoating pump conveys the suspensions into the filter, where they form an even precoat on the horizontal filter elements. Then dosing is prepared in the dosing unit.

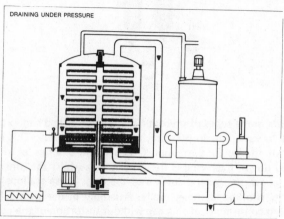

Pressure draining and filling of filter

The filter vessel is emptied and the precoating fluid forced out with pressurized gas. The filter vessel is then filled with unfiltered feedstock from below. This method not only ensures filtration without the need for any pre-runnings, but also prevents consumption of oxygen.

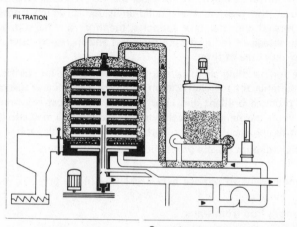

Filtration

During filtration, unfiltered feedstock flows into the filter vessel from above. A wear-resistant dosing piston pump with dose control feeds the desired quantity of kieselguhr into the supply line. A distributor under the cover of the vessel ensures even utilization of the filter elements. The trub is separated and the filtrate is directed into the vertical hollow shaft.

Operational sequence of a modern precoat filter.
(Seitz-Werke GmbH).

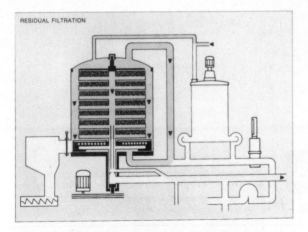

Residual filtration

The residual filtration elements are arranged directly above the flat bottom of the vessel. Via these elements, the contents can be removed in the filtered state without residues. This means a virtual elimination of product losses. The filter system can be drained under pressure with pressurized gas. This makes it possible to influence, within broad limits, the moisture content of the trub to be discharged.

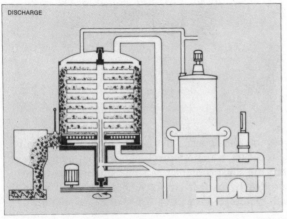

Discharge of trub

The trub is flung off the elements by centrifugal force when the whole filter pack is rotated. A discharge mechanism rotating on the bottom of the vessel carries the trub out via a nozzle arranged at a tangent. It can then be collected in a tank, for example, and piped to a transport container by means of a slush pump. This method saves manpower and is also harmless to the environment. There can be no loading of the sewer network because of the dry discharge.

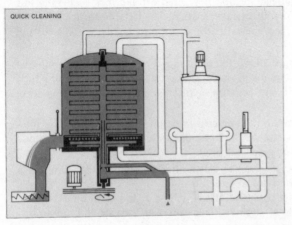

Quick cleaning by backwashing

The dry discharge is immediately followed by quick cleaning. Here, water flows counter to the direction of filtration, *ie* from the filtrate to the unfiltered feedstock end, and removes any trub residues which may still be present. The whole cleaning process takes very little time, and so the system is available for filtration again after a brief interruption.

Operational sequence of a modern precoat filter. (contd).
(Seitz-Werke GmbH).

Stationary, fully automatically operating unit for precoating and continuous body feed of filter aids such as for example kieselguhr, perlite, activated charcoal or stabilizing agents — comprising mixing tank, agitator, precoating pump, metering pump, flow fitting, illuminated sight glass and wiring cabinet.
(Seitz-Werke GmbH)

In addition to diatomaceous earth (diatomite or Kieselguhr) a number of other media may be employed for precoated filters. Chief of these is perlite, which is processed from a vitreous rock of organic origin. This again is basically silica, but the silica content is less than diatomaceous earth. Various grades of perlite are produced, controlled by particle size blendings, and the variety of particle shapes in any one grade is less than with diatomaceous earth.

Other precoat media which may be employed include powdered organic rock (generally less suitable for strong acid or alkaline solutions); and activated carbon. The latter is particularly suitable for decolourization and taste removal, and special carbons are also highly suitable for the filtration of strongly alkaline solutions.

Cellulose media may also be employed, particularly for the removal of colloidal and compressible solids. Various grades of suitable cellulose media are made by micronizing or grinding high grade cellulose fibres. These media are soft and resilient, with the advantage that migration products will not abrade pumps or valves.

Many other types of mechanical filters work on the precoat principle — *ie* whilst basically they are either surface filters or depth filters in themselves, build-up of contaminant produces a porous coating or bed which acts in a similar manner to a precoat filter.

The term 'precoated filter' is also sometimes given to other filter elements which comprise a coating material permanently bonded to a mechanical screen or mesh. In this case the coating is employed to protect the metallic mesh against corrosive attack, whilst at the same time reducing the pore size. Such elements have limited use as strainers. It is generally cheaper and more satisfactory to select the metal for the screen or mesh on the basis of chemical compatibility.

See also chapters on *Media* and *Vacuum Belt Filters*.

Sintered Metal Filters

SINTERED METAL filters provide the possibility of closer control of pore size, shape and uniformity than can be achieved with plastics and the resulting matrix is much stronger, rigid, and more resistant to heat than cellulosic materials, *etc*. Pore size may range from atomic dimensions of the order of 10^{-8} centimetres, through sub-micron size up. Thus, theoretically at least, virtually any cut-off down to the finest ultra-fine filtering requirements can be provided by a sintered metal element. In practice, however, this is modified by the increasing resistance to flow with diminishing pore size, which naturally tends to decrease porosity.

Porosity, or the proportion of voids to solid matrix volume, can also be controlled over a wide range. Whilst increasing porosity decreases resistance to through flow, strength of the matrix decreases rapidly. For reasonable mechanical strength it may therefore be necessary to restrict porosity; or in the case of filters adopt a suitable compromise based on strength/permeability requirements. In terms of practical possibilities, porosity may range from as low as 10% (typical of mass produced sintered components) through 20—30% (typical for sintered metal bearings), up to as high as 95%. In the case of filter elements porosity may range up to 70%, or possibly higher for low pressure elements. The particular advantage of sintered metal filter elements, apart from the fine cut-off which can be provided, is their high strength and rigidity compared with non-metallic media, which makes them particularly attractive for high pressure applications.

Sintered metal filters fall broadly into two categories; those produced by sintering loose powder in a mould, and those produced by compaction. Spherical particles are preferred because they pack more uniformly and thus provide more uniform pore sizes.

The coarser grades of sintered metal filters are produced from particles with a particle diameter of about 1 mm. Since pore size is usually about 15% of the particle diameter, this would yield a pore size of 150 μm, equivalent to a 100-mesh woven wire filter. Such sintered metal filters are expensive to produce and thus not competitive at this level. Manufacturing costs of sintered metal filters is rather less with smaller particle diameters, whereas the cost of woven wire mesh increases with decreasing pore size (and at the same time strength and rigidity are reduced).

Sintered metal filters, therefore, become increasingly more competitive from pore sizes of about 100 μm down. At the finer end, however, spherical metal particles of the order of 5—10 μm diameter are expensive to produce and costly to classify, although they have been produced down to 1 μm size.

Being depth-type filters, sintered metal media are subject to initial losses proportional to the square of the velocity of fluid through the filter and the fluid density. This is normally only significant with fluids with high flow velocities.

Permeability can be expressed in terms of viscous permeability, proportional to pressure drop; and inertial viscosity, proportional to fluid density. Typical values for sintered metal elements are:-

Pore size (μm)	Viscous permeability (Darcy units)	Inertial permeability μm
1	0.6	0.2
2	0.2	0.3
5	1.0	0.7
10	3.0	1.3
20	10.0	2.5
50	50.0	5.0
100	160.0	10.0

For most general purposes sintered bronze filters are suitable. For particularly arduous duties involving very high pressures, high temperatures or corrosive fluids, the filter elements may be sintered from stainless steel, monel, pure nickel, Hastelloy, titanium, or even tungsten.

Bronze and cupro-nickel sinter readily at low temperatures and thus a whole variety of shapes can be produced directly from metal powder in stainless steel or carbon moulds. The mould is then passed through a furnace with a protective atmosphere to sinter the powder together. Pressed or machined shapes may require subsequent treatment to open up surface pores. Filters can be machined to closer tolerances than can be produced by direct moulding, but machining is eliminated whenever possible, or confined to non-effective areas of the filter element, such as the finishing of shoulders for registering purposes.

Typical characteristics of a range of porous bronze filters in seven different grades are given in Table I.

TABLE I – PERFORMANCE OF TYPICAL POROUS BRONZE FILTER ELEMENTS

Cut-off μm	Permeability coefficient x 10^{10} in^2	Minimum recommended thickness	Air flow at 0.1 lb/in^2 differential ft^3/min/in^2	Water flow at 5 lb/in^2 differential gal/h/in^2
90	2 300	5/32	2.44	655
60	1 300	5/32	1.38	450
35	450	1/8	0.478	168
18	100	7/64	0.106	50
10	35	3/32	0.037	21.8
6	14	1/16	0.015	11.2
2	4	1/16	0.004	6.2

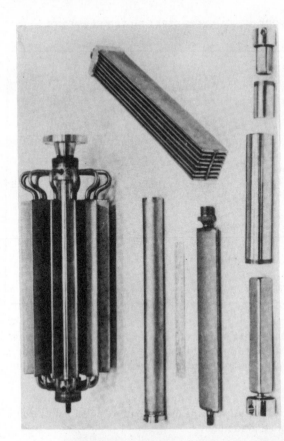

Porous stainless steel filter elements.
(BSA Metal Components Division)

Examples of sintered filter elements.

Porous stainless steel elements may be employed where high strength, greater resistance to temperature and high resistance to corrosion is required. Porous stainless steel elements are commonly produced in the form of plates or discs used directly for filter element construction, or further reworked as necessary *eg* to give a 'star' filter element. The material commonly employed is a stainless steel equivalent to BS 304S15 composition but with a maximum carbon content of 0.05%. The porous material is then equally resistant to corrosion as solid austenitic stainless

TABLE II – PERFORMANCE OF TYPICAL POROUS STAINLESS STEEL FILTER ELEMENTS

Permeability coefficient x 10^{10} in^2	Approximate mean pore size μm	Air flow at 0.1 psi differential through 1 sq ft plate 1/8 in thick	Water flow gpm/sq ft/1/8 inch thickness at differential pressure (psi)					
			0.1	2	5	10	20	30
5	6.5	0.75 cfm	—	4.5	9.5	18	33.8	49
10	12	1.5 cfm	—	6	12.5	23	43.5	63.5
20	18	3.0 cfm	0.055	7	15.5	30	53.5	75
40	28	6.1 cfm	—	8.5	20.5	38	62.5	86
50	33	7.6 cfm	0.46	9	23.5	42.5	66.5	92
100	46	15.3 cfm	1.30	17.5	32.5	55	87	116
150	56	22.9 cfm	1.43	25	46	70	106	138
200	67	30.6 cfm	—	32	55	81	119	151
200	70	38.2 cfm	—	39	62.5	89	127	160

steel to chemicals which do not attack the solid metal. Where the solid metal is subject to some attack, corrosion of the porous metal will be greater because of the greater surface area exposed. This characteristic, in fact, applies to the corrosion resistance of all porous metals, compared with the behaviour of the same metal in solid form.

Typical characteristics of porous stainless steel filter element materials are summarized in Table II. Other metals used for making porous metal elements include cupro-nickel, gold, iron, inconel, monel, nickel, platinum, silver, tantalum and titanium.

The fine filtering provided by sintered metal elements, together with controlled porosity ensuring a true absolute rating, make them an attractive choice for high-duty, high-temperature applications. For general fluid filtering requirements at temperatures above that which can be accommodated by simple fabric or paper element, however, satisfactory performance can usually be achieved with a similar or identical design of general filter fitted with a metallic element, normally in the form of a wire mesh. Again bronze or stainless steel is a typical choice for the mesh, depending primarily on the possible corrosive action of the fluid being handled. Cost is directly proportional to the fineness of the mesh and the complexity of the element design. For very fine filtering, 'microweave' metal wire mesh can provide a performance direcly comparable to that of sintered metal elements.

Candle Filters

TUBULAR FILTER elements contained in a matching vessel are known as *candle filters*. The actual filter vessel may contain one or more filter candles and may be used as pressure (usually) or suction filters for the filtration of liquids and gases. A particular advantage offered is that candles may readily be changed to a different type to suit particular requirements or applications.

Filter candles made from wound textile fibres are used for fine filtering of acids and alkalis in chemical solutions, lacquers, galvanizing baths, demineralized water, *etc*; and also for the sterilizing filtration of air, steam and other gases (see Fig 1). Materials used include cellulose or cotton, nylon, resin-bonded cellulose, glass fibre and PTFE, offering filtration within the range 0.5—100 μm. Textile candles may also be strengthened with a covering of fine gauze and/or also contain absorbent media (*eg* activated charcoal).

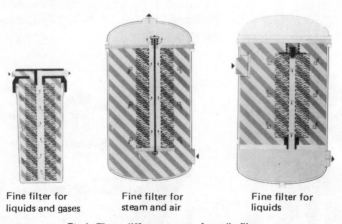

Fine filter for
liquids and gases

Fine filter for
steam and air

Fine filter for
liquids

Fig 1 Three different types of candle filters.

Filter candles made from metallic mesh or gauze (*eg* stainless steel or bronze) offer rather coarser filtration — typically 15 μm to 2 500 μm — and may be used with or without precoat. They are particularly suited for process filtration involving back-washing. Metallic filter candles may also be made from sintered metal.

Examples of products which can be handled effectively by candle filters for clarification filtration, alluvial filtration and liquid/solid separation are:-

Photographic emulsions
Solvents
Hydrofluoric acid
Paints
Mains water
Sulphuric acid
Water for washing gases
Galvanizing baths
Boiler feed water
Degreasing baths
Cooling water
E-water
Mordant baths
Factory water
Iron chloride
Rinsing baths
Varnish
Pigmented lacquers
Fuels
Wire lacquers
Developers
Synthetic resin lacquers
Electrolytes
Miscella
Fixing baths

Glycerine
Mineral oil
Wetting agents
Glazes
Can lacquers
Polyalcohols
Gelatine
Polyester
Glue
Styrenes
Suspensions
Gold salts
Hydrochloric acid
Ammonium nitrate
Potassium hydroxide
Radioactive residues
Phosphoric acid
Zinc chloride
Phosphate baths
Sodium chloride
Ethanol
Chromic acid
Fixing baths
Methanol
Acetone

Benzol
Nitric acid
Butanol
Oil lacquers
Chloroform
Glycol
Toluol
Enamels
Trichloroethylene
Hexane
Methyl-iso-buthylketone
Steam
Potassium bromide
Sodium bichromate
Glycerine water
Acetic acid
Bleaching lyes
Detergents
Dekalin
Diazo solutions
Glacial acetic acid
Stand oil
Silver salts
Test petrol
Tetrahydrofurane

Double filters with changeover fitting.
(Seitz-Werke GmbH)

'Funda' Candle-filter. The textile candles, supported on the downstream side by plastic gridsystem,
are affixed to registers with easy release devices.
Register design permits easy cut-off of separate
stream in case of breakthrough, as well as elimination of heavy headplate.   Cake discharge as
slurry by backwash.   Materials of construction
selected to fit process. Available with filter area
up to 200m^2.

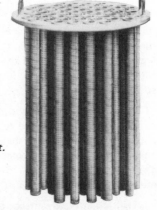

*Example of candle filter insert.
(Seitz-Werke GmbH)*

Filter Tubes

So-called *filter tubes* are basically cartridge elements wound layer-on-layer from yarn fibre in such
a manner as to produce a series of diamond shaped openings. A build-up of anything up to 20
layers may be employed to yield a substantial thickness for filtering in depth. The specific
advantage they offer is compactness — *eg* a 10 inch by 2½ inch diameter filter tube can present the
same filter area as a surface filter over 1 foot in diameter.

Wound filter tubes (cartridges) can have normal pore sizes from 1 μm up to 100 μm. In practice
fairly coarse ratings are normally employed to allow for the fact that with considerable depth of
filtration a precoat effect will be present as contaminants collect and build up in the filter. Too
fine a pore size would lead to early clogging of the surface layers. For handling solutions which
may have slimy contaminants, pore sizes as large as 75—100 μm may be used.

Filter tubes are designed to be fitted in matching cylindrical filter diameters, typical tube
lengths being 10 in, 20 in, 30 in and 40 in. Chambers may be constructed of metal or plastic —
eg high temperature vinyl (CPVC), polypropylene or acrylic. A particular application of filter
tubes in plastic chambers is for filtration and clarification of plating solutions.

See also chapters on *Cartridge Filters* and *Filters and Treatments for Industrial Chemicals.*

Media

Paper

PAPERS ARE essentially sheets of fibrous materials made from organic fibres. In their basic form they are essentially absorbent materials since they will 'swallow up' liquids and may well disintegrate under such action if the liquid is a solvent for the binder. Untreated paper elements used as filters, therefore, have very low mechanical strength and so their application as mechanical filters is strictly limited.

By nature papers have a random fibre structure, although this can be controlled to a large extent in manufacture, and relatively low permeability. Due to the tortuous nature of the through-path, only relatively thin sheets can be used for practical filtering and even then the specific resistance is high. However, treated papers have two great advantages as filter media — (i) they can be given a nominal cut-off of 10—20 μm or better, with a capability of removing a high proportion of much finer particles; and (ii) they are quite inexpensive materials.

Their chief disadvantages are (i) high specific resistance and (ii) limited mechanical strength. To offset the former paper filter elements are most commonly used in pleated form, considerably increasing the superficial area for a given size of element. This substantially reduces the flow velocity through the paper, and hence the effective or overall resistance to flow. Pleating also improves the rigidity of the element, although it is normally fully supported at the ends and inner surface. Flow with a pleated paper element is usually from the outside to the inside, the inner edges of the pleats being supported by a perforated inner tube. Depth of pleating is usually of the order of one quarter the diameter of the element.

Variations on the simple pleated form include corrugating as well as pleating the paper which has the effect of increasing both the surface area and to some extent the stiffness; or dimpling of the surface or the attachment of separator strips to maintain constant spacing and prevent collapse of the pleats. Collapse of a pleated element will reduce the effective surface area and, if excessive, may lead to tearing.

Mechanical strength limitations of paper elements normally set a maximum working pressure for such types of about 100 lb/in^2 (7 bar). This can be improved by rigid reinforcement — for example, a wire mesh backing, but higher pressures also increase the chance of element migration. This is always a possibility with paper elements, especially if they become choked and the system does not incorporate a pressure relief valve to bypass the element.

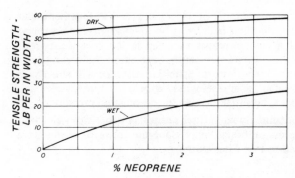

Strength of Kraft paper with neoprene
impregnation.

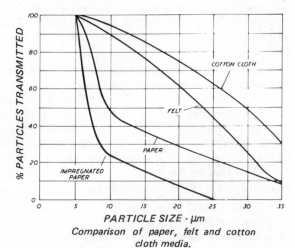

Comparison of paper, felt and cotton
cloth media.

Another inherent limitation with paper elements is that the very nature of the material does not provide an absolute cut-off figure. There will almost certainly always be larger pore sizes than the nominal rating and so random larger particles may be passed by the filter. This limits the suitability of paper elements for ultra-fine filtering. On the other hand the performance of paper, and particularly resin-impregnated paper elements can be superior to felts, fabrics, cotton cloths, and similar media.

Although paper elements are invariably thin the tortuous path provided by the layer of fibres does, in fact, mean that they filter in depth instead of acting as simple mechanical screens. At the same time contaminants will collect mainly on the outer surface and the accumulation of such contaminants will progressively increase the efficiency of the filter by acting as a filter bed.

The fact that some solid contaminants will tend to penetrate into the depth of the paper and become lodged can make cleaning difficult, or even impractical. In the case of 'dry' fluids, such as air, adequate cleaning may be provided by a back flow of air. Paper elements may be reusable in such cases. With 'wet' fluids it is more usual to employ disposable filter elements which are simply replaced when clogged.

A stronger form of paper element employs a large number of paper discs stacked together under compression. This produces an edge type filter, the filter path being between adjacent discs rather than through the discs themselves. By adjusting the compression applied to the stack a cut-off of down to 1 μm or below can be achieved, with true filtering in depth. Such filters, however, have a high specific resistance, proportional to the stacking pressure. Specific resistance will also rise if the element is absorbent — for example, untreated paper discs would absorb moisture present as a contaminant, causing swelling of the discs and a substantial increase in compression pressure.

Papers are also used to a limited extent for filter cloths in filter presses. A paper cloth air filter, for example, is basically a single-cell filter press, although more elaborate forms of element are normally used in panel filters. Paper is also used to face filter cloths.

Fabrics

Fabrics can be considered as a direct, and physically stronger, alternative to papers and are employed in a similar manner for pleated elements, *etc*. Since fabrics lack the rigidity of papers, however, they normally need to be supported by a wire screen or mesh or similar back-up. Where cleaning by back-washing is to be utilized it may be necessary to back-up the fabric element on both sides.

Fabric elements were originally the most commonly used type for fine filtering and are generally comparable with modern paper elements as regards performance achievable. Until the appearance of treated paper elements they were regarded as a superior type, although the two are now strictly competitive for similar duties. Treated papers are the more common because of lower cost, but fabric elements are capable of withstanding higher working pressures with similar geometry. On the other hand, fabric elements have a lower specific resistance than paper elements and, being thicker, can also carry a heavier load of contaminant per unit area. This latter advantage is normally offset by the fact that for the same overall size the surface area of a fabric element is reduced because of its greater thickness.

Possibly a major distinction between the two is that for a similar design of element, fabric would be preferred for larger sizes of filter, or where a degree of true absorption is required as well as mechanical screening. The description 'fabric' is, however, rather loose, compared with papers which imply use of a specific material. Fabrics can comprise a whole range of woven materials, (*eg* see Table I) and properties may be further modified by impregnation with a synthetic resin or similar treatment. The description 'fabric' is also given to filter elements which are really felted fibres rather than true fabrics (that is, felts). Equally, when the term 'cloth' is used to describe the element material this may be a natural or synthetic woven fabric; or even woven wire cloth.

Felts

Natural felts are produced by compressing wool or hair or wool/hair mixtures, yielding a wide range of densities and permeabilities. A cross section through such materials would show successive layers or irregular mesh with an extremely tortuous path for filtering in depth. The random size of the pores makes it virtually impossible to establish even a nominal rating or specific resistance by direct practical tests.

Modern felts are produced from synthetic fibres or mixtures of synthetic and natural fibres, with close control of manufacture to yield consistent density, pore size, and mesh geometry so that cut-off performance is reasonably predictable. The structure of felts is considerably more open than papers, so that whilst filtering in greater depth (thicknesses), specific resistance is lower and high rates of flow can be achieved with smaller element areas and low pressure drop.

TABLE I – APPLICATIONS OF FILTER CLOTHS

Material	Suitable for:-	Maximum Service Temperature °C	Principal Advantage(s)	Principal Disadvantage(s)
Cotton	Aqueous solutions, oils, fats, waxes, cold acids and volatile organic acids	90	Inexpensive	Subject to attack by mildew and fungi
Jute wool	Aqueous solutions / Aqueous solutions and dilute acids	85 / 80	East to seal joints in filter presses	High shrinkage subject to moth attack in store
Nylon	Acids, petrochemicals, organic solvents, some alkaline suspensions	150	High strength or flexibility. Easy cake discharge. Long life.	Absorbs water; not suitable for alkalis
Polyester (Terylene)	Acids, common organic solvents, oxidizing agents	100	Good strength and flexibility. Initial shrinkage	Not suitable for alkalis
PVC	Acids and alkalis	up to 90		May become brittle. Heat resistance poor.
PTFE	Virtually all chemicals	200	Extreme chemical resistance. Excellent cake discharge.	High cost
Polyethylene	Acids and alkalis	70	Easy cake discharge	Softens at moderate temperatures
Polypropylene	Acids, alkalis, solvents (except aromatics and chlorinated hydrocarbons)	130	Low moisture absorption	
Dynes	Acids, alkalis, solvents, petrochemicals	110		
Orlon	Acids (including curomic acid), petro-chemicals	over 150		
Vinyon	Acids, alkalis, solvents, petroleum products	110		
Glass fibre	Concentrated hot acids, chemical solutions	250	Suitable for wide range of chemical solutions, hot or cold (except alkalis)	Lacks fatigue strength for flexing. Abrasive resistance poor.

The wide variety of materials from which synthetic felts can be made has also considerably increased the application of such media through the chemical and petro-chemical industries, breweries, paint industry, food processing, plastics, and dyestuff industries, *etc*, since the material can be chosen specifically on the basis of compatibility and its mechanical properties controlled during manufacture. Synthetic materials used in the manufacture of felts include nylon, regenerated cellulose (rayon), polyethylene, polypropylene, acrylics and polyesters, some of which have general, and others specific, applications.

None of these is an absorbent material as such, so synthetic felts are, basically, mechanical filters. The same is true of metal felts. Natural felts, on the other hand, are hygroscopic and tend to absorb moisture as well as remove solid particles by screening and mechanical retention.

Felts are most commonly used in the form of filter pads, area and thickness being selected on the basis of specific resistance as against flow rates required and acceptable pressure drop. With filter pads there is usually an optimum thickness for efficient filtering and any greater thickness is usually unnecessary, except for purely physical considerations such as ease of handling, *etc*. Thinner felts, particularly synthetic felts, are similar to cloths and may in fact be used as alternatives to cloths for other forms of filter elements, *eg* cartridge filters.

Mineral Wools

Mineral wools are rather akin to 'unfelted' natural felts with random fibre distribution in three dimensions offering a tortuous path for filtering in depth. Density is low and permeability high and with suitable packing very fine filtering can be provided with minimum pressure drop. It is generally necessary, however, that flow velocities be kept very low in order to avoid bunching of the fibres with a consequent drop in efficiency. This somewhat limits their application with liquid filtering, although they are widely used for pure air filtering and the removal of solid particles from gases. In the latter respect mineral fibres may be used at working temperatures well above those possible with other non-metallic filters, for example, at temperatures of 500°C, or even higher for short periods.

Performance down to sub-micron size is possible with mineral wool filter pads. In the case of ultra-fine gas or air filtration, a nominal optimum velocity for flow rate is 30 feet per minute, decreasing to 15 feet per minute at a working temperature of 300°F. Flow velocities in excess of 45 feet per minute will normally promote bunching, but velocities as high as 120 feet per minute may be accommodated where some loss of filtering efficiency can be tolerated.

Typically, a very fine asbestos fibre filter pad of ½ inch (12.7 mm) thickness should be capable of removing solid particles from gases down to 0.1 μm at gas velocities of the order of 30 feet per minute through the pad, with only nominal resistance. Increasing the filter pad thickness above an optimum does not necessarily increase filter efficiency although it increases the possibility of trapping still finer particles. Thus for sterile air and similar applications the filter pad thickness may be as great as 4 or 5 inches (100 or 125 mm).

When used for ultra fine and sub-micron filtering in this way it is also desirable that the air be prefiltered to remove coarser particles, leaving the pad itself to deal with the finer contaminants. This will increase the life of the filter pad which may then be as high as three to six months under continuous use.

COMPARATIVE PROPERTIES OF FILTER CLOTH MATERIALS

	Wool	Cotton	Polyester	Acrylic	Nylon	Aramid	Polypropylene	PVC	PTFE	Glass Fibre
Yarn type *	S	S	S,F,MF	S,F	S,F,MF	S,F	S,F,MF	S,F,MF	S,F,MF	S,F
Specific gravity	1.30	1.52	1.38	1.15–1.17	1.04–1.14	1.38	0.91	1.35	2.1	2.1
Tensile strength (relative) Wool = 1	1	2–4	3.75–6.25	1.85–3.75	3.75–6.5	5–20	3.75–6	2.2	1.3	8–15
Elongation at break %	30–40	5–7	11–14	17–42	18–20	18–20	35	35–40	15	2–4
Maximum continuous service temp. °C	80–90	90–100	130–135	130–135	100–110	200–220	80–90	80–90	240–260	280–300
Maximum service temperature °C	100	110	140	140	120	260	90–100	90–100	280	320
Chemical resistance†										
Strong acids	F	X	G	G	X	F	E	E	E	G
Weak acids	G	F	E	E	F	G	E	E	E	G
Strong alkalis	X	G	X	G	G	G	G	E	E	E
Weak alkalis	F	E	F	G	G	G	G	E	E	G
Solvents	G	G	G	G	E	G	E	F	E	E
Oxidizing agents	X	F	E	G	F	G	X	E	E	E
Resistance to moist heat†	F	G	X	E	F	F	F	G	E	G
Specific solvents for fibre			$C_6H_5NO_2$ C_6H_5OH	$CHON(CH_3)_2$	CH_3COOH $HCOOH$ C_6H_5OH			CH_3COCH_3 $CHCl_3$ CS_2		HF
Trade Names			Dacron Terylene Terital Diolen Tergal Trevira	Orlon Dralon Redon Crylor Zerran Leacril	Nylon Perlon Rilsan Nailon Lilion	Nomex Kevlar	Courlene Merkalon Hostalen Pylen	Saran Harlan Rovyl Leavil	Teflon Fluon	Fibreglass Vetrotex

Key to symbols:

* S = Staple element
M = monofilament
MF = millifilament

† E = excellent
G = good
F = fair
X = dissolved

Diatomaceous Earth

Diatomaceous earth — also known as kieselguhr — is almost pure silica, being fossil diatoms which have collected on the bottom of seas and lakes over a period of tens of millions of years and are, subsequently exposed and accessible for quarrying where the water has receded or been displaced by eruption. These fossils are of tiny size — a typical mean being about 1/200 of an inch — and are characterized by being riddled with minute holes, known as punctae. Some 93% of the volume of a diatom fossil, in fact, is void space, comprising interconnected cavities and pores.

Diatomite is a true fossil diatom, found mainly in California, Nevada and Washington, and in small localized areas in Europe. There are two distinct types — freshwater diatoms and marine diatoms. Freshwater diatoms (with large deposits in Nevada) have a slightly thicker wall than marine diatoms, are more uniform in shape and size and generally less brittle. Marine diatoms consist of disc-shaped diatoms and needle-shaped spicules, yielding particles which bridge more easily. As a result their wet density tends to be higher — *ie* more dry weight of material is needed to form a particular area of filter cake.

Used as a filter bed material, diatomaceous earth can provide extremely fine filtering with relatively low resistance to flow and is often used where the highest purity is required, such as the filtering of sugars, edible oils, water, *etc*. The fineness of the material is emphasized by the fact that it may take 40 million fossils to fill one cubic inch; and a ton of diatomaceous earth can have a volume of 260 cubic feet.

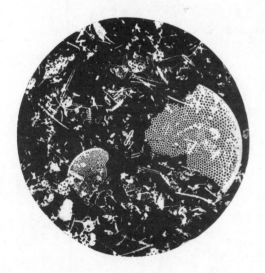

Photomicrograph X200 magnification showing the structure of diatomaceous particles.

Perlite (magnification X1500) top; and fresh water diatoms bottom.

(TR International (Chemists) Ltd)

Perlite

Perlite is a glassy, igneous rock which expands when heated quickly to its softening point, yielding bulkier and more flaky particles than diatoms. These are less effective in thin layers for filtering than diatoms and so normally need to be used in greater bed thicknesses. Even then perlite is regarded as less suitable than diatoms for clarifying. The particular advantage of the material is that it has high bulking value (*ie* low wet density).

Applications

Diatomaceous earth (and to a lesser extent perlite) is widely used as a precoat material on vacuum drum filters, and also in clarifying processes employing filter presses using cloth, paper or pad media; pressure-leaf filters with metal screens; and candle filters.

An alternative method of employing diatomaceous earth as an integral element rather than a coating is to render it in sheet or solid form. This can be done by mixing the diatomaceous earth with cellulose wood pulp which, in effect, acts as a bonding agent. Mechanical strength of such an element depends primarily on the proportion of cellulose pulp present in the mixture. This must be adjusted with regard to the graded size of diatom fossils employed; thus finer fossils would need a higher proportion of binder for the same mechanical strength, but the higher the proportion of binder the less the permeability. It is thus possible to provide grades of different strength (governed by binder proportion and diatom size), different cut-off (governed by diatom size) and different permeability (governed by diatom size and binder proportions). A typical mixture would employ about 20% binder.

Strength can also be enhanced by impregnation with a suitable resin. This is commonly done to add wet strength to such filter sheets, the cellulose binder not being water resistant on its own. Strength can also be improved by corrugating or ribbing the sheets, or even employing a pleated form of element. For other duties it may be possible to 'cast' the material in more solid forms although development with diatomaceous earth/cellulose mixtures is as yet still rather limited.

Glass Fibre

Glass fibre in 'blanket' or 'pad' form is widely used as primary stage air filters. By modification of the conventional spinning process the blanket as manufactured can have progressively increasing density from one side to the other — *eg* sparsely packed large diameter fibres on the dirty air side gradually giving way to more densely packed small diameter fibres towards the inner surface. This effect is produced by an ageing process which 'conditions' the blanket, followed by a further operation to expand the fibres.

Clean 80-85% DRI-Pak Media
200 X Magnification - Note the fineness of the fibres and extremely high fibre content.

Loaded 80-85% DRI-Pak Media
2000 X Magnification - Dirt accumulation from actual atmospheric conditions can be seen in this photo. Particles are trapped along the length of the fibres and at fibre intersections.

Loaded 80-85% DRI-Pak Media
5000 X Magnification - This extreme close-up of a single fibre shows how individual dirt particles collect along the fibres. Particles less than 0.2 μm can be seen on this fibre.

Dirt-holding characteristics of micro-glass fibres.
(AAF Limited)

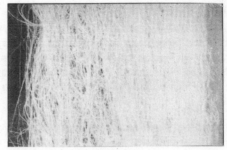

Progressive density is clearly visible in
this sample.

*Expansion of glass fibre blanket during
production.
(AAF Ltd.)*

Expansion produces an aerated filter medium of greatly increased volume and thus high porosity. Binders added prior to this stage can act as fibre lubricants to assist expansion. The expanded blanket can then be oven treated to cure the binder and cement the fibres together to produce a rigid, lightweight mass.

Medium and fine glass fibre filter pads are produced from a blend of glassfibre strands and glass microfibres bonded together with a binder to form thin sheets. A typical media pad is then constructed by interleaving a continuous length of medium folded backwards and forwards over wire mesh or perforated aluminium separators.

Ultra-fine (HEPA) filters use a sheet form medium, produced only with microglass fibres. The complete element may be constructed as previously mentioned, interleaved with spacers cut from microglass 'paper'.

Charcoal Cloth

Charcoal cloth is a new medium developed at the Chemical Defence Establishment at Porton Down and first licensed for production in 1977. It comprises 100% activated charcoal fibres in the form of woven cloth with up to twenty times the absorption properties of granular charcoal and several times greater than those of other cloth, foam or non-woven products coated with fine carbon granules. It also has the advantage of being a strong, flexible material with good resistance to shock and vibration and hence can provide a self-supporting filter element.

Charcoal cloth is manufactured from pretreated woven cellulose fibre cloth, reduced to 100% carbon in a controlled ambient furnace, maintained to ensure the desired strength and absorptive capacity. The process reduces the cellulose cloth to a quarter of the original weight, yielding an activated charcoal cloth with high porosity and high surface area.

The material is expensive to produce but cost should fall with increasing demand. Specific industrial applications include filters for odour control, face masks, respirators, *etc*; filters for air conditioning; and water and chemical treatment filters. In the medical field, particular potentials are air filters for face masks, *etc*, and charcoal cloth bandages for removing offensive odours. The material is also regarded as having high potential in the civil/military defence field, *eg* for respirators, protective clothing and combat gear.

Physical characteristics of charcoal cloth developed primarily for use in respiratory filters are:-

C-Tex (Siebe-Gorman)

Bulk density	0.3 g/cm^2
Surface density	$0.008-0.014$ g/cm^2
Cloth thickness	$0.040-0.050$ cm
Breaking strain	1 kg/cm width
Air flow resistance	$0.007-0.014$ cm wg/cm/sec of flow

The adsorption under steady flow conditions is illustrated in the following table extracted from a series of experiments comparing C-tex to the equivalent granular material.

RESULTS COMPARING C-TEX TO EQUIVALENT GRANULAR MATERIAL

Adsorbent	Specific weight of bed (mg/cm^2) %	Relative humidity %	Linear flow (cm/sec)	Vapour and concentration	Vapour Adsorbed at Penetration (% W/W)
Coal charcoal	17 000	80	9	Carbon Tetrachloride at 6 mg/lit	1.8
Coal charcoal	13 000	80	6	Carbon Tetrachloride at 6 mg/lit	3.0
Nut charcoal	17 000	80	9	Carbon Tetrachloride at 6 mg/lit	4.4
Nut charcoal	12 000	65	8	Trichlorethylene at 5 mg/lit	7.9
C-Tex	35 (4 layers)	80	8.8	Carbon Tetrachloride at 5 mg/lit	8.7
C-Tex	70 (8 layers)	80	8.8	Carbon Tetrachloride at 5 mg/lit	8.0
C-Tex	140 (16 layers)	80	8.8	Carbon Tetrachloride at 5 mg/lit	7.7
C-Tex	60 (9 layers)	80	1.22	Trichlorethylene at 30 mg/lit	37
C-Tex	40 (5 layers)	70	0.75	Trichlorethylene at 5.5 mg/lit	27
C-Tex	40 (5 layers)	80	1.4	Carbon Tetrachloride at 6 mg/lit	14

C-tex actuated carbon cloth
(Siebe Gorman Ltd)

Carbon Fibre

Commercial carbon fibre is produced in fibre diameter sizes of the order of 5–10 μm, from a variety of starting materials, *eg* acrylic textile fibres, cellulose-based fibres or even pitch. They offer a possible alternative to organic fibres and glass fibres for filter pads and felts for extreme chemical and temperature duties, with the additional advantage that the material can be activated and thus also perform as an absorbent filter.

The main limitation of carbon fibre as a filter medium at present is expense, coupled with the fact that the current fibre diameter sizes available means that they cannot achieve the performance of current HEPA filters using microglass fibres. Carbon fibres of suitable size to achieve such ratings are even more expensive to produce and to date have only been prepared by laboratory processes. Larger scale production is certainly feasible, however, although the starting point material can present some limitations. Carbon fibres produced by the carbonization of cellulose wool, for example, are not chemically clean.

Specifically, the main potential applications of carbon fibre as a filter medium would appear to lie in the filtration of inert or reducing gases at high temperatures; filtration processes involving fume and odour removal; and in processes involving hot and/or corrosive gases. Present commercial production of the material limits application to medium efficiency filters. Future production may extend this to performances equivalent to current HEPA high efficiency air filters, extended to higher working temperatures. Carbon fibres are resistant to temperatures up to about 400°C in air, and up to 3 600°C in reducing atmospheres. Resistance to chemical vapours and nuclear radiation is also high.

Anthracite

Anthracite is a suitable medium for gravity and pressure filters for the treatment of hard and soft waters, sewage, oils, and acids and alkalis. Preferably it needs to be treated to produce maximum hardness to ensure minimum wastage by attrition, and be free from water soluble constituents and any other minerals. Such treated anthracite contains over 90% pure carbon and has a low silicon content, making it particularly suitable for the treatment of alkaline waters for boiler feed duties.

The filter medium normally used is a multi-layer of selected anthracite particles and sand. Anthracite particles are lighter and larger than sand, such a mixture providing good filtration in depth in dual-media beds. The larger spaces between the anthracite particles enable high flow rates to be achieved with low load losses. The large surface area of the anthracite is also efficient in removing algae, bacteria and turbidity.

Examples of media size and filtration rates achievable are given in the following Table:-

	Potable Water	Tertiary Treatment of Sewage
Media size	Filtracite* (mean particle size 0.8 mm) Sand around 0.6 mm	Filtracite* (mean particle size 3.0 mm) Sand 1.0 mm
Filtration rate	Up to 2 mm/sec, normally 1.6 mm/sec to produce less than 0.5 units of turbidity	Up to 4 mm/sec to produce less than 4 units of turbidity
Depth of each layer	Standard 1 metre. Filtracite bed to be twice the depth of sand.	Standard 1.5 metre

*Anthracite filter medium ex Thomas Ness Ltd.

The density of filter sand is 2 650 kg/m^3, while Filtracite is 1 400 $\pm$ 20 kg/m^3 yielding in water a ratio of effective density of sand to anthracite of 2 650/1 400 or two to one, and allowing good separation.

Pennsylvania (USA) anthracite weighs 1 600—1 700 kg/m^3, yielding density ratios with sand between 2.4 and 2.8 so that separation is less easily achieved.

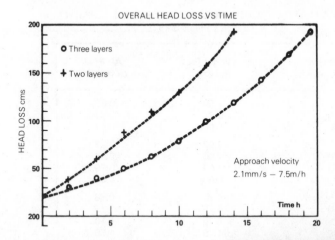

OVERALL HEAD LOSS VS TIME

○ Three layers

✝ Two layers

HEAD LOSS cms

Approach velocity
2.1mm/s — 7.5m/h

Time h

Anthracite grains, lighter and larger (one to two millimetres average diameter) than sand, offer filtration in depth in dual-media beds while their particle shape provides good void space for deposits plus a tortuous flow-path.

Ceramic Filter Elements

Ceramic filter elements have particular application for higher fluid temperatures and for handling corrosive fluids. Elements made from vitreous bonded refractory ceramic aggregate also have a high resistance to physical and thermal shock.

Ceramic elements can be cast or moulded in various element forms, with varying degrees of porosity and uniformity of structure. Void areas are typically up to 50%. Microporous types can be produced with pore sizes down to 1 μm. Ceramic elements can be used for filtering both air and liquids. They are particularly suitable for use with acids and alkalis. Typical pressure drop and flow capabilities of ceramic filter elements are shown in Table II.

TABLE II — FLOW RATES FOR A MICRO-POROUS CERAMIC CYLINDRICAL ELEMENT
10 inch long x 2 inch o.d. x 1½ inch nominal bore

Pore Diameter μm	Pressure Differential lb/in^2	Water Flow gall/hr	Air Flow cu ft/min
1	10	2.50	0.33
	15	3.75	0.50
	20	5.00	0.67
2	5	2.00	0.27
	10	4.00	0.54
	15	6.00	0.80
	20	8.00	1.08
3	5	2.85	0.38
	10	5.70	0.75
	15	8.75	1.13
	20	11.40	1.50
5	5	3.80	0.50
	10	7.60	1.00
	15	11.40	1.50
	20	14.20	1.90
10	5	8.90	1.18
	10	17.80	2.36
	15	26.70	3.54
	20	35.50	4.74

SECTION 2

Sub-section (b)

Bag Filters

BAG FILTERS are widely used for dust removal in industrial atmospheres, the most common form being a cylindrically shaped woven fabric sleeve, with or without stiffening rings. Dust capture can be provided on the internal or external surface of the sleeve, as best suited to the application. Different systems can also be used for removal of collected dust, *eg* mechanical shaking, back-washing with compressed air, or collapsing the sleeve and shaking (see also Fig 1).

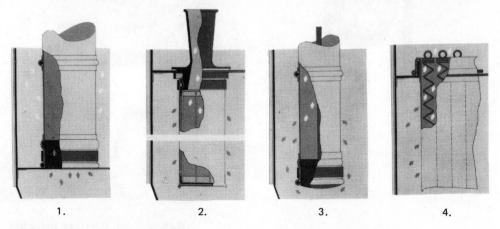

1.   2.   3.   4.

1. Bag filter with mechanical shanking.
2. Bag filer with shaking by compressed air (high pressure jet pulse).
3. Sleeve filter with shaking by air inversion (collapsing).
4. Panel filter.

Fig 1 (Testori)

Fabric fibre and construction can be selected to suit the nature and characteristics of the dusts to be handled, the main parameters being particle size, density, abrasive nature, hygroscopy and tendency to form agglomerates, *etc;* also electrostatic properties, particularly when filtering potentially explosive dust/gas mixtures. In the latter case auto-ignition or explosion due to sparking from electrostatic charges can be eliminated by the use of antistatic materials — *eg* synthetic fibres interwoven with metallic or carbon fibres and connected to earth potential when *in situ*. Bag fabrics can also be treated for water repellance, fire resistance or special surface anti-adhesive characteristics.

Currently available synthetic fibres offer working temperatures with gas up to 230°C; or 300°C in the case of glass fibre fabrics. Metallic and ceramic fibres offer even higher working temperatures, but their application is strictly limited at present.

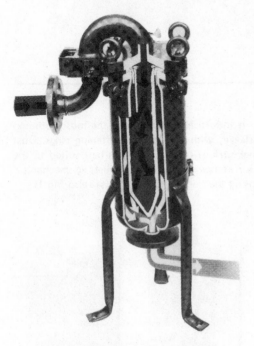

Flow pattern through GAF bag filter for liquid filtration.

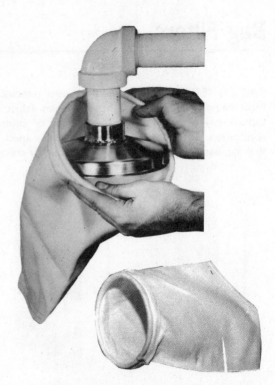

GAF snap-ring filter bag and adaptor head assembly.

Fibre media employed are divided broadly into fabrics and felts. Fabrics are by far the more numerous, with a very wide range of combinations of staple, monofilament or multifilament yarns in various weaves. The weave determines the interlacement between warp and weft, governing both strength and pore openings and the flatness of the fabric surface. Felts are made of wool or synthetic fibre and are characterized by a more homogeneous construction, giving them greater dust retention capacity with generally lower pressure drop. However felts clog more readily than fabrics and felt bag filters require more energetic backwashing.

Bag filters are described in more detail in the chapter on *Fabric Dust Collectors*.

Rotary Drum Filters

ROTARY DRUM filters may be of vacuum type (rotary drum vacuum filters) or pressurized type (pressure drum filters). The former are by far the more common and are produced in a large variety of types and sizes capable of meeting a very wide range of liquid/solid separation requirements in process industries, mineral engineering, effluent treatment plant, *etc*; right down to laboratory sizes. Such filters have continuous operation with high wash efficiency at low specific power requirements. They can be used with a wide variety of filter cloths or filter beds, and with various discharge methods for solids of various consistencies.

Basically a *rotary drum vacuum filter* consists of a cloth-covered drum suspended over a trough containing the suspension, with approximately one-third of the filter area immersed in the suspension. The trough may or may not include an agitator. The drum is commonly divided into three sections known as the cake-building, dewatering and removal zones. The first two zones are under vacuum, whereby water in the material being handled is sucked through the filter cloth and the solid particles build up as a cake on the cloth. The third zone is under pressure and is utilized for the removal of the filter cake. Compressed air used for cake removal can also be employed for clean-blowing the filter cloth.

Dorr-Oliver vacuum drum sugar cane filter.

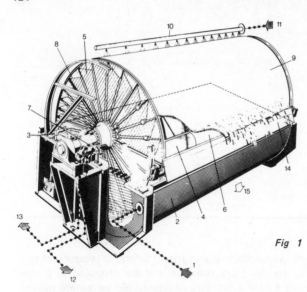

1 Suspension
2 Filter trough
3 Pendulum agitator
4 Filter cells
5 Drum
6 Filter cloth
7 Control head
8 Filtrate pipes
9 Filter cake
10 Washing device
11 Wash liquid
12 Mother filtrate
13 Wash filtrate
14 Discharge device (*eg* Scraper discharge)
15 Solid

Fig 1   *Typical operation of vacuum
drum filter.
(Krauss-Maffei)*

A specific example of a rotary drum vacuum filter is shown in Fig 1. The drum rotates at 10–60 revolutions per hour. A vacuum of approximately 400 to 160 torr is built up with a liquid seal pump which is connected to the drum cells via the control head and filtrate pipes. This causes the liquid to filter through the filter cloth. The solid contained in the suspension is deposited, in a uniform layer, on the filter cloth.

The control head divides the filter drum into different sections for filtration, washing, suction drying and cake discharge, *ie* in the course of one revolution each point of the drum area passes through these zones in succession. The filtrate runs off via the separator reservoir and is discharged either by pumping or by utilization of atmospheric pressure. The filtered solid layer emerges from the suspension due to rotation of the drum, and following its emergence as the drum rotates, is washed, suction dried, and discharged from the filter cloth. The wash liquid is fed onto the cake either directly via wash devices (*eg* weirs and/or spray nozzles); or via a wash belt lying on top of the solid layer.

*'Combibloc' Dorr-Oliver system vacuum
filter in fruit juice design with scavenging filtration and eccentric worm pump.
(Seitz-Werke GmbH)*

The filtrate from the wash zone can be drained off separately from the mother filtrate. The filter cake is discharged by means of a discharge device, covering the entire drum width, specially suited to the cake thickness, consistency, structure, *etc*, (scraper, roller, string, *etc*, — see later).

The filter cloth can be cleaned before re-immersion, either with water jets or with cleaning brushes. As the drum rotates, the cleaned filter is once more immersed in the suspension.

An example of a complete installation for filtration, washing and filtrate separation is shown in Fig 2. If the filter cake is not washed, or if separation of the main and wash filtrate is not required, then the plant is equipped only with a filtrate separator. Instead of the filtrate pump, atmospheric pressure can be utilized for discharging the filtrate.

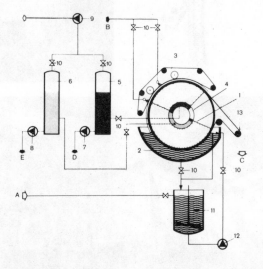

1 - Filter drum
2 - Filter trough
3 - Wash apparatus
4 - Control head
5 - Separator for wash filtrate
6 - Separator for mother filtrate
7 - Filtrate pump for wash filtrate
8 - Filtrate pump for mother filtrate
9 - Vacuum pump
10 - Valves
11 - Suspension container
12 - Suspension pump
13 - Solid discharge device

A - Suspension
B - Wash liquid
C - Solid
D - Wash filtrate
E - Filtrate

Fig 2 Complete installation for a rotary drum filter.

Filter Media

As noted previously, various types of filter cloth can be used on drum filters, depending on the specific application. Precoat filters may also be used, *eg* for treatment of suspensions with a very low solids content and/or where very fine solid particles have to be filtered and an absolutely clear filtrate is required. Diatomaceous earth is the most common precoat material used, but carbon, sawdust, PVC and other substances may also be employed.

Initially a slurry of the precoat is filtered producing a cake of up to 100 mm thickness on the filter cloth. Then the filter trough is drained and filled with the suspension to be filtered. This is now filtered in the normal way through the precoat layer. The filtered cake can be washed and discharged with a scraper knife. At least 0.05 mm of the precoat layer may be scraped off along with the product cake. The precoat layer is then still thinner. When it has reached a variable minimum thickness, product filtration is interrupted. The suspension is drained out of the trough and a new precoat is applied.

With precoat filtration, the filtered solids produced still contain precoat material. Filtrate separation is only possible given certain conditions. However, this process is distinctive on account of the high filtrate quality achieved.

Cake Discharge Methods

The most suitable discharge method depends on the form and characteristics of the cake formed in the filter. This can vary in consistency, thickness and structure according to the product being handled — *eg* from a paste-like substance to a consistent solid. Various discharge methods are shown in Figs 3—7.

1 - Drum/filter cell
2 - Filter cloth
3 - Filter cake
4 - Ventilation
5 - Scraper
6 - Cake release

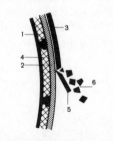

Fig 3 Scraper discharge.

Stockdale scraper knife discharge filter for beet sugar, with cake washing facilities.

Scraper discharge is widely used for effluent sludge, mineral ore dressing or metallurgical working, chemical process slurries and similar products. The scraper blade itself may be fixed or self-adjusting. A fixed (adjustable) blade with high pressure blow back is more or less traditional in certain applications (*eg* coal slurry dewatering, metallurgical processing, *etc*). The blade itself is set a small distance away from the surface of the drum, the actual separation of the cake being achieved by blow back pressure, the scraper thus merely guiding the filtrate away from the drum.

A fixed blade may also be used without blow back. In this case the blade height is set to skim a certain thickness of the cake, leaving the rest on the drum surface. It has the advantage of providing a dryer discharged cake with enhanced filtrate characteristics as well as subjecting the cloth to minimal wear. It is used particularly with crystalline solids and certain types of metallurgical slurries; and for discharge from a precoat filter. In the latter case the blade is set to remove all the cake thickness plus a small thickness of precoat.

1 - Drum/filter cell
2 - Filter cloth
3 - Precoat layer
4 - Filter cake
5 - Scraper
6 - Cake release

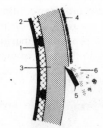

Fig 4 Precoat - scraper discharge.

Self-adjusting scraper blades provide a better performance on thin filter cakes which crack readily. Here flexible plastic or spring-loaded blades are used and the filter cloth caulked so that under low pressure blow back it balloons outwards against the blades so that blade and cloth remain in light, intimate contact. With proper technique, cloth wear is minimal.

Filter fitted with string discharge used to process china clay during production of whitenings.
(Stockdale Engineering Ltd.)

1 - Drum/filter cell
2 - Filter cloth
3 - Discharge string
4 - Filter cake
5 - Discharge and
    return rolls
6 - Guide comb

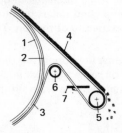

Fig 5 String discharge.

String discharge involves the addition of a number of endless strings spaced at about ½ inch (12 mm) pitch over the width of the filter drum, the run of these strings being extended to form an open conveyor system passing over a discharge and return roller. Effectively these strings lift the cake off the filter cloth at the point where they leave the drum tangentially, the cake falling off where the strings loop back around the discharge roll. A guide comb may also be incorporated between the discharge and return rolls to retain string alignment and remove any residual cake adhering to the strings.

String discharge minimizes mechanical wear on the filter cloth (enabling thinner cloths to be used); avoids the need for blow back; and provides continuous, steady discharge at any suitable point away from the drum. The strings are normally synthetic fibres (*eg* nylon, terylene, poly-propylene, *etc*), chosen according to the product being handled. They can also be in the same material as the cloth; or in specific cases, in the form of metal mesh rather than individual strings.

Stockdale belt discharge filter with acid wash and water rinse.

1 - Drum/filter cell
2 - Filter cloth
3 - Filter cake
4 - Reversing cylinder
5 - Cake release
6 - Washing device/filter cloth washing

Fig 6 Belt discharge.

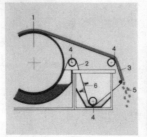

Belt discharge is similar to string discharge in operating principle except that in this case the cloth itself is led off the drum around rollers to form a conveyor run, with the cake automatically tumbling off the cloth at the extremity of the run. The return run of the cloth then passes through a washing device.

This method provides complete support of the cake to the point of discharge and thus is capable of handling all types of cakes and cake thicknesses. It does not need blow back and mechanical wear on the cloth is minimal. The wash on the return run also eliminates any tendency for the cloth to become plugged.

1 - Drum/filter cell
2 - Filter cloth
3 - Filter cake
4 - Discharge roller
5 - Scraper
6 - Cake release

Fig 7 Roller discharge.

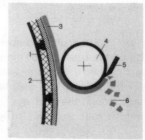

Roller discharge is limited to cakes of an adhesive nature which will transfer from the cloth to a roller. The cake is then released from the roller by a scraper blade. In effect this is a form of scraper discharge, but eliminating any contact between the scraper blade and cloth.

Pressure Drum Filters

In a *pressure drum filter* the rotating drum carrying the filter cloth is contained within a sealed housing divided into chambers to which the different treatment media are fed under pressure. The essential operations correspond to those of a vacuum drum filter, but filtration is under positive pressure and the product and filtrate can remain fully enclosed. Cake discharge then takes place on a zone at atmospheric pressure, normally by a self-adjusting scraper.

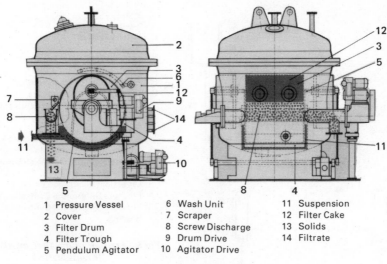

1 Pressure Vessel	6 Wash Unit	11 Suspension
2 Cover	7 Scraper	12 Filter Cake
3 Filter Drum	8 Screw Discharge	13 Solids
4 Filter Trough	9 Drum Drive	14 Filtrate
5 Pendulum Agitator	10 Agitator Drive	

Fig 8 Pressure drum filter.
(Krauss-Maffei)

An example of a pressure drum filter is shown in Fig 8. The drum filter is a cellular construction for continuous mechanical separation of solid-liquid mixtures by filtration under pressure. The pressure differential necessary for filtration is effected by means of gas pressure in a pressure vessel in which the filter drum rotates. The suspension is fed to the filter through a feed pipe. An operational filling level control device situated on either the feed pump or the feed valve ensures constant filling of the trough. An additional overflow pipe can be employed to ensure against overfilling.

Unlike the vacuum drum filter, the pressure differential necessary for cake formation is positioned and controlled between the filter pressure vessel and the filtrate separator. The filtrate from the cake formation and wash zone and gas from the cake drying zone flow over the control head and into the separator via the filter cloth covering, cell inserts and filtrate pipes as in the vacuum drum filter.

The filtered cake can be washed as in the vacuum drum filter. The separated filtrate can also be discharged at this stage.

The filter cake can be separated from the drum by means of the discharge methods described previously for vacuum drum filters. Doctor blade, precoat doctor blade and roller removal are preferred for reasons of construction. The solid is removed from the volute in the surge chamber and transported to the laterally positioned discharge chute. Depending on the mode of operation and the consistency of the filter cake, a pump, pressure lock or a valve is employed.

Pressure drum filters are suitable for processing at high pressures and/or high temperatures. They are particularly suited for solvent filtrate, (eg hot saturated solvents such as boric acid), smelt, products from SRC processes (solvent refined coal), waxes, oils and grease, paraffin and all high viscosity solvents at normal temperature. The range of application extends to bright filtration with the use of filter aids and to filtration processes in protective gas atmospheres.

A complete installation is shown in Fig 9.

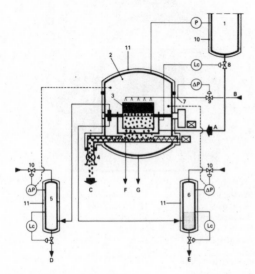

A   Suspension
B   Wash Liquid
C   Solid
D   Main Filtrate
E   Wash Filtrate
F   Suspension (overflow/outlet)
G   Tank Outlet (eg: condensate)
1   Suspension Feed Vessel/Autoclave
2   Filter Pressure Vessel
3   Pressure Filter TDF
4   Screw Discharge with Pressure Valve
5   Filtrate Separator for Main Filtrate
6   Filtrate Separator for Wash Filtrate
7   Washing Device
8   Level Controlled Feed Valve
9   Pressure Differential Controlled Wash Valve
10 Pressure Differential Controlled Gas Valve
11 Heating

Fig 9   Pressure drum filter installation.
(Krauss-Maffei)

Belt Discharge Rotary Drum Filters

In the dewatering of flotation concentrate slurries, produced during minerals dressing, the objective is to recover the maximum amounts of solids, produce a saleable product, where possible, and thus increase plant capacity at the most economic cost. During recent years there has been a significant improvement in process efficiency, at this stage, by the use of belt discharge type drum filters in place of disc vacuum filters and string/knife drums.

The success of the belt type drum filter is based on the simple premise that if filter cakes can be removed completely and continuously from a vacuum filter, then this must give the best possible conditions for high capacity and good cake drying. To achieve this, the filter media must be kept in a clean condition and the discharge system must not rely on the filter cakes having high mechanical strength. These requirements can be met completely by a belt discharge system. On this type of filter, the filter cake is positively supported on the filter media, which acts as a conveyor, carrying the cake from the filter drum to the discharge point. The filter media, after removal of the filter cake, can be washed to maintain it in a clean state before it returns to the drum.

Belt discharge rotary drum filters can give throughputs of up to 30% over the throughputs previously given by rotary drum vacuum filters fitted with knife or string discharge. Even more dramatic improvements are being achieved as compared to rotary disc filters previously used, where past experience has shown that this type are prone to poor discharge and filter cloth binding. Where this occurred, 50% or more of the cake often fell back into the filter bowl, causing a decrease in throughput which was soon reflected in the separation efficiencies of the larger capacity processes. Appreciably lower moisture contents on the filter cakes are also obtained. This can give significant reductions in costs for subsequent drying and in some cases, it allows the drier filter cake to be handled on conveyors, and blended with other material as saleable product without difficulty.

Belt discharge filters also give much greater capability to deal with variations in the filter feed material and this is of particular importance when a filter is handling a natural material or effluent — in which appreciable variations can occur.

Stockdale belt discharge filter installed in coalwash plant. Note the clean state of the cloth following discharge of the cake.

Belt discharge filters are now widely used in coal washing and preparation plants where units in operation are generally large, having areas of 55—75 m^2.

To ensure optimum performance of the filter, it is critical that the belt in operation is trouble free. It is important that the belt lies flat on the drum (it must not fold or crease) and the filter media, in addition to having the right filtration characteristics, must also have the correct mechanical characteristics. The whole system (drum, discharge rolls, wash roll) must be constructed to a high degree of accuracy.

In general the life of the filter (*ie* the filter cloth) is in the range of 6 to 12 months, although cases of 18 months have been reported and this contrasts with other types of vacuum filters where the cloth life can be only three to four months.

Key points to be considered in the design of belt discharge vacuum filters are as follows:-

1) Accuracy on the fabrication of the filter drum.
2) Specially designed internal drainlines to minimize velocities, minimize wear and ease maintenance.

3)   Accurately manufactured discharge rolls mounted in self-aligning bearings with only one roll arranged for adjustment.

4)   Simple and effective tracking system and belt tensioning system on one roll.

5)   Full width washing of belt using spray pipes designed to suit the circuit in question.

6)   Heavy duty sloping collection trough for belt washings.

7)   Availability of additional discharge roll for extra heavy duty.

8)   A facility to use air knife not in contact with the belt to remove difficult cakes.

9)   Availability of full width weir overflow on the filter trough to handle heavily frothed materials effectively and prevent spillage.

10)   Standard fitting of wide range heavy duty variable speed drum drive gear box for maximum flexiblity and service.

11)   Availability of the manufacturer's total back up services at all stages of design, construction, commissioning and operation of the plant to ensure optimum performance of the filter and complete system.

Rotary Disc Vacuum Filters

ROTARY DISC vacuum filters have the advantage, compared with rotary drum filters, of giving a much larger filter area per unit of floor area. They are thus particularly suitable for the processing of bulk products, *eg* in coal preparation, ore dressing, pulp and paper processing, *etc*.

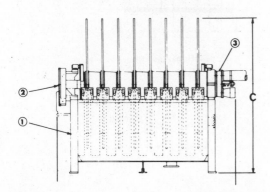

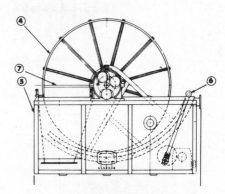

1 - Main drive
2 - Worm reduction
3 - Valve
4 - Disc and shaft assembly
5 - Trough and frame
6 - Agitator
7 - Scraper discharge

Rotary disc vacuum filter.
(Stockdale Engineering Ltd.)

The principle of construction of a rotary disc vacuum filter is a number of discs mounted on a horizontal shaft, each disc having interchangeable elements which can be changed for fitting and removing filter cloths. Conventional disc filters rotate the discs in a sump into which the suspension is fed (the sump may also have an agitator to provide even cake formation), and apply vacuum through the core of the shaft. Cake collected on the emergent sector of the disc is treated as necessary (*eg* washed) and removed by wash and/or scraper just before re-entering the trough. In other designs each disc rotates in its own narrow trough, effectively sub-dividing the filter into a number of individual cells (see Fig 1). In this case agitation is not necessary and the wetted area of disc can be greater (*eg* typically 50% as opposed to 35—40% with an open trough). Also it is possible to isolate sets of troughs from one another so that two or more different products can be handled simultaneously by the same filter.

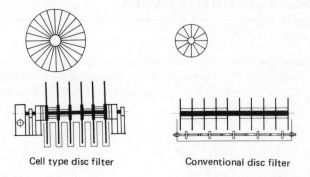

Cell type disc filter   Conventional disc filter

Fig 1

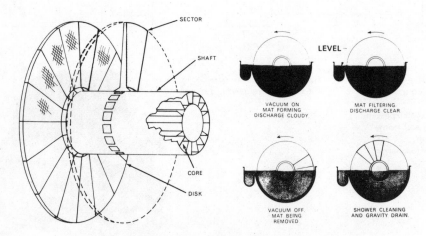

'Polydisk' filter and automatic operating cycle.
(Beloit-Walmsley International)

The filter area, and thus filtering capacity, of a rotary disc filter can be increased by increasing the number of discs in the complete unit. Standard units available may have from one (single-disc filter) up to ten or more (multi-disc units). Each disc in turn may have up to 30 filter cells, depending on diameter size.

An example of a complete system with washing features illustrated is given in Fig 2.

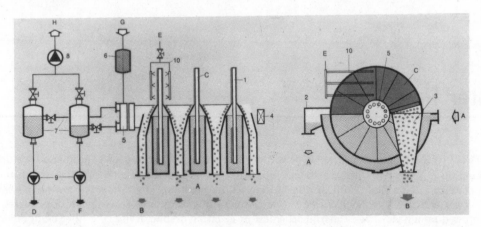

A - Suspension	1 - Filter disc
B - Solids	2 – Filter trough with overflow duct
C - Filter cake	3 - Solids chute with 'scraper'
D - Mother liquor	4 - Filter drive
E - Wash liquor	5 - Control head
F - Wash filtrate	6 - Compressed air container
G - Compressed air	7 - Filtrate separator
H - Vacuum	8 - Vacuum pump
	9 - Filtrate pump
	10 - Washing equipment

Fig 2 Krauss Maeffi disc filter.

Filter Presses

FILTER PRESSES consist of a series of vertical chambers arranged in parallel produced by either stacking flush plates with distance frames separating them, or stacking a series of recessed plates; each plate carrying a filter cloth or other suitable filter medium. The former is known as a *frame filter press* and the latter as a *chamber filter press* — Fig 1. In both cases the stack of plates is compressed by a handwheel, electromechanical or electrohydraulic device, the filter cloth serving as a gasket between individual chambers.

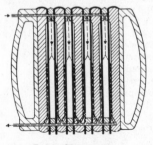

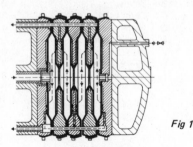

Fig 1

Frame filter press   Chamber filter press

The product to be filtered is fed into the press under pressure, the filtrate passing through the filter media and out of the press whilst solids are retained in the form of a cake on the filter media, each chamber of the press performing as a separate unit. A filter press is, therefore, essentially a pressure filter with separation at the filter faces rather than a press operating on a squeezing action.

Initially the cloth acts as the filter, but as solids are collected and build up on the surface these themselves gradually assume the function of the primary filter medium. Filtering then continues with increasing efficiency until the cake has built up to an optimum thickness.

Pumping pressure progressively builds up to compensate for loss of flow rate until eventually the cake is fully formed and filtrate flow is negligible. The press is then ready to discharge, which is performed by separating the plates and allowing the cake to drop out. If necessary, cake removal may be initiated by mechanical scrapers. The press is then reclosed ready for the next cycle — see Fig 2.

1. Closure of filter.
   The filter cells, covered on both sides with filter cloth, and the smooth removal plates of the filter package, are brought together hydraulically thus forming filter chambers.

2. Filling of chambers with suspension filtration.
   The filter chambers are filled by opening the filling valve and switching-on the feed pump. The pressure in the pump enables the liquid to filter through the filter cloth into filter cells and to be drained off into a collecting channel. In the chambers, the solid thickens into a 'cake'.

3. Compression of the plate package pressure filtration
   The filter package is compressed hydraulically after the feed pump has been shut off and the filling valve closed. As a result, the filter cake in the chambers is compressed and strongly dewatered.

4. Opening of the filter pack
   On the termination of pressure filtration, the plate package unfolds hydraulically. The compressed filter cake adheres to the removal plates.

5. Removal of filter cake.
   The removal plates with the adhering filter cake move hydraulically downwards from the filter package. The filter cake is removed by means of scrapers. A conveyor, installed beneath the filter, transports the filter cake away. After the removal plates have returned, the next filtration cycle commences.

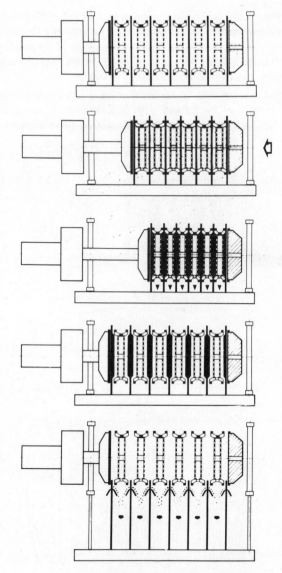

Fig 2 Typical filter press working cycle.
(Krauss-Maffei)

For drainage the filter plates may be formed with vertical grooves, corrugations, pyramid surfaces, and other configurations. In some cases vertical grooves are used in conjunction with a wire mat or perforated metal screen, or a wire mat employed without any grooves at all. A pyramidal surface is generally to be preferred, particularly as this provides the most uniform distribution of wash water over the cake should it be desirable to wash the cake.

Plate sizes range from as small as 4 in x 4 in (100 mm^2 plate area) up to over 4 feet^2 (1.2 m^2). A square shape is virtually universal on modern filter presses although many of the earlier designs employed circular plates. For the retention of large quantities of solids, or incorporation of pre-coat materials (*eg* kieselguhr), plate filters may be equipped with wide, hollow frames. Some presses may contain both types of filtering.

For dealing with materials that need to be handled at a controlled temperature the frames of the press may be formed with jackets through which cooling or heated water can be circulated to maintain a specific temperature during filtration and, if necessary, washing. These are normally referred to as jacketed presses.

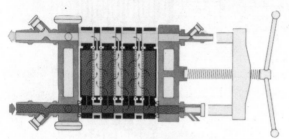

Filter press designed for Kieselguhr precoat filtration for clarifying, etc.

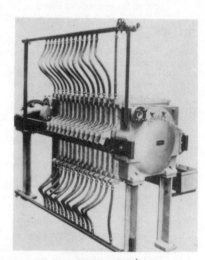

Jacketed type filter press. (S.W.Johnson & Co.Ltd.)

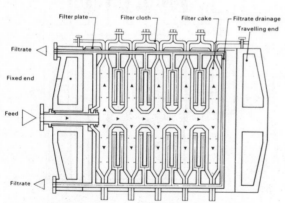

Fig 3

Chamber Filter Presses

An example of a simple form of chamber filter press is shown in Fig 3. The depth of chamber formed is equal to twice the depth of the recess on individual plates, this recess depth being varied to provide a range of cake thicknesses. The object is to obtain as thick a cake as possible without exceeding economic limitations — a typical maximum being about 1½ inch (38 mm). In special cir-cumstances where very thin cakes are called for cake thickness may be 3/8 inch (9.5 mm) or even less.

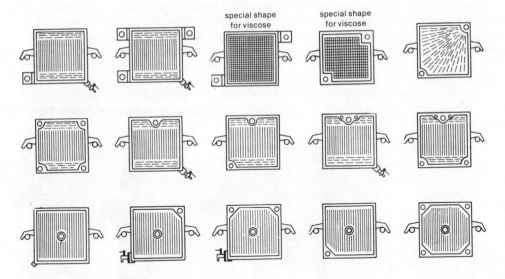

Fig 4 Examples of filter press plate forms.

(Rittershaus & Blecher)

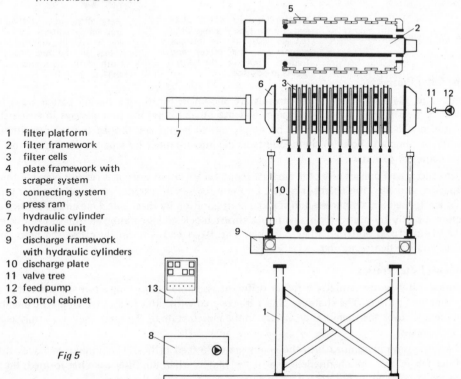

1 filter platform
2 filter framework
3 filter cells
4 plate framework with
scraper system
5 connecting system
6 press ram
7 hydraulic cylinder
8 hydraulic unit
9 discharge framework
with hydraulic cylinders
10 discharge plate
11 valve tree
12 feed pump
13 control cabinet

Fig 5

Recessed plates normally have the feed inlet placed centrally, but this may be varied according to the material being treated and its ability to cake. Thus for materials which do not form a solid cake a bottom corner inlet may be used to enable liquid to be drained out before opening the filter. Alternatively for materials which cake readily the inlet hole may be located near the top of the plate. Where it is not desirable for the filtrate to come into contact with air the eyes may be joined to form a continuous passage. With any of these variations the filter cloths which are hung over the top of the plates have holes punched in them corresponding to the feed hole position in the plate. The more typical forms employed in the modern chamber press are shown in Fig 4. (See also Fig 5).

Fig 6 (S.H.Johnson & Co.Ltd.)

Metal filter press of the plate and frame type having the passage ways in the internal corners of the plates and frames, showing the filter cloths in position.

Metal filter press of the plate and frame pattern with passage ways in external lugs. Joints in the lugs made by cloth cuffs or lipped rubber collars.

Frame Filter Presses

Examples of plate-and-frame filter presses are shown in Fig 6, one having passageways in the internal corners of the plates and frames and the other having the passageways in external lugs. The latter enables the filter cloths to be simply cut to length and draped in position without the necessity of punching holes in them. Joints in the lugs are made by separate cloths, cuff or lipped rubber collars or gaskets.

Plate and frame presses offer the greatest scope for variation since it is readily possible to adjust the spacing, and thus the chamber depth, by the thickness of distance pieces. With either type the frames are locked and compressed in stacked configuration by mechanical closure in a longitudinal direction, usually by pressure obtained by a thrust block and a rotating central screw, one end of the bed being fixed and the other movable. The fixed end is normally called the head and the movable end the tightening end.

Membrane Filter Presses

Membrane filter presses employ a rather different assembly comprising alternating chamber plates and membrane carriers. The chamber plates are covered with filter fabrics whilst elastic membranes are suspended over the membrane carriers. In the closed state of the press they are firmly clamped and hence sealed.

The suspension is pumped into the chambers via a feed orifice. The liquid is led away through the filter fabric over the channelled area of the plates. When the filter cake has formed, the membranes are inflated with compressed air to expand and compress the cake.

Pressure is then released from the membranes, a gap forms between the filter cake and the membrane, and the wash liquid is fed into this gap. After the washing process the membranes are again inflated. The remaining washing liquid is displaced and the residual moisture in the cake is reduced. After again releasing the pressure from the membrane, the filter press is opened and the cake is expelled.

The particular advantages of a membrane filter press are the considerably lower residual moisture in the cake and the saving in wash time and amount of wash liquid required.

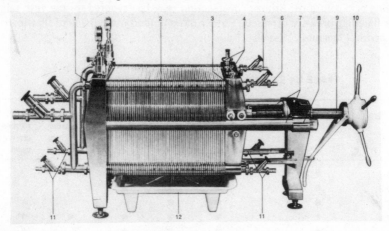

1 fixed filter cover
2 filter pack
3 movable filter cover
4 vent valves
5 vent valve (also steam connection)

6 vent valve (also pressure gas connection)
7 support rods
8 filter cross member
9 tightening spindle

10 hand-wheel with two-stage planetary gears
11 drain valves
12 plastic collecting tray

Leitz Orion filter press.

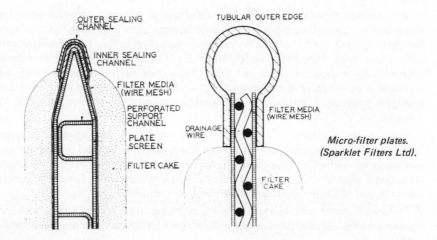

Micro-filter plates.
(Sparklet Filters Ltd).

Plate Materials

Originally cast iron was commonly employed for the frames, spacers, carrier members, and head, this material being relatively inexpensive and strong as well as being resistant to a wide range of chemicals, particularly alkalis. Wooden presses were also favoured as a low cost solution where metallic contact with the filtrate was to be avoided. Modern filter press plates and frames are more usually made of stainless steel; or aluminium alloy with synthetic resin coating. Cast iron, where employed, may be coated for compatibility with the product being handled, or rubber covered for accommodating acid solutions. Bronze construction may be favoured for use with salt brines, and gunmetal for handling brewery products. Rather more limited use is made of plastic materials — eg ebonite for chemical inertness. (See also Table I).

TABLE I — EXAMPLES OF MATERIAL APPLICATIONS

Plate Size		Cast iron	Welded steel	Stainless steel cast/welded	Non-ferrous metal	Plastics	Shaped rubber	GG rubber-covered steel	Wood
m^2	ft^2								
0.02	0.2	●		●	●	●			
0.06	0.6	●		●	●	●			●
0.125	1.25	●		●	●	●		●	●
0.25	2.5	●		●	●	●	●	●	●
0.4	4	●		●	●	●		●	●
0.5	5	●	●	●	●	●	●	●	●
1.0	10	●	●	●	●	●		●	●
1.6	16	●	●	●	●	●	●	●	●
2.5	25	●	●		●	●	●	●	●
4.0	40	●	●		●				●

Filter Cloths

A wide variety of filter cloths may be used although the most common woven materials are now nylon and polypropylene where the smooth surface gives easy cake removal, helped by the good flexibility of such cloths. Cloths woven from monofilament or multifilament yarns also discharge cakes more easily than those woven from staple yarns. Weave also affects the tendency for the cake to key or clog the cloth, so that satisfactory performance can only be established on empirical lines. Much of the economy of operation may depend on continued usage of a relatively expensive filter cloth, and with proper attention to cleaning so that the individual cloths are not damaged.

Paper is not excluded and can prove attractive for certain applications because of its lower cost. It is more likely, however, that paper filters will only be used once and then discarded whilst cloths can be washed and used over and over again provided they are not damaged in removing the cake. Some plain cloths may be discarded after a single use when handling materials which tend to adhere to and block the cloth and are difficult to remove by washing.

Perforated metal screens may be used in frame filter presses where additional strength and rigidity are required; and plastics can provide low cost screens which are easy to clean and sterilize.

Mechanization

Many modern filter presses include the application of full mechanization to filter presses to close, seal and open the press mechanically or hydraulically, and also to move the filter plates during the cake discharge period of the cycle. This is normally associated with various safety devices to stop movement should an operator accidentally make contact with the press during the period when the plate-moving mechanism is working. Mechanization or automation has considerably enhanced the value of the filter press for modern batch treatments requiring a more or less continuous flow.

Pressure Feed

Pressure feed of the liquor to be handled can be by gravity, hand pump, power driven pumps of any suitable type or even compressed air for materials that are difficult to pump. Much depends on the product being handled. Each product will have a typical *filtration curve* with rapid filtering materials having a steep slope and more sludge-like materials a shallow slope — Fig 7. Basically, therefore, rapid filtering materials need high pumping rates, which may be best provided by a centrifugal pump, or even gravity flow with a sufficient head. With longer filtering cycles positive flow pumps are employed.

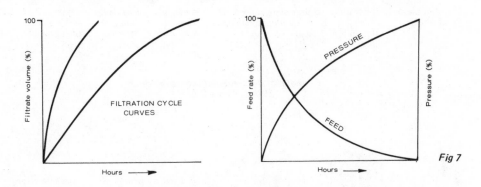

Fig 7

Reciprocating (plunger) pumps are widely favoured, modern types developed expressly for filter press feeds having the plunger directly coupled to (and operated by) a hydraulic cylinder. Such pumps incorporating a relief valve in the hydraulic circuit can follow closely the shape of the filtration curve. A pulsation damper may be a desirable addition to eliminate pressure pulses generated by the reciprocating motion.

Diaphragm pumps are also widely used for filter press feeds and again are usually of hydraulically operated type with two diaphragm chambers for continuous discharge. A pulsation damper is virtually essential with such pumps.

The flexible rotor pump is also attractive as a low cost alternative but for optimum performance needs to be associated with a pressure relief valve, pressure vessel and variable speed drive.

Operating pressures required are not high, but generally range between the equivalent of 10 and 50 feet (3 and 15 m) head of liquor. Filter presses are normally designed for working at pressures of up to 100 lb/in^2 (7 bar), although special types may be produced for very much higher working pressures; for example, up to 1 000 lb/in^2 (70 bar). Wooden presses are not normally suitable for working pressures exceeding 80 lb/in^2 (5.6 bar) and even lower ratings may be adopted with rubber or plastic covered presses.

| Filter plate of plastic | Filter plate of lacquered aluminium alloy | Filter plate of stainless steel | End plate of stainless steel | Kieselguhr frame of lacquered aluminium alloy | Kieselguhr frame of stainless steel | Kieselguhr end frame of stainless steel |

Examples of different plate constructions.
(Seitz - Werke GmbH.)

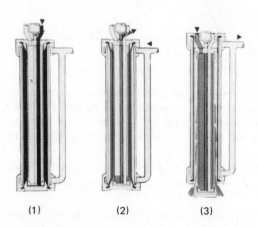

(1)   (2)   (3)

Tube press filter - comprising a steel cylinder casing lined with a tough rubber bladder in the centre of which is filter tube.
(British Separators Ltd.)

1. Slurry is fed into the space between the bladder and filter tube.

2. Hydraulic fluid is then pumped between bladder and casing at up to a remarkable 2000 lb/in^2. The bladder contracts, forcing the liquid out of the sludge or slurry through the filter, from where it is siphoned away for treatment if needed.

3. After high pressure de-watering the residue becomes solid and easily handled. The central filter core is then lowered by pneumatic jack, air is blown through to decake its surface, and the solids simply fall away.
   The whole cycle takes not more than seven minutes, ready for the next load.

TABLE II – TYPICAL EXAMPLES OF FILTER PRESS PERFORMANCE ON DEWATERING OF WASTES IN THE MUNICIPAL, POTABLE WATER AND INDUSTRIAL EFFLUENT TREATMENT FIELDS*

Type of Material	Nature and level of conditioning	Filtration cycle time (Hr)	Solids feed Wt/Wt (%)	Cake Wt/Wt (%)	Cake thickness (mm)	Remarks
Fine waste slurry	Polyelectrolytes 0.05–0.3 lb/ton	0.5–2	15–35	75–82	25–40	More than 80% below 240BS mesh
Frothed tailings	Polyelectrolytes 0.05–0.3 lb/ton	1–2.5	15–35	73–80	25–40	
Primary sewage sludge	5–25% lime with 5–15% copperas, 5–25% lime and 3–6% ferric chloride	3–7	4–7	40–55	25–32	
Digested sewage sludge	or 1-2% ACH(Al_2O_3)	1.5–2 / 2–3	3–6	35–50	25–32	
Heat treated sludge		1–2	12–15	50–70	32	
Mixed sewage sludge including surplus activated	Up to 3% aluminium chlorohydrate (Al_2O_3 basic) or 30% lime with 30% copperas or 3–8% $FeCl_3$	3–6	up to 4	30–45	32	Proportion of surplus activ. sludge is 40% by weight
		2–4	up to 4	30–40	25	
Paper Mill Humus sludge	1% ACH	8	0.5–1.5	30–45	25	
Paper Mill pool effluent sludge	10% lime, 10% copperas of 1% $FECl_3$	1–3	1–1.5	40–55	25	
Pickling and plating sludge	Up to 10% lime if required	1.5–3	2–3	30–45	25–32	
Potable water treatment sludge	In some instances no conditioning is required 0.2–1.5% polyelectrolyte (Frequently it is possible to decant large quantities of clarified water after conditioning and before filtration).	3–8	0.5–3	25–35	19–25	
Brine sludge		1.5–3	10–25	60–70	20–25	
Hydroxide sludge	1 mg/l polyelectrolyte or 10% lime	1.5–3	0.5–1.5	35–45	25–32	
Lead hydroxide sludge		0.5	45	80	32	

*Edwards & Jones Ltd

Application Industries (See also Table II).

In general, filter presses represent low initial and operating costs for batch and process filtering and require a minimum of maintenance. Capital cost is the lowest of any type of filter per unit area of filtering area, with low depreciation and long life. Possible applications cover a wide range of industries, some of which are summarized below:

Brewery industry — bronze or coated presses; sterilizing filters in stainless steel.

Bleaching — deodorizing and filtering of oils, fats and waxes.

Clarification of syrups, juices, wines, oils, varnishes, synthetic resins, viscous and acetate dope.

Dewatering of sludges and slurries — major application.

Filtering pressing of mineral ores, yeast, china clay and clay slip.

Filtration of materials containing solvents and other volatile, hazardous, inflammable and toxic liquids.

Filtration and thorough extraction washing of chemical precipitates, metallurgical slimes and pigments.

High pressure filtration.

Purification and disposal of sewage, industrial and mining effluents, *etc*, — using recessed presses.

See also chapter on *Leaf Filters*.

Belt Filters

BELT FILTERS working on the vacuum principle were originally developed for process applications where intensive washing is required, but are now also employed for a wide variety of horizontal filtering requirements. The principle of operation is simple. A trough-shaped (vacuum) tray supports a filter cloth which is transported horizontally (conveyor belt fashion) over a roller drive. On the vacuum stroke the vacuum tray is evacuated producing filtration down onto the vacuum tray which is carried along by the belt — Fig 1.

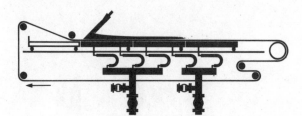

*Fig 1 'Pannevis' vacuum belt filter -
suction stroke.*

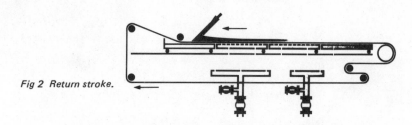

Fig 2 Return stroke.

At the end of the stroke the vacuum is released and the tray aerated. The cloth 'unsticks' and continues moving forward whilst the tray is pulled backwards to its original position — Fig 2. This cycle of vacuum-stroke/return stroke is then repeated. Although working under intermittent vacuum, filtration is continuous in that the suspension feed, the wash liquor feed and the cake discharge and cleaning of the cloth are continuous.

*Fig 3 'Adpec' horizontal vacuum band
(suction belt) filter.
(Pierson & Co (Adpec) Ltd).*

Suction belt filters can be made in a wide variety of sizes and can also incorporate specific treatment/washing processes to meet individual process or cleaning requirements. Normally such filters are produced in open configuration. However, the filter can be provided with a fume hood or even total enclosure if necessary (*eg* for handling toxic or inflammable products).

*Fully automatic suction belt filter for small and medium seal applications.
(Seitz-Werke GmbH)*

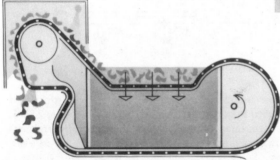

*Leitz 'Polo' suction belt filter.
(Seitz-Werke GmbH)*

'Pannevis' suction belt filter

1. Filtercloth
2. Cloth washing device
3. Cloth tracking device
4. Cloth drive
5. Vacuum hose
6. Vacuum tray
7. Overflow weir
8. Vacuum manifold
9. Vapour hood
10. Pneumatic control panel

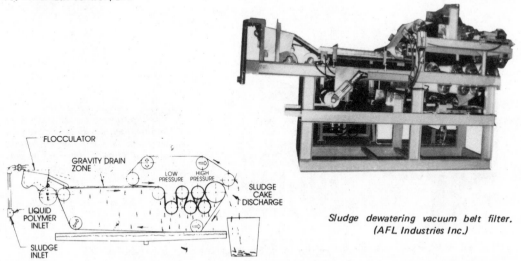

Sludge dewatering vacuum belt filter.
(AFL Industries Inc.)

An alternative method of working a vacuum belt filter is to employ a filter cloth traversing stationary vacuum trays. The cloth is then moved through the filter in short steps during which period the vacuum is switched off. This eliminates the need for a rubber carrier belt and is a much simpler system — *eg* the Adpec horizontal vacuum belt filter has only five moving parts.

Leaf Filters

LEAF FILTERS employ a nest of filter discs spaced on a common shaft and fully enclosed within a pressure-resistant casing. Overall configuration may be vertical or horizontal. The filter nest is normally static for filtration, the suspension being passed through the nest under positive (usually) or negative (vacuum) pressure. Filtrate is withdrawn separately, with solids remaining on the filter discs as cake. Various methods of cake removal may be employed, depending on the type and configuration of the filter discs, *eg* jet washing with or without rotation of the filter nest. Leaf design also varies widely, from simple to complex mesh forms, with or without filter cloths fitted, and for use with or without precoat. A precoat is normally employed where fine filtering is required.

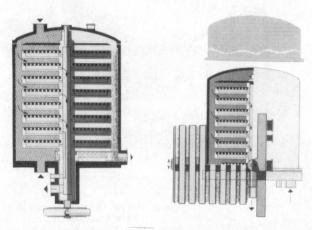

Precoat pressure leaf filters.
For fine filtration, a precoat composed of fibres or filter aids such as kieselguhr or perlite etc, is applied which permits retention of turbid matter in low concentrations or down to particles of colloidal size.

Turbo cleaning filter Seitz Sirius®   Swivel disc filters Seitz Cosmos®

Configuration description normally applies to the arrangement of the casing, *eg* a vertical leaf filter has horizontally arranged leaves; and a horizontal leaf filter vertically arranged leaves. Some manufacturers reverse these descriptions and describe the type of leaf (not casing) orientation. The basic type of filter may also be described as a plate filter (continental European practice) or a disc filter (American practice).

An illustrative working model of the Dorr-Oliver disc pressure filter system.

A typical chemical installation of a bank of Dorr-Oliver pressure filter systems.

Vertical plate filter. (Sparklet Filters Ltd).

Vertical pressure-leaf filter with rectangular leaves mounted vertically on a horizontal discharge manifold at the bottom of the tank. (Stockdale Engineering Ltd)

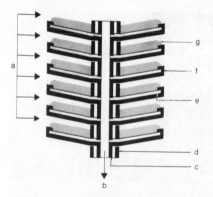

a) unfiltered product
b) filtered product
c) filter shaft
d) spacer ring
e) filter screen
f) filter disc
g) filter cake

Fig 1 Filter nest

An example of a vertical leaf filter is shown in Fig 1. This has a number of circular filter discs with filter screens on the upper side only. These filter discs are fitted on top of one another on a hollow, vertical, filter shaft which supports the filter nest. The spacing between the discs can be varied by spacer rings, depending on the type and quantity of cake to be retained on the disc. The filtrate passes down the conical part of each disc into the hollow shaft.

During filtration, the filter nest is static. Discharge of solids is by rotation of the filter nest, when dry solids are spun off by centrifugal force. Alternatively the filter can be back-flushed when spun to wash and discharge the solids as a slurry.

Particular advantages of vertical leaf filters are good cake consistency with freedom from cracking or channelling because the filter cake is not affected by pressure variations.

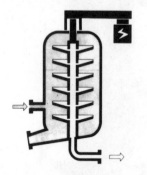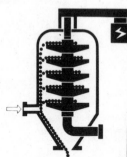

*Funda vertical leaf filter provides filtration
(left) and automatic extraction (right)*

*Fig 2 Filtra-Matic horizontal with
leaf pack withdrawn for discharge of the
dry filter cake.
(United States Filter Corporation)*

Fig 2 shows an example of a horizontal leaf filter which is opened for discharge of dry filter cake. Other horizontal leaf filters have bottom discharge where the cake is removed from each leaf by rotation against a scraper blade (cake cut-off blades) to fall into the bottom chamber from where dry cake is discharged by a slow speed screw conveyor or similar system.

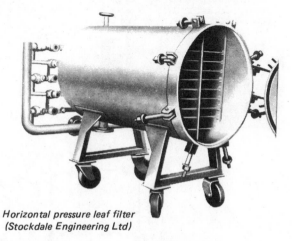

FUNDA® Filter type R cut-away picture, showing the dished horizontal plates, perforated central collecting shaft for the filtrate and the top and bottom seal systems. The filter-nest is rotated for cake discharge by a hydraulic drive. The design shown, is for dry cake discharge.

Horizontal pressure leaf filter (Stockdale Engineering Ltd)

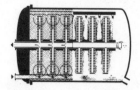

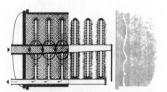

Leitz horizontal pressure leaf filters. (Seitz-Werke GmbH)

Pressure leaf filter with rigid, round, vertically arranged elements in a horizontal pressure container that can also be heated or cooled. For cleaning, the filter is opened by horizontal motion of the filter vessel, and the dry spent cake manually removed from the elements by tapping. Large filters are fitted with a vibrating device.

Pressure leaf filter with rigid, round elements arranged horizontally on a collecting shaft in a vertical pressure vessel. Filter, together with feed pump and dosing unit complete with fittings and pipework as well as switch cabinet form a mobile unit. For cleaning, the filter vessel is lifted off, the element pack swivelled by 90° and the dry spent cake manually removed with the aid of a scraper.

Rosenmund horizontal-plate filter with
scraper peeler and screen conveyor
discharge.

Filtration

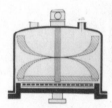

Drying (tilted)

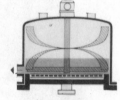

Discharging (tilted)

Horizontal single plate pressure filter
(Seitz-Werke GmbH)

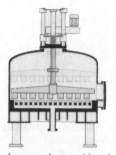

Discharge and smoothing device.

Tipping Pan Filters

TIPPING PAN filters are particularly suitable for handling rapid settling coarse crystalline solids, particularly since settling aids the formation of the filter cake. Very sharp separation of the mother and wash liquors is readily obtained, greatly facilitating wash liquor recirculation. By applying multi counter-current washing techniques, maximum extraction of solubles is possible, with minimum dilution.

Stockdale 15 sq ft totally enclosed stainless steel single tipping pan.

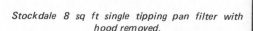

Stockdale 8 sq ft single tipping pan filter with hood removed.

Tipping pan filters are available as single and multi pan units. They are normally open vessels with a false bottom supporting the filter fabric. This bottom unit is pivoted to provide 180 degrees rotation (tipping) for discharge of solids.

Feed is loaded into the pan and filtration takes place either by gravity or under vacuum, depending on the design of the unit. Cake washing can be followed by air drying, if required, prior to removal of the cake by tipping. When the pan(s) are in the inverted position the filter fabric can also be washed.

SECTION 2

Sub-section (c)

Separators

THE GENERAL classification *separators* covers a variety of devices, the chief of which are centrifuges, cyclones, wet scrubbers, coalescers and hydrostatic precipitators; all of which form the subject of separate chapters which follow in this section. Centrifuges predominate, particularly because of the flexibility of the principle in adapting to specific media, volume and separation requirements, when they may be specifically described by duty — *eg* separators, purifiers, clarifiers, *etc*, together with their characteristics. On account of their operating characteristics, *pusher centrifuges* are particularly suitable for solids, giving rapid filtration. Their filterability is strongly dependent upon the particle size distribution of solids. Systems having a particle in excess of 0.2 mm can be readily treated in pusher centrifuges whereas much finer products require more complicated machines or machine combinations.

As the gap width of the screens cannot be reduced arbitrarily without impairing the processing capacity, it is inevitable that during the cake formation in the feed region very small particles will pass through the screens together with the filtrate. To recover these fines it may be necessary to use settling tanks with partial recycling, centrifugal disc separators, or other special machinery.

In many cases it is advisable to separate excess liquid prior to centrifugal drainage. The more important devices used for this purpose are hydrocyclones, curved screens, and static thickeners (Fig 1) the first two being particularly attractive because of their simplicity and small size.

In a *hydrocyclone,* the product to be processed is concentrated into a solids concentrate and a thinned suspension of fines. The concentration is achieved by a combination of centrifugal and gravitational action. The product is introduced tangentially at high velocity into the cyclone head from where it descends on a helical path. The circular motion provides a sizeable centrifugal acceleration causing the large particles to be impelled towards the wall and discharged at the bottom of the cone. The residual liquid and the fines ascend in axial direction and leave the system through the centre of the head.

Hydrocyclones have no moving parts and can be fabricated from materials resisting both abrasion and corrosion. They require an operating pressure between 1 and 2 bar, usually provided by a centrifugal pump.

Cyclones are also used as de-aeration devices with centrifuges. Because of ventilation, the filtrate leaving the centrifuge is mixed with a large volume of air. Cyclones directly attached to the filtrate outlet provide effective de-aeration.

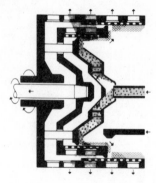

Pusher Centrifuges

Pusher centrifuges apply a continuous filtration process to separate crystalline and fibrous solids from suspensions.

The slurry to be separated flows from the feed pipe through a rotating feed cone and accelerates the material outwards to the basket wall. The solids retained, build up as a cake which is moved axially towards the discharge end of the basket by means of a reciprocating action of the pusher plate. If the basket consists of more than one rotor, the solids are forced to cascade over the basket stages of successively larger diameter until they are ejected from the front end of the final stage. A liquid can be sprayed onto the cake to effect a wash.

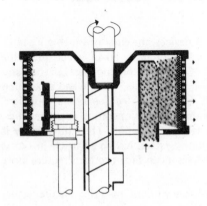

Peeler Centrifuges

Peeler centrifuges apply a discontinuous filtration and sedimentation process to separate solids from suspensions.

The suspension controlled by an adjustable opening shut-off valve, enters the basket via a stationary feed pipe. Centrifugal action forces the liquid through the peripheral filter while the solids are retained. A wash liquid can be introduced through a suitable spray pipe. After spinning dry, the solids are peeled out at full speed and discharged by means of a screw conveyor or a chute. If filtration is impossible or uneconomically slow then the peeler centrifuges can be used with imperforate basket to give accelerated sedimentation of the solids with the liquid phase being removed by overflow or intermittent skimming.

(Alfa-Laval)

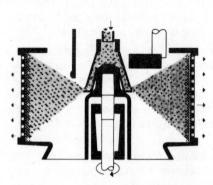

Three-Column Basket Centrifuges

Three-column centrifuges apply a discontinuous filtration process to separate solids from suspensions.

The suspension enters the basket via a stationary feed pipe or a rotating feed cone. When the machine is charged, the feed is shut off to allow drainage. A wash liquid can be introduced through a suitable spray pipe. In bottom discharge as shown in the sketch, the solids are discharged by means of a paring knife. In top discharge machines the solids can be removed pneumatically, mechanically, by hand, or by withdrawal of the filter bag.

Fig 1

Curved Screens

A curved screen has a lamellar filter medium similar to that of the pusher centrifuge, but there are no moving parts and the gaps are at right angles to the direction of particle movement. Depending on the individual requirements, the suspension to be concentrated enters the apparatus via a weir or by being injected through nozzles in tangential direction. On passing over the screen, a portion of the liquid phase and fines escape through the gaps, thus leaving a concentrated suspension of improved filterability. To prevent clogging of the screen, the back can be flushed as indicated in Fig 2.

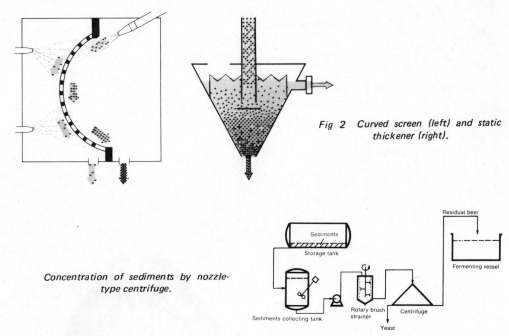

Fig 2   Curved screen (left) and static thickener (right).

Concentration of sediments by nozzle-type centrifuge.

Static Thickeners

In a static thickener, the solids settle within the cone under gravity allowing clarified liquid to overflow.

Separators

Centrifuges designed as separators commonly employ a disc type bowl — Fig 3. Physical separation of the two liquid components occurs within the disc set. The light liquid phase builds up in the inner section, and the heavy phase builds up in the outer section.

The dividing line between the two is called the 'separating zone', this should be located along the line of the 'rising channels' for most efficient separation. The rising channels are a series of holes in each disc, arranged so the holes provide vertical channels through the entire disc set.

These channels also provide the entrance for the liquid mixture into the spaces between the discs. As centrifugal force separates the two liquids, the solids move outward to the sediment-holding space. The location of a separation zone is controlled by adjusting the back pressure of the discharged liquid phase(s) or by exchangeable ring dams.

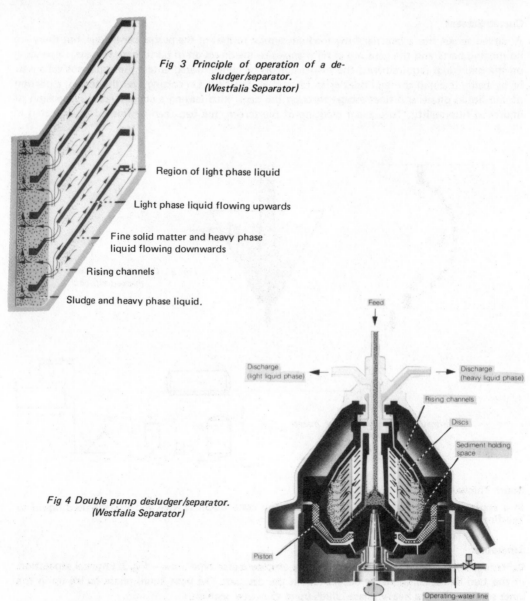

Fig 3 Principle of operation of a de-
sludger/separator.
(Westfalia Separator)

Region of light phase liquid

Light phase liquid flowing upwards

Fine solid matter and heavy phase
liquid flowing downwards

Rising channels

Sludge and heavy phase liquid.

Fig 4 Double pump desludger/separator.
(Westfalia Separator)

Double pump de-sludger / separators separate immiscible liquid mixtures containing solids, with both liquids discharged enclosed and under pressure. They are used primarily for mixtures where the heavy and light liquid components are approximately equal in volume (Fig 4).

Double pump separators are particularly suited for separation of volatile mixtures containing solids, where valuable products might evaporate. The double pump configuration also minimizes danger of oxidation of either liquid phase. Pressurized liquid discharge has the additional advantage of reducing or eliminating pumping requirements downstream of the centrifuge. Fig 5 shows a nozzle type (centrifuge) separator.

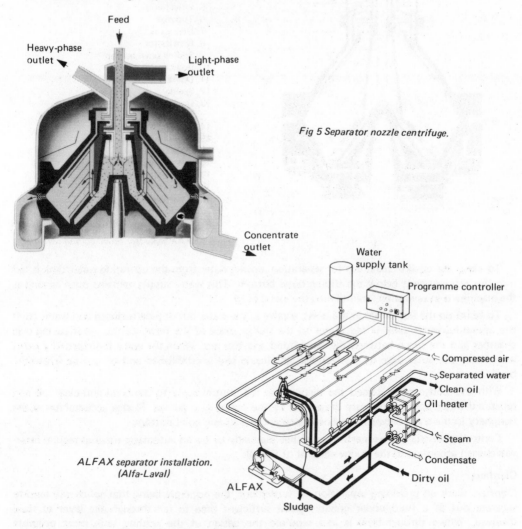

Fig 5 Separator nozzle centrifuge.

ALFAX separator installation. (Alfa-Laval)

Separators may also be designed for specific duties. An example of a separator designed for three-phase separation of oil-water-sludge mixtures is shown in Fig 6.

The separator bowl is equipped with a conical disc stack, a wide top disc for the liquid seal, and interchangeable gravity discs at the water outlet covering the normal range of specific gravities likely to be encountered for the application in question. Dual built-in paring disc pumps are provided for pressurized discharge of both the clean oil and water phases. A gear-type feed pump on the lower frame is driven from the wormwheel shaft.

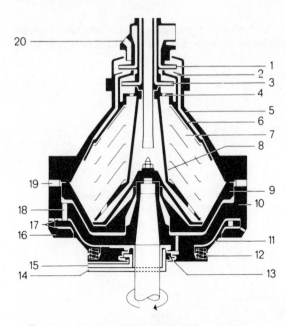

1. Water paring disc
2. Gravity disc
3. Oil paring disc
4. Level ring
5. Bowl hood
6. Top disc
7. Disc stack
8. Distributor
9. Sliding bowl bottom
10. Bowl body
11. Operating slide
12. Spring
13. Operating water
    paring disc
14. Opening water supply
15. Closing and make-up
    water supply
16. Dosing ring
17. Dosing ring chamber
18. Drain valve
19. Sludge port
20. Liquid seal and
    flushing water supply.

Fig 6 ALFAX separator bowl: components

To close the bowl in readiness for separation, dosing water from the operating water tank is fed into the compartment below the sliding bowl bottom. This water supply remains open as long as the machine is in operation, maintaining the static head.

To build up the liquid seal in the bowl, a valve in the water outlet pipe is closed and water from the operating water tank is fed direct to the sludge space of the bowl via the water paring disc chamber and the space between the bowl hood and top disc. When the water has reached a radial level inside the outer edge of the top disc, the liquid seal is established and oil can be fed to the bowl.

With the sludge ports closed the dirty oil is fed continuously to the bowl and clean oil and separated water are continuously drawn off by the paring disc pumps. Sludge accumulates at the periphery in the angle between the bowl hood and the sliding bowl bottom.

Controlled discharges are performed either manually or by an automatic timer at regular intervals chosen according to the sludge content of the oil.

Clarifiers

Clarifiers work on providing separation by settlement, the principle being that solids will tend to separate out of a fluid under gravity, given sufficient time to fall through the layer of fluid involved. Where through-flow is also required the design of the settling tank must promote hydraulic conditions consistent with high clarification efficiency. This leads to considerable variety in detail design.

An example of a circular settling tank is shown in Fig 7. This particular clarifier embodies a feed channel around the outer periphery of the tank. This channel is uniform in width but depth varies from a maximum at the input end to a minimum at the extreme end. A series of specially sized and spaced ports are provided on the bottom of the feed channel, arranged so that each port takes its proper proportion of the total flow. A constant forward flow is maintained, even though the flow volume is reduced at each port.

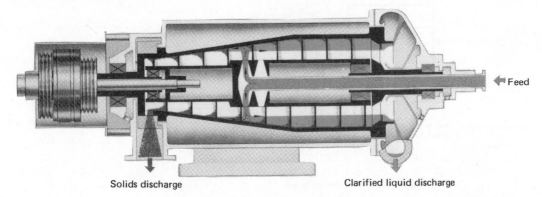

Solids discharge   Clarified liquid discharge

Fig 7 Decanter centrifuge clarifier.

Hermetic clarifier
(Westfalia Separator)

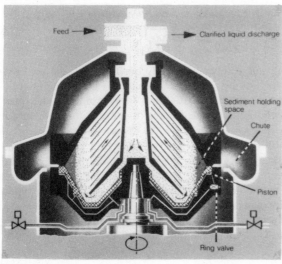

Typical clarifier bowl.
(Westfalia Separator)

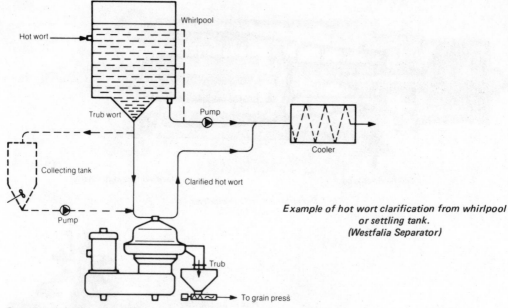

Example of hot wort clarification from whirlpool or settling tank.
(Westfalia Separator)

Centrifugal clarifier with
self-cleaning bowl

Comparative sizes of filter press and decanter centrifuge installation for dewatering sewage sludge from a town with a population of about 150 000.
(Alfa-Laval)

Flow is fed uniformly downward into the tank, discharging evenly between the tank wall and baffle skirt. This area serves to reduce the effect of the discharge through the ports, to minimize fluid velocity approaching the bottom of the tank and diffuse the flow. Flow into the tank proper is thus gentle across the entire tank cross section and directed upwards towards the tank centre where an effluent trough is located.

With a conventional horizontal tank, flow is horizontal, tending to limit flow rates so that the flow velocity is low enough to allow adequate settling to take place. A variation is to divide the tank up with a series of baffles to form, in effect, a series of small vertical flow cells associated with collecting troughs. Flow from one cell to the next is by overspill, flow rate being controlled by the weir length. Thus weir length can be increased by incorporating a series of V-notches in the periphery instead of overspilling from a plain rim. This method is used to control the flow in each cell so that the full tank volume can be used, at the same time minimizing the risk of short-circuiting the flow.

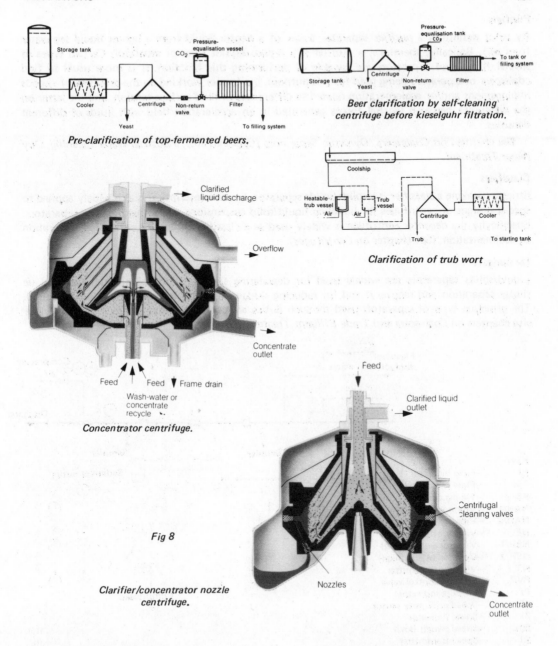

Pre-clarification of top-fermented beers.

Beer clarification by self-cleaning centrifuge before kieselguhr filtration.

Clarification of trub wort

Concentrator centrifuge.

Fig 8

Clarifier/concentrator nozzle centrifuge.

Centrifuges may also be designed as clarifiers, concentrators or clarifier/concentrators and described as such — see Fig 8.

Equally mechanical filters are also used for the clarification of liquids, particularly *filter presses* and *precoat filters* for the clarification of beers, wines and similar liquids.

Purifiers

By strict definition a *purifier* separates traces of a denser liquid from a lighter liquid (*eg* water from oil). Basically, therefore, a purifier is a liquids/liquids filter or separator. Certain types of special filters and separators are capable of performing this function. It is more usual to find *coalescers* or *separators* being used for this purpose, the former working on the principle of viscous impingement and/or agglomeration related to differences in fluid surface tension; and the latter on the difference between inertial forces generated in an acceleration field with fluids of different densities.

See chapters on *Coalescers, Dynamic Separators (Cyclones etc), Industrial Water Cleaning, Oily Water Treatment.*

Classifiers

Strictly speaking a *classifier* is a solids/solids separator, but the description is also widely applied to special designs of centrifuges for handling liquid/solid suspensions, and other types of separators. Specifically the *decanter* centrifuge is widely used as a classifier, providing continuous separation by sedimentation. (See chapter on *Centrifuges*).

De-sludgers

Liquid/solids separators are widely used for dewatering sludges, both for product recovery (*ie* sludge separation and recovery) and for reducing sludge waste to 'dry' cake for ease of disposal. The principal type of separators used for such duties are centrifuges and coalescing units — (see also chapters on *Coalescers* and *Trade Effluent Treatment).*

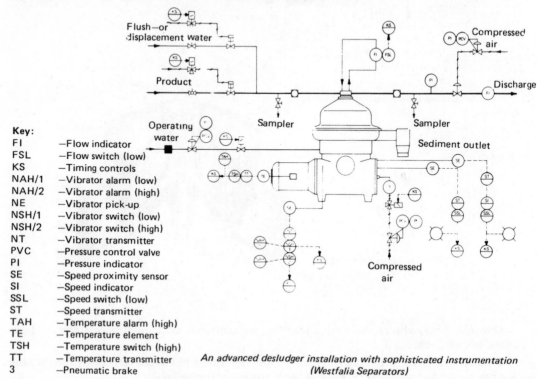

Key:
FI   —Flow indicator
FSL   —Flow switch (low)
KS   —Timing controls
NAH/1   —Vibrator alarm (low)
NAH/2   —Vibrator alarm (high)
NE   —Vibrator pick-up
NSH/1   —Vibrator switch (low)
NSH/2   —Vibrator switch (high)
NT   —Vibrator transmitter
PVC   —Pressure control valve
PI   —Pressure indicator
SE   —Speed proximity sensor
SI   —Speed indicator
SSL   —Speed switch (low)
ST   —Speed transmitter
TAH   —Temperature alarm (high)
TE   —Temperature element
TSH   —Temperature switch (high)
TT   —Temperature transmitter
3   —Pneumatic brake

An advanced desludger installation with sophisticated instrumentation (Westfalia Separators)

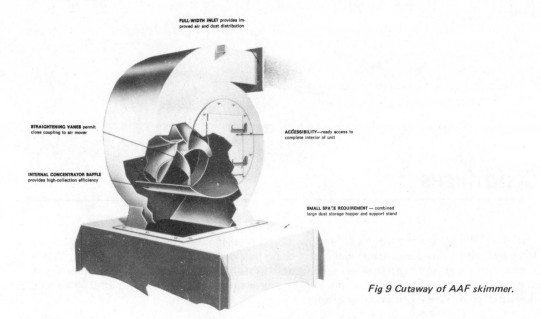

Fig 9 Cutaway of AAF skimmer.

Skimmers

The description *skimmer* is used in different senses. Basically it is a mechanical device for removing scum separated and on the surface of a liquid by flotation (*eg* in a settlement tank). The term is also used, however, to describe low pressure centrifugal precipitators designed to remove dust from dry air or gases (*eg* as an alternative to cyclones).

An example of a centrifugal skimmer is shown in Fig 9. Dust laden air enters the skimmer tangentially. Centrifugal forces, created by this inlet, compel the dust particles to follow the involute curve of the wrapper sheet. The bulk of the dust is skimmed from the air stream through a wide slot. The remaining dust enters the specially shaped secondary air system within the unit and is blended with incoming dust laden air.

This secondary system, with its continual cyclonic force, eventually deposits the collected dust through the slot into the storage hopper. Cleaned air is exhausted to the atmosphere or, in many cases, to a secondary cleaner.

Typical applications of low pressure centrifugal skimmers include:

(i)   Primary collectors in pneumatic conveying.

(ii)   Primary collectors where atmospheric pollution will not be created.

(iii)   Reduction of dust loading to more efficient final collectors.

(iv)   Reclamation of the large size fraction of the dust in a dry state where wet collectors are used.

Centrifuges

THE CENTRIFUGE is primarily a device providing a mechanical acceleration field via centrifugal force and which can thus separate solid particles suspended in a fluid of lower density. This is similar to the action of separation by settlement in a gravitational field but very much more rapid since the mean centrifugal acceleration generated in centrifuges is of the order of 5 000–8 000 times greater than acceleration due to gravity.

Specifically the separating rate (V_S) in a centrifuge is given by

$$V_S = \frac{K \cdot d^2 \, (\Delta_1 - \Delta_2)}{\nu} \times R\omega^2$$

where d = particle diameter

$(\Delta_1 - \Delta_2)$ = difference in density of solids and fluid

ν = fluid viscosity

R = effective radius of centrifuge

ω = rotational velocity

K is a constant whose value depends on units employed

Bracketed quantities relate to the product involved. Parameters governing the separating rate of a centrifuge handling a particular product are thus R and ω, or basically the effectiveness of the centrifuge is directly proportional to $R\omega^2$. Thus the performance of a centrifuge is dependent only on the design and the permissible stressing of the rotating bowl. Bowl stress, in turn, comprises two components:

(i)   stress due to rotation of its own mass

(ii)   stress due to liquid pressure

In smaller bowls (i) accounts for about one half the total stress, but becomes increasingly significant with increasing bowl size. Liquid pressure (ii) is dependent on bowl radius and may approach 100 bar in modern centrifuges. Thus bowl form and size (diameter), rotational speed and choice of bowl material are primary design parameters.

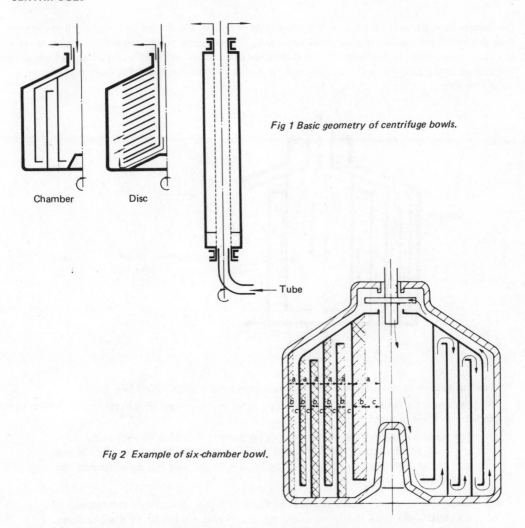

Fig 1 Basic geometry of centrifuge bowls.

Chamber   Disc

Tube

Fig 2 Example of six-chamber bowl.

This has led to the development of three basic bowl shapes (Fig 1), viz:

(i)   *Chamber-type bowl* — with a number of concentric chambers aimed at providing a series arrangement of centrifugation spaces.

(ii) *Disc-type bowl* — containing a series of conical discs providing a parallel configuration of centrifugation spaces.

(iii) *Tube-type bowl* — providing highest speed of rotation, and thus strongest acceleration field, for the same material stress.

Chamber-type Bowl

Typical form of a chamber-type bowl is shown in Fig 2. The distance *a* between the cylindrical inserts consists of the thickness of the trub space *b* and axially flowing layer *c*. The layer thickness diminishes from chamber to chamber the further they are from the bowl centre; it is greatest in the central chamber and smallest in the outermost chamber. Hence the effective settling distance also declines from the central chamber outwards. The effective acceleration field increases from chamber to chamber, hence with a given difference in densities and feed liquid of a given viscosity the coarser solid particles will separate out in the inner chambers and the finer particles in the outer chambers.

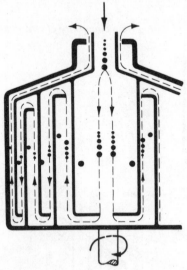

Fig 3   Classifying effect of a chamber bowl.

Thus the solid matter is classified to some extent in a bowl of this kind (see Fig 3).

The clarification efficiency of a chamber-type bowl is influenced by several factors, which can be divided into three groups:

(a)   The factors affecting the rate of settling, *eg* particle size d, difference in densities $(\triangle_1 - \triangle_2)$ and viscosity ν. If the feed liquid contains solid particles of different size, the smaller particles are deposited on the larger ones and are separated out with them.

(b)   Design factors such as the strength of the acceleration field $R\omega^2$, the number of chambers and thus the layer thickness c, and also the height of the chambers. (The latter cannot be increased arbitrarily because the ratio of bowl outside diameter to bowl height must not fall much below 1 in order to ensure good balancing and good operation).

(c)   Rate of axial flow in the chambers

This axial flow rate depends on the centrifuge output (through-put per unit of time). The greater the through-put, the higher is the axial flow rate in the chambers and the shorter the time available for a particle to cover the necessary settling distance c. With a lower axial flow rate the retention time is longer and clarification efficiency better.

Specific advantages of centrifuges with a chamber-type bowl are:-

(a)   Clarification efficiency remains consistently good until the trub spaces are filled with solid matter.

(b) Large trub capacity, hence liquids containing relatively high proportions of solid matter can be processed (*eg* when using 2-chamber bowls).

(c) Compact trub cakes, hence hardly any liquid loss.

The disadvantage of this type of bowl is that when the trub space is filled with solids the centrifuge must be stopped and cleaned manually.

Disc-type Bowl

The disc-type bowl contains a large number of conical discs with a suitable wall thickness to provide good rigidity, spaced at intervals of 0.016—0.03 in (0.4—0.75 mm) depending on the liquid to be processed and the consistency of the solids to be removed from it (*eg* see Fig 4). Each space between adjacent discs forms an individual centrifugation space. The liquid entering the bowl distributor at the centre is split up into many thin layers. The *settling distance* of a particle is therefore made very small, so that high speed and an extremely strong acceleration field can be dispensed with.

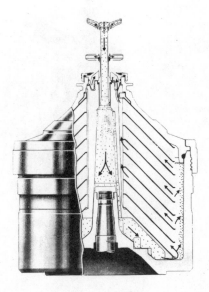

Fig 4   Disc-type bowl of a hermetic
centrifuge.

The angle of tilt of the discs is limited by the angle of slope of the solid matter removed in the centrifugal field. To enable the solids to slide down the underside of the discs, the angle of tilt of the discs must be equal to or smaller than the angle of slope of the solids in the centrifugal field.

The number of discs depends primarily on the overall height of the bowl. To ensure good balancing the ratio of the outside diameter of the bowl to the bowl height must not be much below 1. The number of discs also depends on the disc thickness, which is limited by the mechanical stability of the discs. The spacing of the discs depends on the concentration of the solid matter in the feed liquid, the particle size and consistency, and must be wide enough to prevent clogging.

Centrifuges with disc-type bowls are particularly suitable for clarifying liquids with a small proportion of suspended solids.

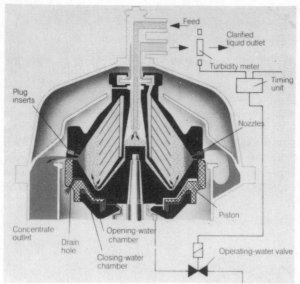

Nozzle centrifuge with automatic de-
sludging.
(Westfalia Separators)

Section through the bowl of Westfalia
nozzle-type centrifuge, model HFH
12.036

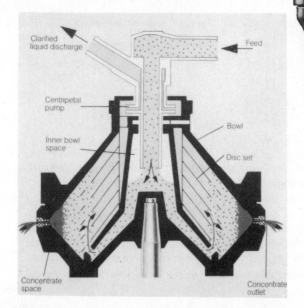

Fig 5 Cross section of a typical nozzle
centrifuge.
(Westfalia Separators.)

Nozzle-type Centrifuges

A nozzle-type centrifuge (Fig 5) is merely a variation on the disc-type bowl. Solid matter is removed from the feed liquid in the disc set of the bowl. The clarified liquid is discharged from the bowl under pressure by means of the centrifugal pump. The separated solids emerge continuously through the nozzles as concentrate (*ie* suspended in part of the feed liquid).

The *quantity* of concentrate is not dependent on the density of the feed liquid, but is a linear function of the bowl speed, the number of nozzles, and the radius on which the nozzle outlet lies, and varies as the square of the nozzle diameter.

The obtainable solids concentration is a function of the volume of concentrate discharged by the nozzles, the initial feed liquid concentration, and the initial feed liquid volume. With a fixed speed, fixed number of nozzles and initial feed liquid concentration, the discharge concentration can be adjusted by varying the nozzle diameter and initial feed liquid volume.

Fig 6 shows a horizontal section through the bowl at the level where the solids enter the nozzle channel, where it will be seen that the solids accumulate in segments. These segments must not be allowed to extend into the disc set, as they would have a deleterious effect on clarification efficiency. Solid matter accumulating in these segments is not discharged from the bowl, which cannot therefore empty itself automatically when the feed is shut off.

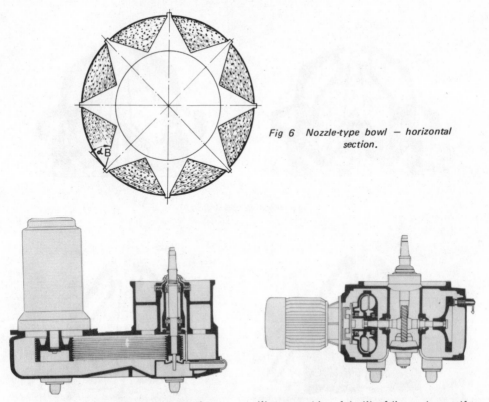

Fig 6   Nozzle-type bowl — horizontal section.

V-belt drive of the Westfalia nozzle centrifuges   Worm gear drive of the Westfalia nozzle centrifuges

Examples of alternative drive systems.

1 feed
2 discs
3 centripetal pump
4 discharge
5 sediment holding space
6 sediment ejection ports
7 timing unit
8 outer closing chamber
9 inner closing chamber
10 opening chamber
11 bowl valve
12 piston

13 opening water
14 closing water
15 auxiliary opening water
16 sensing zone disc
17 sensing liquid clarifying discs
18 sensing liquid pump
19 flowmeter
20 sensing liquid pump
21 switch

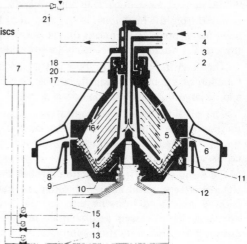

Fig 7   Example of centrifugal clarifier
with self-cleaning bowl.

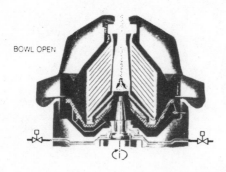
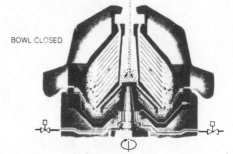

Fig 8 (Westfalia Separators)

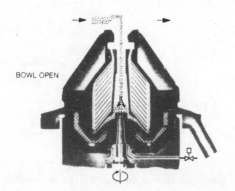
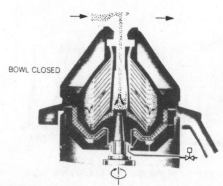

Fig 9 (Westfalia Separators)

Prestrainers are included in the feed lines of nozzle-type centrifuges to retain coarse impurities likely to clog the nozzles. The diameter of strainer holes should be about 10% smaller than the diameter of the nozzles.

Self-Cleaning Centrifuges

Centrifuges with disc-type bowls are also produced in self-cleaning form, using various different principles, *eg* internal sliding piston (Fig 7), external sliding piston, removable chamber bottom, *etc*. The process can be automated and controlled by time, monitoring of discharged liquid or autonomous control.

Two basic types of self-cleaning bowls are shown in Figs 8 and 9. In Fig 8, the piston which controls the open/close action of the ports is the bottom of the centrifugation chamber. While the bowl is spinning, the piston is kept in the raised position (ports closed) by pressure (created by centrifugal force) of the operating liquid (usually water); the action of this liquid is controlled by a ring valve, which is, in effect, a second piston. To open the bowl ports, an automatic valve feeds operating water to the ring valve, forcing it downward. This drains the operating water from underneath the piston, and the centrifugal pressure of the rotating product in the bowl then forces the piston downward, thus opening the ports in the bowl periphery through which the solids are discharged.

To close the bowl ports again, operating liquid flow to the ring valve is halted and the remaining liquid under the ring valve forces it to close. Operating liquid is then fed into the chamber below the piston, causing it to move upward, thus closing the bowl.

In Fig 9, the piston is also held in the raised position (closed bowl) by centrifugal pressure of the operating liquid; this liquid is contained in a chamber under the piston called the "closing chamber". To open the bowl ports, operating liquid is fed into the "opening chamber" above the piston, forcing the piston downward, thus opening the ports in the bowl wall.

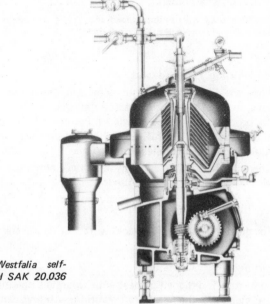

Section through the Westfalia self-cleaning centrifuge, model SAK 20.036

To close the bowl again, the flow of operating liquid is halted, allowing the remaining liquid in the "opening chamber" to drain out through a small orifice. The pressure of the remaining operating liquid in the "closing chamber" then forces the piston upward, thus closing the ports.

Hermetic Centrifuges

Totally enclosed or *hermetic centrifuges* with chamber or disc-type bowls are used for clarifying feed liquids whose pressure must not be allowed to fall. The feed and discharge connections are attached to the rotating bowl by airtight mechanical seals which move in accordance with the eccentric rotation of the bowl. Either collars made of flexible material or sliding ring seals made of carbon are used (*eg* see Fig 10). The bowl head contains rotary feed and discharge pumps. Hermetic centrifuges may be used in pressure systems up to 8 bar.

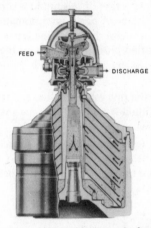
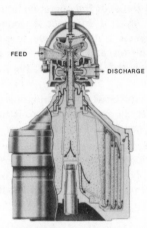

Disc-type bowl with hermetic feed and discharge and built-in feed and discharge pumps.

Chamber-type bowl with hermetic feed and discharge and built-in pumps

Fig 10

Hermetic centrifuges are also used:

(a) When the feed liquid cannot withstand the impact on entry into the rotating bowl, *ie* when the particles to be removed are liable to be destroyed at the inlet (*eg* protein). Since the bowls of hermetic centrifuges are filled right to the centre, the feed liquid is gently brought up to the bowl speed by means of the liquid friction immediately on entry.

(b) When the feed liquid is easily oxidated, emits gas or evaporates. In breweries hermetic centrifuges can be used:

For preclarification of beers ready for racking   (No carbon dioxide losses, no destruction of protein)

For the clarification of the cold wort   (Good clarification efficiency, because protein particles are not destroyed)

Peeler Centrifuges

A peeler centrifuge is designed to deal with separate suspensions discontinuously in batches. Each batch is subdivided into the necessary operations — filling, centrifuging, washing, peeling.

This adjustable batch cycle is in most cases controlled automatically. The various operations within a batch can be performed at constant or varying speed of the centrifuge drum. An example of a peeler centrifuge is shown in Fig 11. The suspension (1) to be separated flows into the centrifuge (5) through the filler pipe (2).

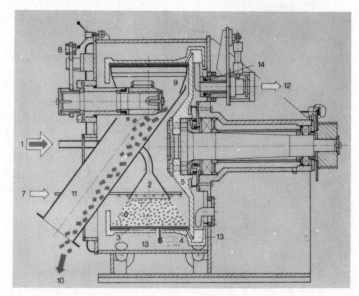

Fig 11

In the filtration process the liquid filters through a filter cloth (3) under the effect of centrifugal force. It is drained through the perforated jacket of the drum (5) or the filtrate bore of the siphon drum into the filtrate housing (4) or ring cup (13) of the siphon drum and leaves the machine through a filtrate shaft or liquid scraper pipe (14). The solid material is retained in the drum by the filter cloth and forms a uniform layer (6). If the solid layer is to be washed, the wash fluid is sprayed on, through the wash pipe (7). The resulting wash liquor leaves the machine in the same manner as the main filtrate. However, it can be separated from the main filtrate in a reversing mechanism. The solids are centrifuged until the desired residual moisture content is reached, and scraped out by a hydraulically operated swivel scraper knife (9) down to a residual layer — the basic layer — which remains on the filter cloth. The solid material (10) which is mostly friable is discharged by means of a chute (11) or screw.

In the sedimentation process, the solid/liquid-mixture is separated in a solid-jacket drum according to the different specific gravities of its components. Due to its greater specific gravity, the solid material settles and concentrates on the drum floor. The clarified liquid forms a layer on top of the solids. It is drained by a swivel-mounted scraper pipe or — if the filling process is continued — flows over the drum rim. The settled solids layer is discharged by means of the scraper knife.

Pusher Centrifuges

Pusher centrifuges utilize continuous filtration for the separation of suspended, fast-draining crystalline and granular or fibrous solids from liquids. In a typical machine the suspension to be separated flows continuously from the stationary feed pipe onto a rotating cone designed to accelerate the material to the speed of the basket. From this acceleration cone, the slurry flows

A   Slurry
B   Solids
C   Filtrate
1   Feed pipe
2   Feed distributor
2a Wash basket
2b Spray nozzle
3   Slot screen
4   Basket
5   Screen retaining ring
6   Pusher plate
7   Pusher shaft
8   Pusher control with
    pusher piston
9   Hollow shaft with
    bearings
10 Disc brake
11 V-belt drive
12 Oil feed bearing
13 Hydraulic pump with
    motor
14 Oil cooler
15 Bearing housing with oil
    pan and motor support
16 Filtrate housing
17 Solids collecting housing
    with volute race discharge

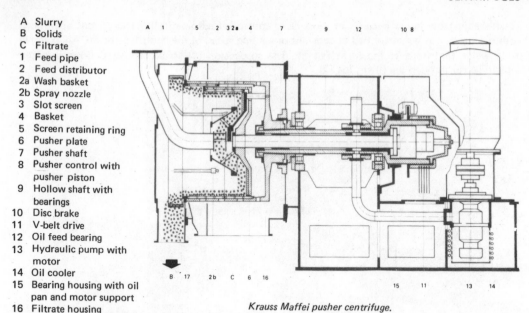

Krauss Maffei pusher centrifuge.

across the face of the pusher plate onto the rear of the basket where most of the liquid phase is drained whilst the solid is retained to form a cylindrical cake. The reciprocating action of the pusher plate causes this cake to be advanced towards the open front end of the basket. During the withdrawal stroke of the pusher plate space is created in the basket which is filled by the incoming slurry solids. On the forward stroke the plate acts on the newly formed bed of solids so that both this and the previous ring of cake is pushed forward.

During the axial motion over the basket screen mother liquor adhering to the particles can be removed by washing. In hydraulic machines, the pusher reciprocation is effected by oil pressure acting on alternate sides of a piston. The oil pressure is provided by a dual screw pump, the pressure distribution on the alternate sides of the piston being controlled by proximity switches.

Both single-stage and multi-stage rotors may be employed — see Fig 12. In a one-stage machine the reciprocating part is the pusher plate carrying the acceleration cone. In a two-stage machine the reciprocating part is the screen of small diameter. During its forward stroke, its front wall serves as

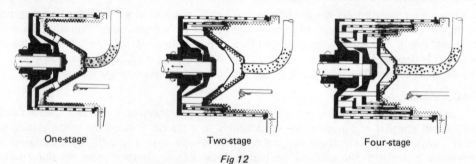

One-stage   Two-stage   Four-stage

Fig 12

the pusher for the screen of large diameter. During the backward stroke, the cake on the screen of small diameter is pushed by the non-reciprocating carrier plate of the acceleration cone.

On the four-stage machine shown, stages 1 and 3 reciprocate (the smallest diameter rotor being stage 1). During their forward stroke, some cake of stage 2 is pushed to stage 3, and some cake of stage 4 is ejected, while stage 1 is replenished from the acceleration cone. During the backward stroke, some cake of stage 1 is pushed to stage 2, and some cake of stage 3 to stage 4.

Tumbler Centrifuges

In a tumbler centrifuge solids are separated into a conical basket and discharged by means of a tumbling action of the rotating drum. An example is shown in Fig 13 where the mixture to be separated is fed to the centrifuge vertically from above through the hopper. By this means, highly concentrated non-flowing mixtures can also be separated. The suspension is evenly distributed to the periphery of the truncated sieve basket by means of a 'pump impeller-like' accelerator.

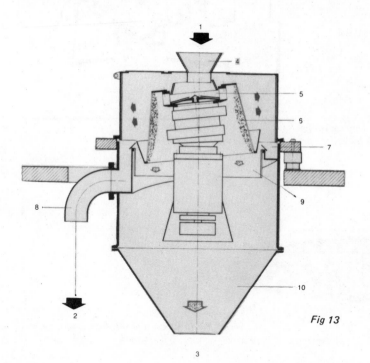

1 suspension
2 filtrate
3 solids
4 funnel
5 accelerator
6 sieve basket
7 filtrate channel
8 filtrate connection
9 rubber apron
10 solids discharge housing

Fig 13

The liquid filters through the sieve slots and is conveyed along the filtrate channel through a filtrate connection. As a result of the tumbler action, the solid moves gradually across the sieve basket forming a filter cake, the thickness being determined by the throughput capacity and the transport characteristics (tumbling angle, alteration in speed). It is discharged from the drum, thrown against the rubber apron and drops down from the centrifuge housing.

Baffle Ring Centrifuges

Baffle ring centrifuges have been specially developed for dewatering plastic pellets through repeated impact of granular particles on baffle surfaces within the machine. Water films developed on the baffles are removed by centrifugal force into a filtrate compartment. Dry pellets meanwhile jump over the filtration gap formed by the baffle rings and are finally discharged into a collection bowl.

An example of a baffle ring centrifuge is shown in Fig 14.

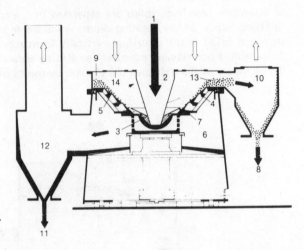

1 granulate-water-mixture
2 feed hopper
3 rotating basket
4 baffle ring insert
5 water film
6 filtrate compartment
7 filtration ring gap
8 granulate
9 granulate collection bowl
10 granulate cyclone
11 filtrate/water
12 filtrate cyclone
13 fan blades
14 ventilating flange

Fig 14 Baffle ring centrifuge.
(Krauss Maffei)

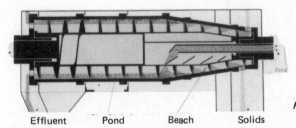

Effluent   Pond   Beach   Solids

Fig 15 Decanter centrifuge section.
(Alfa-Laval)

Decanter Centrifuges

A decanter centrifuge is basically a settling tank of circular form mounted on an axis and spun at high speed to produce separation of solids in the decanter bowl. A screw type conveyor carried internally and rotated relative to the bowl provides continuous discharge — Fig 15.

A common use of decanter centrifuges is for separating slurries into one or two liquid phases and a solid phase. They can handle feeds containing up to 60–70% solids in particle sizes from about 5 μm upwards. Various types are also used for a wide range of other duties — see Fig 16.

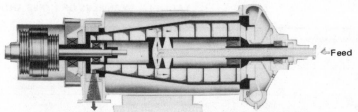

Solids discharge   Clarified liquid discharge

Gravity discharge decanter — used where exposure of the liquid to
atmosphere is not detrimental.

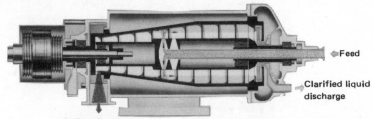

Solids discharge

Pressure discharge decanter — used where foaming, evaporation, vapour
loss or oxidation of the liquid is to be avoided. Typical applications
include chemical suspensions, pharmaceutical extracts, citrus and other
juices, coffee and tea extracts and others.

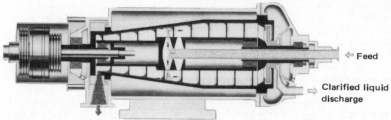

Solids discharge

Gas tight decanter — used in processes involving volatile solvent suspensions, or where aroma loss or oxidation is to be prevented, or in
handling products associated with toxic or explosive gases. Typical
uses include certain instant beverage applications, as well as special
chemical and pharmaceutical suspensions.

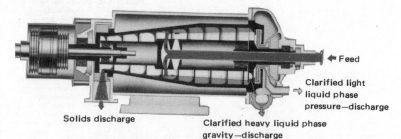

Solids discharge   Clarified heavy liquid phase
gravity–discharge

*Fig 16 Examples of different
types of decanters.*

Separator decanter — modified form providing separator action, used to
separate two immiscible liquids from each other.

TABLE I – EXAMPLES OF TYPES AND

Diagrammatic representation				
Type	Peeler Centrifuge	Peeler Centrifuge with rotary siphon	Three-Column Centrifuge	Pusher Centrifuge one-stage drum
Separation method	filtration sedimentation discontinuous	filtration discontinuous	filtration discontinuous	filtration continuous
Granulation of separated solids	>0.01 mm	>0.01 mm	>0.005 mm	>0.08 mm
Consistency of processed suspension	flowable, pumpable	flowable, pumpable	flowable, pumpable, pasty	flowable, pumpable, conveyable by screw
Thickness of solid layer	up to 250 mm basic layer 5–15 mm	up to 250 mm basic layer 5–15 mm	up to 240 mm	15–100 mm
Form of solids layer				
Consistency of separated solids	friable	friable	friable – punctureproof	friable
Washing possibility	very good unlimited	very good unlimied circuit system	very good unlimited	good
Separation filtrate/wash filtrate	possible, very good	possible, very good	possible, very good	possible, less good
Filtrate quality solids output	>99%	>99%	>99%	>95%
Dwell time of product	unlimited usual up to 30 min	unlimited usual up to 30 min	unlimited usual 20–120 min	7–50 sec
Filter area/unit clarifying area/unit	0.1–6.3 m^2	0.1–6.3 m^2	1.6–6.3 m^2	0.2–2.4 m^2
Drum volume/unit	2–1400 litre	2–1400 litre	63–800 litre	
Drum diameter	0.25–2.0 mm	0.25–2.0 mm	0.5–1.6 mm	0.3–1.1 mm
Filtering medium	textile or metal cloth, basic product layer on filtering medium	textile or metal cloth, basic product layer on filtering medium	all textile and metal cloths, filter bags	slotted metal screens
Discharge element	peeler knife, peeler spoon	peeler knife, peeler spoon	peeling-off with reduced drum speed or removal of filter bag	piston (pusher bottom)
Most important fields of application	products with extreme demands to residual moisture and wash results	further developed peeler centrifuge, Considerable increase in filtration speed and extended basic layer dwell time to assure efficient washing and extracting processes	pharmaceutical industries for numerous products on one machine. No crystal breakage by reduced speed during peeling	coarse, quickly filtering products. Subsequent de-watering of filter cake from vacuum filters

CHARACTERISTICS OF CENTRIFUGES*

Pusher Centrifuge multi-stage	Tumbler Centrifuge	Decanter Centrifuge	Screening Decanter	Baffle-Ring Centrifuge
filtration continuous	filtration continuous	sedimentation continuous	sedimentation + filtration continuous	filtration continuous
$>$0.08 mm	$>$0.02 mm	$>$0.005 mm $<$0.005 mm (flocculation)	$>$0.01 mm	$>$1.0 mm
flowable,pumpable conveyable by screw	flowable to bulky pumpable	flowable pumpable	flowable pumpable	pumpable
15—80 mm	5—50 mm	depending on capacity	depending on capacity	
friable	friable	friable pasty	friable	friable
good	but little	but little	good	not possible
possible, less good	not possible	not possible	with reservation possible	not possible
$>$92%	$>$92%	$>$99%	depending on separation problem	depending on separation problem
7—50 sec	3 10 sec	3—6 sec	up to 5 sec	up to 2 sec
0.14—2.25 m^2	0.4—3.2 m^2	0.2—2.5 m^2	0.9 m^2	
0.3—1.1 mm	0.5—1.4 mm	0.25—0.8 mm	0.5 mm	0.5—0.75 mm
slotted metal screens	slotted metal screens		perforated metal plates	perforated plates for preliminary dewatering, ring slot for subsequent dewatering
piston pusher bottom and pusher ring	tumbling motion (changement of screen angle all around)	screw	screw	
simular one-stage pusher centrifuge for products which may give compressed hard filter cakes.	well filtering mass products like coal, ore, sand, salt.	polymeric suspensions PVC, PE, etc. sludges, fine-crystalline products, classifying	polymeric suspensions crystalline products	special centrifuge for plastic pellets

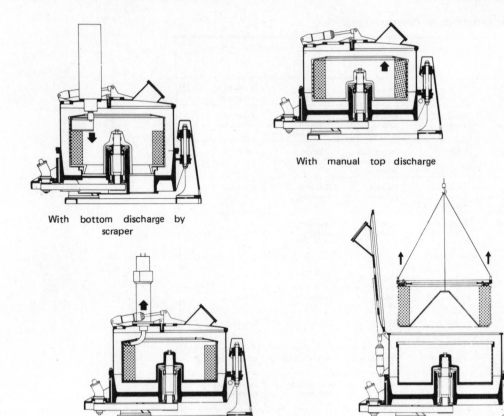

With bottom discharge by
scraper

With manual top discharge

With pneumatic top discharge

*Fig 17   Three column basket
centrifuges.
(Alfa-Laval)*

With top discharge by bag
withdrawal

Three-Column Centrifuges

A three-column basket centrifuge can be equipped to handle various filling, washing and discharge requirements in a discontinuous filtration process with minimum attrition of the solids. The suspension to be separated enters the machine via a stationary feed pipe or a rotating feed cone (Fig 17). The latter is designed to effect very gentle acceleration of the suspension. When the basket is filled, the feed valve is closed by automatic control. The subsequent treatment consists of drainage of the mother liquor, washing of the solids, drainage of the wash liquid, and discharge of the cake.

In the case of bottom discharge, a paring knife removes the cake towards the open centre, leaving a thin residual heel in the basket. In top discharge machines, the solids are removed pneumatically, mechanically, manually, or by withdrawal of the entire filter bag.

After removal of the cake, the centrifuge is ready for another charge. Programming the sequence of events can be accomplished by a fully automatic control unit.

Suspension of the machine on three columns provides extensive compensation of any imbalances of the system, thus dispensing with concrete or damper foundations.

Dynamic Separators (Cyclones)

SEPARATORS WORK on gravitational and/or inertial forces as opposed to mechanical separation such as that provided by filtration or screening. The simplest form of separation is by *settling* which relies purely on gravitational force for the separation of solids from a fluid in which they are suspended. Provided the solids are of greater density than the fluid gravity will give the solids a *settling velocity* proportional to the density of the solid and the square of the particle diameter, and inversely proportional to the viscosity of the fluid, *ie*

$$\text{settling velocity} \propto \frac{\rho \, d^2}{\nu}$$

where ρ = particle density
d = particle diameter
ν = fluid viscosity

Specifically settling velocity (V_s) under gravity only is given by:

$$V_s = \frac{d^2 \times (\Delta_1 - \Delta_2)}{K \nu} \cdot g$$

where $(\Delta_1 - \Delta_2)$ = difference in densities
K is a constant, depending on units for d and ν

In the presence of dynamic/inertial forces

$$V_s = \frac{d^2 \times (\Delta_1 - \Delta_2)}{K \cdot \nu} \cdot f$$

where f is the dynamic force involved, *eg* for a centrifuge $f = R \, w^2$

where R = effective radius of centrifuge
w = angular velocity

The relationship between particle density, diameter and fluid viscosity governing settling velocity holds true as long as the particle size is not so small that its motion is affected by Brownian movement of the molecules of the fluid in which it is carried. When this is so the terminal velocity can be substantially reduced and at a certain particle size Brownian movement is sufficient to keep the particles suspended indefinitely. This may be taken as the case with particles of 1 μm size or smaller in air.

It also applies only to a fluid in a perfectly static condition. Movement of the fluid which produces local vertical velocities will affect the falling velocity of particles accordingly. With pure translational velocity the effect of fluid velocity can be neglected, although absence of vertical velocities is only likely to occur with laminar flow. With turbulent flow conditions are indeterminate, except by purely practical tests.

The significance of the above is that settling can be used as a method of separating solid particles from a fluid, provided the terminal velocity of the particles is high enough for the particle to settle out in the time that 'parcel' of carrier fluid takes to pass between two points. This is the general principle of working of clarifiers and settling tanks. (Fig 1).

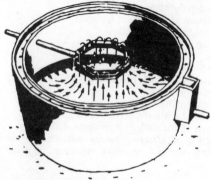

Fig 1 Circular settling tank/clarifier.

Gravitational Plus Inertial Effects

Settling rate may, however, be increased by artificial means, such as deliberately introducing a vortex motion in the fluid. The increased 'g' force applied to the particles increases their velocity relative to the bulk of the fluid, which principle is used in simple vortex flow separators, centrifuges, and cyclone separators.

Another method of producing increased settling rates without introducing motions in the carrier is to cause the particles to agglomerate and thus increase their effective diameter. The effect can be considerable, since terminal velocity is proportional to the square of the diameter. Thus agglomeration of particles which increases the effective diameter size by ten times, say, will increase the settling rate by 100 times. This is the principle employed in ultrasonic fluid clearers and separators, the ultrasonic waves promoting agglomeration of particles suspended in the fluid. Mechanical separators may work on a similar principle of promoting agglomeration by the use of coalescing materials.

Cyclones

Cyclones are basically aerodynamic or hydrodynamic separators where the fluid being handled is caused to develop a vortex flow, literally throwing out more dense particles from the main fluid stream. Since cyclones work according to the mass of the particles involved they may also be applicable to the separation of light and dense solids in mixtures, as well as solids from gases or liquids, or liquid particles from gases. The same principle is also utilized in pipeline air filters for separating out water and oil droplets and heavier solids before the contaminated air actually reaches the filter element.

Cyclones may be of 'dry' or 'wet' type. Dry cyclones provide solids/gas separation — *eg* air or gas cleaners. Wet cyclones provide solids/liquid separation — *eg* separation of solid particles present in liquids. Wet cyclones are specifically described as hydrocyclones.

Cyclones operate under pressurized conditions and where sufficient pressure is not already available in the feed pumping is required. Capital and operating costs are, however, generally low and cyclones are particularly suitable for 'classification' as well as basic filtering duties on batch processing.

TABLE I — SOME APPLICATIONS OF CYCLONES AND HYDROCYCLONES

1. Sizing of particles	a) Removal of sized crystals from crystallizing systems, the overflow returning for further concentration. b) Removal of coarse particles from thickener feeds with substantial reduction in consumption of flocculants. c) Preparation of filter feeds. d) Preparation of finely sized abrasives. e) Preparation of ceramic clays. f) Cleaning of filter bed sand.
2. Degritting of water or suspensions	a) Desanding of water supplies. b) Removal of grit from paper pulp. c) Degritting of clays. d) Degritting of milk or lime. e) Removal of grit and dirt from fruit juices. f) Removal of grit and dirt from wool scour liquor. g) Degritting of effluents before discharge to settling ponds, to eliminate silting with great reduction in wear on pumps and pipelines.
3. Desliming	a) Removal of ultra fine particles from granulated materials. b) Desliming ahead of leaching processes. c) Removal of clay from building sands. d) Preparation of mine backfill.
4. Closed circuit grinding	This is the most important application of hydrocyclones. They are far cheaper than gravity settlement type classifiers, occupy much less space and give more accurate separations. The high separating forces in a cyclone often enable separations to be made that are impossible in any other type of classifier or filter.
5. Preparation of solutions or suspensions	By feeding controlled quantities of water and solids to a pump sump and pumping through a cyclone, solutions and suspensions can quickly be prepared without a mixer. This system works well in conjunction with a density controller supplying a signal to operate the adjustable apex value in the cyclone.
6. Separation by specific gravity	a) Removal of organic matter from sugar beet effluent. b) Removal of peat from sand. c) Separation of shells from nut kernels. d) Separation of light and heavy minerals, using a heavy suspension as the 'medium'.

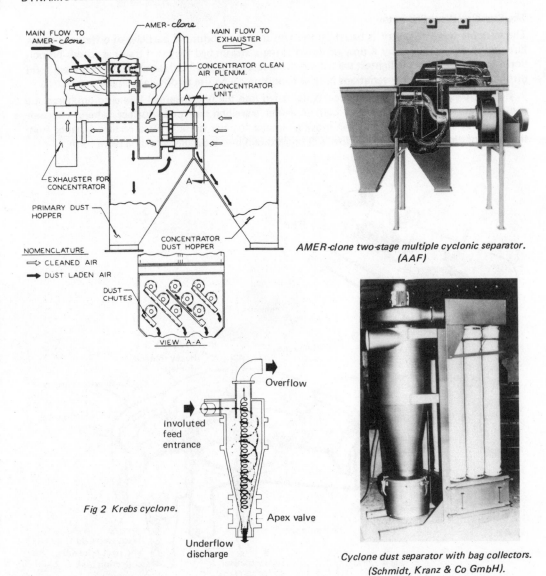

AMER-clone two-stage multiple cyclonic separator.
(AAF)

Fig 2 Krebs cyclone.

Cyclone dust separator with bag collectors.
(Schmidt, Kranz & Co GmbH).

Hydrocyclone/Classifiers

Modern classifiers of this type commonly operate on the hydrocyclone principle. They differ in detail from conventional cyclones although the basic operating principle is the same. The main advantage offered by hydrocyclones is better entry flow control and elimination of turbulence and greater freedom to adjust proportions and shapes to suit the material being handled. The use of liners also ensures a smooth and regular internal surface which is of great importance in critical separations.

A typical design of hydrocyclone is shown in Fig 2 whilst Table I summarizes typical applications of such units.

The Standing Wave Separator

The *standing wave separator* is based on the fact that if a mixture of particles of different density but similar size is moved by a flow of liquid along a stream bed they will travel at speeds proportional to their weights, the lightest particles moving fastest. In practice, each weight group will form distinct ripples or mounds, variations in flow condition giving rise to different ripple shapes.

Fig 3 shows this applied in practice. Water is fed into the first (nearest) funnel to discharge at a constant rate onto a flat conveyor belt or similar travelling horizontal surface, where it spreads radially away from the pipe in a fast moving circular laminar pattern. At a certain distance from the point of discharge the laminar flow will break down into a circular standing wave form.

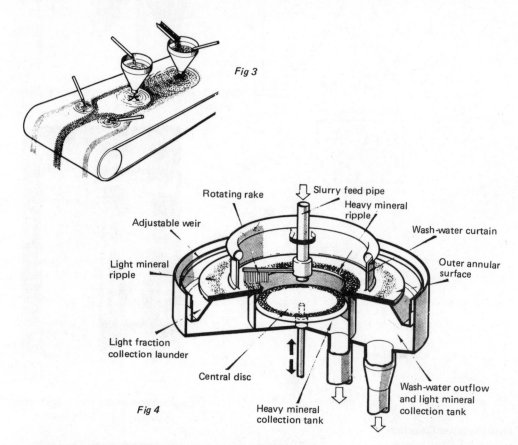

Fig 3

Fig 4

A graded mixture of light and heavy particles introduced into the inflow of water from the second funnel will become separated around the circumference of the standing wave form, the heavy particles being deposited as a ripple at this point whilst the lighter particles are carried into and beyond the wave to form a second circular ripple. Effectively, with the translational velocity produced by the travelling belt the different weight particles will separate into two distinct ribbons on the belt.

The same standing wave principle applied to a bath feed separator is shown in Fig 4.

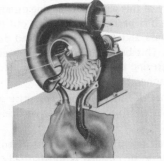

*Roto-clone dry centrifugal dust collector
operates on centrifuge principle.
(AAF)*

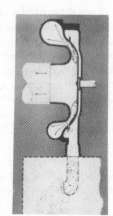

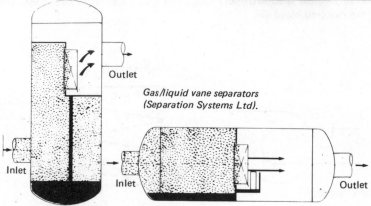

Outlet

*Gas/liquid vane separators
(Separation Systems Ltd).*

Inlet

Inlet

Outlet

Aerodynamic Cleaners

A simple form of air cleaner based on a wedge shaped aerodynamic cell is shown in Fig 5. The cell comprises sides of identical, equally spaced slats providing narrow passages through which emergent air can flow, entry air being directed into the face of the cell and the converging volume produced by the convergent sides. To complete the cell is a closed section into which dirt particles and bleed air can pass, forming in fact a duct to collect and carry away such particles.

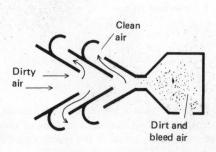

Clean
air

Dirty
air

Dirt and
bleed air

Fig 5 'Dynavane' air cleaner.

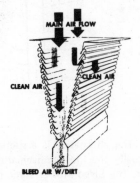

MAIN AIR FLOW

CLEAN AIR

CLEAN AIR

BLEED AIR W/DIRT

Fig 6 Operation of 'Dynavane' cell.

Operation of the cleaner is shown in Fig 6. The main air flow passes directly into the wedge shaped cell, the majority of this air then changing direction abruptly to escape through the louvred sides. At the same time dirt particles are thrown out of the main stream by inertial separation to continue in a straight line and collect in the bleed duct together with some 10% of the airflow representing 'bleed' air. This bleed air continually sweeps the bleed duct and thus promotes a self cleaning function by carrying the dirt particles out of the duct into a suitable collector (or simply returning them to atmosphere).

A complete air cleaner of this type may comprise one or more individual cells and can operate in any plane, except that with vertical or near vertical positioning the bleed duct must be located lowermost.

The same type of cell operating under pressurized conditions is shown in Fig 7. This can be employed where the air to be cleaned is substantially static and thus must be inducted into the cleaner in order to supply the required bleed air.

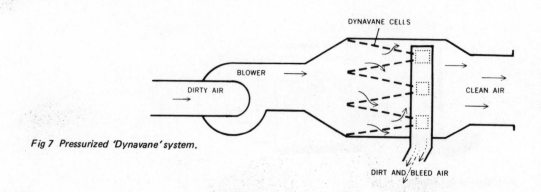

Fig 7 Pressurized 'Dynavane' system.

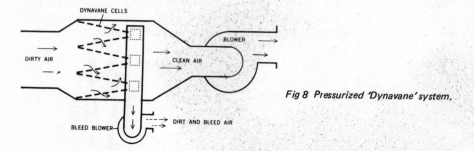

Fig 8 Pressurized 'Dynavane' system.

The alternative is a suction system, shown in Fig 8. In this case a small auxiliary blower is usually the most convenient and most practical method of providing the required flow of bleed air. The bleed blower static pressure required will be approximately equal to the resistance of the cell plus friction and other losses present in the bleed ducting.

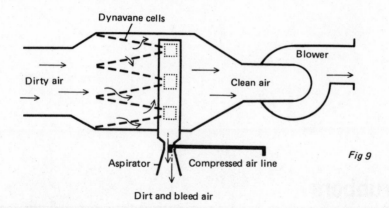

Fig 9

A further variation on the suction system is shown in Fig 9. This system can be employed to advantage where the air cleaning device is to be applied at the air inlet of a gas turbine or similar type of machine where compressed air or fast flowing exhaust gases are available as a power source for bleed-off air flow.

See also chapters on *Centrifuges, Separators* and *Bulk Air Filters.*

Wet Scrubbers

WET SCRUBBERS are designed to wash fume or dust laden air or gases with a spray or sheet of water and remove such contaminants as are present, leaving only clean air or gas to be exhausted from the system. They are capable of handling many fume and dust control problems arising from industrial processes and are particularly applicable to hot gas processes where it is possible to quench the gas stream by direct introduction of water as close to the process as possible. Quenching in this manner makes the dusty gas stream easier to handle.

Scrubbers may be open (vented) or fully enclosed. An example of the former type is shown in Fig 1, applicable to a process or storage tank which needs to 'breathe' but as a consequence can release objectionable fumes. The action of water sprayed into a venturi section creates suction, drawing the fumes into the scrubber where they are removed and carried down by the scrubbing water, leaving only clear gases together with entrained moisture to be exhausted.

Fig 1 Open scrubber designed for use on
acid tanks.
(Rigidon (UK) Ltd).

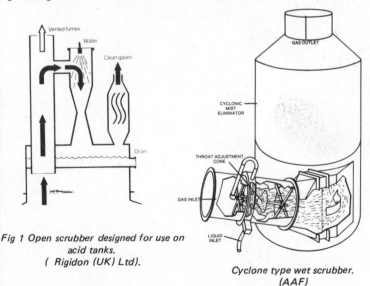

Cyclone type wet scrubber.
(AAF)

The efficiency of such an arrangement is largely dependent on the venturis design and the forced water injection system yielding maximum scrubbing energy (*ie* maximum pressure drop). With venturi type scrubbers high water feed rates are necessary, but savings can be realized by recirculating the water through a suitable water cleaning system.

AAF 'Kinpactor' venturi-type wet dust collector. This unit accomplishes intermixing of dust particles and water droplets. Water introduced ahead of the throat is atomized by the high velocity air stream, and dust particles collide with and are captured in the millions of small droplets. The water-laden gas stream then enters the separator tangentially where droplets are removed by centrifugal force. Clean, droplet-free air passes through the separator outlet and slurry is continuously drained from the separator.

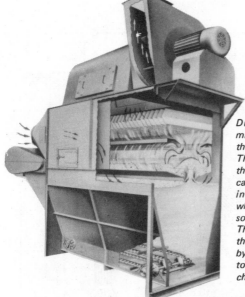

DCE Wet Deduster

Dust laden air is brought down two vertical headers on to the main water surface where the two streams are deflected through a right angle to a zone where violent collision occurs. The combined air streams are then entrained upwards through a turn of very small radius, into the inner chamber carrying with them a considerable volume of water. The intermixed water and air impinge on a central deflector plate which deflects the water to the sides of the inner chamber, so causing the air to pass through an intense spray curtain. The air then separates from the bulk of the entrained water, the fine water drops retained in the air stream being caught by spray eliminators, which ensure negligible water carry over to the fan and air outlet. All water drawn into the inner chamber returns to the bottom tank through flutes spaced at regular intervals.
(Dust Control Equipment Limited)

Entrained moisture in the exhaust gases will be in droplet form or mist which may or may not be acceptable. In some processes, for example, the scrubbing liquid may not be water but an aggressive fluid (*eg* acid) where it is obviously necessary to eliminate this from the final exhaust by some form of demister, *eg* by *mist eliminator pads* or *mist eliminator blades*. The latter are more efficient, have a lower pressure drop across the eliminator, and are better able to handle any dust remaining without clogging. Alternative demisting units include elementary centrifuges, cyclones, *etc*.

An example of non-vented venturi-type scrubber is shown in Fig 2, designed for handling boiler flue gas cleaning and capable of operating with any of several sulphur dioxide scrubbing agents. Scrubbers of this type are normally designed for specific applications, differing in detail

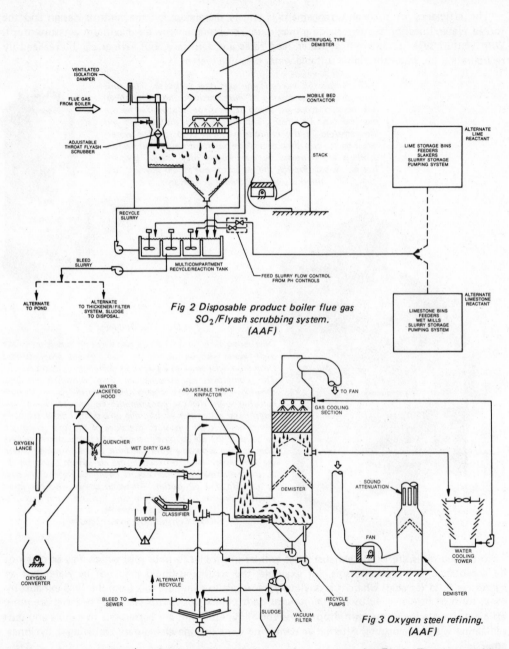

Fig 2 Disposable product boiler flue gas
SO₂/Flyash scrubbing system.
(AAF)

Fig 3 Oxygen steel refining.
(AAF)

mainly in the gas cooling/condensing and demisting section —*eg* see also Fig 3. This is a scrubber specifically designed for an oxygen steelmaking plant which produces a gas stream consisting primarily of nitrogen, carbon dioxide, and oxygen at temperatures in excess of 3 000°F. The gas stream contains dust-loadings as high as 20—40 grains per cubic foot dry gas which consist of slag,

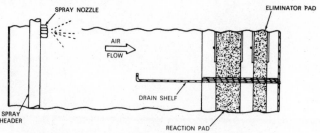

*Principle of operation of extended-surface scrubber
(AAF)*

*Self-cleaning nozzles spray water parallel to the air stream
and directly onto the reaction pads. This water is distributed
uniformly across the face of the pad and saturates the entire
depth of the pad for maximum liquid-to-air contact. Liquid
droplets which pass from the reaction pad are trapped by the
eliminator pads. Water flows, by gravity, from the pads onto
the drain shelf and from there by internal drain piping to the
bottom of the unit where drain connections are provided.*

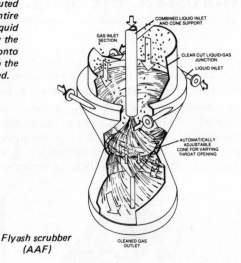

*Flyash scrubber
(AAF)*

iron oxide and other metallic oxide fumes. In order to properly capture all generated fume within
the metal shop, design gas-flow quantity and hood configuration must be carefully considered.
System gas-volume cannot be simply based upon a certain percent of theoretical air requirements.

Normally the gas stream is quenched or saturated as quickly as possible. In the quencher, the
larger dust particles are collected and the gas stream is cooled to 200°F or less by direct water
contact. This pre-cleaned gas is then drawn through one or more venturi where the energy
utilized will produce exit dust loadings of 0.02 grains or less per standard cubic foot dry gas.
Due to the very high gas volumes involved, it is normally most practical to after-cool the gas, or
condense most of the water vapour, in order to both reduce the gas flow and increase the gas
density prior to the system fan, thereby keeping system fan requirements at a minimum. The
resulting stack effluent is essentially free from a water vapour plume under most conditions.

Other Types

Other types of scrubbers in common use include spray towers, vertical and horizontal packed
towers, jet ejectors, venturi scrubbers, extended surface scrubbers, fan spray scrubbers and various
individual designs (some of which may be described as 'cleaners').

Hydrostatic Precipitators

A HYDROSTATIC precipitator can be described as a centrifugal scrubber, or a wet centrifuge. It is essentially a wet-type dust collector (separator) where dust is washed out of air or gas by the combined action of intermixing of water and dust-laden gas and centrifugal force.

An example is the Roto-Clone, shown in cutaway section in Fig 1. Air, flowing through the stationary impeller at high velocity, carries the water in a heavy turbulent sheet. The centrifugal force exerted by the rapid changes in direction of flow causes the dust particles to penetrate the water film and become permanently trapped. The water is continually re-used and since the water curtain is produced by the air-flow, no pumps or nozzles are required.

Fig 1 'Roto-Clone' hydrostatic precipitator with detail of impeller.
(AAF)

Regardless of the volume of air handled, the water level is maintained at the same elevation on the clean air side. As air flow reduces pressure loss through the Roto-Clone impeller decreases causing make-up water to raise the water level on the dirty air side. This higher operating level throttles the air passage in the impeller and increases the air velocity through the narrowed opening. An almost constant approach velocity therefore causes the same volume of water to be impelled through the passages by the air stream so the scrubbing action and collection efficiency at reduced air flow ratings are maintained.

Water level control is an important feature of this design. With baffle or stationary-impeller type dust collectors, the water level must be synchronized with the amount of air flowing through the unit if constant collection and reasonable pressure drop are to be maintained. Roto-Clone water-level control automatically adjusts the operating water level when the exhaust volume varies. Collection efficiency and pressure drop are not sensitive to variations in volume. The same high degree of dust removal is maintained over a range of 60% to 100% of rating.

The water level control is located external to the circulating water in the Type N Roto-Clone. Make-up water slightly in excess of the quantity evaporated in the Roto-Clone is added in the control box, while excess goes directly to drain connected to overflow weir without intermixing with the dirty water in the Roto-Clone itself. As a result dirty water with its solids cannot overflow and plug drains or sewers or contaminate streams. No adjustments need be made to keep the operating level at the proper height for different exhaust volumes or gas densities.

See also chapters on *Centrifuges, Dynamic Separators* and *Wet Scrubbers.*

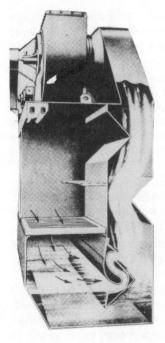

Cutaway type N Roto-Clone. Bench showing water reservoir beneath grilles and location of impeller.

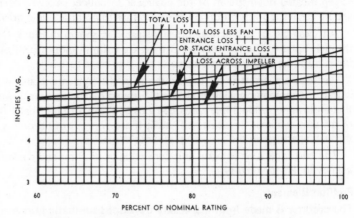

Typical chart of AAF Roto-Clone pressure losses for variation in exhaust volume from nominal rating. Size number multiplied by 1 000 gives nominal rating in ft³/min of Roto-Clone.

Coalescers

COALESCERS ARE a special type of separator designed to collect highly dispersed droplets present in a carrier fluid and form or coalesce these droplets into large drops which will rapidly separate out. Specifically they are used to separate water from fuel oils — originally aviation fuels, but now widely applied for water removal from diesel fuels and other liquids.

The principle by which this is done is to pass the water contaminated fuel through a dense, inorganic fibre bed or filter mat. Water droplets are intercepted by and impinge on the fibres, the oil film between the two being thinned by displacement and the effect of viscous drag. Ultimately the oil film ruptures allowing the water droplets to attach themselves completely to the fibre with the fuel film dispersed and passed on through the mat. Other water droplets are collected by the fibres in a similar manner and will join up (coalesce) with each other forming streams along the fibres — Fig 1.

The droplets continue to grow in size until drag and gravity forces break them away and they drop off the filter mat into a sump. In practice a final stripping stage is desirable — *eg* a fine mesh screen located downstream of the coalescer to collect smaller water droplets which may spin free and be carried along with the oil stream rather than settle under gravity. (Fig 2).

An example of a practical filter/coalescer is shown in Fig 3. Contaminated oil fountains out through holes in the top section of a centre column mounted through the division plate. Oil then flows from the inside to the outside of the two-stage cartridge.

Particles are arrested by the synthetic prefilter element and water is coalesced from the oil within the inorganic coalescer element. Filtered oil then passes through a PTFE coated metal mesh that ensures no residual free water carry over. Clean, dry oil finally flows up to an outlet at the top of the unit, whereas the coalesced and stripped water forms droplets large enough to fall by gravity through apertures in the division plate into the sump.

The cartridge is an integral unit consisting of prefilter and coalescer elements encased in perforated cylinders for rigidity.

Prefilter Element

The prefilter is made from a specially developed synthetic fibre medium which is pleated, and the folds separated, by means of spacers. The structure provides maximum dirt holding capacity, eliminates element distortion and ensures that the complete filter area is utilized to maintain maximum flow.

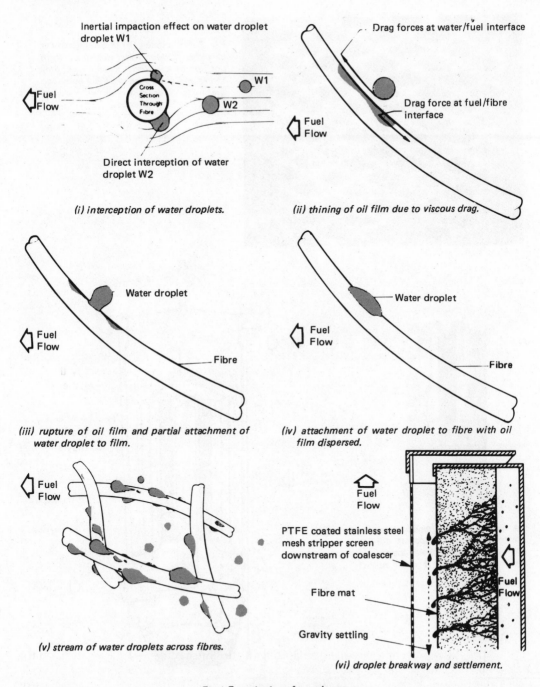

(i) interception of water droplets.

(ii) thining of oil film due to viscous drag.

(iii) rupture of oil film and partial attachment of water droplet to film.

(iv) attachment of water droplet to fibre with oil film dispersed.

(v) stream of water droplets across fibres.

(vi) droplet breakway and settlement.

*Fig 1 Functioning of a coalescer
(Vokes Ltd).*

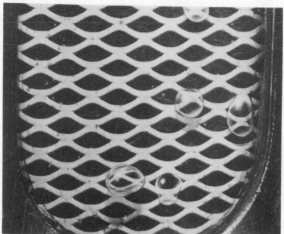

Fig 2 The outside of a filter/coalescer cartridge showing water droplets held in position by interfacial tension until drag forces and gravity breaks them away and the water falls onto the sump below. (Vokes Ltd).

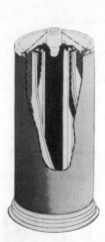

A typical Vokes filter/coalescer cartridge. The cartridge is disposable because once loaded with contaminant it is of no further use.

Fig 3 Vokes filter/coalescer.

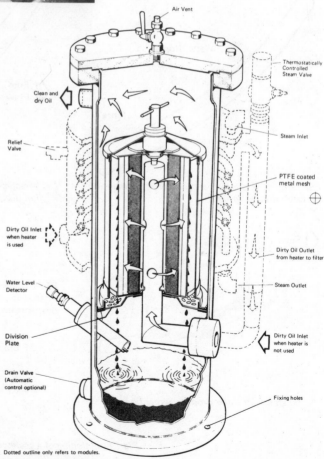

Air Vent

Thermostatically Controlled Steam Valve

Clean and dry Oil

Relief Valve

Steam Inlet

PTFE coated metal mesh

Dirty Oil Inlet when heater is used

Dirty Oil Outlet from heater to filter

Steam Outlet

Water Level Detector

Dirty Oil Inlet when heater is not used

Division Plate

Drain Valve (Automatic control optional)

Fixing holes

Dotted outline only refers to modules.

In addition to removing particulates down to 5 μm, the prefilter protects the coalescer element from excessive quantities of particulate contaminant. This is especially important in applications treating diesel fuel where pipe scale, rust, waxes and asphaltenes might otherwise block the fine pores of the coalescer element.

Coalescer Element

This second stage consists of a cylinder of fine inorganic fibres pressed to a predetermined density and depth sufficient to ensure maximum water coalescing action. The element is also designed to maintain a flow of relatively low velocity through its depth to ensure efficient water removal.

Flow rates that can be achieved through a cartridge measuring 435 mm long x 216 mm diameter are approximately 1 400 litres/hour for diesel fuel and 500 litres/hour for lubricating oil. Higher flow rates can be accommodated by using a multiplicity of cartridges in an appropriate vessel to give up to 16 800 litres/hour for fuel and up to 4 000 litres/hour for lubricating oil when using steam jacketed modules.

Other designs of coalescers employ plate or tube elements instead of cartridges — *eg* see Figs 4 and 5.

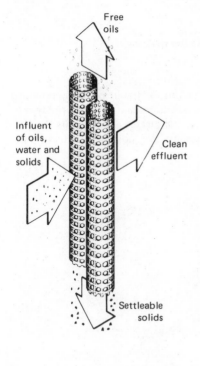

Tubes reduce free oil content of effluent to 10 mg/litre or less because microscopic oil particles agglomerate on the surface. The growing oil globules either wick up or, if sufficiently buoyant, break free to rise to the surface.

*Fig 4 Vertical tube coalescer
(AFL Industries Inc).*

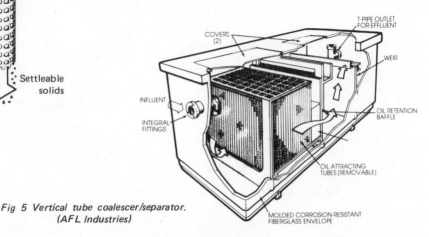

*Fig 5 Vertical tube coalescer/separator.
(AFL Industries)*

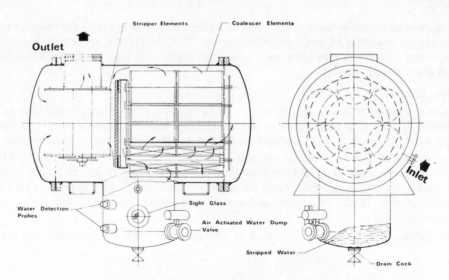

High capacity coalescer filters have horizontal element stacks,
whereas in smaller units the cartridges are installed vertically.
(Vokes Limited)

Coalescers can also be used to remove water from lubricating oils, hydraulic oils, *etc*, provided these contain no detergent additive. Detergents reduce interfacial tension, and inhibit formation of large droplets on the coalescer. The same is true of fuels containing surface active agents (surfactants), although in this case a prefilter can usually limit or eliminate the 'poisoning' effect on the coalescer stage.

See also chapter on *Oily Water Treatment.*

Homogenization

HOMOGENIZATION IS basically a blending process whereby agglomerates in a fluid are broken down and uniformly dispersed throughout the body of the fluid. In a sense it is the opposite of filtering, but is a directly related subject since it can offer an alternative form of treatment for specific products by breakdown and dispersion of solids contents rather than solids removal. A particularly significant field of application is the treatment of heavy fuel oils.

Heavy fuel oil is residual fuel, often cut back with a lighter distillate, and consequently has a very wide variety of viscosity and composition depending upon the original blend of crude oils and the proportion of cut back oil. In many respects the oil may be likened to a soup of waxy lumps and bunches of fibre, being of course the agglomerates of asphaltenes and bituminous matter derived from the residual. It is not easy to disperse residual thoroughly in a cut back oil and very often bunker oil becomes stratified, particularly if the wax content is relatively high.

Heating the fuel dissolves the wax, but the asphaltene agglomerates are not broken down by this means, and since they can be of the order of 100–200 μm in size they represent sizeable lumps, in combustion terms, relative to the average size of hydrocarbon chains in the bulk of the fuel. These asphaltene agglomerates are very slow burning in comparison to the rest of the fuel, and generally are not completely burned either in a diesel engine cylinder or in a boiler. The mechanism of burning particles starts by evaporation of the lighter fuel fractions leaving a perforated shell of carbon within which is trapped a sticky mixture of heavy hydrocarbons, ash and the complex vanadium salts which are responsible for the high deposition rates on piston crowns, valve seats and boiler tubes.

To convey some idea of the relative speed of combustion of different size droplets, if a droplet of 100 μm diameter in size is broken down into small droplets of 5 μm diameter, then the total surface area increases 20 times and the number of these small droplets is 8 000. If those are reduced to 2 μm diameter, the total surface area increases 50 times and the number of smaller droplets to 125 000. For complete combustion in a diesel engine the maximum possible surface area must be presented by the fuel droplets and although the injector decides the spray pattern, the size of drop depends primarily upon the viscosity of individual fuel particles, or the treatment to which it has been subjected.

Centrifuging is an obvious way of removing unwanted solids, but such treatment not only removes unwanted water and solids but also the heavy asphaltene agglomerates.

When fuel was relatively cheap this action could be economically justified, but it is not now economically viable to throw away ½% to 2% of good fuel by the separator, as this represents not only a direct increase in fuel costs but also an indirect one in respect of the cost of centrifuge maintenance and cleaning and the disposal of sludge. The trend is clearly towards the burning of heavier fuels, partly to keep running costs down, but mainly because of the shrinking availability world wide of good quality crudes. It becomes wasteful to burn the good quality oils when more economic and socially acceptable uses present themselves.

Whereas, at the present time, fuels generally available for bunkers are in the range 1 000 to 3 500 secs Redwood No 1, it is predicted that in the 1980's the viscosity range will rise to 6 000 secs Redwood No 1, and, furthermore, sulphur, vanadium, ash and water content will inevitably rise. Also the treatment, by centrifuging, of 6 000 secs Redwood No 1 fuel becomes extremely difficult.

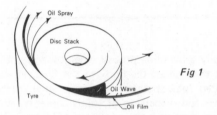

Fig 1

Homogenization offers an alternative approach. A homogenizer operates on the principle of passing fuel oil through a housing where a series of rolling discs subject the fuel to a shearing and crushing force (see Fig 1). Under this force, any large clusters of heavy hydrocarbons present in the fuel are reduced to particles or globules of effectively the same size (5 μm or less). The mixing action of the homogenizer then disperses these particles, and any water present, evenly through the fuel. The rolling action of the discs on the integral tyre within the homogenizer housing induces a highly turbulent wave of oil ahead of each disc stack, locally intermixing the oil. As the discs rotate away from the tyre, oil adhering to the disc surface is sprayed across the unit, mixing the fuel on a macroscale.

Reducing the particle size to the order of 5 μm, which is about the same size as the base oil particles, means there is no basic change in the fuel itself, but its burning characteristics are much more uniform. Only the fuel viscosity will be changed slightly, depending on the nature of the residual fuel, the oil used to cut back viscosity, and the degree of mixing as bunkered. Also homogenized fuels have good stability, with initially no evidence of water separation.

Water in fuel is a normal occurrence and gross amounts may be gravity separated in a settling tank leaving a residue of about 1% in the fuel. Centrifuging removes the majority of this, but then condensation due to storage in a daily use tank adds further quantities. An advantage of using the homogenizer is that small slugs of water present in the fuel, taken from the settling tank, are thoroughly dispersed in the fuel such that the injector will not experience cycling of oil and water.

Commercial Homogenizers

The Vickers Fuel Oil Homogenizer developed through prototype ball and disc mills is produced in module form comprising a homogenizer bowl, motor, coupling, control tank, level controller and contents gauge on a common base — Fig 2.

The working system comprises three separate circuits: the main engine supply, engine spill and homogenizer recirculation. Fuel is drawn from a conventionally heated settling tank and passed

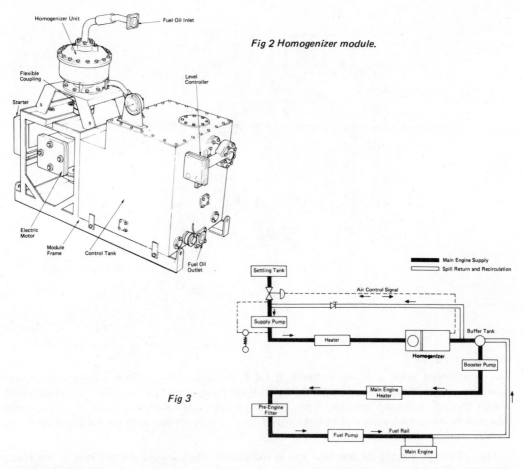

Fig 2 Homogenizer module.

Fig 3

through a heater capable of heating to a viscosity of between 150 and 200 Redwood No 1 seconds. Fuel is homogenized and is drawn from the control tank through the buffer tanks by the booster pump, and onwards to the main engine. All components after the homogenizer are conventional to a marine engine system as is the engine spill return to the buffer tank.

When a reduced quantity of fuel is required by the booster pump, so the in-built level controller signals closure of the homogenizer control valve. On stopped engine conditions this effectively isolates the homogenizer bowl from the settling tank and to prevent the machine running dry, fuel is taken by the supply pump through the recirculation system. The homogenizer control system is pneumatically operated. In vessels operating with a conventional centrifuge as a back-up system the supply pump and heater can be of that system, thereby eliminating duplication.

During prolonged shut down the fuel in the control tank may be heated by built-in steam coils prior to recirculation and thus re-homogenization. In this case the tank vent connection prevents gassing of the fuel.

A diagram of a basic installation is shown in Fig 3.

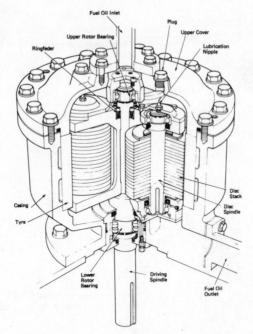

Fig 4 Homogenizer unit.

Homogenizer Bowl

The homogenizer bowl is shown in detail in Fig 4. Basically this comprises a rotor that encompasses sets of flat circular discs supported by shafts that rotate on bearings. The rotor is driven by a shaft through a flexible coupling from an electric motor. As the rotor starts to rotate, radial clearance between each shaft and its discs allows them to gain contact with the hardened steel tyre thereby crushing the fuel film.

Fuel enters at the top of the unit and is radially distributed onto the top face of the rotor, where centrifugal force causes it to be discharged onto the disc/tyre interface. The oil is subjected to several passes of the disc stacks that cause intimate shearing and crushing. Heavy hydrocarbons are completely distributed into the bulk of the fuel and the removal of local concentrations reduces the possibility of re-agglomeration occurring.

Other Types of Homogenizer

Other types of homogenizer (*eg* those developed primarily for process duties) utilize the nozzle principle for breakdown and dispersion of agglomerates. Whilst nozzles can be equally effective for such duties, they do require filters before and after the homogenizer unit and consequent filter servicing.

See also chapters on *Coalescers, Centrifuges, Oil Cleaning* and *Oily Water Treatment*.

SECTION 3
Applications

Sub-section (a)

Bulk Air Filters

FILTERS DESIGNED for the treatment of large volumes of air fall broadly into three categories:-

(i)   Primary filters designed to trap the majority of larger airborne dust particles have high dust holding capacity. These are usually of dry panel type or roll filters capable of working with relatively high airflow velocities (see also Fig 1).

Fig 1 Examples of primary air filters
(AAF Ltd)
Left: Disposable panel filters — glass fibre pad curved back
and front with metal grilles. Initial resistance 0.16" wg. Final
recommended resistance 0.5" wg.
Centre: Dry pad or roll glass fibre filters. Initial resistance
0.15" wg. Final recommended resistance 0.5" wg.
Right: Pad type filter (alternative to panel filter). Initial
resistance 0.10" wg. Final recommended resistance 0.5" wg.

(ii)   Second stage filters with finer media for trapping and retaining finer particles passed by a primary filter — eg particles of 5 μm diameter and smaller. These smaller particles (0.5–5 μm) are the most damaging as regards staining of decor in buildings, harmful effects on machinery and pressure equipment, etc. Again these may be of unit or panel type, or bag type, with extended depth of filtration. Maximum air velocities are generally low, *eg* of the order of 0.5 ft/sec (0.12 m/sec) or less.

(iii)   Ultra fine or final stage filters yielding very high efficiencies (*eg* 99.95% or better) even with sub-micron particles. The chief type here is the high efficiency particulate air filter (HEPA) employing a high density medium built up from glass fibres with a sub-micron diameter and rendered in the form of a closely pleated pack. Air velocity in this case is limited to about 0.1 ft/sec (0.03 m/sec). Electrostatic precipitators also come into this category because of their capacity for ultra-fine dust filtering. They can operate with much higher air velocities.

Luwa fine dust aid filters — efficiency rating 85% or 95% to ASHRAE 52-76 and DIN 24185.

'Air' filter *types* can be categorized as follows:-

(i)   *Cartridge filters* — mainly applicable as engine intake filters and filters for compressed air systems.

(ii)   *Pad filters* — disposable elements mounted in frames or panels.

(iii)   *Panel filters* — unit filters which may be disposable (*eg* using synthetic fibre or spun glass media); washable (*eg* using polyurethane foam or a similar material); or cleanable (*eg* woven steel mesh cleaned by immersion in an oil bath).

(iv)   *Viscous panel filters* — employing screens or media wetted with oil; or dry fibre coated with an adhesive gel.

(v)   *Roll filters* — which are basically panel filters, with the filter media automatically fed from a 'clean' roll to a 'dirty' roll.

(vi)   *Rotating viscous panel filters* — in the form of a continuous curtain 'loop' of metal slats or similar, automatically rotated and passing through an oil bath. The oil acts both as a viscous impingement and cleaning agent.

(vii)   *Bag filters* — normally arranged in bag form to provide high efficiency filtering with high dust retention. There are also other forms of extended surface/extended depth filters which can be included in this category.

(viii) *Particulate air filters* — for final stage filtering, as noted above.

(ix)   *Electrostatic precipitators* — which may be of dry type (agglomerators), or have the plates periodically cleaned by water washing. In the dry type dust is collected in filter bags or a separate downstream filter.

(x)   *Louvres* — aerodynamic type separators which also have a capacity for collecting liquid mist particles.

(xi)   *Separators* — various types working on aerodynamic principles.

(xii)   *Scrubbers* — 'wet' dust separators.

Pad and Panel Filters

Simple screens are of elementary construction and comprise a pleated or corrugated element mounted in a square or rectangular frame. They can be classified under three headings, depending on whether or not the element is reusable. Thus in the case of elements which cannot be cleaned the complete panel is disposed of and replaced with a new one when the pressure drop has risen to an unacceptable level (usually 0.5 inches wg above the initial pressure drop). Other panels may be designed with *semi-permanent* elements, when cleaning can be accomplished by removing the panel, laying face downwards and tapping gently to remove dust; or possibly the dust removed with a vacuum cleaner. The number of cleaning cycles which can be achieved without damaging the element is limited, hence the type is referred to as a semi-permanent panel.

Permanent panels have stronger elements which are readily cleanable by removal and washing. These may be dry filters or, more usually, viscous panel filters employing metallic elements with or without fibrous interlayers. A particular advantage with viscous panel filters is that they can be designed to have constant or even reducing efficiency characteristics so that pressure drop will not rise excessively even if cleaning of the filter is neglected.

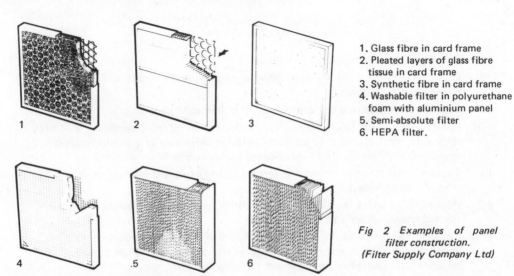

1. Glass fibre in card frame
2. Pleated layers of glass fibre tissue in card frame
3. Synthetic fibre in card frame
4. Washable filter in polyurethane foam with aluminium panel
5. Semi-absolute filter
6. HEPA filter.

Fig 2 Examples of panel filter construction. (Filter Supply Company Ltd)

Various cloth, fabric or even paper media may be employed for dry panel filters. Most favoured materials are synthetic fibres and glass fibre in pad, multi-layer or pleated form. It is becoming increasingly common practice to coat media with a viscous agent to ensure high dust retention. Examples of various types are shown in Fig 2. Most panels of this type are disposable.

With a semi-permanent panel the element can employ a similar medium, but supported between fine fabric gauze for additional strength and backed with scrim to facilitate cleaning.

Fully cleanable (permanent) filters normally employ elements formed by woven metal mats which may be reinforced with wires or layers of corrugated expanded metal, the whole being assembled in a metal frame for durability. Characteristics vary widely with the actual form of element construction employed and so direct comparison cannot be drawn with other types.

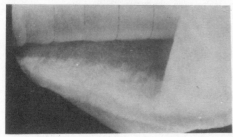
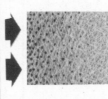

'Kompak' composite glass and filterdown filter media. (Vokes Air Filter Ltd).

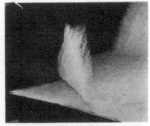

Two-layer 'Vee-Glass' air filter media. (Vokes Air Filter Ltd)

Graduated density glass fibre panel media. (AAF Ltd).

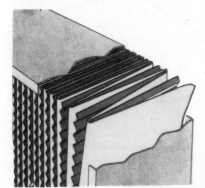

Vokes 'absolute' or HEPA filter construction using pleated synthetic fibre media ('Super Vee') or continuous filament glass fibre bonded strata ('Vee-Glass').

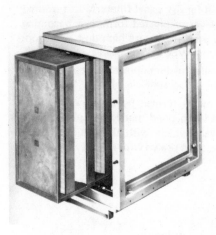

Luwa composite panel and fine dust filter.

Luwa panel filters.

Vokes Supervee panel filter.

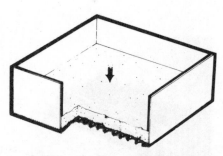

Capillary air filter comprising knitted polypropylene or demembraned polyurethane media in aluminium sheet housing.
(Filter Supply Company Ltd).

Viscous Panel Filters

Viscous panel filters provide dust retention by the effective impingement of dust on a large area of oily surface. In this respect they can have a superior performance to dry filters (particularly in heavily contaminated atmospheres). Their effectiveness, however, will also rely on adequate particle retention properties to eliminate subsequent re-entrainment of particles as the oil is dried up by collected solids. In practice the retention properties can be adjusted, in design, to give constant efficiency or falling (reducing) efficiency.

This is controlled by the operating characteristics of the viscous panel. If wetting characteristics are adequately maintained efficiency remains high and substantially constant. In certain circumstances efficiency may increase, as with conventional dry filters, if the presence of oil on the element assists the formation of a porous bed of solids. If the degree of wetting decreases markedly with build up of contaminant, however, the retention properties of the filter will fall, and hence its efficiency will also fall.

A simple viscous panel filter comprises one or more layers of wire mesh, usually in crimped or deeply pleated form, or even wire wool housed between two layers of mesh. Such types tend, generally, to have relatively low efficiency and only moderate retention properties. They may also be subject to 'channelling' where the airflow is directed through particular, and individual, paths rather than distributed over the whole filter area. Better performance is usually achieved by sandwiching a layer of cotton gauze or similar absorbent medium between layers of wire mesh, the gauze both decreasing the average air passage dimension for increased filtering efficiency and also increasing the effective mass of oil which can be retained by the panel (that is, increasing the degree of wetting).

Viscous panel elements incorporating absorbent media layers will normally have constant (or even increasing) efficiency characteristics. Reducing efficiency characteristics are usually given by all-metal construction. Here efficiency is high as long as the wire surfaces remain tacky, but as the oil is absorbed by accumulating dust retention capacity falls. This can be advantageous in applications where it is more important that lack of attention to filter cleaning does not generate excessive high back pressure than the fact that high filtering efficiency is always maintained. On the other hand, with regular cleaning and re-wetting at suitable intervals, the performance of a reducing efficiency filter can remain high in service. An example of a viscous panel filter is shown in Fig 3.

Fig 3 Viscous impingement
panel air filter
(AAF Ltd).

Panel and roll filters illustrat-
ing wide variety of types
available.
(AAF Ltd).

Roll Filters

Roll type filters are normally automatic. The filter medium may be a woven or non-woven synthetic cloth or glass fibre mat, or similar, possibly backed with mesh for added strength or even carried on a screen. The filter cloth itself may be treated with special wetting fluid to improve dust capacity and efficiency. The cloth roll is simply spooled from top to bottom, being replaced with a new spool when the whole length has been run through (Fig 4).

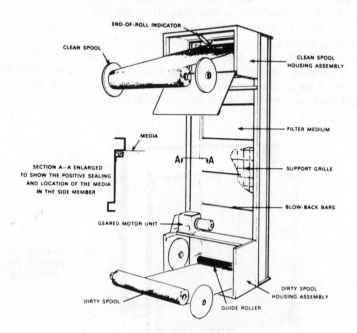

Fig 4 Typical automatic roll filter.

Various forms of automatic control are possible, the most common being to actuate movement of the filter cloth by a pressure differential system. This can be preset to operate at a specific differential pressure (typically 0.45 to 0.55 inches wg with a synthetic fibre cloth element), and start the drive motor. The motor is then triggered off to stop the cloth in position when sufficient new area is exposed to lower the differential pressure to the original (clean) figure. A separate inching control is also usually provided for operating the filter during service; also an 'end-of-roll' indicator to show when the upper spool is running empty.

Instead of a flat traverse the filter cloth may be run in a vee-shaped path to increase the effective filter area. The unit may also operate horizontally, or vertically face downwards, as well as straight up — Fig 5. Units may also be made self-cleaning by continuous recirculation of the filter element.

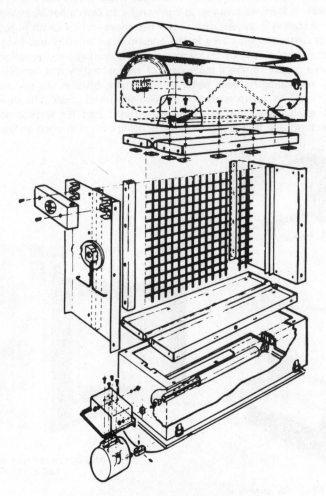

Fig 5 Farr 'Mini-clean' automatic type air filter.

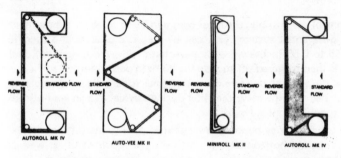

Fig 6 Self-cleaning roll type
filters.
(Vokes)

An automatic self-cleaning rotary screen is shown in Fig 6. The filter medium in this case consists of separate panels, formed from layers of crimped metal plates laid with the lines of corrugations at right angles to form air passages at right angles to each other. A number of such panels is built up to form a complete screen, each supported on an endless chain in such a manner that each panel always presents the same face to the oncoming air whether travelling up or down the filter frame. The chains are driven by an electric motor operating through reduction gearing and controlled by a timer preset to give a movement of approximately one complete revolution per day. Cleaning is accomplished by each panel, in turn, being tilted in the oil tank at the bottom whilst the oil is agitated by compressed air, flushing the panel clean. The design of the screen plates is such that when the cleaned screen is again raised into the vertical position excess oil drains back into the sump and thus eliminates any oil being carried through on the airstream.

Horizontal roll-type filter.
(AAF Ltd).

Vertical roll-type filter with automatic
precleaner.
(AAF Ltd).

Fig 7 Vokes multi-layer bag air filter, front withdrawal.

Bag Filters (Fig 7)

Bag filters take various different forms but all work on the same principle. The filter medium is in the form of a bag, closed sleeve or envelope attached to a rigid front member which holds the bag open. One or more such bags can then be assembled in a holding frame from which they can be withdrawn for disposal.

Bag filters provide an extremely high filter area for a given entry or panel size. The bags, which form the filter element, need to be of somewhat stronger construction than panel elements, but may range from impregnated paper through natural and synthetic fabrics to glass cloth, depending on the application involved. For industrial applications, and where very fine filtering is required, the bags are often made from glass wool protected on both sides with scrim. Multi-layer construction is also employed with different filter media — eg an inner layer of rather more open form for dust retention, an intermediate layer for fine filtering and an even closer outer layer to prevent filter fibre migration.

Very high filtration efficiencies are possible with filter bags, depending on the media used — eg up to 99.8% efficiency with BS2831 No 1 Test Dust or an ASHRAE/EUROVENT average atmospheric efficiency of 90—95%. Performance also depends on the bags remaining rigid and 'inflated', even at reduced or nil airflow. Some bags are self-supporting by their construction; others require hooks, loops or wire mesh for support.

Bags are invariably disposable rather than re-usable, so material cost can affect the choice of bag. Any additional cost, however, is often recoverable since in many applications a bag filter can provide both primary and second stage filtering (ie does not need to be preceded by a coarse primary filter).

A properly designed bag filter, too, can perform efficiently with from 25–30% up to 150% of the normal airflow, *ie* is particularly suitable for variable air volume systems.

Electrostatic Precipitators

See separate chapter on *Electrostatic Precipitators*.

Louvres

Louvres work on the principle of inertial separation but the aerodynamic design involved is somewhat critical. A highly successful example is shown in Fig 8. This comprises a V-shaped 'pocket' of all-welded construction. The ends of the pocket are solid, with one or both sides of the V made up of the formed louvre slits. Dirty air enters the open end of the V pocket. The dust is separated from the air as the air turns to pass through the open louvred slits in the side of the V. The dirt continues on in its original direction and is concentrated at the apex of the V. To provide continuous removal of the separated material, the V apex contains a 'slot' the entire length of the louvre sheet. This slot allows the separated material to enter the 'dust chute' which collects this discharged dirt from one or more slots and conveys it to the desired point of disposal. In order to convey the separated material, a small amount of air passes through the slot as secondary air movement.

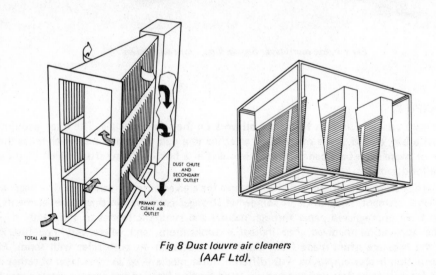

Fig 8 Dust louvre air cleaners
(AAF Ltd).

Such a louvre will operate over a wide range of velocities through the louvre blades without a loss in efficiency, provided the proper relationship of secondary to primary air is maintained. Normally, the secondary air is 10% of the primary air. However, this proportion can be changed to provide, within limits, desired changes in cleaning efficiency. The velocity through the louvre blade which is used on any one installation is determined by the allowable pressure drop across it. Thus, a Dust Louvre of a given area may have an infinite range of ft^3/min (CFM) capacities as determined by the allowable pressure drop allocated to the Dust Louvre. It has been applied with primary air pressure drops from 0.3 in to 9½ in water gauge.

See also chapters on *Dynamic Separators (Cyclones etc), Wet Scrubbers, Filters for I/C Engines* and *Filter Selection Guides*.

Air Filter Services

SERVICES IN which air filters play a prominent part can be categorized as follows:-

(i)   Building Services
(ii) Heating and Air Conditioning
(iii) Industrial Ventilation
(vi) Clean Rooms

The principal duties of the filters used in these services are described in this chapter.

BUILDING SERVICES

In building services a primary consideration of a filtration system is to achieve the optimum balance between capital cost and running costs. The latter is particularly important in times of rising costs, both as regards maintenance, labour costs and replacement of expendable filter media (disposable filter elements). The trend, too, is towards the adoption of pre-engineered package units for air handling rather than piecemeal installation on site. In general this proves to be more economic and is more readily analyzable in terms of likely future material costs — *ie* such figures should be available from the manufacturer of the central station unit including fans, heat exchangers and humidifiers in addition to the air filtration system.

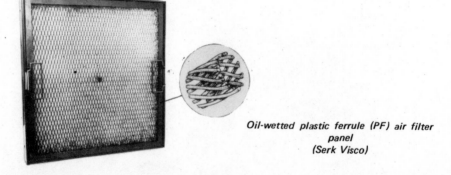

Oil-wetted plastic ferrule (PF) air filter
panel
(Serk Visco)

Air conditioning of British Rail Mk IIID
coach using Vokes panel filter.

Luwa filtrasept wall air outlet with
perforated plate.

A further advantage of the package deal is that panel filters, automatic roll filters and various combinations of filters provided by a systems supplier are designed to match standard dimensions for air-handling units. It remains, however, to decide which types of filters are best suited and most cost-effective for the performance required.

Specifically a basic question to be answered is whether primary (relatively coarse) filters are suitable on their own or need to be backed up by second stage filters at additional cost. Primary filters normally only remove dust particles down to the order of 5 μm. Applied to centrally heated offices and similar buildings the amount of finer dust particles remaining in the air can be considerable, calling for interior cleaning/redecoration at relatively close intervals — typically on a 2-3 year/5-6 year cycle in urban areas.

Second stage filtration using finer media to filter down to 1 μm could considerably extend these periods with reduced building maintenance costs, at the expense of increased capital and operating costs for the filter system. Potential savings can be even more significant in large department stores, *etc* for reducing both redecorating costs and the amount of shop soiled goods. Unfortunately there is no short-cut to filter cost savings here as it is impractical to provide ultra-fine filtering at a primary filter stage. Equally, to dispense with primary filtering and rely on fine filters only would materially reduce the performance and life of disposable elements used with fine filters.

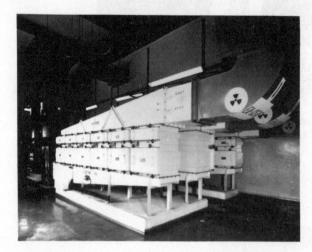

Vokes Unipack filter used for pile cap extract at CEGB Hinkley Plant.

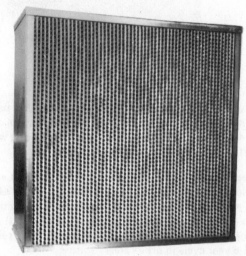

Vokes absolute panel air filter.

Primary Filters

For primary filters the choice will normally be between panel filters and automatic roll filters. The former are cheaper to install but generally more expensive to maintain. Efficiencies of both types are relatively low, but with automatic roll filters generally slightly better than panel types. Increasing use is being made of automatic viscous screen filters where efficiencies generally lie mid way between the other two types.

As a general guide line, panel filters are almost universally used for building systems handling air volumes up to 10 000 ft^3/min; and automatic roll filters with disposable media, or automatic viscous screen filters for larger installations.

Secondary Filters

Where cost effective, or where initial capital cost is not a critical factor, these can be combined with bag type filters for second stage filtration; or electrostatic filters for retention of even finer particles. If the latter are of the dry type, collection of dust from these filters must be by bag or automatic roll filter. Dry type electrostatic filters normally combine such dust collectors in an integral unit. Both bag type filters and electrostatic filters are particularly suitable for variable air volume systems where air volumes can vary from 20% to 110% of design value. Other types of filters are less effective for variable volume flow. Variable air volume systems are becoming increasingly prominent because of the energy savings possible.

Serk Visco dry static type air filters. Micro-cube (left) and MV glove-type (right).

Systems and Filter Limitations

Apart from the effect of variable air volumes on the effectiveness of certain types of filters, other system characteristics may dictate the choice of filter type, particularly as regards flow velocities. In general the higher the efficiency of a filter the lower the permissible (design) flow rate, hence in many cases it may be necessary to downgrade filter performance to accept necessary operating parameters; *eg* rule out the possibility of employing a two-stage in-line filter package.

HEATING AND AIR CONDITIONING

Broad requirements have been described previously under *Building Services.* Basically the system is called upon to induct atmospheric air, clean and heat or cool it, and circulate the treated air throughout the premises. The amount and type of contaminants present in the air will vary widely with the site. In rural areas dust concentration is likely to be of the order of 0.05–0.5 mg/in^3 and to comprise mainly soil erosion particles, vegetable matter, seasonal pollens and a minimum of carbonaceous matter. In metropolitan areas dust concentration is likely to be 0.1–1 mg/in^3 with a high proportion of carbonaceous matter, ash, silicon and other granular products. In industrial areas the dust concentration can be expected to be of the order of 2–5 mg/in^3 with a large content of carbonaceous matter as well as tarry oils and waxes, mineral and chemical dusts and sulphurous gases and acids. Typical 'average' dust content of atmospheric air is likely to be that shown in Fig 1.

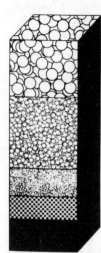

Range of particle sizes (μm)	Average particle size (μm)	Proportionate quantities by particle count per cubic foot of air	Per cent by particle count	Per cent by volume (or by weight for uniform specific gravity)
30–10	20	500	0.005	28
10–5	7½	17 500	0.175	52
5–3	4	25 000	0.25	11
3–1	2	107 000	1.07	6
1–½	¾	676 000	6.78	2
½–0	¼	9,140 000	91.72	1

Fig 1 Size distribution of a typical atmospheric dust sample
(AAF Ltd)

The standard normally accepted for intake filters in the UK is an efficiency of 95% against BS2831 Test Dust No 2. This is readily achieved by a number of dry, viscous treated or wet media, with high flow rates. Glass media are widely favoured and can be produced with a graduated matrix to provide extremely high dust retention capacities. There is, however, always the possibility of element migration (more so with chopped strands than continuous filament glass fibres) and for this reason glass media are not permitted in certain installations – eg hospitals and pharmaceutical and food factories, computer suites and clean rooms.

Such installations also normally employ two-stage (or even three-stage) filtration as standard in air conditioning systems – eg panel or roll filters now largely replacing other fine filter types because of the high airflow rates they can accommodate in a compact size. Bag filters are also suitable for handling recirculated air.

Alternatively, fine filtering can be provided by individual air outlet filters where flow volumes and flow rates are lower (and higher pressure drop is tolerable). Here HEPA (high efficiency particulate filters) are a particularly attractive solution, although many outlet filter modules are designed to take alternative types of pod of cartridge media. The greater resistance to flow of an ultra-fine filter medium can be offset by increasing the filter area as the actual size of the module is not critical.

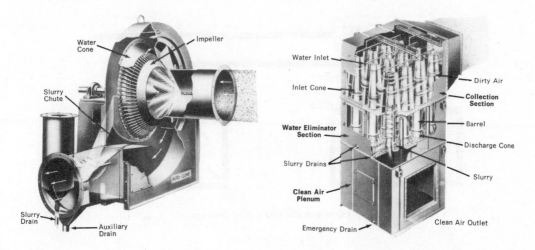

Roto-Clone wet dynamic dust collectors for control of air pollution from incinerators
(AAF Ltd)

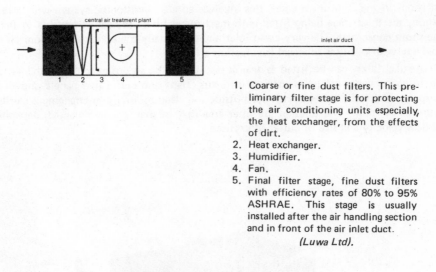

1. Coarse or fine dust filters. This preliminary filter stage is for protecting the air conditioning units especially, the heat exchanger, from the effects of dirt.
2. Heat exchanger.
3. Humidifier.
4. Fan.
5. Final filter stage, fine dust filters with efficiency rates of 80% to 95% ASHRAE. This stage is usually installed after the air handling section and in front of the air inlet duct.

(Luwa Ltd).

Fig 2 Basic air filtration system.

An example of a typical arrangement of filters in a central air treatment plant is shown in Fig 2. The primary filter (1) serves the main purpose of protecting the air conditioning units, particularly the heat exchanger (2) from dirt. This is followed by the humidifier (3) and the fan (4). The second stage filter (5) can provide finer filtering as required (also dictated by flow rate required) and is usually installed after the air handling section and in front of the inlet air duct.

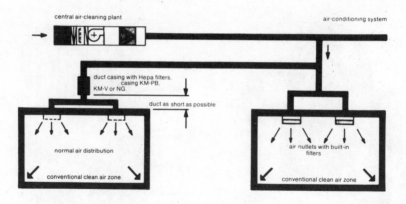

Fig 3 Conventional clean room filtration.

This basic system is shown extended to cover the filtration requirements for a conventional clean room in Fig 3. In most cases, this involves an air conditioning system with three stages of filtration, the third stage being fitted with mechanical filters as near as possible to the air outlet in the room concerned. The very clean inlet air is optimally mixed with the room air so that the desired degree of purity is achieved (rarefaction effect).

Mechanical filters can be fitted as near as possible to the air outlet to enable the air to be distributed using conventional units such as diffusors, flaps and perforated panels, shown in the left hand room. The technical equipment is outside the clean room. Filter changing is carried out outside the clean room. The duct in the filter area may or may not be enlarged, depending on the rated flow velocity and size of outlet filters used.

HEPA filter outlets for clean rooms.
(Luwa Ltd)

Replaceable cartridge HEPA filter module for clean room systems. Air leaving side shown on right. (AAF Ltd).

An alternative system is shown by the right hand room. This method of fitting filters gives several advantages: the air filtration takes place directly at the point of room entry; the filters also fulfil the function of distributing the air. This arrangement is of particular benefit for up-dating existing systems.

Possible arrangements for filters in laminar flow clean rooms are shown in Fig 4. Such systems incorporate low-turbulence displacement flow (*ie* laminar flow). Air is initially fed from a conventional central air cleaning plant. Second stage filtering/conditioning is then applied and air fed to the room through a filter wall or ceiling, providing a third stage of filtering (right hand room).

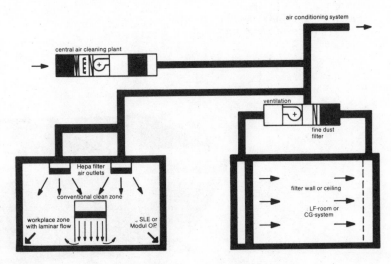

Fig 4 Laminar flow clean room filtration. (Luwa Ltd)

This stage is also designed to provide laminar flow which implies a flow velocity between 0.25 and 0.5 m/sec. A large outlet filter area is therefore necessary to provide high volume flow, *eg* occupying the whole area of the wall or ceiling.

Alternatively where only a small part of the overall clean room requires laminar flow, such systems may be formed, as in the left hand room. Here the bulk of the room is fed via conventional air outlet filters with the workplace zone fed by a separate laminar flow filter.

Vokes grease filters installed in the kitchens of a large hotel.

Grease trap filter.
(Serk Visco)

INDUSTRIAL VENTILATION

In factories a dirty atmosphere can produce an unpleasant , working environment reduce operator efficiency, shorten the life of machines, increase maintenance costs and contaminate products. The problem of air treatment is aggravated by the abnormally high concentration of heavy and/or abrasive contaminants in an industrial atmosphere. Full control may be beyond the scope of conventional filtration systems (or be uneconomic to apply). In this case special dust collecting treatment may need to be applied to specific areas.

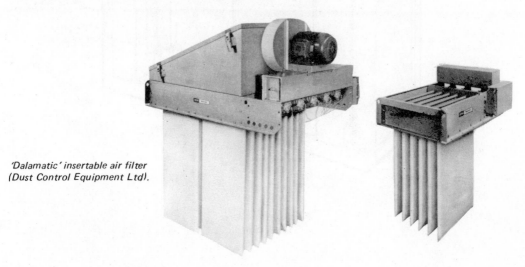

'Dalamatic' insertable air filter
(Dust Control Equipment Ltd).

Vokes 'Unipak' filter installation at a
nuclear power station.

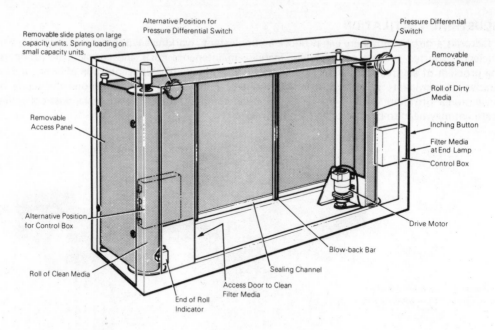

Automatic roll filter
(AAF Ltd)

Industrial dusts may range in particle size from 1 000 μm down to about 1 μm, or even down to 0.1 μm in the case of cupola dust, foundry dust, electric arc furnace dust and paint pigments. The various types of dust collectors which may be used are:-

(i)   *Fabric collectors* — relatively inexpensive units available in a wide range of types and sizes with a capture range from 100 μm down to about 0.05 μm.

(ii) *Cyclones* — working on aerodynamic principles with no moving parts and particularly suitable as primary collectors for dusts of moderate to coarse particle size (capture range down to 10 μm); or as precleaners for more efficient final collectors.

(iii) *Multicyclones* — with high collection efficiency for large exhaust gas volumes containing dust in medium concentrations (capture range down to about 8–10 μm).

(iv) *Centrifugal Skimmers* — and other similar dry working collectors operating on aerodynamic principles.

(v)   *Wet Collectors (scrubbers)* — working on aerodynamic principles in conjunction with a water spray or water wash. These include cyclone and jet type scrubbers (capture range down to 1–2 μm); and venturi-type scrubbers (capture range down to 0.1 μm with high efficiency types).

(vi) *Viscous impingement filters*

(vii) *Electrostatic precipitators* (capture range down to 0.1 μm).

(viii) *Oil Bath Dust Collectors* (capture range down to 1 μm).

(ix)   *Oil Mist Collectors* — specifically designed to trap and remove oil mist.

(x)   *Fume Extractors* — hoods, fishtails and enclosures.

(xi)   *Fume Collectors* — *eg* activated charcoal or similar absorbent filters.

See also chapters on *Filter Ratings, Contaminants, Electrostatic Precipitators, Dynamic Separators (Cyclones), Fabric Dust Collectors, Fume Extraction and Filtration, Sterile Compressed Air and Gases* and *Filters for I/C Engines.*

Fabric Dust Collectors

FABRIC FILTER collectors have a wide range of applications for dust removal from air or gas streams with a potential performance superior to that of most other types of separators and collectors — see Fig 1.

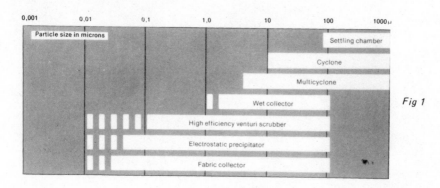

Fig 1

Actair Dynaclone dust filter installation at Fisons' Immingham fertilizer plant. It is used to prevent air pollution from the production of Nitrotop fertilizer and to recover raw materials.

Actair 130/360 dust filter installation at A. Schulman Inc. Ltd, Crumlin, Gwent. This unit is part of a new £50,000 air pollution control plant which ensures clean working conditions and prevents dust reaching local residents. It collects an average of 200 kg (440 lb) of dust each week and has a flow capacity of 36 000 m³/h (21 300 ft³/min)

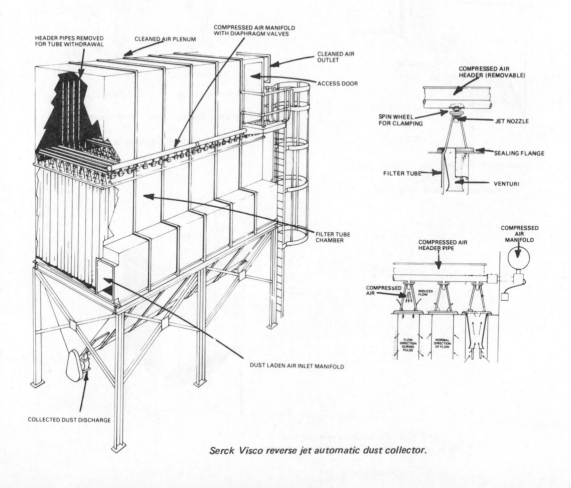

Serck Visco reverse jet automatic dust collector.

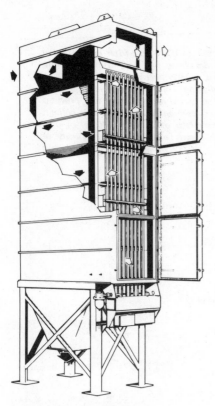

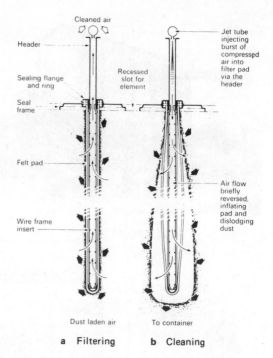

Cleaned air

Header

Sealing flange
and ring

Seal
frame

Recessed
slot for
element

Jet tube
injecting
burst of
compressed
air into
filter pad
via the
header

Felt pad

Wire frame
insert

Air flow
briefly
reversed,
inflating
pad and
dislodging
dust

Dust laden air

To container

a   Filtering   **b**   Cleaning

*Section through filter elements of
'Dalamatic' dust collector.
(Dust Control Equipment Ltd).*

*'Dalamatic' reverse jet fabric dust
collector.
(Dust Control Equipment Ltd).*

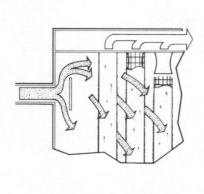

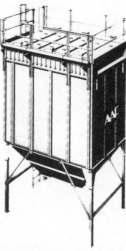

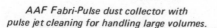

*AAF Fabri-Pulse dust collector with
pulse jet cleaning for handling large volumes.*

All fabric collectors employ the same method of separating particulate from the air stream. Dust-laden air flows through a cloth tube or envelope, where particles larger than the fabric interstices are deposited by simple sieving action. A mat or 'cake' of dust is quickly formed on the air-entering surface of the fabric. The dust cake acts as a highly efficient filter, capable of removing sub-micron dusts and fumes, while the fabric serves principally as a supporting structure for the cake.

In terms of efficiency rating, non-woven (felted) fabrics are more efficient than woven fabrics since the open areas are smaller. Similarly any type of fabric can be made more efficient by using smaller fibre diameters, closer weaving or packing and a greater weight of fibre per unit area of fabric. Increasing *efficiency*, however, naturally means a reduction in *permeability* and also in *cleanability*. Also efficiency is not a constant parameter. Efficiency increases (and permeability decreases) in service because of the cake effect, and normally is higher than new (as made) efficiency after use and cleaning. The selection of fabric is thus essentially a compromise between efficiency and cleanability and permeability.

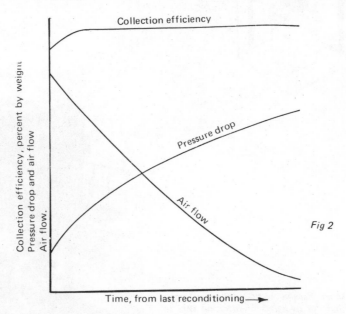

Fig 2

No fabric dust collectors can be made 100% efficient but with proper fabric selection, adequate sizing and good design they can operate at efficiencies well in excess of 99%. Typical performance characteristics are as shown in Fig 2; the end point of use (where the fabric must be cleaned) is when the resistance to flow causes a reduction in airflow to a figure below an acceptable minimum.

Types of Fabric Collectors

The two most common forms of fabric collectors are tubes (or stockings), and envelopes (or flat bags). Pleated cartridge forms are also used, but to a lesser extent. The performance of tubes and envelopes is essentially similar for the same materials and air-to-cloth ratio, the main difference being in the usual method of cleaning.

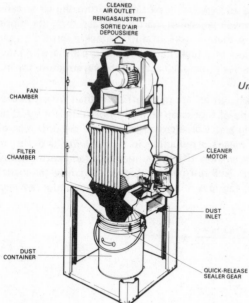

Unimaster UMA 152 dust control unit.
(Dust Control Equipment Ltd).

Actair Pacetecon PC 200 model dust filter has two tiers of filtration cells to give a flow capacity of up to 60 000 m³/h (35 400 ft³/min) within the minimum floor area.

The sizing or rating of the fabric filter is given directly by the air-to-cloth ratio expressed in terms of ft³/min per ft² of cloth (or other consistent units). This ratio, in effect, represents the average velocity of the gas stream through the filter medium and thus can also be expressed directly as *filtration velocity*. Typically this may range from 1 ft/min to 12 ft/min — see also Table I.

TABLE I — CHARACTERISTICS OF FABRIC TYPE COLLECTORS

	Interruptable Operation Light to Moderate Loading	Interruptable Operation Heavy Loading		Continuous Operation Any Loading	
Fabric reconditioning requirement	Intermittent	Continuous			
Type of reconditioning	Shaker	Shaker	Reverse Air (Low Pressure)	Reverse Pulse — (High Pressure) Pulse Jet or Fan Pulse	
Collector configuration	Single Compartment	Multiple Compartments with inlet or outlet dampers for each		Single Compartment	
Fabric Configuration	Tube or Envelope	Tube or Envelope	Tube	Tube or Envelope	Pleated-cartridge
Type Fabric	Woven	Woven		Non-Woven (Felt)	Non-Woven (Paper Mat)
Air Flow	Highly Variable	Slightly Variable		Virtually Constant	Virtually Constant
Normal rating (filtration velocity, ft/min)	1 to 6 ft/min	1 to 3 ft/min	1 to 2 ft/min	5 to 12 ft/min	$<$1 to 2.5 ft/min

AAF Amertherm high efficiency reverse air collapsing tube fabric collector. Suitable for handling large volumes of hot gases.

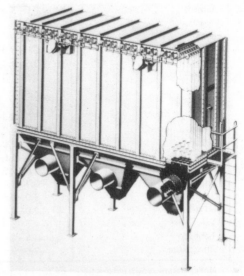

AAF Amertube snaker collector, especially suitable for the handling of fumes.

TABLE II — TYPICAL AIR TO CLOTH RATIOS (AAF Limited)

Dust	Usual Air—Cloth Ratio ($ft^3/min/ft^2$)		
	Shaker Collector	Pulse Jet	Reverse Air Collapse
Alumina	2.5–3.0	8–10	—
Asbestos	3.0–3.5	10–12	—
Bauxite	2.5–3.2	8–10	—
Carbon black	1.5–2.0	5–6	1.1–1.5
Coal	2.5–3.0	8–10	—
Cocoa, chocolate	2.8–3.2	10–12	—
Clay	2.5–3.2	9–10	1.5–2.0
Cement	2.0–3.0	8–10	1.2–1.5
Cosmetics	1.5–2.0	10–12	—
Enamel frit	2.5–3.0	6–8	1.5–2.0
Feeds, grain	3.5–5.0	14–15	—
Feldspar	2.2–2.8	9–10	—
Fertilizer	3.0–3.5	8–9	1.8–2.0
Flour	3.0–3.5	10–12	—
Graphite	2.0–2.5	5–6	1.5–2.0
Gypsum	2.0–2.5	10–12	1.8–2.0
Iron ore	3.0–3.5	10–12	—
Iron oxide	2.5–3.0	6–8	1.5–2.0
Iron sulphate	2.0–2.5	6–8	1.5–2.0
Lead oxide	2.0–2.5	6–8	1.5–1.8
Leather dust	3.5–4.0	10–12	—
Lime	2.5–3.0	10–12	1.6–2.0
Limestone	2.7–3.3	8–10	—
Mica	2.7–3.3	9–11	1.8–2.0
Paint pigments	2.5–3.0	6–8	2.0–2.2
Paper	3.5–4.0	10–12	—
Plastics	2.5–3.0	7–9	—
Quartz	2.8–3.2	9–11	—
Rock dust	3.0–3.5	8–10	—
Sand	2.5–3.0	10–12	—
Sawdust (wood)	3.5–4.0	10–12	—
Silica	2.3–2.8	7–9	1.2–1.5
Slate	3.5–4.0	10–12	—
Soap, detergents	2.0–2.5	5–6	1.2–1.5
Spices	2.7–3.3	10–12	—
Starch	3.0–3.5	8–10	—
Sugar	2.0–2.5	8–10	—
Talc	2.5–3.0	10–12	—
Tobacco	3.5–4.0	10–12	—
Zinc oxide	2.0–2.5	5–6	1.5–1.8

Note: Values tabulated are based on light to moderate loadings of granular dust having particle size and shape characteristics typical of the specific material. Ratios will normally be less when dust loading is very heavy, temperature is elevated, or particle size is smaller than commonly encountered.

Typical average figures as a general guide for sizing are of the order of 2—4 ft/min. The lighter the dust concentration and/or the more frequent the cleaning interval the higher the filtration velocities that may be employed. Air-to-dust ratio is also influenced by the type of dust involved and the method of cleaning employed — see Table II.

Reconditioning (Cleaning)

Common methods used for cleaning are by mechanical shaking, low pressure-reverse air, and high pressure-reverse jet (pulse jet). Which method is used depends on the fabric used, the configuration and the design duty cycle, and housing configuration. As regards material effect, non-woven (felted) fabrics are more difficult to clean and thus normally require high pressure-reverse jet cleaning. Woven fabric tube or envelope collectors are normally adequately cleaned by shaking or reverse flow.

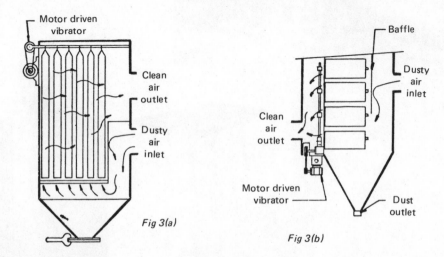

Fig 3(a)

Fig 3(b)

With a tube type collector (Fig 3a), air enters at the bottom of the tubes and dust is collected on the inside of the tubes. Gas flow is from inside to outside so that the tubes inflate during operation and do not require internal support. Used for intermittent duty cycling, air flow is stopped when cleaning is required and the tops of the tubes shaken by a vibrating mechanism to shake off collected dust. This operation can be carried out with airflow present, *ie* with the collector in continuous service, but in this case there is a distinct possibility of dust being carried through to the clean air outlet. Also cleaning will be less effective.

Shaker cleaning applied to an envelope type collector is shown in Fig 3b. With an envelope collector airflow is from outside to inside the bags causing a collapsing effect. To resist this the bags are normally supported internally with a wire mesh or fabricated wire cage. Dust collects on the outside of the bags and is readily removed either by shaking or reverse airflow. With shaker cleaning the shaker mechanism may be located in either the dirty air or clean air side compartments.

Reverse airflow cleaning may be used with tube type collectors to deflate and collapse the tubes causing the dust cake to collapse and break away. It is employed particularly with tube fabrics which could be damaged by repeated shaking, thus reducing their service life — *eg* glass fibre fabric tubes.

*Delamatic DLM 8/4/10 installed at
asbestos plant.
(Dust Control Equipment Ltd).*

*Econo-Mizer automatic dust collector.
Removable bag plate shown in smaller
detail photograph.
(Provenan Ltd).*

Continuous Duty Reconditioning

Multiple compartment collectors can be employed to provide continuous collection with automatic cleaning simply by isolating one compartment at a time for cleaning in sequence — *eg* see Fig 4. A further advantage is that since cleaning can be performed at shorter intervals higher filtration velocities can be employed.

TABLE III – CHARACTERISTICS OF FILTER FABRICS

Generic Name	Max. Temp. °F, (°C)		Physical Resistance					Chemical Resistance				
	Continuous	Intermittent	Dry Heat	Moist Heat	Abrasion	Shaking	Flexing	Mineral Acid	Organic Acid	Alkalies	Oxidizing	Solvents
Cotton	180 (80)	–	G	G	F	G	G	P	G	F	F	E
Polyester	275 (135)	–	G	F	G	E	E	G	G	F	F	E
Acrylic	275 (135)	285 (140)	G	G	G	G	E	G	G	F	G	E
Modacrylic	160 (70)	–	F	F	F	P–F	G	G	G	G	G	G
Nylon (Polyamide)	240 (115)	–	G	G	E	E	E	P	F	G	F	E
Nomex*	400 (205)	450 (230)	E	E	E	E	E	P–F	E	G	G	E
Polypropylene	200 (95)	250 (120)	G	F	E	E	G	E	E	E	G	G
PTFE	500 (260)	550 (290)	E	E	P–F	G	G	E	E	E	E	E
Fluorocarbon	450 (230)	–	E	E	P–F	G	G	E	E	E	E	E
Vinyon	350 (175)	–	F	F	F	G	G	E	E	G	G	P
Glass	550 (290)	600 (315)	E	E	P	P	F	E	E	F	E	E
Wool	215 (100)	250 (120)	F	F	G	F	G	F	F	P	P	F

*Du Pont

Key: E = Excellent   F = Fair   G = Good   P = Poor

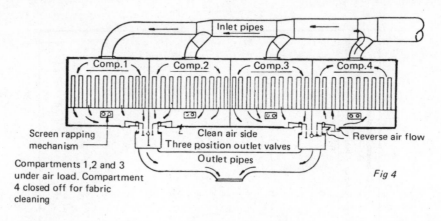

Screen rapping mechanism

Clean air side
Three position outlet valves
Outlet pipes

Reverse air flow

Compartments 1,2 and 3 under air load. Compartment 4 closed off for fabric cleaning

Fig 4

Reverse-Pulse Cleaning

Cleaning by the application of reverse-pulses of high pressure air is normally applied to tube and envelope collectors employing felted fabrics (and to pleated cartridge collectors). The high pressure pulses may be created by a pressure blower (fan), or come directly from a compressed air supply. In the latter case the type is normally called a *pulse-jet* collector.

For reverse-pulse cleaning all types, including tube collectors, collect dust on the *outside* and have flow from outside to inside (see Fig 5). Internal supports are thus necessary to prevent the bags from collapsing. The pulse of cleaning air is then introduced at the clean air side, the resulting

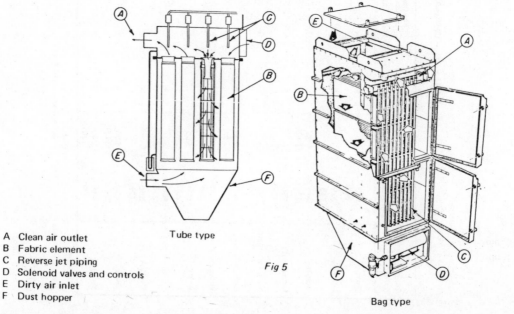

A Clean air outlet
B Fabric element
C Reverse jet piping
D Solenoid valves and controls
E Dirty air inlet
F Dust hopper

Tube type

Fig 5

Bag type

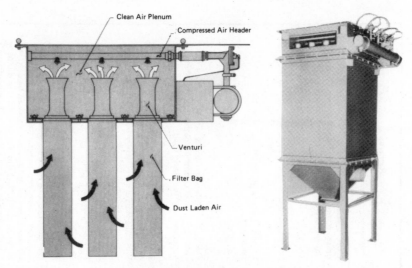

AAF Fabri-Pak dust collector with pulse jet cleaning.

reverse flow snapping the bags away from their supporting cage, breaking the dust cake and blowing the fabric clean. At the same time the severe flow deposits the removed dust in the collector or dust holder, preventing any outflow during the cleaning interval.

The complete pulse cleaning cycle occurs very rapidly — *ie* within a tenth of a second or less — after which normal flow is restored. Effectively, therefore, the collector operates continuously, with pulse cleaning frequency adjusted as required — *eg* typically at one to ten minute intervals. Only a small percentage of the fabric is cleaned at one time (typically 10%), which, together with the very short reconditioning cycle, makes high filtration velocities possible. Actual filtration velocity employed may, however, need to be limited to minimize re-entrainment of dust from a cleaned area onto adjacent fabric surfaces. This effect is more marked with cartridge type collectors than tube or envelope types.

TABLE IV — COMMON APPLICATIONS OF FABRIC DUST COLLECTORS

Steel Making
Electric arc furnaces
Open-hearth furnaces
Basic oxygen furnaces
Sintering machines
Kish collection

Rock Products
Cement kilns
Clinker coolers
Perlite expanding furnaces
Asphalt plants
lightweight aggregate kilns

Mining
Smelters
Ore roasters
Calciners
Crushing and screening
Materials handling
Pelletizing plants

Foundries
Cupolas
Sand systems
Abrasive cleaning
Reverbatory furnaces
Induction furnaces

Other Industries
Food processing
Pharmaceuticals
Metalworking
Woodworking
Chemical processing

Coal and coke handling
Grain handling and storage

TABLE V – FABRIC COLLECTOR SELECTION GUIDE (AAF)

Operation	Dust Loading*	Particle Size	Tube or Envelope Collectors	Pulse Jet Collectors	Remarks
Ceramics					
Materials handling	Light	Fine	Occasional	Usual	Dust released from bin-filling, weighing, mixing, pressing, and forming. Refractory products screening and dry pan operations more severe.
Felting and grinding	Med-Hvy	Fine-Med	Occasional	Usual	
Spraying	Lt-Med	Medium	Occasional	Occasional	
Chemicals					
Materials handling	Lt-Hvy	Varies	Frequent	Usual	Includes conveying, elevating, mixing and packaging.
Crushing and grinding	Med-Hvy	Varies	Usual	Usual	
Weighing and screening	Lt-Mod	Fine-Med	Rare	Usual	
Roasters, kilns, dryers	Heavy	Med-Coarse	Frequent	No	Gas stream cooling is usually necessary when fabric collector is used and/or insulated housing. Wet collectors are frequently used.
Bin ventilation	Light	Fine-Med	Rare	Usual	
Foundry					
Abrasive cleaning	Mod-Hvy	Fine-Med	Frequent	Frequent	Wet collectors are frequently used.
Swing frame grinders	Moderate	Med-Coarse	Rare	Occasional	High-efficiency dry centrifugal collectors are frequently used.
Shakeout	Lt-Mod	Fine	Occasional	Occasional	**Wet collectors are frequently used.**
Sand Handling	Moderate	Fine-Med	Rare	Rare	Wet collectors are frequently used.
Tumbling mills	Heavy	Med-Coarse	Occasional	Occasional	Wet collectors are frequently used.
Cupola	Moderate	Varies	Frequent	No	Gas stream cooling is usually necessary when fabric collector is used and/or insulated housing. High-efficiency dry centrifugal collector can be used when codes permit 0.20 grains per cubic foot in discharge. Venturi-type high-energy scrubber frequently used.
Non-ferrous melting	Varies	Ext-Fine	Usual	Occasional	Gas stream cooling is usually necessary when fabric collector is used and/or insulated housing. Venturi-type high-energy scrubber frequently used.

cont...

					Remarks
Grain					
Materials handling	Light	Medium	Rare	Usual	
Feed mill	Moderate	Medium	Rare	Usual	
Coolers	Moderate	Medium	Rare	Usual	
Bin-ventilation	Light	Medium	Rare	Usual	
Metalworking					
Production grinding	Light	Coarse	No	Occasional	High-efficiency dry centrifugal collectors are frequently used.
Tool room	Light	Fine	No	Occasional	High-efficiency dry centrifugal collectors are frequently used.
Polishing and buffing	Light	Varies	No	Rare	Wet collectors are frequently used.
Cast iron machining	Moderate	Varies	No	Occasional	Oil-bath air cleaning is preferred collection method.
Pharmaceutical and Food Products					
Mixing, grinding, weighing, blending, packaging	Light	Medium	Occasional	Usual	
Coating pans	Varies	Fine-Med	Occasional	Frequent	Wet collectors are frequently used.
Sugar handling	Light	Fine-Med	Rare	Usual	
Sugar granulators	Moderate	Fine-Med	No	No	Wet collectors are frequently used.
Rock Products and Metal Mining					
Materials handling	Mod-Hvy	Fine-Med	Rare	Frequent	Wet collectors are frequently used.
Crushing and screening	Heavy	Medium	Rare	Frequent	Wet collectors are frequently used.
Dryers, kilns	Mod-Hvy	Med-Coarse	Frequent	Frequent	Gas stream cooling is usually necessary when fabric collector is used and/or insulated housing. Wet collectors are frequently used.
Coolers	Moderate	Coarse	Frequent	Frequent	Wet collectors are frequently used.

cont...

TABLE V – FABRIC COLLECTOR SELECTION GUIDE (AAF) (contd.)

Operation	Dust Loading*	Particle Size*	Tube or Envelope Collectors	Pulse Jet Collectors	Remarks
Rubber and Plastic Products					
Mixers	Moderate	Fine	Rare	Usual	Wet collectors are frequently used.
Batchout rolls	Light	Fine	Rare	Frequent	Wet collectors are frequently used.
Talc dusting	Moderate	Medium	Rare	Frequent	
Grinding and buffing	Moderate	Coarse	Rare	Occasional	High-efficiency dry centrifugal collectors are frequently used.
Plastics material handling	Moderate	Medium	No	Frequent	Includes conveying, elevating, mixing and packaging.
Plastic finishing	Light	Fine-Med	No	Frequent	
Steel Mills					
Basic oxygen furnace	Med-Hvy	Ext-Fine	Occasional	No	Venturi-type high-energy scrubber frequently used.
Electric arc furnace	Light	Ext-Fine	Usual	No	Gas stream cooling is usually necessary when fabric collector is used and/or insulated housing. Venturi-type high-energy scrubber frequently used.
Open hearth	Med-Hvy	Fine	Occasional	No	Venturi-type high-energy scrubber frequently used.
Blast furnace	Heavy	Varies	No	No	Venturi-type high-energy scrubber frequently used.
Kish	Medium	Med-Coarse	Rare	No	Graphite particles formed when pouring high-carbon iron. Dry centrifugal cyclone is a popular and economical choice.
Coal and coke handling	Moderate	Medium	Usual	Frequent	Wet collectors are frequently used.
Sintering machines	Med-Hvy	Fine-Med	Frequent	No	Gas stream cooling is usually necessary when fabric collector is used and/or insulated housing. Wet collectors are frequently used.
Coke screening	Med-Hvy	Med-Coarse	Rare	No	Wet collectors are frequently used.
Materials handling	Med-Hvy	Fine-Med	Rare	Usual	Wet collectors are frequently used.
Woodworking					
Saws	Moderate	Varies	Frequent	Usual	High-efficiency dry centrifugal collectors are frequently used.
Sanding	Moderate	Fine	Frequent	Usual	High-efficiency dry centrifugal collectors are frequently used.
Hogging	Heavy	Varies	Frequent	Frequent	High-efficiency dry centrifugal collectors are frequently used.

cont...

	Dust Loading	Particle Size			
Miscellaneous					
Bakeries	Moderate	Medium	No	Occasional	High-efficiency dry centrifugal collectors are frequently used.
Brake lining sanding and grinding	Heavy	Medium	Occasional	Occasional	Wet collectors are frequently used.
Bronzing machines	Moderate	Medium	Occasional	Occasional	High-efficiency dry centrifugal collectors are frequently used.
Coal					
Material handling	Moderate	Medium	Usual	Frequent	Wet collectors are frequently used.
Dedusting	Heavy	Medium	Frequent	Frequent	Wet collectors are frequently used.
Bunker ventilation	Light	Fine	Occasional	Frequent	High-efficiency dry centrifugal collectors are frequently used.
Cosmetics	Varies	Fine-Med	Usual	Usual	
Cotton flocking	Light	Medium	No	Rare	High-efficiency dry centrifugal collectors are frequently used.
Lead battery plants	Light	Fine-Med	Usual	Frequent	Wet collectors are frequently used.
Leather buffing	Moderate	Medium	No	Occasional	Wet collectors are frequently used.
Leather sanding	Moderate	Fine-Med	Rare	Occasional	Wet collectors are frequently used.
Metal powders	Varies	Fine-Med	Usual	Usual	
Metal reclaiming	Varies	Ext-Fine	Usual	Occasional	Gas stream cooling is usually necessary when fabric collector is used and/or insulated housing. Venturi-type high-energy scrubber frequently used.
Paper cutting	Moderate	Medium	No	Occasional	
Paper grinding	Mod-Hvy	Medium	No	Rare	
School woodworking	Moderate	Varies	Rare	No	High-efficiency dry centrifugal collectors are frequently used.

*The listings under 'Dust Loading' and 'Particle Size' are averages and will vary from job to job. The ranges are as follows:-

Dust Loading

Light .... ½ to 2 grains/ft³
Medium .... 2 to 3 grains/ft³
Moderate .... 3 to 5 grains/ft³
Heavy .... Over 5 grains/ft³

Particle Size

Extremely Fine .... 50% in ½ to 2 µm range
Fine .... 50% in 2 to 7 µm range
Medium .... 50% in 7 to 15 µm range
Coarse .... 50% above 15 µm

Fume Extraction and Filtration

INDUSTRIAL FUMES may consist of *'dry smoke'* (*eg* given off by welding operations, certain machining operations, *etc*), or *'wet smoke'* aerosols — such as oil mist or other liquid products in mist form, or mixtures of both. Such contaminants can be removed from the immediate atmosphere by extraction, which to be properly effective must collect the fumes at source. The heavily contaminated extract must then be filtered to provide a non-polluting exhaust.

There are three basic methods of extracting unwanted fumes:-

(i)   *Hoods* — As a general solution, large hoods are not an efficient way of collecting fume. They require large volumes of air and often restrict light from the working area. Most hooded systems require airflows of at least 2000 ft^3/min, and as such tend to cost more than the ducted system which may only need to employ about 350 ft^3/min. Hoods are sometimes unavoidable, but should generally be used only as a last resort.

(ii) *Fishtails* — Fishtails provide a relatively high velocity of extraction over a small area. Typical applications include extraction of welding fume and the removal of oil mist for certain types of unguarded machine tools. They can be mounted so that they may be moved, either on a swinging arm or by a magnetic clamp, and should in no way adversely affect the operation undertaken. These usually have a slotted area equal to the cross sectional area of the extract duct (say 12 in x 2.3/8 in for a 6 in duct). Such a fishtail extracting between 400—500 ft^3/min may solve most problems if mounted approximately 9 in away from the source of fume emission. Welding fumes, because of the small area over which they are generated, may have extraction rates as low as 120 ft^3/min drawn through extraction slots no more than 3 in x 1 in. In collecting fume directly at source, it is sometimes necessary to ensure that solid matter such as swarf, or indeed liquid droplets, are not entrained, and accordingly it will be necessary to experiment with the positioning of the fishtail to produce optimum results. The object of the exercise is to create an extraction velocity of approximately 100 ft/min at the source of emission. Cross draughts, heat and other factors will also have a bearing on the positioning and extraction rate.

(iii)   *Enclosure* — Ideally fume created by operations such as machine tools should be enclosed. Such enclosures help to prevent splashing and contain fume. In the case of machine tools many machine tool manufacturers fit oil mist extraction and filtration equipment as standard. Here again, the degree of extraction is important. The object is to design a system having an extraction rate so that relatively clean workshop air is drawn into the fume generating area rather than allow the fume to escape around the sides of the enclosure or when the doors are opened.

In order to keep the working area under a negative pressure, approximately 150 ft^3/min is required for every square foot of open area around the guards. The size of the enclosure may also have a bearing on the extraction rate as very large enclosures will naturally require a higher rate of extraction to obtain the same air change rate. The figure quoted above will, for most applications, provide a satisfactory solution, but again the point of extraction may require minor adjustment. The extraction point should, where possible, be away from the working area and so reduce the possibility of drawing off unwanted solid matter, liquid, *etc.*

There are other methods of extraction which are less commonly employed. These include lip extractors which may often be used around fume creating tanks, and powerful floor mounted ducts such as may be adopted in certain foundries. These are the exception rather than the rule, and expert advice should be sought if considering these methods.

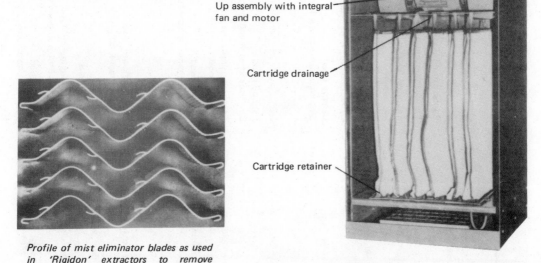

Up assembly with integral fan and motor

Cartridge drainage

Cartridge retainer

Profile of mist eliminator blades as used in 'Rigidon' extractors to remove moisture carry-over from wet scrubber exhausts.

AAF Oil-Pak oil mist collector with forced flow incorporates pre-filter and large efficiency bag type filter cartridges.

RECOMMENDED VELOCITIES FOR EXHAUST HOODS*
Area of slot or face (sq ft) × Velocity (ft/min) = ft^3/min

Process	Type of Hood	Required air velocity, ft/min
Aluminium furnaces	Enclosed hood, open one side	150–200 over open face
	Canopy hood	200–250 over face
Bottle washing	Enclosed booth, open one side	150–250 over face
Brass furnaces	Enclosed hood, open one side	200–250 over open face
	Canopy hood	250–300 over face
Chemical laboratories	Enclosed hood, door front	100 over door opening
	Enclosed hood, open front	100–150 over face
	Down draught, table type	150–200 over table area
Degreasing	Canopy hood	125–150 over face
	Slot type, tanks up to 4 ft wide	2 ft wide, 1500–2000 through 2 inch slot one side
		3 ft wide, 1500–2000 through 4 inch slot one side
		4 ft wide, 1500–2000 through 6 inch slot one side
		Over 4 ft wide, use slots on four sides
Driers	Canopy hood	125–150 over face
	Slot type at each end, continuous dryer	150–200 over 6 to 8 inch slot
Electric welding	Enclosed booth, open front	100–150 over face
	Canopy hood	125–150 over face
Electroplating	Canopy hood	125–150 over face
	Slot type, tanks up to 4 ft wide	2 ft wide, 1500–2000 through 2 inch slot one side
		3 ft wide, 1500–2000 through 4 inch slot one side
		4 ft wide, 1500–2000 through 6 inch slot one side
		Over 4 ft wide, use slots on four sides
Foundry shakeout	Enclosed booth, open front	150–200 over face
	Down draught, grill type	300–500
Grain dust, wood, flour, etc.	Slot type	2000 through 2 to 4 inch slot
	Canopy hood	500–600 over face
Grinding (disc) and sanding	Down draught, grill type	250–300 over open face
	Bench type with slot one side	2000–2500 through 4 inch slot
Hand forge	Canopy hood	150–250 over face
	Enclosed booth, open one side	200–300 over face

Kitchen range	Canopy hood	125—150 over face
Metal spraying	Enclosed booth, open one side	200—250 over face
Paint spraying	Enclosed booth, open one side	125—200 over face
Paper machine	Canopy type	200—300 over face
Pickling tanks	Canopy hood	250—350 over face
	Slot type, tanks up to 6 ft wide, slot one side	Minimum 4 inch slot 2000—5000 through slot
Quenching tanks	Canopy hood	200—300 over face
Rubber mixing rolls	Canopy hood	200—300 over face
	Slot type	2000—2400 through 2 inch slot
Soldering booths	Enclosed booth, open one side	150—200 over face
Steam tanks	Canopy hood	200 over face
	Slot type, tanks up to 6 ft wide, slot one side	1500—2000 through 4 inch minimum slot
Stone cutting	Enclosed booth, open face	400—500 over face
Turning tanks	Slot type, tanks up to 4 ft wide, slot one side	2 ft wide, 1700—2500 through 2 inch slot 3 ft wide, 1700—2500 through 4 inch slot 4 ft wide, 1700—2500 through 6 inch slot
Varnish kettles	Canopy hood	250—300 over face
	Slot type, all round slot	2 inch minimum slot, 2000 through slot

*Vokes Limited

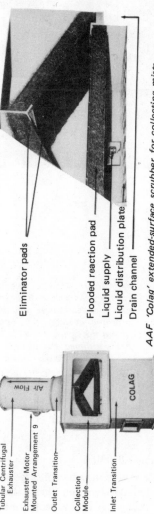

Eliminator pads
Flooded reaction pad
Liquid supply
Liquid distribution plate
Drain channel

Tubular Centrifugal Exhauster
Exhauster Motor Mounted Arrangement 9
Outlet Transition
Collection Module
Inlet Transition
Air Flow
COLAG

AAF 'Colag' extended-surface scrubber for collecting mists, vapours and fumes.

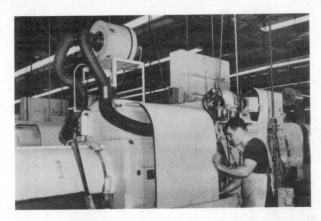

AAF Dynapure centrifugal oil mist collector with dual take-offs exhausting large screw machine.

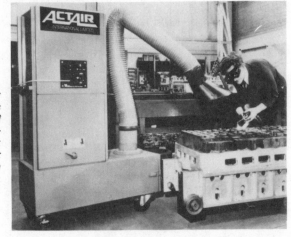

An Actair Traveller electrostatic air cleaner used by C & B Smith Foundries Ltd to collect power welding fumes and overspray at source. The operator working on this cylinder head jacket core box has positioned the flexible intake duct so that pollution is drawn away from him.

Fume Filtration

Dry smoke may be collected by impingement — bag and paper type filters, as well as electrostatic and electrodynamic filters. Very high efficiencies may be obtained by either method. In the case of paper/bag filters, replacement becomes necessary from time to time, whereas on the electrostatic type of unit regular cleaning is most important. There are, however, some electrostatic units which have automatic or semi-automatic wash facilities, which, although desirable, may prove an expensive option.

Wet smoke — or aerosols — are liquid droplets ranging from $10-0.5$ μm suspended in air. These may be filtered by bag-type filters, electrostatic/electrodynamic filters or centrifugal impaction units. Bag-type filters prove effective and have the advantage of being cheap. However, bag changing is not an enjoyable experience and moreover the filtrate then requires disposal. Electrostatic units are more expensive and more effective with very light contamination as the liquid collected drains off the collection plates under gravity. This builds up a stain on the plates and regular cleaning becomes necessary if the filtration efficiency is to be preserved.

Industrial electrostatic collector cell with slide rails.
(AAF Ltd)

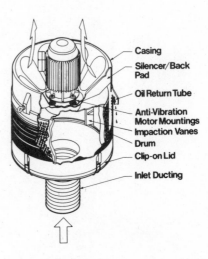

Casing
Silencer/Back Pad
Oil Return Tube
Anti-Vibration Motor Mountings
Impaction Vanes
Drum
Clip-on Lid
Inlet Ducting

Filtermist centrifugal impaction filter drawing off oil fumes from a rivet-making machine, eliminating workshop pollution and allowing the operator a clear view of the task in hand.
(The Filtermist Company Limited)

A schematic diagram of a Filtermist centrifugal impaction filter. Directly driven by an electric motor, a drum filter with impaction plates draws off oil mist and forces the particles to impact and coalesce before being drained off for reuse.
(The Filtermist Company Limited)

Centrifugal impaction units offer certain advantages. Filtration efficiency, although not as high as clean electrostatic filter, still provides very high efficiencies down to 0.5 μm without any deterioration in use. The centrifugal action imposes approximately 1 000 g on the aerosol, and consequently the collectors become self cleaning. By their very simplicity they are easy to look after and cost little when compared with electrostatic systems.

Centrifugal Impaction Filters

Unlike other filtration systems, the centrifugal impaction filters are self-cleaning and a high filtration efficiency is constantly maintained. A perforated steel drum is directly driven by an electric motor while blades in the drum's interior generate suction to draw in the oil mist via ducting. Oil mist is impacted by the blades at velocities in excess of 50 metres per second and particles are forced to coalesce before being thrown by centrifugal force against the inner surface of the outer casing. Cleaned air is returned to the workshop while pressure within the casing ensures that the liquid oil is continually drained away via a discharge duct for re-use.

See also chapters on *Wet Scrubbers, Electrostatic Precipitators, Fabric Dust Collectors* and *Dynamic Separators.*

Machine Intake Air Filters

THE SIMPLEST form of an effective machine intake filter is an element of pleated paper housed in a suitable casing. The pleats provide both rigidity for the element, so that it requires a minimum of support, and at the same time a large surface area. This area may further be increased by corrugating as well as pleating the paper.

A typical filter of this type is shown in Fig 1. Air is invariably drawn from the outside to the inside, so that dust particles and other solid contaminants are trapped or stopped by the outer surface of the element, where they may cling or fall to the bottom of the casing. Filters of this type are widely used for air cleaning on internal combustion engine air intakes and similar duties where flow rates are moderate and pressure drop must be kept to a low figure (normally not more than 2 to 5 lb/in^2 (0.1 to 0.3 bar)).

Variations include the use of pleated felt and other media although these do not have any specific advantages over impregnated paper for light duty applications. Felt elements normally need support with wire mesh or similar reinforcement to withstand pressures up to 100 lb/in^2 (7 bar) — pleated paper is capable of withstanding pressures of that order without reinforcement.

Fig 1 Pleated paper element and (right) cartridge type pleated paper filter.

Neither type is suitable for higher pressures, even with reinforcement, without danger of disruption, or at least migration, of the element.

In the case of fabric filters for air, detail design of the filter element may differ appreciably from the standard pleated form. An example is shown in Fig 2 where the fabric is mounted on wire gauze and folded into a star shaped formation. This results in a very high surface area and consequently low flow velocities over the surface of the fabric. A fabric element may also be preferred to a paper element for heavy duty industrial filters.

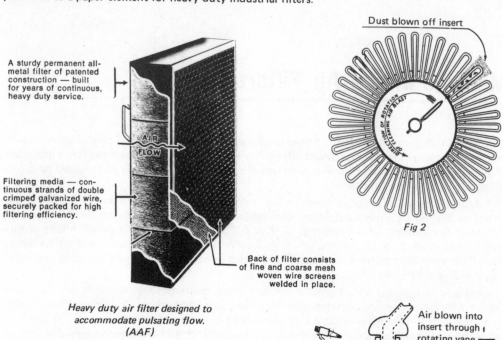

A sturdy permanent all-metal filter of patented construction — built for years of continuous, heavy duty service.

AIR FLOW

Filtering media — continuous strands of double crimped galvanized wire, securely packed for high filtering efficiency.

Back of filter consists of fine and coarse mesh woven wire screens welded in place.

Heavy duty air filter designed to accommodate pulsating flow. (AAF)

Dust blown off insert

Fig 2

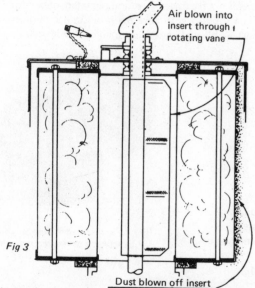

Air blown into insert through rotating vane

Fig 3

Dust blown off insert

Simple dry filters may have replaceable or cleanable elements, depending on the size and design duty. Some designs provide for cleaning *in situ* (without removal of the element) this normally being accomplished by reverse flow. Others may provide *in situ* cleaning by reverse flow accompanied by mechanical agitation. A typical example is shown in Fig 3 where a vane is incorporated in the centre of the filter. For reverse flow cleaning an air supply is connected to the top of the hollow central bolt and at the same time this bolt is turned by hand to rotate the vane. A blast of air is thus directed into each pleat of the element in turn, blowing off dust which has collected on the outer surface.

Where flow rates are relatively high, or the air pressure is in excess of, say, 40 lb/in^2 (3 bar) there is some advantage in deflecting the incoming air by louvres or vanes, or by the shape of the entry so that it enters the filter body with a swirling motion. The centrifugal flow pattern resulting will carry solids and moisture in suspension outwards to impinge on the casing walls. The resulting loss of particle velocity will then cause the suspension to drop to the bottom of the casing whilst the remainder of the air passes through the filter element from the outside to the inside in the normal manner. This is the principle employed in compressed air line filters.

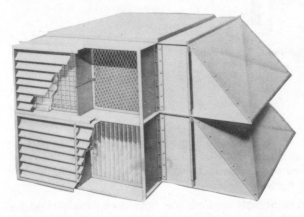

Filters and filter housing for engine or compressor house intake air cleaning. (AAF)

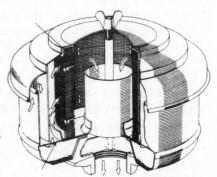

Fig 4 Oil-bath air filter.

Oil Bath Filters

The oil bath filter — Fig 4 — combines both 'wet' filtering and viscous-impingement action. In this case air is initially drawn through the oil in the bottom of the housing, the oil separating out and retaining a proportion of the solid contaminants. Air and remaining contaminants together with an oil mist are then drawn upwards to impinge on the filter element, which is usually made of woven steel wire. This element or screen is continuously wetted by the oil mist and thus acts as a viscous-impingement filter. At the same time, since there is a continual feed of oil mist to the filter, condensation of oil takes place on the surface and the oil will fall back into the oil bath carrying some dust with it. The actual filter element in this case is partially self-cleaning whilst contaminants continue to collect in the oil bath.

Provided the oil level is properly maintained, and the contaminants removed or the oil changed when necessary, the performance of an oil-bath filter should be high and consistent. It has, however, largely been replaced by other types for specific duties, such as 'dry' air intake filters on modern internal combustion engines.

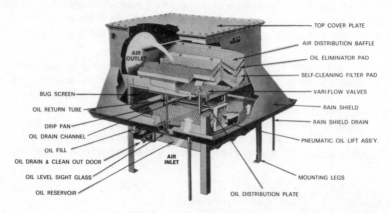

AAF 'Cycoil' intake filter for larger marine engines.

Stationary Installation

Stationary machines installed in factories, *etc,* are normally located in machine houses or separate rooms, taking intake air via ducting from an outside wall with suitable filter(s) incorporated. Alternatively the complete machine house is treated as a 'clean room'. In this case conventional panel type intake filters are normally installed in the wall.

Care is necessary to ensure that the type of filter used matches both the equipment and the characteristics of the application. Specifically a more robust filter is needed where pulsatory air flow has to be accommodated — see Table I.

See also chapters *Filters for I/C Engines, Compressed Air Treatment* and *Bulk Air Filters.*

TABLE I — MACHINES CHARACTERIZED BY INTAKE AIR FLOW

Pulsating Air Flow	Smooth Air Flow
Reciprocating compressors	Centrifugal fans
Naturally aspirated engines	Centrifugal blowers
Pump scavanged engines	Centrifugal compressors
Crankcase scavanged engines	Rotary lobe type blades
	Axial compressors
	Sliding vane compressors
	Rotary screw compressors
	Naturally aspirated engines

Compressed Air Treatment

THE CONTAMINANTS likely to be found in compressed air fall into the following categories:

(i)   Atmospheric dust, smoke and fumes inducted by the compressor;
      atmospheric bacteria and viruses.

(ii) Water vapour inducted and passed through the compressor.

(iii) Gases generated in the compressor.

(iv) Oil carried over from the compressor.

(v)   Solid contaminants generated within the system.

A pair of fabricated housing filters for the removal of contaminants from compressed air systems.
(Domnick Hunter Filters Ltd).

The degree of treatment required depends on the application. For general industrial applications, *eg* using mains for compressed air supplies, partial water removal by aftercooling the air delivered by the compressor followed by filter treatment to remove solid contaminants down to a specific size may be adequate. At the other extreme two or more stages of filtering may be required, including oil removal after which the air may be further conditioned by drying to provide humidity control.

Inducted Contaminants

Industrial stationary compressors are normally installed in separate rooms divorced from factory-generated contaminants and drawing air from the outside atmosphere. The level of dust concentration present is likely to be of the order of 0.6 to 3.0 x 10^{-6} lb/ft^3 (10 to 50 mg/m^3). More or less standard practice is to fit the compressor with an intake filter (panel filter down to paper cartridge type depending on the size of the compressor) having an efficiency of 99.9% based on the following likely dust concentration present in ambient air:

The air intake filter can, therefore, be expected to pass all particles smaller than 5 μm, (as well as a proportion of larger sizes), in addition to atmospheric water vapour. It will also pass all gases, vapours, odours, bacteria and viruses.

Dust size (μm)	% total weight
5	12
5 – 10	12
10 – 20	14
20 – 40	23
40 – 80	30
80 – 200	9

Water

Ambient air always contains water vapour. After leaving the compressor the air is fully saturated with water vapour, the actual amount of water vapour present being directly proportional to the temperature of the air and inversely proportional to the pressure (see Tables IA, IB, IC). Thus liquid water is best removed when the temperature of the air is lowest and the pressure is at its highest — *ie* immediately on leaving the compressor.

TABLE IA – MOISTURE CONTENT OF SATURATED COMPRESSED AIR

Air Temp °F	Air Pressure – Pounds per Square Inch (lb/in^2) gauge												
	0	30	40	50	60	70	80	90	100	110	120	130	150
32	4.34	1.43	1.16	0.98	0.85	0.75	0.67	0.61	0.55	0.51	0.47	0.44	0.38
40	6.00	2.09	1.60	1.36	1.16	1.03	0.91	0.84	0.77	0.70	0.65	0.60	0.52
50	8.69	2.87	2.35	1.93	1.70	1.52	1.43	1.23	1.12	1.02	0.95	0.89	0.79
60	12.41	4.10	3.32	2.80	2.35	2.13	1.90	1.77	1.58	1.46	1.35	1.26	1.10
70	17.85	5.90	5.05	4.08	3.52	3.10	2.66	2.52	2.28	2.10	1.95	1.82	1.59
80	24.97	8.25	6.80	5.70	4.87	4.35	3.88	3.52	3.20	2.93	2.78	2.53	2.23
90	30.81	10.20	9.33	7.90	6.78	6.00	5.33	4.90	4.42	4.06	3.76	3.50	3.13
100	43.40	14.30	12.70	10.80	9.28	8.25	7.32	6.93	6.03	5.57	5.15	4.80	4.20
110	64.50	21.30	18.80	14.60	12.60	11.10	9.85	8.98	8.12	7.46	6.93	6.45	5.66
120	87.00	28.70	23.20	19.70	16.80	14.80	13.30	11.60	10.90	10.10	9.30	8 67	7 56

TABLE IB – MOISTURE CONTENT OF AIR
(pounds of water per 1 000 cubic feet of air)

Relative Humidity (%)	Air Temperature (°F)										
	50	55	60	65	70	75	80	85	90	95	100
10	0.06	0.07	0.08	0.10	0.12	0.14	0.16	0.19	0.22	0.26	0.31
20	0.12	0.14	0.17	0.20	0.24	0.28	0.33	0.38	0.45	0.52	0.61
30	0.18	0.21	0.25	0.30	0.35	0.42	0.49	0.58	0.67	0.79	0.92
40	0.24	0.28	0.34	0.40	0.47	0.56	0.66	0.77	0.90	1.05	1.22
50	0.30	0.35	0.42	0.50	0.59	0.70	0.82	0.95	1.12	1.31	1.53
60	0.36	0.43	0.50	0.60	0.71	0.83	0.98	1.15	1.34	1.57	1.84
70	0.42	0.50	0.59	0.70	0.83	0.97	1.15	1.34	1.57	1.83	2.14
80	0.48	0.57	0.67	0.80	0.94	1.11	1.31	1.53	1.79	2.10	2.45
90	0.54	0.64	0.75	0.90	1.06	1.25	1.58	1.72	2.02	2.36	2.75
100	0.60	0.71	0.84	1.00	1.18	1.39	1.64	1.92	2.24	2.82	3.06

TABLE IC – MOISTURE CONTENT OF SATURATED COMPRESSED AIR

Example – 1 m^3 of air at atmospheric conditions fully saturated at 20°C contains 17.4 g of water vapour. When compressed to 6.3 bar and 50°C it can only retain 11.2 g as vapour ∴ 6.2 g (17.4–11.2) is released as liquid water. If cooled down to 25°C a further quantity of 7.93 g (11.2–3.27) of water will condense out

WATER VAPOUR CONTENT OF FULLY SATURATED COMPRESSED AIR
Grams of water vapour per cubic metre (g/m^3) of air at standard atmospheric pressure of 1013 mbar (0 bar gauge) and saturation conditions and when compressed to the pressure and temperature shown

Air Temp °C	AIR PRESSURE IN BARS												
	0	0.4	0.63	1.0	1.6	2.5	4.0	6.3	8.0	10.0	12.5	16.0	20.0
0	4.82	3.45	2.97	2.42	1.87	1.39	0.97	0.67	0.54	0.44	0.36	0.29	0.23
5	6.88	4.93	4.24	3.46	2.68	1.99	1.39	0.95	0.77	0.63	0.52	0.41	0.33
10	9.41	6.74	5.80	4.73	3.66	2.72	1.90	1.30	1.06	0.87	0.70	0.56	0.45
15	12.7	9.08	7.83	6.39	4.94	3.67	2.56	1.76	1.43	1.17	0.95	0.76	0.61
20	17.4	12.5	10.7	8.75	6.77	5.02	3.51	2.41	1.95	1.60	1.30	1.04	0.84
25	23.6	16.9	14.6	11.9	9.18	6.82	4.77	3.27	2.65	2.17	1.77	1.40	1.14
30	30.5	21.8	18.8	15.3	11.9	8.81	6.16	4.22	3.43	2.81	2.29	1.81	1.47
35	39.0	27.9	24.0	19.6	15.2	11.3	7.87	5.40	4.38	3.59	2.92	2.32	1.88
40	49.6	35.5	30.6	24.9	19.3	14.3	10.0	6.87	5.57	4.55	3.72	2.95	2.39
45	63.5	45.5	39.2	31.9	24.7	18.3	12.8	8.79	7.13	5.84	4.76	3.77	3.06
50	81.0	58.0	49.9	40.7	31.5	23.4	16.4	11.2	9.10	7.45	6.07	4.82	3.90

Standard practice is to follow the compressor with an aftercooler which should be of sufficient size and cooling capacity to reduce the temperature of the outgoing air to within 8–10 degC of the temperature of the water entering the aftercooler. Cooling in the aftercooler may be by ambient air or water. In the latter case approximately 20 litres of water will be required for every 2.5 m^3 of free air being cooled in a typical system to realize the above performance.

A receiver following the aftercooler, and located in the coolest place possible, will permit further cooling and water condensation.

For compressors operating at pressures in the region of 7 bar gauge the size of the receiver in litres should be approximately equal to thirty times the rated free air delivery of the compressor in dm^3/s, ie a compressor rated at 50 dm^3/s free air delivery requires a receiver of approximately 1 500 litres capacity.

As further cooling may occur in the distribution mains themselves, these should be laid out with a pitch in the direction of air flow so that both gravity and air flow will carry water to drain legs located at appropriate intervals. These should be fitted with automatic drain valves to prevent them becoming flooded.

Any downloops in the distribution mains should be avoided if possible but if this cannot be arranged then drain legs should be located at the downloop.

Except for the drain legs, all take off points from the distribution mains should be taken from the top of the main to prevent liquid water from entering the take off lines – see Fig 1.

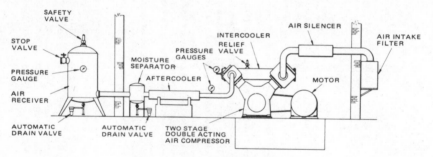

Fig 1 A typical compressor installation.
(IMI Norgren)

Because of the possibility of cooling occurring during the passage of air through the distribution mains, it is preferable to install individual smaller filters as near as possible to the actual point of use of the air rather than a single large filter adjacent to the air receiver. These filters should also be located upstream of any pressure reducing valves.

Particularly important today is the availability of several types of automatic-drain air filter which completely and automatically dump collected fluids. A typical float-operated automatic-drain mechanism is illustrated in Fig 2. The operation is such that, when the liquid level in the bowl reaches a predetermined height, the float A opens a pilot valve B, to admit air above the piston C and cause the drain valve D to open. The liquid is expelled by air pressure to a drain, whereupon the float closes the pilot valve and so the drain valve. Its operation does not depend on flow, and so it can be used effectively on drain legs and other 'dead end' services. This particular mechanism is designed to open when there is no air pressure in the line, so overnight draining of the system is possible. Such filters effectively reduce maintenance costs, eliminate human forgetfulness and are particularly useful for inaccessible or remote locations.

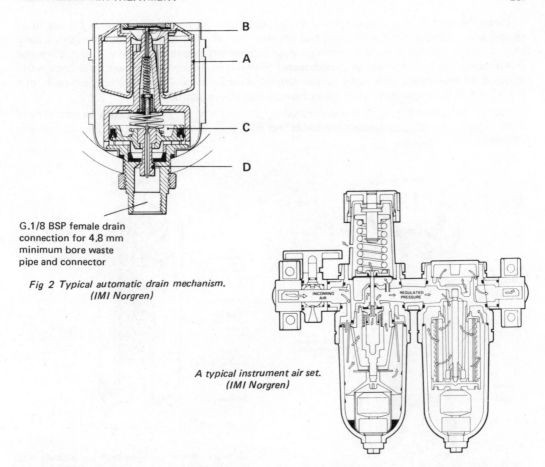

G.1/8 BSP female drain connection for 4.8 mm minimum bore waste pipe and connector

Fig 2 Typical automatic drain mechanism.
(IMI Norgren)

A typical instrument air set.
(IMI Norgren)

A properly designed air line filter of the correct size for the rate of air flow will effectively remove the liquid water, but cannot reduce the water vapour content of the air. If the air is subjected to further cooling after it has passed through the filter more water may condense out. If complete freedom from water contamination is essential then steps must be taken to ensure that the water vapour content of the air is lowered to the point at which the 'Dew Point' of the air is lower than any temperature that can be attained by the air itself. (See later under *Humidity Control*).

Oil

When the air is compressed in a lubricated compressor small amounts of oil will inevitably leave with the compressed air. Since this oil has been subjected to high temperatures during air compression it will have been oxidized and will no longer be suitable as a lubricant — hence the necessity of injecting a separate oil supply into a system that needs lubricant. However, the amount of degraded oil leaving a modern lubricated compressor is relatively low and partially separated out in the aftercooler anyway. The small residual of degraded oil is normally quite acceptable for general industrial systems; or equally can be removed in sufficient quantities by normal air line filters.

Certain systems demand pure, oil-free air, in which case the choice lies between the use of an oil-free compressor or further treatment of the delivered air. The former is not necessarily a complete solution. Oil-free compressors still produce compressed air contaminated with dirt and water and it can be more economical to use lubricated compressors, in conjunction with aftercoolers and standard air line filters, and to fit special Ultra High Efficiency filters to remove oil only from those parts of the compressed air system where oil free air is essential.

The problem of oil removal is complicated by the fact that oil in compressed air can exist in three forms — liquid oil, oil/water emulsions and oil vapour. Special filters are required to remove oil vapour and oil aerosol.

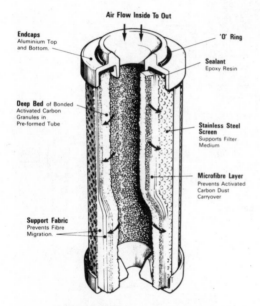

Domnick Hunter general purpose protection filter capable of particle removal down to 1 μm with maximum remaining oil content of 0.5 ppm.

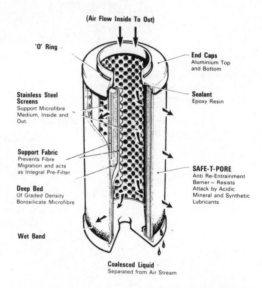

Domnick Hunter oil-X grade AA coalescing filter capable of oil removal down to 0.003 ppm.

Removal of Oil Aerosols

Modern oil removal filters are of the coalescing type commonly using glass fibre elements. Oil particles of varying sizes impinge on and adhere to the fibres resulting in a gradual build up of coalesced droplets. These droplets are driven to the outside of the filter by the air stream. When the oil comes to the outside of the material it is stopped in a porous sock covering the element. It then flows by the force of gravity down to the bottom of the sock where it drops to the filter bowl. The oil is then automatically drained from the filter. These filters are capable of removing the oil content in the compressed air down to a level of 0.1 mg/m^3 or less.

In addition to removing oil droplets, such filters have an equally high efficiency in removing minute water droplets but they should be protected against gross dirt or water contamination by means of standard air line filters mounted upstream.

The critical oil particle size is 0.1 to 0.5 μm droplets. Some manufacturers state 0.3 μm but the figure is slightly dependent on the kind, viscosity, temperature and quantity of the oil particles fed to the filter. Filters capable of retaining this size will also retain any other sized droplets. Smaller particles will be captured by the fibres due to their Brownian movements and the bigger droplets mainly by inertia effect.

It is advisable to ensure that these prefilters, fitted in the line ahead of the Ultra High Efficiency filter, are capable of removing dirt particles down to 5 μm or less as otherwise the coalescing filter may quickly become choked with dirt.

As a matter of principle high efficiency oil filters should also always be installed downstream of a dryer, where used. A high concentration of water in liquid form will not only give a higher load to the filter; an element saturated with water will even tend to allow easier passage of oil particles.

As with standard air line filters, the size of the Ultra High Efficiency filter should be selected in accordance with the air flow through it — see Table II.

TABLE II — TYPICAL SIZING OF COALESCING FILTERS FOR OIL REMOVAL

Nominal Port Size		Air Flow at 6.3 bar gauge
ISO/7	ISO/R228	dm^3/s A.N.R.
R$_c$ 1/8	G 1/8	up to 1
R$_c$ 1/4	G 1/4	up to 4
R$_c$ 3/8	G 3/8	0.25 to 8
R$_c$ 1/2	G 1/2	1 to 22
R$_c$ 3/4	G 3/4	3 to 35
R$_c$ 1	G 1	5 to 55
R$_c$ 1.1/4	G 1.1/4	7.5 to 80
R$_c$ 1.1/2	G 1.1/2	10 to 100

Oil removal filters on Consolidated Pneumatic stationary compressors are capable of removing 100% of liquid oil and water as well as particles down to 0.01 μm.
(Domnick Hunter Filters Ltd).

Under normal operating conditions the continuous rate of air flow through the filter should not be permitted to exceed 75% of the maximum rated capacity of the filter as excessive continuous flow results in excessive air velocity with a risk of reintroducing oil into the air stream.

Coalescing filters must be Ultra High Efficiency filters to accomplish their purpose and although standard filter tests exist there is no accepted standard laid down to establish the efficiency of a coalescing filter in removing oil.

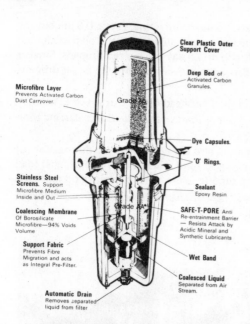

Clear Plastic Outer Support Cover

Deep Bed of Activated Carbon Granules.

Microfibre Layer Prevents Activated Carbon Dust Carryover.

Grade AA

Dye Capsules.

'O' Rings.

Stainless Steel Screens. Support Microfibre Medium Inside and Out

Sealant Epoxy Resin

Coalescing Membrane Of Borosilicate Microfibre—94% Voids Volume

Grade AA

SAFE-T-PORE Anti Re-entrainment Barrier — Resists Attack by Acidic Mineral and Synthetic Lubricants

Support Fabric Prevents Fibre Migration and acts as Integral Pre-Filter.

Wet Band

Coalesced Liquid Separated from Air Stream.

Automatic Drain Removes separated liquid from filter

Domnick Hunter 'Oil-X' combination filter capable of particle removal down to 0.01 μm and removal of oil vapour down to 0.003 ppm

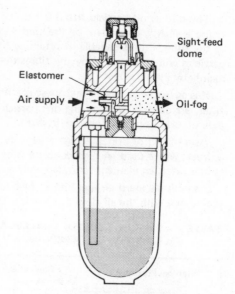

Sight-feed dome

Elastomer

Air supply

Oil-fog

A typical oil-fog air line lubricator. (IMI Norgren)

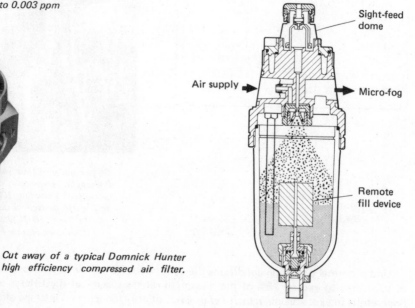

Cut away of a typical Domnick Hunter high efficiency compressed air filter.

Sight-feed dome

Air supply

Micro-fog

Remote fill device

A typical micro-fog lubricator

Oil Vapour

For most processes the removal of oil vapour is unnecessary since, unlike water vapour, oil vapour exists only in minute quantities and is not objectionable except in those circumstances where its odour is unacceptable.

For certain processes in the food, pharmaceutical and beverage industries, or where air is being used to supply breathing masks, it is strictly necessary to remove oil vapours. This is most commonly done by passing the air through an adsorbing bed, usually of activated carbon, although other materials can be used.

Combination filters incorporating both coalescing elements and adsorbent beds are available to supply Ultra Clean Air which will satisfy the requirements of BS4275 for breathing quality air as far as freedom from oil is concerned, but special filter units are required to remove carbon monoxide or carbon dioxide and odours.

Solid Contaminants

Standard air line filters for distribution lines generally remove particles down to about 40–50 μm in size, or lower in some cases. Finer filters can be used for better protection where required, but it is more usual to use these for second stage filtering at the take-off point to individual supplies. In this respect line filters fall into four categories, viz:

(i)   'Roughing' filters for distribution mains, capable of removing particles down to 50 μm.

(ii) 'Medium' efficiency filters capable of removing particles in the range 5–40 μm.

(iii) 'Fine' filters capable of removing particles in the size range 1–5 μm.

(iv) 'Ultra-fine' filters capable of removing particles down to 0.1 μm or better.

Fine and ultra-fine filters are normally only used for second and third stage filtering, respectively, ie should be preceded by a coarser filter to remove coarser contaminants and protect the finer filter from gross dirt contamination. Some specific recommendations for the filter rating required are given in Table III — see also Fig 3.

Part of the Domnick Hunter filter range.

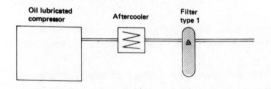

GENERAL PURPOSE PROTECTION *eg*

General industry ring mains
Civil Engineering
Highway maintenance
Rock quarrying
Drilling
Shotblasting
Pre-filtration for finer filters,
oil removal filters, dryers.

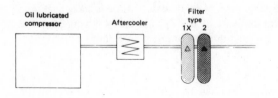

ALTERNATIVE TO OIL-FREE COMPRESSOR, *eg*

Instrumentation
Spray painting
Advanced pneumatics
Air gauging   Air bearings
Air conveying   Air motors
Low cost automation   Purging pipelines
Process control   Blow moulding

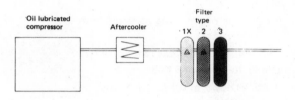

CRITICAL APPLICATIONS REQUIRING OIL-FREE AND ODOUR—FREE AIR, *eg*

Breathing air
Cosmetics
Film processing
Bottling
Fluidics   Pharmaceutical
Air blast circuit breakers   Dairy
Decompression chambers   Breweries
Foodstuffs   Medical

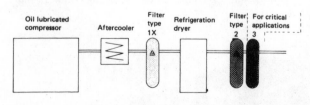

REDUCED DEW POINT SYSTEMS

where Dew Point is not
required to be less than
2—4°C and ambient
temperature does not
approach within 5—10°C
of this. For example interior
of factories.

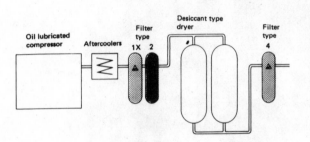

EXTREMELY LOW DEW POINT SYSTEMS

where Dew Point must be
below 0°C. For example external
installations or applications
involving rapid expansion of
the compressed air

Filter types:
1 — Rotating, medium efficiency or fine,
       depending on system
1X — Fine
2 — Oil/removing filter
3 — Odour removing filter
4 — Ultra fine filter

Fig 3 Guide to filter selection.

TABLE III — SUGGESTED DEGREE OF CLEANLINESS REQUIRED
((IMI Norgren Limited)

Type of Industrial Process	Water Removal		Oil Removal		Particulate Matter Removal			
					Above 40	μm 10–25	3–5	Below 1
	Liquid	Vapour	Aerosols	Vapour				
Air agitation	E	C	E	E	NS	NS	E	C
Air bearings	E	C	E	X	NS	NS	E	C
Air conveying and flotation								
Foodstuffs	E	E	E	E	NS	NS	E	C
Powders	E	E	E	C	NS	NS	E	C
Granular products	E	C	E	X	NS	E	C	X
Air motors: rotary, reciprocating, linear (air cylinders)								
Heavy duty	E	X	X	X	E	X	X	X
Light duty	E	X	X	X	E	X	X	X
Miniature	E	X	X	X	E	C	X	X
Ultra high speed (above 100 000 rev/min)	E	X	X	X	NS	NS	E	X
Blow guns, cleaning and cooling nozzles								
Cleaning of electronic equipment	E	E	E	C	NS	NS	E	C
Cleaning of food or pharmaceutical containers	E	E	E	E	NS	NS	NS	E
Cleaning of machine parts	E	X	X	X	NS	E	X	X
Cooling of glass and plastics	E	C	E	X	NS	NS	E	X
Cooling of metals	E	X	X	X	E	X	X	X
Film processing	E	E	E	C	NS	NS	NS	E
Breathing masks and protective clothing	E	C	E	E	NS	NS	NS	E
Fluidics								
Input sensors, logic circuit, output devices	E	X	E	C	NS	NS	E	X
Power circuits	E	X	X	X	E	C	X	X
Food, drink and tobacco processing general machinery	E	E	E	E	NS	NS	NS	E
Boot and shoe machines	E	X	X	X	E	X	X	X
Brick, clay and tile machines	E	X	X	X	E	X	X	X
Foundry machines	E	X	X	X	E	X	X	X
Glass machines*	E	X	X	X	E	X	X	X
Laundry and dry cleaning machines*	E	C	C	X	E	X	X	X
Machine tools	E	X	X	X	E	C	X	X
Packaging, paper and printing machines*	E	X	C	X	E	X	X	X
Shot blasting plant	E	C	X	X	E	X	X	X
Textile machines*	E	X	C	X	E	X	X	X
Welding machines	E	X	X	X	E	C	X	X
Instrumentation								
Pneumatic gauging equipment	E	X	E	X	NS	E	C	X
Precision pressure regulators	E	X	E	X	NS	NS	E	X
Process control instruments	E	C	E	X	NS	E	C	X
Pneumatic circuits and valves								
Directional control, flow control pressure control valves excluding precision type	E	X	X	X	E	X	X	X
Spray guns†	E	C	E	X	NS	NS	E	C
*If air comes into contact with product	E	C	E	X	NS	NS	E	X

Key:

C — should be considered; E — essential; NS — not suitable; X — not normally required

† Size of particulate matter should not exceed 50% of the thickness of the paint layer in order not to roughen the finish.

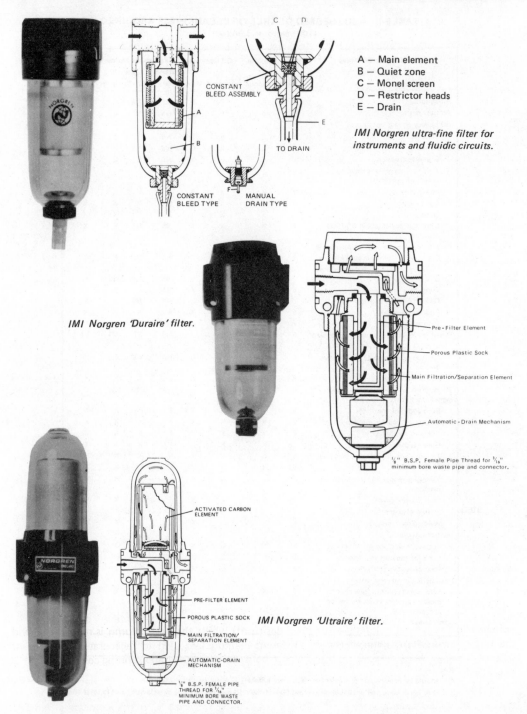

A – Main element
B – Quiet zone
C – Monel screen
D – Restrictor heads
E – Drain

CONSTANT
BLEED ASSEMBLY

TO DRAIN

CONSTANT
BLEED TYPE

MANUAL
DRAIN TYPE

*IMI Norgren ultra-fine filter for
instruments and fluidic circuits.*

IMI Norgren 'Duraire' filter.

Pre - Filter Element

Porous Plastic Sock

Main Filtration/Separation Element

Automatic - Drain Mechanism

1/8" B.S.P. Female Pipe Thread for 1/16"
minimum bore waste pipe and connector.

ACTIVATED CARBON
ELEMENT

PRE-FILTER ELEMENT

POROUS PLASTIC SOCK

MAIN FILTRATION/
SEPARATION ELEMENT

AUTOMATIC-DRAIN
MECHANISM

IMI Norgren 'Ultraire' filter.

1/8" B.S.P. FEMALE PIPE
THREAD FOR 1/16" MINIMUM
BORE WASTE PIPE AND
CONNECTOR.

Humidity Control

Removal of water from the compressed air to a level where no new condensation can be formed in the compressed air system (*ie* the dew point is made lower than ambient temperatures) can have specific advantage in any industry, and in some can be an essential feature. Examples of the advantages of 'dry' compressed air are:-

(i)   Supply to air tools making it possible to lubricate them more efficiently.

(ii)   The lubrication of all pneumatic components is improved when dry compressed air is used, and servicing intervals are increased.

(iii)   The use of dry compressed air in spray painting equipment eliminates any risk of damage to the paint finish from water droplets.

(iv)   In blast cleaning units the reliability of the equipment is improved and risks of icing under outdoor conditions are eliminated when using dry air.

(v)   In a dry compressed air system there is no corrosion, which can lead to loss of pressure and leaks; there is also no need for draining off of the condensed water.

Air drying is also desirable in conditions of high ambient temperatures and local humidity, such as laundries, *etc*, where it may otherwise be difficult to secure sufficiently low compressed air temperatures to provide ideal conditions for air line filters.

Different degrees of dryness (dew points) are required, depending on the use of the compressed air, the ambient temperatures and humidity. Different types of air dryers with varying dew point performances are therefore available.

Refrigeration dryers use the simplest drying method; the air passes through an aftercooler but the coolant is maintained at a much lower and constant temperature. The coolant is produced by a closed refrigeration circuit (incorporating compressor, condenser, *etc*) adjusted to cool down the air to a temperature just above $0°C$. The limitation for these dryers is the freezing point of water.

Cooling is done in two steps, first in a precooler (cooling with the cold air leaving the dryer) and then in the main cooler (cooling with the coolant). All water condensed in these coolers is separated and removed from the air. The lowest obtainable dew point with a refrigeration dryer is approximately $+2°C$. This dryness is quite adequate for most common uses of compressed air. In fact, by drying the air to a dew point which is approximately 10 deg C below the lowest possible prevailing ambient temperature in the air system, all risks of getting condensate have usually been eliminated.

Lower dew points are required when the compressed air can be cooled to temperatures below $0°C$, *eg* in compressed air pipes outdoors in winter time. Certain processes, pneumatic instruments *etc* often require dew points below $0°C$. For such applications adsorption dryers should be used. With these dryers, dew points down to $-40°C$ can be obtained.

The adsorption dryer consists of two drying columns filled with desiccant. The compressed air passes through one column where the desiccant adsorbs the water vapour in the air, and this process continues until the desiccant is saturated with water vapour. The air flow is then automatically switched to the second column (with active desiccant) whilst the first column is regenerated and the water removed from the desiccant. Different methods are used to regenerate the desiccant (choice normally being determined by a balance between investment and running costs).

In the heat regenerated adsorption dryer the water vapour is removed by heating the desiccant. The released water vapour is then taken away from the drying column in a current of air. In one type of heat regenerated dryer the heat is generated by external band shaped heaters clamped

Compressed air filter with built-in heater.
(Domnick Hunter Filters Ltd).

A range of cast housing compressed air filters capable of being bolted together to operate in tandem.
(Domnick Hunter Filters Ltd).

A typical selection of the air service units being offered by Kay Pneumatics Limited. Features of this range include metal bowl guards for safety and high flow performance.

around the columns. The released water vapour is removed by a small amount of expanded dried air (approximately 1.5%). Large heat regenerated adsorption dryers are regenerated with ambient air sucked in by a blower. This air has been heated up by an external heater before entering the desiccant bed.

The heat regenerated type of adsorption dryer is most suitable for medium to large compressed air installations. For small air flows the so called heatless dryer, which is regenerated with cold air, is more suitable.

The technique of expanding a part of the dried compressed air gives a very dry regenerating air which can remove the adsorbed water from the desiccant. This type of adsorption dryer is of a very simple construction since no heater is required. The amount of compressed air used for regeneration (approximately 15%) limits their use to small rates of consumption.

The *sorption* dryer is based on a new drying method for compressed air and is so far only employed in a range of dryers specially designed for use together with oilfree screw compressors. The drying is achieved by passing the wet air through a drying material impregnated with a hygroscopic salt.

The drying material is folded into a honeycomb pattern and shaped into the form of a rotor.

Drying takes place by two simultaneous processes:

(i)   Adsorption of moisture to the surface of the drying material.

(ii)   Absorption of moisture by the hygroscopic salt.

The combination of these two processes is termed sorption. The rotor slowly turns passing through two separate sections. In three quarters of the rotor section the air is dried and in the remaining section it is regenerated by hot compressed air. As this air has a very low relative humidity, no additional heating is required; therefore, the only power requirement is the small amount of electricity needed to drive the rotor and the control circuit (approximately 0.06 kW). All air used for regeneration is recycled back to the main stream of compressed air.

The dew point after passing through this type of dryer is approximately 50 degC below the temperature of the compressed air entering the dryer.

See also chapters on *Compressed Air for Breathing* and *Sterile Compressed Air and Gases*.

Compressed Air for Breathing

PURITY REQUIREMENTS for breathing air supplied by compressed air systems demand high standards of installation and ultra high efficiency filters. Maximum acceptable levels of impurities laid down in BS4275:1974 are

> carbon dioxide 500 ppm (900 mg/in^3)
> carbon monoxide 5 ppm (5.5 mg/in^3)
> oil mist 0.5 mg/in^3

Breathing air must also be free from odours and contamination by dust or metallic particles and any other irritating or toxic contaminants.

Commonly in industrial systems the breathing air supply is tapped directly from the working compressed air line. This places a premium on correct airline installation, even though the breathing air is necessarily separately filtered. Where there are multiple working points demanding breathing air supplies it is preferable, however, to install an air line for breathing systems separate from the normal air line or working supply line.

The type of compressor used is not particularly significant since the concentration of oil vapour in air delivered from oil-lubricated compressors at temperatures acceptable for breathing air will be well below the acceptable level for tolerance (600–1 300 mg/in^3). Reduction of oil mist is essential, however, with such types. With all compressors the main requirement is that it should be installed so that it can only induct clean, uncontaminated air.

A combination of filters is required following the take-off point for each breathing air line. The first can be a standard airline filter capable of removing solid particles and water. This will substantially improve the service life of a following high efficiency filter for removing oil mist. Such a basic filtering system — normally quite adequate for all industrial applications — does not remove odours or gases, hence the importance of the compressor inducting only clean air. The only other proviso is that the compressor should be adequately sized so that it does not overheat, which could possibly result in the generation of carbon monoxide or even toxic vapours in the case of PTFE ring compressors. For the latter reason, many authorities designate PTFE ring compressors as unsuitable for providing breathing air.

Ultra high efficiency filters are required for oil mist removal — *ie* those with an efficiency in excess of 99.9%. This will ensure minimal contamination and also eliminate build-up of oil contamination in downstream pipelines (which can be considerable over a period with, say, a filter having only 99% efficiency).

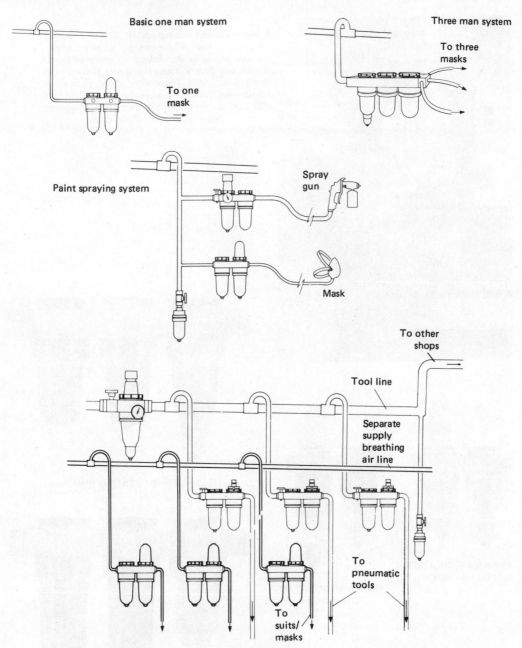

Basic one man system

To one mask

Three man system

To three masks

Paint spraying system

Spray gun

Mask

To other shops

Tool line

Separate supply breathing air line

To pneumatic tools

To suits/masks

Compressed air installation where personnel are engaged in work requiring a breathing air supply and pneumatic tool supply

Examples of recommended systems.
(IMI Norgren Ltd)

A Siebe Gorman Powermask Mk III with one-piece PVC suit — one of two versions of this positive-pressure respirator that have been approved by the Health and Safety Executive under the Asbestos Regulations, 1969. Respirators of this type are in regular use in defined areas by the UKAEA and BNFC at Windscale for the protection of workers exposed to radioactive dusts.

Model M8R-461-F2XD for three masks.

Model M4R-201-A2XD for one mask.

Model M4R-301-A2XD for two masks

Norgren breathing air sets.

Model M8R-661-F2XD for four or five masks .

Minimum delivery requirement for breathing air is 4.2 ft^3/m (120 lit/min) free air per person, with a higher figure being desirable. Pipelines, filters and pressure reducing valves must be sized accordingly. Relative humidity of the air should be between 25% and 80% at atmospheric pressure. Acceptable temperature for breathing air is between 15 and 25°C. Humidity requirements largely rule out the use of dryers in the system; alternatively a humidifier may be included in the system if a dryer is essential for other purposes. Continual breathing of dry air can cause discomfort or even respiratory troubles. Certain types of airline lubricators can be used as humidifiers, if necessary (*ie* 'fog' type lubricators which would then generate only water vapour). Temperature requirements may or may not call for cooling equipment.

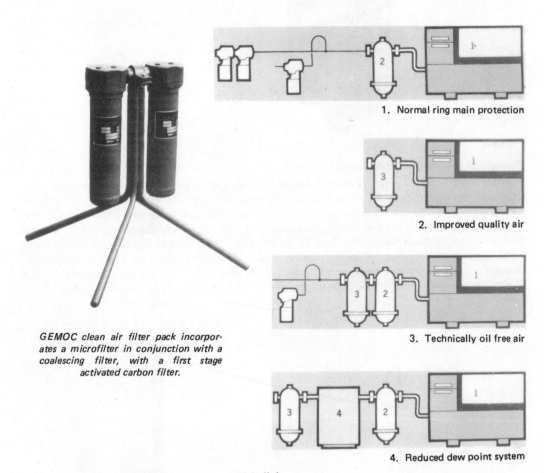

1. Normal ring main protection

2. Improved quality air

3. Technically oil free air

4. Reduced dew point system

GEMOC clean air filter pack incorporates a microfilter in conjunction with a coalescing filter, with a first stage activated carbon filter.

1. oil-lubricated compressor with built-in attenuator.
2. air line filter
3. oil-removal filter
4. refrigeration dryer

Examples of levels of protection.
(Consolidated Pneumatic Tool Co. Ltd)

*Oil-removal filter incorporating oil trap.
(Consolidated Pneumatic Tool Co.Ltd).*

Removal of Odours and Toxic Vapours

As mentioned previously, this is not necessarily a problem when the compressor·is correctly sized, sited and well maintained. If strictly necessary, most odours can be removed by activated charcoal filters, and carbon monoxide by special absorbent media filters. In both cases such filter elements have a limited effective life and need replacement at regular intervals (depending on the concentration of vapours present which they have to absorb). The need for this will become obvious with odour-removing filters, but not so with carbon monoxide which is odourless. Where objectionable or toxic gases are known to be present in the supply from a compressor (*eg* the compressor is sited in a position where it can inhale such gases), the use of respirators or bottled air supplies is to be preferred.

Sterile Compressed Air and Gases

THERE ARE many applications for sterile compressed air and gases. The production and packaging of many dairy and food products such as beer, yoghurt, creams and cheeses all use compressed air or carbon dioxide. Fine chemicals such as enzymes, antibiotics and vaccines all use large quantities of compressed air during their production process. Unfortunately the nature of these products makes them susceptible to contamination by micro organisms held in the compressed air or gas.

Any product that can be contaminated by airborne bacteria must be protected. In the case of foods and chemicals produced by fermentation, ingress of bacteria would cause serious defects if not complete rejection of the finished product. Beer is pumped and held under pressure by CO_2 protecting it from the atmosphere, and of course it must be free from any bacteria or degraded yeast cells.

BIO-X air sterilization filter on a yeast
propagation fermentor.
(Domnick Hunter Ltd).

*Typical single element BIO-X air
sterilization filters.
(Domnick-Hunter Ltd).*

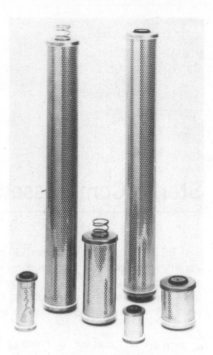

*Selection of BIO-X air sterilisation
elements
(Domnick Hunter Ltd)*

Compressed air originating from the atmosphere can contain all types of micro organisms. These are not killed in the heat of compression and remain in the compressed air. Their very small size, for example, (bacteria are in the region of 0.2 to 5 μm), makes their removal a difficult problem. These micro organisms can pass through conventional filter materials, around sealing mechanisms and grow through wet filters.

Carbon dioxide in its normal supply form is quite clean and does not normally constitute a problem. However connections made during transfer allow ingress of micro organisms through dirty connections and downstream pipe work quite often contains back flow of product providing an almost ideal breeding ground.

The solution to all of these problems is to sterilize the gas. This can be accomplished by mechanically removing the micro organisms by filtration in what is known as 'cold sterilization'. The equipment necessary is relatively simple to install and operate and represents a very economical investment.

In order to understand 'cold sterilization' it is first necessary to appreciate the basic principles used in the filtration of gases. To be effective the filter material must be capable of removing very small particles whilst causing the minimum of obstruction to the flow of the gas. The most modern filter material used which has these properties is borosilicate micro fibre. This is typically a randomly dispersed bed of fibres of mean diameter 0.5 μm with a voids volume or free space between fibres of 94%.

In removing micro organisms or any other particle the filter material utilizes three main mechanisms of filtration, which are direct interception, inertial impaction and Brownian motion or diffusion. Considering direct interception first, this affects the larger particles in a gas stream which are literally sieved out. These are very easy to remove and present no real problem other than clogging the filter material. Inertial impaction occurs when a particle travelling in the gas stream is deflected around the first, second or even third fibres in the filter material and is eventually unable to negotiate the tortuous path presented to it and cannot change direction as quickly as the gas stream. It therefore collides with a fibre and remains attached to it. The third mechanism, Brownian motion or diffusion as it is sometimes called, affects the very fine particles which are subject to intermolecular and electrostatic forces which cause them to actually spiral in the gas stream thus increasing their effective diameter and causing them to collide with and be trapped on a fibre. In analyzing the three mechanisms it can be seen that a critical particle size could exist which is the most difficult to remove due to it falling 'between' mechanisms. This particle size is in fact 0.3 μm. It is a very relevant size especially considering that small bacteria are in the same order.

Micro organisms trapped on and within the filter material by the aforementioned mechanisms remain trapped and cannot pass through the filter. They cannot grow on the filter material as it is inert; or grow through it, providing that the material does not become contaminated by back flow of product or saturated with water.

Having the correct filter material is only part of the story as this filter material must be formed into a filter element that can be fitted easily in a housing and which can be relied upon to operate under arduous system conditions. To achieve this the filter material must be intimately supported on both sides and then encapsulated in end caps to prevent any possible bypass. This construction provides a cylindrical element of exceptional strength and reliability.

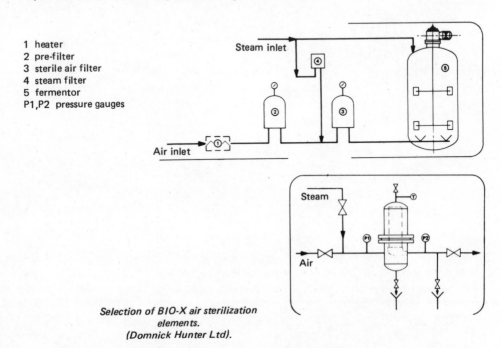

1 heater
2 pre-filter
3 sterile air filter
4 steam filter
5 fermentor
P1,P2 pressure gauges

*Selection of BIO-X air sterilization
elements.
(Domnick Hunter Ltd).*

In setting up filters to sterilize a gas some method must be found of initially rendering the whole system sterile and also carrying this out on a routine basis. This is most often done using steam and sterilizing at approximately $125°C$ for a period of thirty minutes. It is normal to sterilize the pipe system from immediately prior to the sterile filter right down to the point of application. In some cases, for example when sterilizing a fermentor it is normal to sterilize the fermentor and then allow steam to pass back down the compressed air supply line to a point past the sterile filter. After steam sterilization the system is allowed to vent to atmospheric pressure which will allow flash drying of the filter element. When this has been accomplished the system is then pressurized with sterile gas to keep any atmospheric pollution out.

When considering the critical nature of gas sterilization using filtration it is essential that any filter used has been previously integrity tested to ensure that it will perform its duty. The best way of integrity testing a filter element and indeed the whole filter is to use a cloud of test particles in the region of the critical particle size of $0.3 \mu m$. Theoretically if a filter is, for the sake of argument, 100% efficient when tested on a cloud of particles of $0.3 \mu m$ size then this filter is capable of removing any particle below this size and any particle above this size. It is possible to create a test cloud of this nature by using DOP (dioctylphthalate). Porton Down Microbiological Research Station have determined that an efficiency of 99.997% on a test of this type does not provide 100% removal of all viable organisms and hence give 100% sterile gas.

Great care is taken in the manufacture of gas sterilization filter elements, involving strict controls on quality and testing. It is essential that every single filter element made is efficiency tested before despatch because even the smallest flaw could cause a problem. To be acceptable gas sterilization filter elements and filters tested with the DOP test should show an efficiency greater than 99.9999% to give a factor of safety acceptable to the manufacturer which will give the necessary security in operation.

Oxygen Filters

OXYGEN IS potentially a dangerous gas, capable of producing violent spontaneous combustion in contact with contaminants such as rust scale and other degradation products in oxygen pipelines; solvents, lubricants, greases, *etc*. Equally, oxygen can lower considerably the ignition temperature of combustible particles. The requirements for oxygen filters are thus stringent and unique, governing material choice and construction of the filter body, choice and form of filter element, and seals and accessories.

Oxygen filter bodies may be made from carbon steel or stainless steel and require high quality construction and cleaning. Carbon steel parts are preferably fine finished and phosphated. Internal fittings may be of non-sparking bronze alloy (*eg* tungum) with complete electrical loading. The design should, also be such as to avoid vortex formation and minimize particle impact (to avoid particle temperature rise); with positive separation of contaminants in a 'calm' region .

Sintered metals are a suitable choice for the filter element; specifically sintered bronze on a stainless steel internal support. Such filters are capable of providing filtration close to 5 μm. Elements are not regarded as cleanable, but may be 'recoverable' in the sense that the support parts may be salvaged and refitted with new bronze elements. An example of such a design is shown in Fig 1.

An oxygen filter should always be fitted with two pressure gauges — one upstream and one downstream; or alternatively a differential pressure gauge. Such gauges must be capable of withstanding the maximum static pressure of the system on one side and atmospheric pressure on the other without damage or losing calibration. Gauges used must also be degreased for oxygen service.

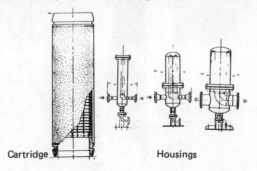

Cartridge   Housings

Fig 1 'Oxopor' oxygen filters.
(BEA Filters)

Dust and Fume Respirators

INDUSTRIAL RESPIRATORS for protection against dust and light fumes generally consist either of a half mask covering the nose and chin or a full face mask connected to a filter. (The latter type also provide eye protection). Half masks are generally suitable for use where the total concentration of contaminants does not exceed ten times the MAC (Maximal Allowable Concentration) or TLB (Threshold Limit Value). Where higher concentrations are present a full face mask should be used.

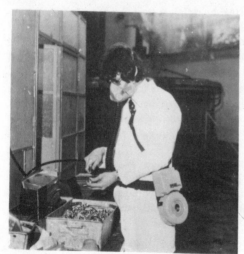

Siebe Gorman Powermask with Orinasal half mask.

Vistarama twin filter mask.
(Siebe Gorman)

All respirator designs should incorporate non-return valves to ensure that most of the exhaled air is passed directly to atmosphere and not re-breathed. Equally, all masks should be formed in a non-irritant material with seals to provide an airtight fit. Full face masks can generally provide a better seal than half masks.

Filters used are invariably disposable. The best type for use with half masks is the cartridge filter. Depending on the design of the mask and the protection provided, one or two filter cartridges may be fitted. (Two cartridges also offer the advantage of reduced resistance to breathing). Different types of filter cartridges may be fitted to provide protection against different toxic gases, vapours, dusts, and combinations of such contaminants. The simpler types of filters may provide varying degrees of dust protection only — typically comprising a cotton wool and gauze prefilter to remove coarse dust followed by a fine dust filter cartridge. Filters for toxic fume protection employ chemical cartridges (absorbent filters) and may or may not incorporate a dust filter.

Examples of different types of respirator filters covering specific requirements are:-

(i)   Dust protection only — Health and Safety Executive approved and BS2091 : 1969 Type B.

(ii)   High efficiency dust protection only — Health and Safety Executive approved and BS2091 : 1969 Type B.

(iii) Acid gas protection for concentrations not exceeding 0.1% by volume (1 000 parts per million).

(iv)   Acid gas and dust protection for concentration of gas not exceeding 0.1% by volume (1 000 parts per million) — Approved to BS2091 : 1969

(v)   Organic vapour protection for concentrations not exceeding 0.1% by volume (1 000 parts per million).

(vi)   Organic vapours and dust protection for concentrations of vapour not exceeding 0.1% by volume, and approved to BS2091 : 1969

(vii) Limited paint spray protection for concentrations not exceeding 0.1% by volume (1 000 parts per million).

(viii) Agricultural dusts and pesticides and all substances listed under Part II of Agricultural (Poisonous Substances) regulations approved to BS2091 : 1969.

(ix)   Ammonia protection for a maximum duration of 60 minutes at 0.1% concentration by volume.

(x)   Dust protection only. NCB approved ADR/SG/6, and approved to BS2091 : 1969 Type A/H.

(xi)   Dust protection to very high efficiency, approved to BS4555 : 1970.

Canister Filters

Canister filters are used with full face masks, the mask being connected to the canister via a flexible hose. The filter canister is thus separate from the mask and can be worn on the chest or back.

The actual life of a canister in service will vary considerably according to the location of the hazard and the method of use of the toxic material concerned. The life of the canister can, therefore, be found only by experience. If, however, the partially used canister is returned to the makers after a measured period of exposure to the gas concerned, an estimation can be made of the remaining life left in the canister.

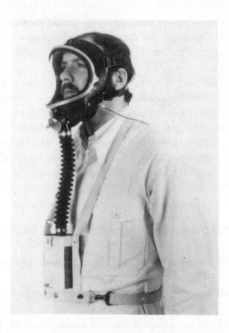

Full face mask with canister filter.
(Siebe Gorman)

It must be emphasized that with a full face mask and canister filter the wearer inhales the surrounding atmosphere via a canister charged with the appropriate filtering material. Whilst a suitable canister will give protection against most known gases, it will not protect against atmospheres deficient in oxygen or (except for a very short time), high concentrations of gases. For such cases breathing apparatus providing air independent of the surrounding atmosphere is required.

Colour Coding

Canisters are identified by colour coding but the protection provided is also listed on the label. Examples typical of British practice and consistent with BS 2091 are:-

Type	Colour	Protection against
A	Blue	Ammonia
C	Black	Organic vapours
CC	Black, grey stripe	Organic vapours and dusts
CG	Red	Acid gases
H	Blue and black	Ammonia and organic vapours
NF	Orange	Nitrous fumes
NFC	Orange, grey stripe	Nitrous fumes and dusts
P	Black, green stripe	Methyl bromide
CGC	Red, grey stripe	Acid gases and dusts
D	White	Hydrogen cyanide
SHC	Red, white and grey stripes	Hydrogen cyanide and dusts

European colour coding differs, the following draft code now being adopted by the majority of European countries:-

Type	Colour	Protect Against
A	Brown	Organic gases and vapours
B	Grey	Inorganic gases and vapours
E	Yellow	Sulphur dioxide and other acid gases
K	Green	Ammonia

Canister respirators must only be used against those gases specifically indicated on the canister. If dusts, mists or fumes are also present in the atmosphere a particulate filter should be used. They may also be used as emergency equipment to enable people to vacate danger areas safely and quickly but should not be used for rescue work in confined spaces.

Half mask and respirator with single filter.
(Siebe Gorman)

Twin filter half mask respirator.
(Siebe Gorman)

Canister respirators are not recommended for routine process work where the likely concentration of gas is not known or where it may exceed 1% by volume or 100 times the acceptable level. Should any doubt exist regarding the use of a respirator in any given conditions then breathing apparatus must be selected or recommended.

Positive Pressure Respirators

In these devices air is drawn through a filter by a battery operated fan and delivered to the facepiece at a flow rate in excess of 120 litres/min, so that positive pressure is always maintained within the facemask even during inhale. Consequently a much greater degree of protection is afforded to the wearer than with negative pressure respirators together with a decrease in the inspiratory effort required. The apparatus was originally designed for working in dust environments such as in those caused by lead and asbestos stripping but this has since been extended to include agricultural spraying, handling people with contagious diseases and radioactive fuel rods.

A Siebe Gorman Powermask Mk III with one-piece PVC suit — one of two versions of this positive-pressure respirator that have been approved by the Health & Safety Executive under the Asbestos Regulations 1969
Respirators of this type are in regular use in defined areas by the UKAEA and BNFC at Windscale for the protection of workers exposed to radioactive dusts.

Siebe Gorman Powermask with hood.

Protection Factor

To make the selection of respirators more precise, the term 'protection factor' has been introduced. This term is derived from the expected inward leakage which may occur for any given respirator and has been defined as:

$$\text{Nominal protection factor} = \frac{\text{Maximum concentration of contamination in working environment}}{\text{Concentration of contaminant inside face mask}}$$

(*ie* that which will be inhaled when wearing the respirator)

Clearly, the concentration in the facepiece which is made up of contaminant leaking in around the face seal, through the face seal, through the exhale valve and through the filter, must not exceed the M.A.C. Therefore with a knowledge of the concentration of contaminant in the working environment and its M.A.C. the minimum protection factor of the respiratory equipment to be selected is derived from the ratio:- •

$$\frac{\text{Maximum concentration of contaminant in atmosphere}}{\text{M.A.C.}}$$

For example, if a dust has an M.A.C. of 0.5 mg/m^3 and the concentration of the dust in the working environment is 20 mg/m^3 then equipment providing the wearer with a minimum protection factor of 40 is required

$$ie \ \frac{20}{0.5} \ = 40$$

A respirator complying with BS2091 type B has a maximum face seal leakage of 5% and a maximum filter leakage of 2%, giving a maximum total inward leakage of 7%. Thus the protection factor is:-

$$\frac{100}{7} \ = 14$$

Such a respirator would not provide adequate protection in the example given earlier.

See also Table I.

TABLE I – NOMINAL PROTECTION FACTORS OF SOME SIEBE GORMAN RESPIRATORS

Respirators	Inward Leakage %		Protection Factor
	Face seal (typical)	Filter (average)	
Filtasafe & FC1	3.0	2	20
Filtasafe & 2 FC2	1.5	0.5	50
Filtasafe & FC6	3.0	5	12 Dust only
Filtasafe & FC6	3.0	Nil	30 Gas only
Vistarama & FC1	0.05	2	48
Vistarama & 2 FC11	0.05	0.001	1960
Puretha 'CC'	0.05	Nil	2000 Gas only
Powermask & VHE filter	Nil	0.01	10000 Dust only
Powermask & Vapour & Dust	Nil	0.1	1000 Dust only

Note: Inward leakages are averaged over ten people with normal features.
Persons with abnormal features could have excessive face seal leakage.

Mist Eliminators for Gases

THE USE of mist eliminators to remove liquid droplets from industrial gases falls broadly into two categories:-

(i)   Process gas cleaning — as a necessary requirement of the process involved.

(ii) Exhaust gas cleaning — for environmental considerations.

Types of eliminators used include:

(a)   Filter packs (fibrous and wire-mesh elements)

(b)   Candle filters

(c)   Cyclones

(d)   Electrostatic precipitators

(e)   Impingement filters (eliminators)

Characteristics of these individual forms of mist eliminators are summarized in Table I. Most are well known (and described elsewhere), except for impingement eliminators. These are based on inertial effects with the gas flow being repeatedly deflected (Fig 1). Three configurations are possible — *horizontal* for vertical gas flow; *vertical* for horizontal gas flow; or *inclined* with gas flow at the same angle to the horizontal.

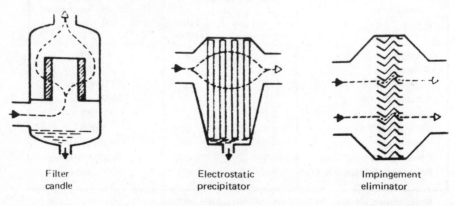

Filter
candle

Electrostatic
precipitator

Impingement
eliminator

Fig 1

TABLE I – TYPES OF MIST ELIMINATORS FOR INDUSTRIAL GASES*

Type	Operating Mechanism	Assembly	Function	Remarks
Settling Tank Knock-out Drum	Gravity	Tank (upright or horizontal).	Slowing down of the gas flow so much that the settling velocity is higher than the gas velocity.	Simple, inexpensive apparatus for very gross drops, poor efficiency, rare use.
Fibre Filter Filtering candle	Mechanical filter	Case with compact packing of fibres or different single or individual filtering candles	Single drops are brought in touch with the fibres, flow together, increase and fall down due to gravity. The filtering candle prevents passing of droplets while gas flows through.	Voluminous apparatus with very low face velocity and low liquid loading preferably for very small drops; danger of clogging and build-up.
Electrostatic Precipitator	Electrostatic forces	Case with electrodes.	The drops are electro-charged and attracted to the collecting electrodes.	Complicated, expensive apparatus for extremely fine drops, very high efficiency, rare use.
Cyclone	Mass moment of inertia	Tank with installation which forces the gas flow to rotate	Based on rotation separation because of varying density, the drops are eliminated along the tank walls.	Simple and voluminous apparatus for middle-sized drops, good efficiency, frequent use.
Wire Mesh	Mass moment of inertia	Tank with pack of several layers of wire mesh of undulating wires; compact wire mesh with high porosity.	The drops are brought in touch with the wire surface, flow together, coalesce and fall down due to gravity.	Voluminous apparatus with low face velocities for low liquid loading and very fine drops, danger of clogging and build-up.
Impingement Eliminator	Mass moment of inertia	Tank with a set of profile plates of different types.	Gas flow is split up into many single flows and repeatedly deflected. Due to inertia the drops cannot follow the flow of the gas and thus are eliminated on the impingement surfaces.	Small compact construction because of high face velocity, very high efficiency even for very fine drops, low pressure drop on well formed profiles, increasing use.

*Euroform

Typically an impingement eliminator is composed of corrugated profile plates assembled with phase separating chambers mounted on a frame with a sump below. (Fig 2).

The profiles split the gas flow into single streams. The corrugated plates produce inertia in the drops and they strike the corrugations, being pushed towards the phase separating chambers. There gravity impels the film of moisture into the sump. The construction of the plane separating chambers aids the flow and reduces waste and eddying. By this means loss of pressure is avoided at high velocities and less energy expended.

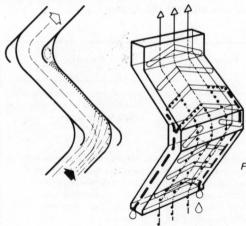

Fig 2 Vertical impingement separator.

Examples of horizontal flow mist eliminator profiles.

Swirl-type mist eliminator with bucket ring.
(Euroform)

Euroform T100 mist eliminator
complete with housing for insertion in
a duct.

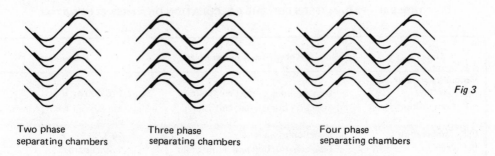

Two phase
separating chambers

Three phase
separating chambers

Four phase
separating chambers

Fig 3

Efficiency can be improved by increasing the number of separating chambers incorporated — *eg* providing two-phase, three-phase or four-phase separation — Fig 3. Specifically, however, the optimum geometry depends on the type of eliminator, *ie* longitudinal, vertical or inclined, as affecting the collection and discharge of the liquid droplets. Theoretically efficiencies of up to 100% are possible, but practical efficiencies realized are lower, *ie* are restricted to a (design) limiting drop size. For a particular mist eliminator the limiting drop size (d^*) is a function of the face velocity, but can be expressed fully as:-

$$d^* = K\left[\left(\frac{\Delta g}{\Delta L}\right) \cdot V_G \left(\frac{1}{V_A}\right) \cdot \left(\frac{ra - ri}{Q}\right)\right]^n$$

K and n are (design) constants

Δg = density of gas

ΔL = density of liquid

V_G = viscosity of gas

V_A = face velocity

ra, ri and Q are empirical measurements of the flow grid.

A mist eliminator designed on this basis will provide 100% efficiency in removal of drop sizes of d^* or greater. Smaller droplets will only be partially removed — *eg* see Fig 4.

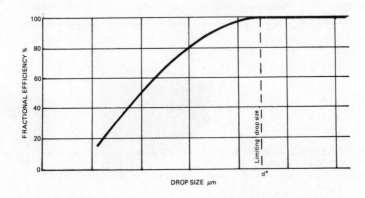

Fig 4

TABLE II – PARAMETERS FOR THE CALCULATION OF A MIST ELIMINATOR

Data	Knowledge is necessary for	Example
Variability state of gas:		
(i) Gas flow	Dimensioning of mist eliminator	210 000 m^{3}h^{-1}
(ii) Composition	Selection of material, corrosion	Exhaust air from phthalic acid plants
(iii) Temperature	Selection of material	40°C
(iv) Pressure	Case-construction and liquid-drain	1 atm approx
(v) Density	Calculation of mist eliminator	1.2 kg m^{-3}
(vi) Viscosity	Calculation of mist eliminator	Approx 15.6 x 10^{-6} m^{2}s^{-1}
(vii) Humidity	Deciding if the drops can evaporate (build-up)	Saturated
Variability of state of the liquid:		
(i) Loading	Dimensioning of mist eliminator	25m^{3}h^{-1}
(ii) Composition	Selection of material, evaluation of build-up danger	Water, enriched with 1–18% of organic acid
(iii) Density	Calculation of mist eliminator	Approx 10^3 kgm^{-3}
(iv) Drop size distribution	Calculation of mist eliminator	Expected distribution: <65 μm
(v) Pollution, *eg* solid particles	Evaluation of danger of build-up and clogging, corrosion	When falling short of saturation, phthalic anhydride is produced
(vi) Surface tension	Evaluation of wetting behaviour	Like water
Operating data:		
(i) Admissible pressure drop	Dimensioning of mist eliminator	Maximum 100 mm water gauge
(ii) Admissible installation area	Dimensioning of mist eliminator	3 500 mm = height 3 200 mm = width
(iii) Desired efficiency	Dimensioning of mist eliminator	99.9% for drops $\geqslant$14 μm 60% for drops = 8 μm 40% for drops = 6 μm
(iv) Velocity distribution in front of mist eliminator	Dimensioning of mist eliminator	Horizontal flow after pre-eliminator (length = 4 m)
(v) Limit drop size	Dimensioning of mist eliminator	As small as possible
(vi) Direction of flow	Selection of mist eliminator type	Horizontal

 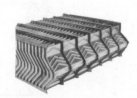

Coarse separator (left) normally used with a fine eliminator following (right).

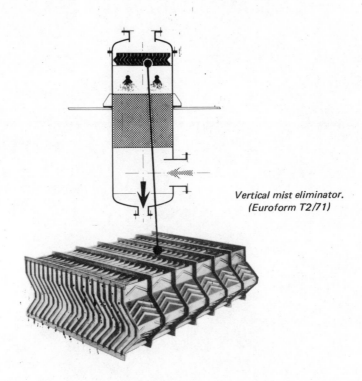

Vertical mist eliminator.
(Euroform T2/71)

Table II summarizes the parameters governing the design of a typical mist eliminator, together with example performance requirements for an exhaust gas cleaning application.

See also chapters on *Dynamic Separators, Candle Filters, Hydrostatic Precipitators, Wet Scrubbers.*

SECTION 3

Sub-section (b)

Water Filters

THE CONVENTIONAL and still the principal type of filter used for cleaning bulk water is the sand bed with back-washing carried out by a backflow of water, or preferably water backwash combined with air scour. The latter results in better fluidization of the bed and more effective cleansing. Conventionally such sand filters are downflow (gravity type), but upflow filters are also used where higher flow rates are required, or where high turbidities make conventional downflow sand filters impractical.

High rate downflow filter.

Conventional downflow filter.

Downflow Filters

Conventional downflow sand filters are effective for liquid-solids separation at flow rates up to about 5 gallons/min per ft^2 of filter area. Higher rate downflow filters are, however, available. With proper selection of media, granular as well as gelatinous suspended matter can be filtered out without a rapid differential pressure build-up. Typical filter media consist of selected silica sand, anthracite, coal, or combinations of these materials. Multiple media filters in discrete layers can provide differential filtration — Fig 1.

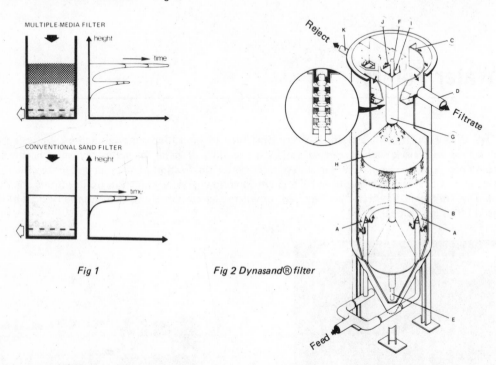

Fig 1

Fig 2 Dynasand® filter

Recent development has concentrated on the moving bed filter where the sand is continually washed and recycled. Apart from providing better cleansing a moving bed filter does not have to be shut down for backwashing; it can operate continuously.

An example of a modern moving bed sand filter is shown in Fig 2. Dirty water is fed to the bottom of the unit and is introduced to the sand bed by a distributor ring (A). Water flows upward through the sand bed (B) which is moving downward. The clear filtrate exits from the sand bed, overflows a weir (C), and is discharged from the unit (D).

Accumulated solids, sand, and water flow into the suction intake of an *air lift pipe* (E). Air is injected into the bottom of the air lift. A turbulent flow of air, water, and sand loosens the impurities as it moves up to the top of the air lift (F). Sand overflows at the top and additional washing takes place as the sand falls through a *washer* (G) where final traces of the impurities are removed. Cleaned sand is returned to the top of the sand bed by means of a cone shaped *distributor* (H).

The impurities removed from the sand are collected in a central compartment (I), *overflow an adjustable weir* (J), and are discharged from the unit (K). Because of the head difference between the filtrate water level and the reject water level, a small amount of filtrate will flow up through the washer into the reject water flume. This prevents any solids but the sand from being discharged into the filtrate compartment.

Only two parameters are required to control the mode of operation of the filter. One is the air flow rate, which determines the sand recirculation rate; the other is the reject weir setting which determines the reject flow rate.

Upflow Sand Filters

With an upflow sand filter flow is from the bottom through to the top of the bed. The main difference is that the entire bed depth is utilized to trap solids with the fine top layer acting as the final clean-up area. This gives a suspended solids capacity of 6–10 pounds per square foot of surface area, depending on the density of the suspended matter; a greater capacity per square foot of surface area than a conventional downflow filter. The upflow bed stabilizer keeps the bed in place during the high on-stream rate in order to take full advantage of the bed solids capacity. Expansion of the bed by air agitation prior to washing assures scrubbing of the bed for maximum cleaning efficiency. This action allows the up-flow to handle highly turbid waters at high flow rates, with longer cycle lengths, while ensuring good cleaning cycles.

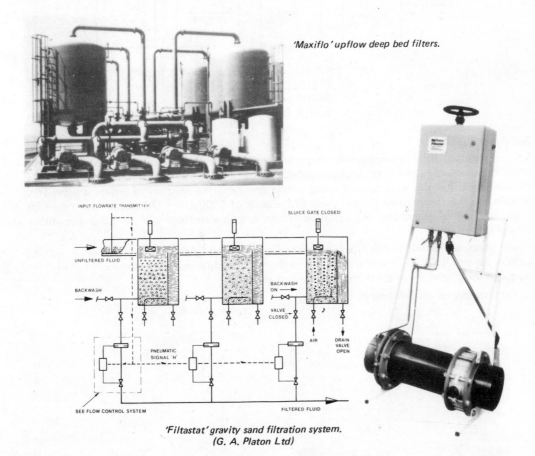

'Maxiflo' upflow deep bed filters.

'Filtastat' gravity sand filtration system.
(G. A. Platon Ltd)

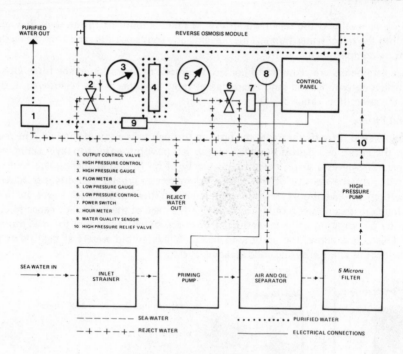

Fig 3 Osmotic water purified system.
(G.M. Power Plant)

Salt Water Purifiers

Various methods from evaporation to chemical treatment may be employed for producing fresh water from sea water and other impure sources. One of the most successful is the reverse osmosis process which has the advantage of being simple and requiring only a low power supply. This process involves compressing the salt water to the order of 1 000 lb/in^2 (70 bar) to pass it through a semi-permeable membrane. The resulting filtrate is then free from salt and other impurities, including bacteria.

An example of a unit of this type is shown in Fig 3. Depending on size, an output of up to 2 160 gallons per day (10 000 litres/day) of fresh water can be obtained from a power input of 3 hp (required for driving the priming and high pressure pumps).

See also chapter on *Drinking Water Filters.*

Drinking Water Filters

IN THE UK alone there are an estimated 350 000 touring caravans together with tens of thousands of boats of all types and sizes which rely on onboard tanks for domestic water supply. The usual source of filling is from mains water via a tap and/or hose which, in the case of marinas can also be used for general wash-down duties. Only on a limited number of marinas is drinking water available from a separate source fitted with hygienic (good quality) hose. The chances are, therefore, quite high that there will be initial contamination when the water tank is filled — certainly so if the tank is not flushed and cleaned at least annually.

Further contamination is then inevitable on standing. A recent test conducted with a large plastic container filled with tap water showed an initial bacterial count of 18 per ml, which after only one week had risen to 45 000/ml. Thus the equipment commonly used to store and dispense fresh water in mobile environments leaves much to be desired unless subject to additional treatment. This may range from the simple use of purifying agents added to the water; filtration; or complete water treatment. Of these filtration is by far the most attractive of the low cost methods.

Contaminants present can range from the objectionable to the harmful. Objectionable contaminants are those which affect the taste and colour of drinking water. Harmful contaminants include all forms of disease-producing bacteria and possible cancer-causing agents. Simple chemical

Safari water purifier.

Safari G.E. filter cartridge.

treatment by 'dosing' the water can kill bacteria, usually at the expense of taste and sometimes colour. Filters are capable of removing suspended matter down to about 0.4 μm in size, which is smaller than the bacteria causing intestinal type disorders, and can also include adsorbent media to remove most taste-producing contaminants and colouring contaminants.

The adsorbent medium most commonly used in such filters is activated carbon. Ultra-fine filtering can be combined with this to ensure maximum water clarity and maximum adsorptive properties. There then remains the desirability of dealing with bacteria removed and held in the filter media. The basic answer is to incorporate an insoluble, non-toxic, sanitizing agent in the filter capable of destroying held bacteria. A charcoal filter on its own is inadequate for dealing with bacteria since it retains them *in situ*.

Other important features are that the filter unit should be sealed, the media non-migrating; and heat-resistant if it is to be used with hot water. It should also be easy to mount as an in-line fitting, and easy to disassemble to change the filter cartridge. Disposable cartridge filters are preferable to 'clearable' filters as it is not generally possible to remove all bacteria by clearing; also filter media may be damaged and lose their efficiency by 'heavy' cleaning. Accepting activated charcoal (usually combined with a silver sanitizing agent) as the main element, the additional elements used for ultra-fine mechanical filtering will finally govern the overall performance. The use of asbestos as a filtering medium is to be avoided as the material is subject to migration and can, in fact, *add* asbestos fibres to water passing through it. It is also desirable to obtain an optimum balance between what is removed and what is passed by the complete filter — *eg* some soluble mineral salt content in the final product may be desirable, rather than removing as much dissolved minerals as possible, *en bloc*. (Sodium fluoride, incidentally, is a dissolved salt which cannot be removed by a filter).

The capacity of the filter also requires to be tailored to specific needs, generally rated in terms of gallons the filter can treat before the cartridge needs replacement — *eg* 400 gallons, 800 gallons, *etc*, depending mainly on filter size. This can only be an approximate rating and is very much

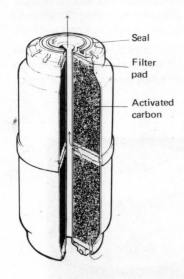

Seal

Filter pad

Activated carbon

Flava-major water filter.

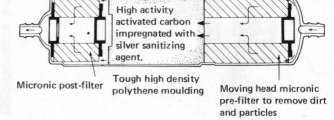

High activity activated carbon impregnated with silver sanitizing agent.

Micronic post-filter

Tough high density polythene moulding

Moving head micronic pre-filter to remove dirt and particles

Fress-ness in-line water filter.

dependent on the condition of the water being treated, the water pressure (in a pressurized system), and pressure cycling. If the same water being handled contains a relatively high proportion of suspended matter, the life of the filter cartridge can be considerably extended by the addition of a relatively coarse pre-filter in the system at a position where it is readily accessible for cleaning. It should be fitted upstream (*ie* near the tank). The main filter should be located as close to the supply outlet (tap) as possible.

In the laboratory, filter life may be assessed in various ways — *eg* chlorine break-through showing end-of-life of the adsorbent element; bacterial counts in the effluent; colour tests; differential pressure (indicating clogging of the filter); *etc*.

Bacterial count tests are obviously of major significance. Amongst the more significant of the harmful bacteria are *salmonella typhi* or S.typhi (the cause of typhoid fever), and *fecal coliform* (a sewage indicator). A satisfactory water filter should provide 100% removal in both cases.

Apart from chlorine and hydrogen sulphide, the origin of bad tastes and odours in raw waters is usually organic contaminants. Here the ability of a filter to remove methylene blue from water is a standard — and demanding — test for organics removal capacity. The longer a filter can continue to deliver clear effluent when fed with methylene blue loaded influent, the better its ability to accommodate organics. This particular test is a simple one to compare the performance of different filters.

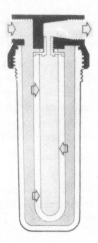

IMI water filter for domestic installations.

Industrial Water Cleaning Treatment

REQUIREMENTS FOR the treatment of industrial wastewater can differ widely from one application to another. The most common problem is the presence of oily contaminants, but suspended and settleable solids may also be present together with other salts, *etc.* in solution over a wide range of pH. The following can, therefore, only be offered as a general guide to treatment of industrial wastewater.

Contaminants and/or problem	Suggested treatment
Oil in globular form circa 150 μm, also settleable solids	Gravity type oil/water separator with internal capacity to store oil. Depending on the permissible oil content of the treated wastewater, flow velocity in separator may need to be limited and oil-skimming incorporated.
Oil contamination in emulsified form; no appreciable solids	Coalescing-type oil/water separator
Settleable solids only	Gravity-type separator. Performance may be enhanced by chemical treatment to provide agglomeration.
Settleable and suspended solids only	Bulk clarifier
Large solids, fibres and waste material. No fines.	Rotating screen
Sludge	Gravity separator or gravity filter. For large volumes, vacuum drum filter, belt filter, etc.
Wastewater requires pH adjustment	Chemical treatment. Other treatment as necessary to deal with other contaminants present

See also chapters on *Oily Water Treatment, Oil Reclamation, Trade Effluent Treatment.*

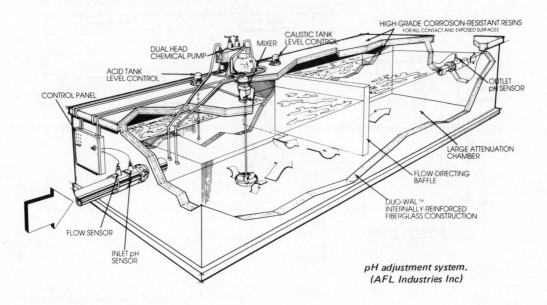

pH adjustment system.
(AFL Industries Inc)

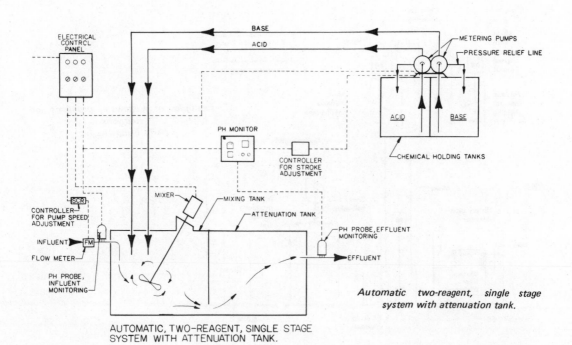

AUTOMATIC, TWO-REAGENT, SINGLE STAGE
SYSTEM WITH ATTENUATION TANK.

Automatic two-reagent, single stage
system with attenuation tank.

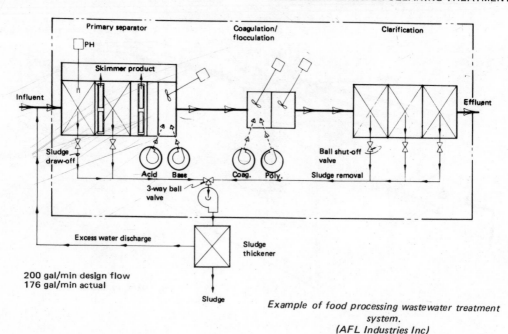

Example of food processing wastewater treatment system.
(AFL Industries Inc)

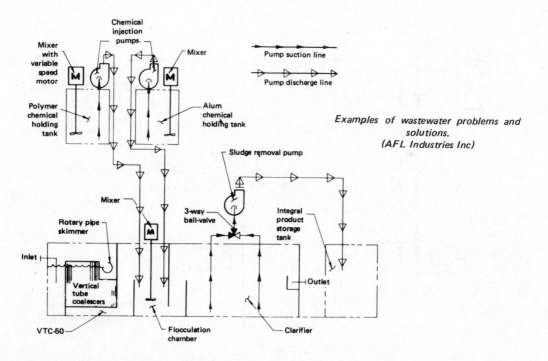

Examples of wastewater problems and solutions.
(AFL Industries Inc)

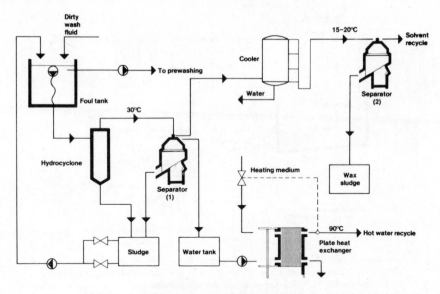

Vehicle dewaxing: system with two separation stages for water and solvent reclamation.
(Alfa-Laval)

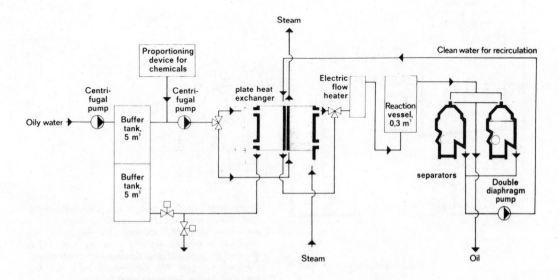

Decontamination of flush water in crude separation plant.
(Alfa Laval)

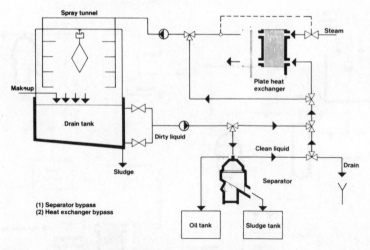

Degreasing: typical regeneration and temperature control system for automated spray line. Contaminated liquid from spray tunnel drains off to collecting tank and is pumped to self-cleaning separator for continuous removal of oil and sludge. Cleaned fluid goes back via plate heat exchanger to spray tunnel. Temperature of liquid leaving plate heat exchanger is monitored and regulated by automatic feedback control loop.
(Alfa-Laval)

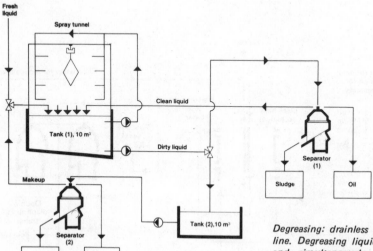

Degreasing: drainless system for automated spray line. Degreasing liquid is circulated from tank 1 and simultaneously cleaned by separator (1) installed in bypass. At end of week, tank (1) is drained to tank (2) and refilled with fresh liquid. Contents of tank (2), cleaned by separator (2), are used during following week as makeup to compensate for daily evaporation of $2\ m^3$.
(Alfa-Laval)

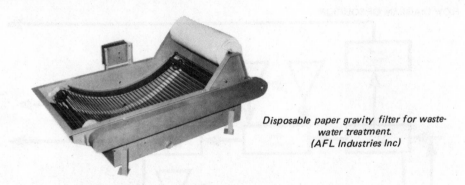

Disposable paper gravity filter for waste-
water treatment.
(AFL Industries Inc)

FLOW DIAGRAM OF SOLUTION

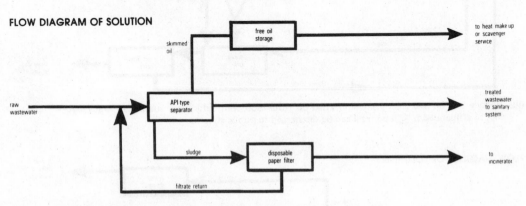

(i) Reduce 400 ppm free oil and settleable solids to less than 100 ppm of oil so effluent can be discharged to municipal sanitary system.

FLOW DIAGRAM OF SOLUTION

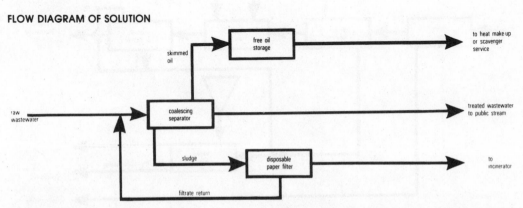

(ii) Reduce 150 ppm mechanically-emulsified oil and settleable solids to $\leq$ 15 ppm (oil) so effluent can be discharged to public stream.

Examples of wastewater problems and solutions
(AFL Industries Inc)

cont...

FLOW DIAGRAM OF SOLUTION

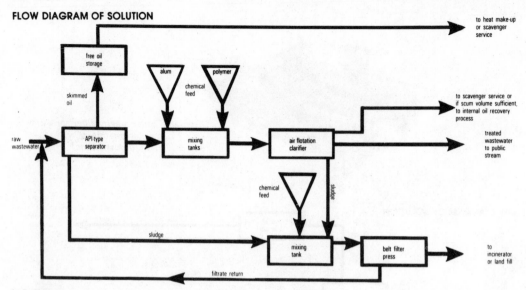

(iii) Reduce free oil and chemically-emulsified oil (total 500 ppm) and heavy suspended solids loading, so effluent with ≤15 ppm oil can be discharged to public stream.

FLOW DIAGRAM OF SOLUTION

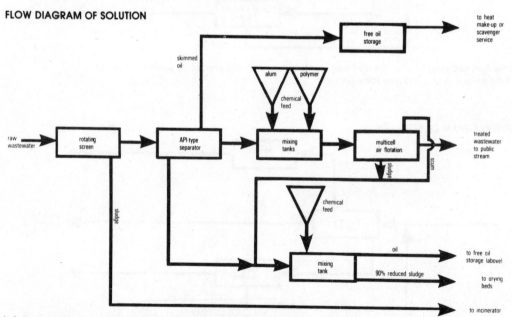

(iv) Remove floating trash, settleable solids, free oil and chemically-emulsified oil (total 400 ppm) to ≤15 ppm oil, so effluent can be discharged to public stream.

Examples of wastewater problems and solutions
(AFL Industries Inc)

cont...

FLOW DIAGRAM OF SOLUTION

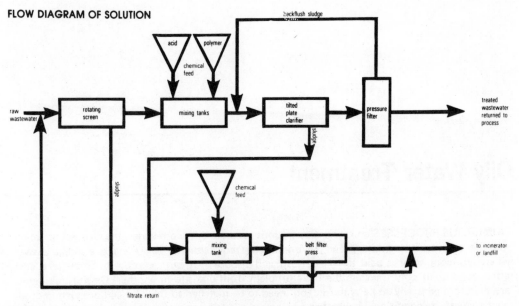

(v) Remove floating trash, settleable solids, suspended solids, and adjust a caustic pH extreme so that wastewater can be recycled to process capable of accepting no more than 5 mg/litre suspended solids.

Examples of wastewater problems and solutions
(AFL Industries Inc)

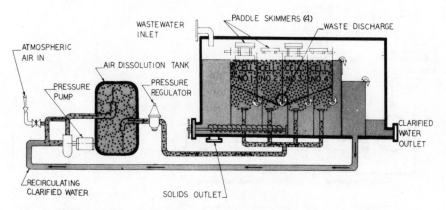

Multicell dissolved air flotation system for removal of
floatable oils and solids from industrial wastewater.
(AFL Industries Inc)

Oily Water Treatment

NUMEROUS PROCESSES and service operations generate oily wastewater, the disposal of which may be subject to legislatory and environmental requirements. *Tankering* is a direct answer whereby a contractor is paid to collect waste and dispose of it, but can prove to be the least cost effective. Also it only transfers the basic problem from one site to another. On-site treatments are therefore generally to be preferred, but need to be matched to the kind and proportion of oil contaminant, its condition (*ie* whether free or emulsified), and the presence of other contaminants.

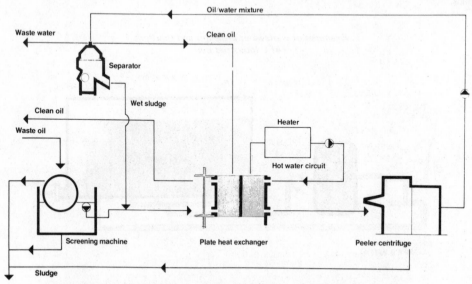

Standard plant developed by Alfa-Laval in Germany for waste oil treatment. Feed is first treated in a rotary screening machine with 3 mm mesh for removal of coarse solids, then heated to 70–75°C in plate heat exchanger. Oil is desludged in peeler sedimenting centrifuge and dewatered in self-cleaning centrifugal concentrator. Heat content of reclaimed oil is recycled to feed in regenerative section of heat exchanger.

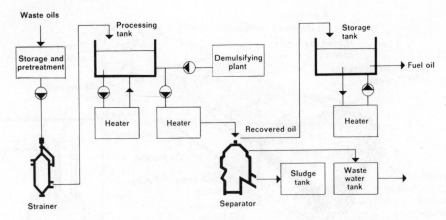

*Example of plant for heating miscellaneous waste oils. Coarse particles are removed
from feed by a self-cleaning strainer, and mixture is heated to 100°C to facilitate
separation of water and sludge in self-cleaning centrifugal purifier.*
(Alfa-Laval).

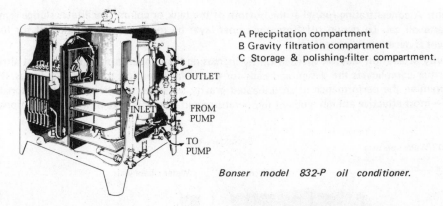

A Precipitation compartment
B Gravity filtration compartment
C Storage & polishing-filter compartment.

Bonser   model   832-P   oil   conditioner.

Incineration is a possible on-site treatment although this may demand the use of special incinerating equipment with gas or fuel oil added to support combustion. Much depends on the proportion of oil present in the waste. Emulsified oil wastes, although containing a high proportion of water, are often more readily incinerated than heavier oily wastewater.

Settlement under gravity is a direct, low-cost solution but involves the use of bulky separator tanks. Also such tanks need to have correct proportions for optimum performance, *eg* a minimum depth-to-width ratio to ensure that linear velocity through the separator is not high enough to cause re-mixing of oil and water. Hence gravity separators are essentially specialized designs, as well as being bulky. A gravity separator to API recommendations for treating 700 gallons/minute of oil needs to be 67 ft long, 11 ft wide and 6 ft deep. This can provide fairly rapid separation of oil to a point where the wastewater is suitable for discharge.

In smaller gravity separators or separation columns the time taken for separation may be as high as two or three days. This will allow the majority of the sludge to settle. Four distinct layers are formed, consisting of an uppermost layer of oil, followed by light sludge, water, and bottom

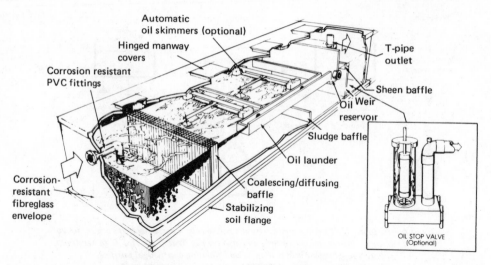

Enhanced gravity separator (EGS) by AFL Industries Inc.

sediment. A concentrating funnel at the bottom of the tank or column facilitates sludge removal, and waste oil can be drawn off from the upper layer by means of a float take-off for further treatment if necessary — *eg* reclaim.

Gravity separation may be speeded up by increasing the temperature of the influent although this further complicates the design and calls for particular attention to avoid heat losses. By the same premise, the performance of an unheated gravity separator will be subject to seasonal variations — most effective at high ambient temperatures and least effective in winter conditions.

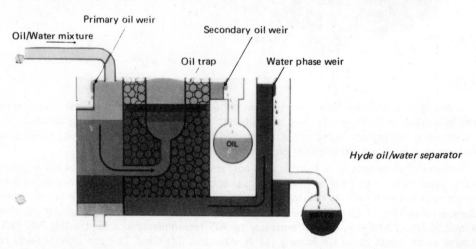

Hyde oil/water separator

Coalescer/Separators

A coalescing medium installed in the separating chamber provides a surface on which oil globules can combine or agglomerate. And the larger the oil globule, the faster its rate of rise. The globules wick-up the coalescing medium and break free to rise through the continuous phase. The faster rate of rise of the larger particles means less retention time is required than for straight gravity separation. The use of a coalescing medium provides another benefit: an API type separator is designed to remove 150 μm oil globules (free oil). A coalescing type separator of the proper design can removal oil globules as small as 20 μm. Further the size of separating chamber is substantially reduced compared with an API separator.

The coalescing medium used needs to have oleophillic properties for optimum oil retention. At the same time such a property usually means that the medium is water repellent. Plastic materials such as polypropylene and PTFE have proved to have excellent coalescing properties used in the form of plates or tubes—Fig 1. The tube type is claimed to have a superior performance.

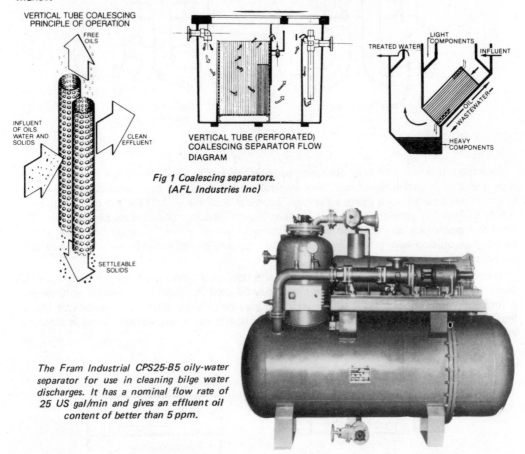

Fig 1 Coalescing separators.
(AFL Industries Inc)

The Fram Industrial CPS25-B5 oily-water separator for use in cleaning bilge water discharges. It has a nominal flow rate of 25 US gal/min and gives an effluent oil content of better than 5 ppm.

Oil Removal

Most separators have an internal collection area or reservoir for accumulating skimmed oil. The simplest method of transferring floating oil to the internal reservoir is to provide an adjustable overweir. This type of skimming device can be adjusted to skim a predetermined level of the top surface as the flow moves through the unit. Oil flows over the weir and into the internal reservoir for removal.

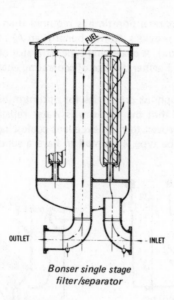

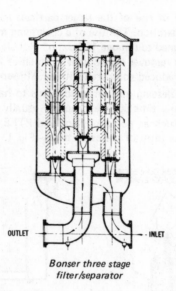

Bonser single stage filter/separator

Bonser three stage filter/separator

Examples of two methods of bulk oil storage are shown in Fig 2, the conventional separate tank and an optional integral tank. The integral oil 'slop' tank is positioned along the entire length of the separator and shares a common inner wall with the unit. The width of the slop tank can be designed to provide the desired product storage capacity. Skimmed oil can be gravity fed from the separator's oil collection sump or internal reservoir to the larger oil slop tank. Incorporating an oil slop tank in the separator means that only one installation site is required and it eliminates interconnecting piping.

If the separator has an oil overweir with a collection sump (and a relatively constant dynamic flow) a skimmer is not essential. A skimmer may be used to advantage in certain applications to overcome the inflexibility of an overweir and may be of adjustable level or automatic (floating) type. The latter can be capable of removing virtually water free oil with possible recovery value.

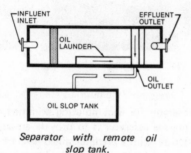

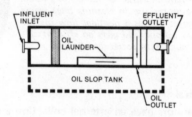

Separator with remote oil slop tank.

Separator with integral oil slop tank

Fig 2

Other Methods

Other methods used include chemical treatment to provide coagulation and/or flocculation followed by sedimentation or flotation, air flotation alone, acid-cracking, thermal splitting and filtration.

In the case of flocculation gravity separation can generally be best accomplished with clarification. Clarifiers usually have an advantage over air flotation if the floc settles. Properly sized they are more efficient in removing some flocs. Also power requirements are less and they are easier to maintain. A clarifier may not be suitable if the floc has a near neutral buoyancy and a very long settling time. In other words, an extremely long detention time would require too large a clarifier. An alternative is air flotation.

The heart of the Fram Industrial oily-water separator system is this unique arrangement of corrugated plates. Oil collects at the peak of each corrugation and weeps upwards due to the differing specific gravities of oil and water until it collects at the top of the unit. The recovered oil contains less than 5% of water and can be reclaimed or used for space heating.

There are two common types of air flotation: dissolved and dispersed. Dissolved air flotation (DAF) involves the use of pressurized water which contains dissolved air. This water is released in the bottom of the tank containing the wastewater. The release of pressure allows the air to separate from the water generating millions of tiny bubbles that lift the floc to the surface. In dispersed air flotation, the air is not dissolved in the water, and the bubbles are larger and fewer in number. The typical bubble size is 80 μm for dissolved air flotation and 1000 μm for dispersed flotation.

Typical air flotation units are made in single- and multi-cell configurations. Stickier scum and sludge can usually be obtained from flotation equipment than a clarifier, but such units are commonly used in combination with a clarifier.

Filtration

Filtration is more normally used as a post-treatment, *eg* further to improve the water quality. Oil-water separators are, however, also designed on a filtration basis.

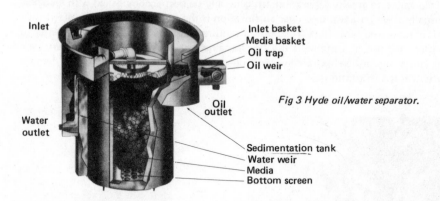

Fig 3 Hyde oil/water separator.

An example is shown in Fig 3, utilizing the principle that when two non-miscible liquids of different densities flow by gravity through a porous medium they will have different penetrability rates. First the oil-water mixture enters a sedimentation tank where heavier particles settle out. The oil-water mixture then enters the inlet basket and flows into the medium where the oil separates from the water at an accelerated rate. The water flows downwards through the bottom screen then up and over a water weir which creates a water table supporting the oil longer. The oil travels horizontally on top of the water into the oil trap and then over an adjustable oil weir which is set at a position slightly above the maximum water level.

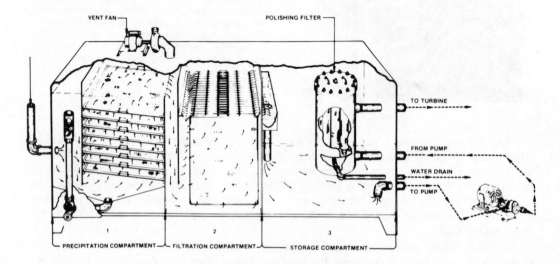

Schematic diagram showing oil flow through a Bonser turbine oil conditioner.

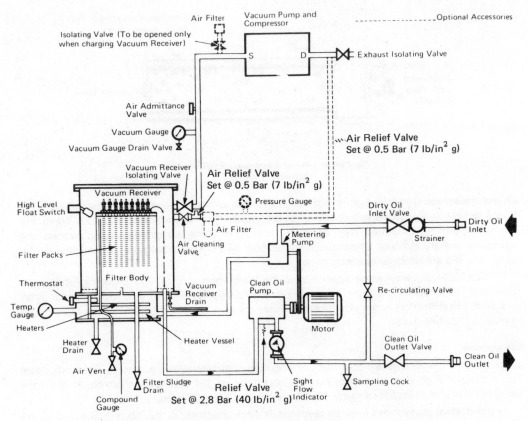

Flow diagram for Vokes medium vacuum MT range filters for transformer oil.

Emulsified Oily Waters

Emulsified oil wastes can present particular problems in handling, particularly those originally intended to behave as emulsions (*eg* machine tool coolants), because of the stable nature of the emulsions involved. Two basic methods are:-

(i)   Chemical treatment to neutralize the emulsifiers, allowing oil to separate out.

(ii) Heating to near boiling point to separate the oil and water phases, together with chemical dosing if necessary.

With chemical splitting (i), final treatment is then in a separator. With thermal splitting (ii), complete process equipment is normally involved incorporating heat exchangers associated with evaporators or centrifuges.

A more straightforward process which can be used is *ultrafiltration* using suitably designed membrane filters. These differ from conventional filters in that the flow is tangential to the filter

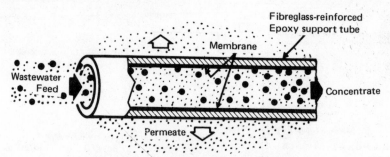

Fig 4 *Hyde tubular membrane ultrafiltration.*
(Zimmite (UK) Ltd)

element (membrane) rather than at right angles to the surface — an example being shown in Fig 4. In a typical unit wastewater feed is introduced into an array of membrane modules. Water and low-molecular-weight solutes (for example, salts and some surfactants) pass through the membrane and are removed as permeate. Emulsified oil and suspended solids are rejected by the membrane and are removed as concentrate.

In ultrafiltration, wastewater flows across the membrane surface. For ordinary filtration, a filter cake builds up on the filter screen, which requires replacement or cleaning at regular intervals. With ultrafiltration, cross flow prevents filter cake buildup, and high filtration rates can be maintained continuously.

Membranes

Ultrafiltration membranes are thin films of proprietary non-cellulosic polymers. The membranes can withstand high operating temperatures, extremes in pH and solvent exposure, and have demonstrated a working life of many years in treating oily wastewaters.

Ultrafiltration membranes have an asymmetric pore structure. A thin 'skin' (<0.5 μm) covers a highly porous substructure. The combination of a thin skin and porous substructure gives the ultrafiltration membranes a low resistance to permeate flow, permitting low-pressure operation. Waste water flows across the skin side of the membrane, which has small pore openings (<0.005 μm). Because all emulsified oil droplets and suspended solids are larger than the pore openings, pore plugging cannot occur.

See also chapters on *Oil Reclamation, Filtration of Metalworking Fluids, Industrial Water Cleaning, Membrane Filters.*

Metal Working Fluids

MOST METALWORKING operations call for the use of lubricants/coolants to lubricate the surface between workpiece and tool and remove heat generated by the process. Additional advantages offered by such fluids are washing away of fine swarf from the work area and corrosion inhibition. The most common choice is an oil/water emulsion, the oil content providing the lubrication and water acting as the main cooling agent, such fluids being generally referred to as *coolants.*

In the majority of cases coolant is contained in a circulating system, either individual to a machine or in a central system supplying a number of machines. Deterioration of such fluids results from:

(i)   Contamination by dirt, metal fines, swarf, chips, *etc;* and foreign liquids — *eg* water in oil-based coolants and tramp oil in water-based coolants.

(ii)   Degradation by bacteria introduced into the fluid from airborne dirt, metal stock, impure water used as a diluent, *etc.*

(iii) Evaporation of water from water-based coolants resulting in an increased concentration of dissolved minerals.

Deteriorating coolant properties can lead to loss of precision in work, reduced tool life and heavy wear on machine parts, need for frequent replenishment of coolant, and unpleasant working environment (smells, fumes, even risk of skin disease). Effective cleaning of the whole circulation system before new fluid is used, and effective methods of purifying and recirculating coolants, are therefore commonsense as well as being good housekeeping and a sound investment.

Where cutting fluids are used in considerable volume, *eg* for groups of individual machines, centralized supply systems are often better than individual circuits. Such a system can also incorporate a centralized cleaning unit for accepting dirty coolant from the machines and returning it clean. Such a cleaning plant can be specifically adapted to the requirements of the machines and plant involved.

Contaminants present may be fluid or solid; and the latter may be fine or coarse, fibrous, chips, slushy or needles, as well as varying widely in size. Grinding operations in particular produce extremely fine particles which are not readily separated out by conventional filters. The water used as a diluent in water-oil fluids can also have a significant effect. Hard water can cause a scum to form which clogs filters; soft water can cause foaming if highly agitated. High mineral content in water can make fluid residues more solid than when pure water is used.

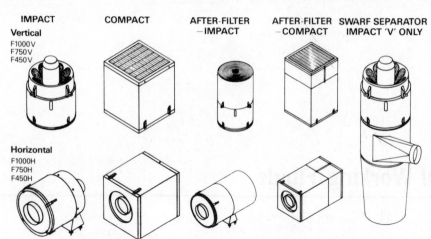

IMPACT   COMPACT   AFTER-FILTER   AFTER-FILTER   SWARF SEPARATOR
                     —IMPACT   —COMPACT   IMPACT 'V' ONLY

Vertical
F1000V
F750V
F450V

Horizontal
F1000H
F750H
F450H

'Filtermist' units for eliminating machine shop pollution at source.

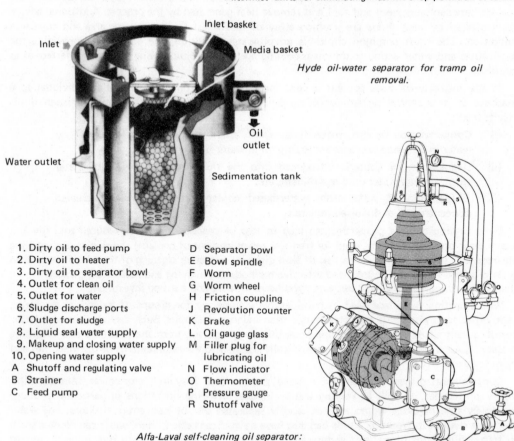

Inlet basket

Inlet

Media basket

Hyde oil-water separator for tramp oil removal.

Oil outlet

Water outlet

Sedimentation tank

1. Dirty oil to feed pump
2. Dirty oil to heater
3. Dirty oil to separator bowl
4. Outlet for clean oil
5. Outlet for water
6. Sludge discharge ports
7. Outlet for sludge
8. Liquid seal water supply
9. Makeup and closing water supply
10. Opening water supply
A Shutoff and regulating valve
B Strainer
C Feed pump

D Separator bowl
E Bowl spindle
F Worm
G Worm wheel
H Friction coupling
J Revolution counter
K Brake
L Oil gauge glass
M Filler plug for
   lubricating oil
N Flow indicator
O Thermometer
P Pressure gauge
R Shutoff valve

*Alfa-Laval self-cleaning oil separator:
principal components.*

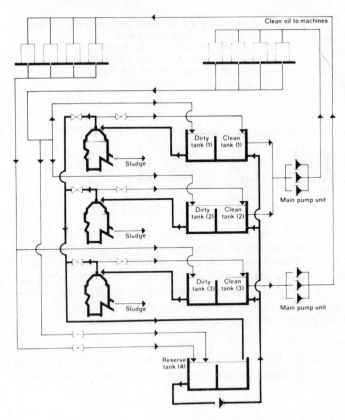

Purification of grinding oil.
Large centralized plant installed in a
Berlin factory. Specifications called
for:

a. *minimum floor space*

b. *ability to cope with high flow*
    rates and wide fluctuations
    while delivering a constant flow
    at constant high pressure.

c. *coolant to be free of moisture*
    and solid particles larger than
    1 μm.

d. *fully automatic operation.*

Three automatic control systems
are installed for different grinder
line pressures. Separate pump units
compensate for fluctuations. Sep-
arators operate in bypass during
day shift and switch automatically
to full-flow operation at night.

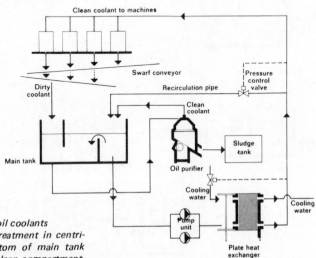

Clarification/purification of neat oil coolants
Standard Alfa-Laval system for bypass treatment in centri-
fugal clarifier or purifier fed from bottom of main tank
foul compartment and discharging into clean compartment.
Cooling water flow to plate heat exchanger and recircula-
tion of clean oil are automatically regulated.

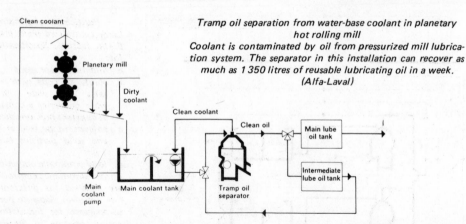

Tramp oil separation from water-base coolant in planetary hot rolling mill
Coolant is contaminated by oil from pressurized mill lubrication system. The separator in this installation can recover as much as 1 350 litres of reusable lubricating oil in a week.
(Alfa-Laval)

Tramp oil particularly should be removed from water-oil coolants as its presence can degrade the coolant properties dramatically, thus considerably reducing its useful life — *eg* it can cause loss of cooling and wetting properties, deplete emulsifiers, nullify rust-inhibitors and impede filtration. In fact for any particular machine there is a maximum tramp oil level which the system can tolerate without requiring the machine or central system to be shut down for cleaning. Ideally a system should have a tramp oil separator which ensures that the tramp oil level left in the system is always below the maximum acceptable limit for the process, *ie* cutting, grinding, *etc*.

Treatment for Water-based Coolants

Water-based coolants are soluble oils in the form of emulsions in water with additives such as emulsifiers, coupling agents (to assist dispersion), corrosion-inhibitors, anti-foaming and wetting agents, and bactericides.

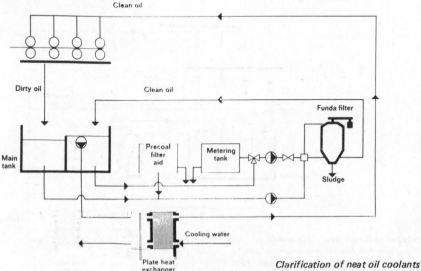

Clarification of neat oil coolants
Standard Alfa-Laval system for full-flow treatment with Funda precoat filter between foul tank and clean tank. Clean oil is recirculated via plate cooler.

The first step towards maintenance of water-based coolant quality is correct mixing. In a good emulsion, the oil droplets should be about 1 μm in diameter and positively charged for mutual repulsion to keep them in a state of colloidal suspension.

The water used must be softened if necessary with sodium carbonate to prevent foreign ions from destroying the droplet surface charges and causing coalescence. The oil must be added to the water (not *vice versa*), and the phases must be mixed quickly to prevent foaming and scum formation.

To maintain the coolant *clear,* the system should provide for continuous removal of solid contaminants and allow fines to settle out.

The solid impurities in water-based cutting coolants are generally coarser than those in, for example, grinding oils. Swarfs are easily removed by straining and medium-sized particles by gravity settling in a 'dirty' tank. The dirty and clean tanks are often combined in a single vessel with a system of baffles, except for applications with low stock removal when the dirty tank may be skimmed or scraped by a drag-link conveyor. However, some fine particles in the micron range still remain in suspension, and these may be removed before the coolant is recycled in order to avoid undue tool wear and impairment of work finish.

Screens, screening machines and rotary strainers can trap solid particles down to about 15 μm, are relatively inexpensive, and can have high capacities. Conventional filters can also perform a

Nickel alloy strip being flooded with coolant from three of 12 jets as it is successively cold-rolled to reduce thickness at the Hereford plant of Henry Wiggin. Squeegee rollers and air-knife are located between snubber roll and coolant.

The installation of a Hyde separator supplied by Zimmite (UK) to remove tramp oil from coolant and avoid bacterial growth has eliminated rejection of rolled strip due to irreparable staining and extended coolant life from three weeks to six months.

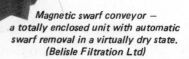

Magnetic swarf conveyor —
a totally enclosed unit with automatic swarf removal in a virtually dry state.
(Belisle Filtration Ltd)

similar duty on low volume systems and are produced in a variety of forms to fit in both centralized and individual systems. They may also be used with, or combined with, magnetic filters to separate and retain ferrous metal particles.

Hydrocyclones are even simpler and cheaper than screens, but are less efficient and less flexible as regards the contaminants they can handle. They are also sensitive to blockage by large particles or tramp oil. Two-stage hydrocyclone treatment can, however, trap particles down to about 5 μm.

Centrifugal separators (disc-bowl type) offer many advantages, but are more expensive. They are advantageously associated with screens and can remove fine particles passing through screens, as well as tramp oil. Both single and two stage units may be employed.

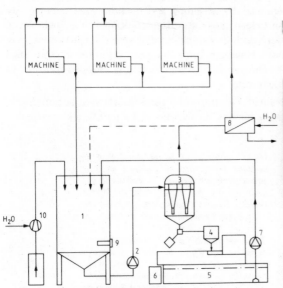

Standard Mann hydrocyclone block plant

Schematic diagram of a centralized Mann hydrocyclone block plant.

1. Round storage container
2. System pump
3. Hydro-cyclone block
4. Discharge cyclone
5. Paper strip filter.
6. Sludge carrier.
7. Lift pump.
8. Heat exchanger.
9. Heater.
10. Emulsion mixer

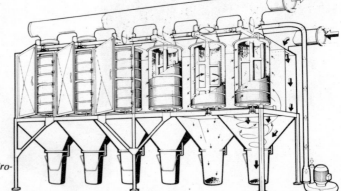

Schematic diagram of centralized hydrocyclone block plant (Mann & Hummel GmbH)

Tramp Oil Separation

Centrifugal separators are generally recognized as the most effective method of removing tramp oil in high volume systems and can reduce tramp oil level to 1% or less as well as removing solids and some emulsified oil. High capital, operating and maintenance costs are less attractive features in the case of smaller industrial plant. Alternatives available are:-

(i)   *Skimmers* — wheel or belt type where floating tramp oil adheres to the wheel or belt which is then wiped clean, transferring the tramp oil to a collecting drain. At best these can be expected to reduce tramp oil level to 2—3%. They will not remove emulsified or suspended tramp oil which may be present in the system.

(ii) *Porous Media Separators* — which are gravity-type filters with a porous medium through which water and oil permeate at different rates. They are relatively inexpensive units capable of separating free floating and suspended tramp oil (as well as solids) and reducing tramp oil level to the order of 0.5—1.5%. They are compact in size and take up minimal floor space.

(iii) *Tube-type Separators* — which are basically separating tanks with nests of conglomerator tubes. They will remove only free floating tramp oil (and some solids by settlement) with a capability, suitably sized, of reducing tramp oil level to the order of 1.25—2%. Their main disadvantage is the large size for effective operation.

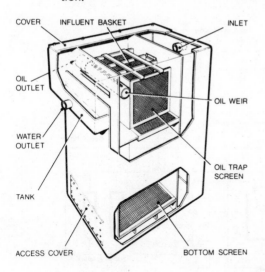

COVER   INFLUENT BASKET   INLET
OIL OUTLET
WATER OUTLET
TANK
ACCESS COVER
OIL WEIR
OIL TRAP SCREEN
BOTTOM SCREEN

Hyde tramp oil remover and oil/water separator

Faudi Feinbau compact precoat filter unit AS 0.8 is designed for use in conjunction with superfinishing machines with low stock removal and volume flows but with exacting purity requirements.

The unit can be supplied in a mobile or stationary version, with one or two filter housings. It is very versatile and is suitable for various operating conditions.

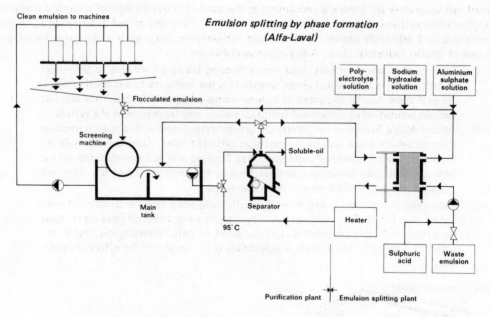

Emulsion splitting by phase formation
(Alfa-Laval)

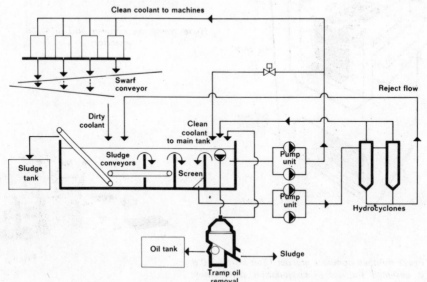

Three-stage emulsion treatment system.
1. coarse sludge settles out on conveyors in main tank.
2. hydrocyclones in bypass circuit remove fine solid contaminants.
3. centrifugal concentrator connected in bypass removes tramp oil and
   ultra-fine particles.

(Alfa-Laval)

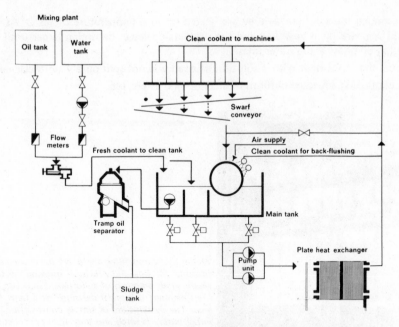

*Mixing, clarification and cooling of emulsion coolant
Installation in a ball bearing works. Full flow of used coolant
returns to main supply tank via screening machine. Automatic mixing system keeps main tank topped up. Tramp oil
separator in bypass
(Alfa-Laval)*

Emulsion Splitting

Ultimately, even with efficient cleaning treatment, emulsions reach the end of their useful life.
Disposal can then be a problem since public health authorities in most industrial countries limit
the permissible oil content of liquid wastes which can be discharged into sewerage systems. These
limits are typically between 10 and 50 mg/litre. To conform to this, it is necessary to split the
emulsions to remove the oil before attempting disposal. Equally, if the volume involved is large,
emulsion splitting may be economic to recover oil to be used as fuel or even a hydraulic fluid.

Emulsions may be split chemically (by flocculation); or by heat (phase formation).

Flocculation processes produce sludge, which entails the use of sludge-handling equipment. On
the other hand, phase formation processes produce little or no sludge, and are generally to be preferred. The sludge that emerges from phase formation usually amounts to only 0.5% of the total
flow. It is formed from any emulsifying agents, cleansing fluids or similar chemicals that may be
present in the emulsion. Small quantities of these substances and even relatively large quantities
of free oil do not affect the results.

The Phase Formation Process

The phase formation method is based on the principle that if the electric charges that keep the oil
droplets apart are reduced or eliminated, the droplets will agglomerate forming larger units. This is
achieved by adding a strong electrolyte, such as 2–3% of a saturated solution of magnesium

chloride, and then mixing the solutions as they are heated up to a temperature of 98°C. At this temperature the surface tension is very low and the droplets coalesce, becoming larger until the emulsion splits into an oil phase and a water phase.

It should be noted that treatment with a solution of a salt will not split purely synthetic emulsions, *ie* emulsions containing aqueous solutions of alcohols and esters, *etc.*

'Mann' micro top filter plants are being used successfully for fine and precision drawing machines where small amounts of solid particles occur. The filter element is a paper cartridge with large filter area. The systems are of simple construction. The initial outlay is small and they feature particularly high separating capacities.

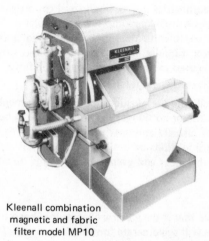

Kleenall combination
magnetic and fabric
filter model MP10

Kleenall plain fabric filter
model P-25

(Gaston E. Marbaix Ltd)

Design Requirements

The design of coolant filters and separators for machine tools is an extremely complex and varied subject. Some of the general aspects which have to be considered before a preliminary appraisal can be made are:-

(i) The purpose or necessity of the filter or separator.

(ii) The viscosities and associated properties of the coolant to be filtered.

(iii) The metal cutting functions.

(iv) The degree of separation required.

(v) The flow rate required.

(vi) The filter capacity.

(vii) The machine type and its physical characteristics relating to outlet heights, operations, table size, *etc.*

(viii) Type and nature of stock produced.

(ix) Space available for the system.

(x) The expansion rate of cut material which will convert the solid material removed into the expanded volume of chips, swarf and slurry, *etc.*

(xi) The target system efficiency and cost effectiveness in terms of total stock introduced related to that remaining in suspension after complete cycling.

(xii) Operating period affecting stability of production and flexibility and durability of system.

(xiii) Protective devices to be incorporated in the system to cover mis-use or mechanical failure.

(xiv) The system is safe and complies with at least the minimum standards laid down by the Health and Safety at Work Act.

Filter Appraisal

Providing all the relevant information is available, the process of individual assessment of the stages necessary can be undertaken. In the process of 'breaking down' we can, by selection and elimination, determine the number of stages required, and the size and types of filter media best suited to provide a filter which invariably combines several distinct functions.

The range of machine tools presently under production is diverse and extensive. The designer's function may thus vary from specifying equipment for a single, small toolroom grinder, up to that for a complicated multi-stage unit requiring detailed site appraisal in addition to a special study of the requirements of individual machines. The latter could call for a central system serving either a line of machines, or a complete section of the working plant. Safeguards would also be necessary on a central system to avoid extremely high production losses which could occur if the system is not fully equipped with full stand-by pumps, auto level monitors, alarms and back-up systems to cover electrical or mechanical failure.

Design Process

The design process is best illustrated by examining a typical machine and its functions. The example chosen for this purpose is a multi-spindle rotary indexing machine, using a water based soluble coolant machining an EN8 vehicle component having a variety of drilling and spot facing operations, with one final burnishing station. Design analysis is as follows:-

(i) **Purpose and need for a filter**

An automatic rotary indexing machine is a very expensive piece of equipment and for an extended tool life and reduced tool wear an optimum separation level is required. In addition such a machine can be adapted to take various machining heads from plain drilling, ejector or gun drilling to fine boring and burnishing tools; this possible variety of configuration determines the positive need for a filter with two distinct levels of separation in the case under discussion.

(ii) **Coolant**

The coolant to be filtered is a soluble water based emulsion and all relevant properties are taken into account when assessing the most suitable materials, pumps and separating devices, which may be affected by its viscosity or any change in properties due to temperature variation, *etc.*

(iii) **Metal cutting operations**

The cutting operations consist of primary stock removal from drilling operations using chip breaker drills, and the use of standard spot facing tools and burnishing rolls, the last of these producing a negligible fraction of the total stock for disposal.

(iv) **The degree of separation**

Here an optimum cut-off of 50 μm is taken, based on an operating efficiency of 98%. The degree of cut-off required for the special burnishing station will be determined by the surface finish specified or the particle size stipulated by the tool manufacturer. Often the requirements are compounded by the need to provide a higher pressure feed to the burnishing station, the system pump for which may have operating parameters needing a cut-off of perhaps, 10 μm. We have, therefore, established two levels of separation, one for machine tool and single point cutting operations and a second for the specialized burnishing tool and its supply pump.

(v) **Flow rate**

The flow rate is dependent upon the number of spindles, the proximity or clustering of drills at certain positions, plus the general configuration of tooling positions and sizes. The total flow can be established by making individual spindle and station assessments and extending these to cover all stations requiring coolant. This provides the basis of flow required for machining operations. The total would probably be some 80 gal/min made up of 10 gal/min for burnishing with the balance for drilling operations, *etc.* To ensure clearance of fixtures and machine slide-ways from swarf on a machine of this size and complexity, a suitable safety factor would be a figure of 20/25% increase on the calculated flow, giving a total flow requirement of approximately 100 gal/min.

(vi) **System capacity**

System capacity is directly proportional to flow. The optimum established many years ago was a ratio of 10:1, capacity to flow, *ie* for every 100 gal/min a capacity of 1 000 gallons was required giving a settlement period of ten minutes. As the development of filters progressed and speed and production rates improved, this cycle time was dramatically reduced. The premium of floor space and the cost of oils together with improved methods of processing have made possible reductions to levels as low as 3:1 on the first stage, *ie* a capacity of 300 gallons. It must, however, be stressed that space permitting or in larger under floor designs where much higher initial losses occur then a ratio of 10:1 is maintained whenever possible.

In addition to the 300 gallons we must provide additional capacity for clean liquid storage.

The sample system having both a low and a high pressure pump, from our total 100 gal/min cycling to the machine tool, 10 gal/min is rated at a cut-off of approximately 10 μm, with the balance rated at a nominal 50 μm.

To house two pumps with different levels of separation requires two holding tanks. The capacities of these, again, are directly related to system pump flows. However, in each of these tanks the same principles of settlement occur, so that extremely fine particles may remain in suspension due to space limitations. The ratio of such storage reservoirs has been reduced where possible, thus producing a fairly rapid turnover. The high pressure pump tank capacity will still be based on a ratio of 10:1, providing a capacity of 100 gallons.

This has been determined because the pump is a low flow unit but high pressure and is, therefore, likely to be fitted with a high kilowatt rated drive motor, thus being a potential heat source. The ratio for the low pressure holding tank is not so critical and we can cycle this in as low a ratio as 2:1 providing low pressure capacity of 180 gallons.

We have now established a dirty tank of 300 gallons and clean tank capacity of 280 gallons, giving a combined capacity of 580 gallons.

(vii) **Machine type**

The machine bed size, shape and configuration will, together with the outlet height, determine   firstly the dirty tank depth, which we will take as 600 mm, providing sufficient depth for an above floor system for a compact holding tank layout. The feed pipework nozzle bends and ring main supply pipework will also provide information to determine theoretical losses which will, in turn, assist in selecting pump duty ratings.

Unit configuration can vary to suit the available space, but alternative rectangular or delta forms can be provided and invariably the overall length and width of systems are determined and vary according to site conditions without compromise to the already determined capacities and flows.

(viii) **Nature of stock**

The material is a machinable EN8. Approximately 95% by volume of stock will be produced by the various drilling operations. Although chip breaker tooling has been specified, this may change at a later date. We can, therefore, expect that 95% of stock produced will be of uniform chip form, the balance being made up of small stringy segments and extremely fine particles.

The nature and volume of the chips will determine that the 300 gallon primary system will require some means of automatic clearance. The finer particles determine the necessity for some secondary separator.

(ix) **The system space**

In order to keep costs low, systems should, wherever possible, be formed of cuboid modules. However, the design may be altered by reduction in length with appropriate width increases and the designer has within the parameters of machine layout and site location certain flexibilities which can be used when necessary.

The various options should be carefully considered and a layout adopted which least compromises the unit efficiency.

(x) **Expansion rate of material**

The majority of stock is producing drilling chips of fairly uniform character. From this we can determine the volume of stock produced by using accepted expansion ratios. If, for example, we were not using chip breaker drills, then it would be expected that an expansion ratio of 80:1 could result. However, due to the relatively uniform nature of chip in question a ratio of 50:1 may be utilized, *ie* for every 1 cubic inch of metal removed, the filter will receive 50 cubic inches of steel chippings.

(xi) **Optimum efficiency**

We have already established that the machine requires a separator device which is automated to some extent. The cost effective section has to an extent already been covered by our decision to have two levels of separation rather than rating maximum system flow *ie* 100 gal/min filtered to a level of 10 μm.

(xii) **Operating period**

Operating period and duration affect selection of electrical control equipment, and motor rating. Where possible, all of these are specified for continuous operation. The operating period will further affect ultimate settlement during shutdown periods and timing delays can be fitted to the primary section to ensure overloads do not occur on recommencement of operations.

(xiii) **Protective devices**

All motors, contactors, together with mechanical overload torque limit on geared reduction units, are fitted to any conveyor drive unit, frequently incorporating integral switch gear in order that mechanical stoppage is monitored by visual or audible alarms. Low level switches also monitor sudden level drops, giving adequate warning to the operator to enable corrective procedure to be implemented.

(xiv) **System safety**

System safety is guided initially by the statutory requirements of the Health and Safety at Work Act 1974, and must in all respects comply with the minimum requirements of this Act, together with more recent innovations which are continually being incorporated.

Selection of Filter Parts and Types

It can be seen that we have basically all the necessary information to commence selection from the various types of systems which we have available. Just as the drilling machine produced in 1948 has progressed to a multi-spindle machine with a variety of almost fully automated operations,

BEL magnaroll magnetic drum filter 15 GDM
(Belisle Filtration)

BEL Hydrocyclone drag link filtration
system incorporating cartridge filter and
clean coolant storage tank 50 GDM
(Belisle Filtration Ltd)

BEL rotary drum filter 50 GDM for
aluminium alloys
(Belisle Filtration Ltd)

so have its settling tanks and suds pump evolved to a multi-stage system. The precise selection of these will be determined by their suitability in each case.

For the design the stages must be analyzed from machine output to the first stage of the filter, ie the 300 gallon primary tank. The requirement is first and foremost to remove a high percentage of solids in order to provide satisfactory levels of secondary and final stage filtration. The options are (a) slat conveyor; (b) magnetic conveyor; (c) drag conveyor; (d) media belt conveyor. The best suited of these on an efficiency and cost effective basis is (c) drag conveyor which, due to the stock density and type of chip form will provide an efficient removal device, raising solids up the conveyor incline and allowing adequate time for coolant drainage. Stock is discharged in a semi-dry state, thus reducing oil loss from the system and producing easily handled waste.

Stage two separation offers several other alternatives — media pressure, pleated paper, permanent media, hydrocyclones, magnetic incline strainer, or magnaroll. From the aforementioned options, only two do not require preventative maintenance or utilize consumables, namely, magnaroll and hydrocyclones.

The decision is very much a matter of personal preference but given the previously stressed condition that the first stage conveyor is operating at the design efficiency, we would not fully utilize the removal capability of magnaroll. The hydrocyclone would, therefore, provide adequate secondary degree separation, being capable of delivering in excess of the full flow requirement of 100 gal/min. The cyclones are also extremely durable due to the abrasive resistant nature of polyurethane together with its high impact resistance — frequently necessary in a workshop environment.

From here we progress to a clean liquid storage tank, but prior to feeding coolant back to the machine tool, we have one other level of separation to provide for, that being the 10 μm cut-off required for the burnishing station. For this we would fit a feed pump supplying the third and final stage high pressure operation.

The alternatives available here are permanent media internally pressure-fed random fibre elements, inline cartridge filter fitted with alternative elements of pleated paper or extended life stainless steel. Both pleated paper and stainless steel provide a positive cut-off. From these options the most suitable is the pleated paper and therefore our final stage of filter is a pleated paper cartridge vessel with optional stainless steel element, if required.

Due to maintenance requirements the final stage filter would be provided in duplex form with rapid changeover valves in order that element change can be undertaken without high pressure pump flow interruption.

Our final design decision is that of determining the pressure required on the low pressure feed pump. The determining factors here are primarily the number of spindles, the size of nozzles, the drops and bends, and size of ring main pipework feeding the various tool stations. From these a theoretical frictional loss can be calculated which can be allowed for when making a final pump selection, thus enabling us to provide a low pressure feed pump of 90 gal/min at an operating norm of 25 to 30 lb/in^2.

Filters and Treatment for Industrial Chemicals

MANUFACTURED PARTS may go through a whole series of chemical and electrochemical operations such as washing, pickling, degreasing, phosphating, galvanizing, plating, *etc*, as well as numerous rinsing stages. Considerable economies can result from effective filtering and clarification of the various fluids involved, and in the case of highly automated systems such treatment becomes essential in order that the fluids used continue to be dependable. Further, many operations may produce sludge, often containing toxic metal salts presenting a difficult disposal problem. Here there can be considerable advantages in employing sludge dewatering to compact a large mass of wet, sticky substance into a much smaller and more easily handled dry cake which may or may not have further value. At the same time process fluid can be recovered.

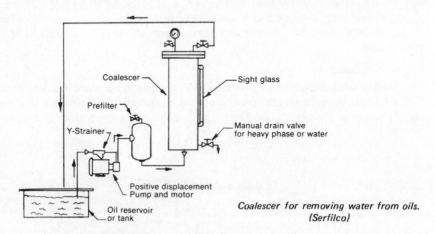

Coalescer for removing water from oils.
(Serfilco)

Water Treatment

Clean water is an essential requirement for anodizing, plating and similar processes which may require softening or carbon purification of the raw water supply. Certain processes also require the use of de-ionized water which can be obtained with ion exchange and/or reverse osmosis treatment. In all such cases *prefiltering* of the water is highly desirable to eliminate solid contaminants which could reduce the efficiency of the water treatment involved, a suitable filter rating being 15 μm. The treated water can then benefit by post-filtering to capture any migration of the treatment medium (*eg* as could occur with carbon purification).

Where there is no stringent demand on water quality for processing a filtered water supply is still desirable to prevent clogging of nozzles, sprays, control valves, *etc,* and reduce wear on pumps. It also becomes essential on recirculating systems, especially where the water is used for washing. The choice of filter in such cases is usually dependent on the amount of solids likely to be present, the degree of protection desirable (filter rating), available space and cost.

Acid and Pickling Baths

Commonly, acid and pickling baths are not filtered in non-automated processes, contaminants being allowed to settle out. Batch filtering can, however, substantially improve acid life and simplify waste treatment.

Cleaning Solutions

Alkaline soak-cleaning solutions and electro-cleaners generally accumulate considerable amounts of solids and organic contaminants as well as floating scum. The latter is normally removed by skimming. Solids can be removed by settlement when the plant is idle, followed by decanting or drawing off the fluid and removal of the settled solids. Fluid itself is replaced periodically, as necessary — *eg* when sample analysis shows that it is reaching the end of its usable life.

Where heavy dust loads are involved continuous or periodic (batch) filtering with a relatively coarse (50 μm) filter can show considerable economic advantages.

Anodizing Solutions

Anodizing solutions are not generally filtered on non-automated plant although periodic batch filtering is desirable. Seal solutions, however, benefit from continuous or bypass filtering and may also require periodic carbon treatment to remove discolouration from the dyes used. A filter comprising a main filter element and an activated carbon chamber can provide continuous protection throughout the life of the element and carbon content. Ideally a separate filter should be used on the seal tank.

Phosphating Solutions

Phosphating solutions contain either zinc, iron or manganese phosphate and phosphoric acid with suitable accelerators. During the process the clean steel parts are immersed in (or sprayed with) the metal phosphate-phosphoric acid bath, iron is dissolved at the surface and a phosphate coating is formed.

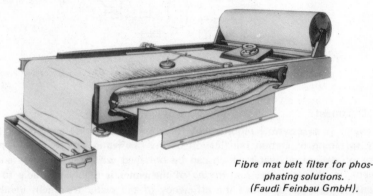

*Fibre mat belt filter for phos-
phating solutions.
(Faudi Feinbau GmbH).*

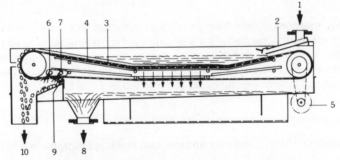

Faude Feinbau continuous belt filter — a type particularly suitable for the continuous cleaning of phosphated baths. The framework of the filter is constructed in unstressed steel, the outer faces tied together by diagonal struts. Collecting sump has an outlet flange connection (8) for the removal of the filtrate; there is a slurry scraper (9) and waste chute (10) for the slurry. The band filter bed is perforated plastic sheet (4) with a continuously circulating filter band (3) above it in plastic material. The solution inlet (2) has an adjustable deflector plate and inlet connection (1) for the unfiltered phosphate solution. A spray installation for water (6) and compressed air (7) consists of two oscillating nozzle jets, two magnetic control valves for controlling the operation. Band transport is through drive motor (5) insulation type 1P54; band speed is 30 cm/minute (optional 60 cm/minute). Control of the band motion and the spray installation is by a time switch.

Operation

The unfiltered solution flows through inlet (1) to an inlet chamber (2) through the plastic filter band (3) into the collecting sump and through the outlet (8) back to the bath. The impurities build up on the bed of the filter band (3) into a slurry layer. Their thickness depends on the Bonderizing method. The layer formation reduces the porosity and raises the quality of filtration. As the filter band (3) moves forward the filtered slurry is dropped out through the waste chute (10). At the same time the forward movement of the band opens two magnetic valves for water and compressed air; two nozzle jets (6 and 7) spray the returning conveyor band from the reverse side to clean off any slurry residue.

The operation of these baths requires even application of solution and good chemical control. Sludge accumulation results in poor quality, lost production and frequent maintenance. The sludge generated will not harm the phosphate process as such, but is detrimental to the operation since it tends to foul and plug heat exchangers, circulating pump and strainers, spray nozzles, *etc*. The sludge must, therefore, be removed, preferably with an automatic separation system.

Zinc phosphate baths require acid resistant materials, such as 316SS. They generate more sludge than the iron phosphate baths which can be handled with carbon steel and cast iron. Two or more tank turnovers per day using medium porosity media (25–40 μm) has proved effective. A tapered bottom phosphate tank aids in conveying the sludge to the pump. Either in-tank or out-of-tank pumps may be used to transfer the sludge laden solutions to the filter. Filtrate is returned to the phosphating tank by gravity or a sump pump in the clean reservoir of the filter.

Plating Solutions

Virtually all plating solutions benefit from continuous filtration. They also require periodic purification to restore their clarity, particularly those solutions containing wetting agents, since any oil introduced with the bath is dispersed throughout the solution and can be deposited on workpieces causing peeling or imperfect plating. Purification is commonly done with activated carbon treatment (see later). General recommendations are summarized in Table I.

TABLE I – RECOMMENDATIONS FOR FILTRATION AND PURIFICATION OF PLATING SOLUTIONS*

Process	pH	Bath Temperature F	Filtration	Filter Rating μm	Carbon Treatment
Anodizing	1	60–90	Optional	15	No
Anodizing Ni seal	5.5	200	Desirable	15	Batch
Brass, Bronze	10	100–200	As required	15	No
Cadmium	12	100	As required	30	No
Chromium Hexavalent	1	110–130	Optional	15	No
Chromium Trivalent	2–3.5	75	Continuous	1–5	No
Copper Acid	1	75–120	Continuous	15	Periodic
Copper Cyanide	11–13	70–150	Continuous	15	As needed
Copper Electroless	14	100–140	Continuous	3	No
Copper Fluoborate	1	70–120	As required	15	As needed
Copper Pyrophosphate	8–9	110–130	Continuous	10–20	As needed
Gold Acid	3–5	80–125	Continuous	1–5	Periodic
Gold Cyanide	7–12	75	Continuous	5	Periodic
Iron Chloride	1	195	Continuous	15	Yes
Lead Fluoborate	1	100	Continuous	15	No
Nickel Bright	3–5	125–150	Continuous	15–30	Yes
Nickel Semibright	2–5	130	Continuous	15	Yes
Nickel Chloride	2	120–150	Continuous	15	Yes
Nickel Electroless	4–11	100–200	Continuous	15	As needed
Nickel Sulfamate	3–5	100–140	Continuous	15	Yes
Nickel Watts	4	120–160	Continuous	15	As needed
Nickel-Iron	3.5–4	135	Continuous	15–30	Yes
Rhodium Acid	1	100–120	As required	5	Periodic
Silver Cyanide	12	70–120	Continuous	5	Periodic
Tin Acid	0.5	70	As needed	15	As needed
Tin Alk.	12	140–180	As needed	30	No
Tin-Lead (solder)	0.5	100	Continuous	15	Periodic
Tin-Nickel	2.5	150	Continuous	15	Yes
Zinc Acid Chloride	3–5	70–140	Continuous	15	No
Zinc Alkaline	14	75–100	As needed	30–50	Optional
Zinc Cyanide	14	75–90	Continuous	30–100	No

*Serfilco (USA)

Chromium Plating

The thickness of chromium deposits from an electroplating solution ranges from light to heavy using bath temperatures from room temperature up to 140°F. Continuous filtration down to 15 μm is desirable to achieve the highest possible clarity and deposit quality. Recently, trivalent chromium plating baths have been introduced. These require continuous filtration with dense media to remove the fine particulate matter formed during plating. Since the bath does not tolerate any metallic contamination, contact with all metals, including lead, must be avoided.

With self-regulating baths, care should be taken to filter the solution off the top only and to by-pass around the filter during agitation of the self-regulating chemicals. Any solids from the self-regulating bath which are picked up by the filter would, in time, be dissolved as required. The purpose in keeping them from the filter in large quantities is to prevent the solids from restricting the flow through the filter and reducing the amount of agitation. However, with an oversize filter, the regulating chemicals can be retained on the surface of the filter medium without reducing flow too much.

Nickel Plating

With nickel plating baths agitation is usually recommended and organic compounds are added to get the best levelling and brightness. Other nickel solutions are used for engineering and salvage applications or electroforming, which demand a near perfect plate. These contain anti-pitting agents instead of organic brighteners. Bright and semi-bright nickel electrolytes require the continuous or periodic removal of organic breakdown products from brighteners with activated carbon. Carbon purification may be desirable for nickel solutions prior to the addition of wetting agents. Initial and continuous carbon treatment with at least two tank turnovers per hour are suggested. The new nickel-iron plating baths must be filtered and purified like any other bright nickel solution.

Electrolytic purification by 'dummy' plating to remove undesirable metallic impurities, such as copper, is frequently employed in conjunction with filtration equipment by either pumping from a separate tank or weir filled with overflow solution, or by recirculating through the slurry tank for this purpose.

Solids can be removed from the bath by recirculating the solution through a filter which employs filter media with an average particle retention of 15 μm down to sub-micron, with or without filter aid. Flow rates per hour will also vary from two up to ten times the volume of the tank. One tank turnover per hour is not sufficient in most cases to remove all the solids in suspension before they settle to the bottom; sedimentation in the plating tank requires periodic cleaning and down time of the tank. Coarser, or slightly denser, media may be used depending upon the dirt load and the degree of clarity required. With a higher flow rate, a coarser filter medium will attain the same degree of clarity as a denser medium, at a lower flow rate. The coarser filter has higher dirt holding capacity and longer life.

Zinc Plating (Acid Baths)

Zinc sulphate baths produce a matt zinc deposit and are primarily used for coating steel wire and strip. Zinc chloride baths produce a lighter deposit. Continuous filtration of the order of 10–15 μm is recommended in both cases. Acid zinc baths are susceptible to contamination with iron which must be periodically precipitated as iron hydroxide by hydrogen peroxide treatment. This precipitate is difficult to filter because of its gelatinous nature.

Hydroxide sludge tank with cylinder-bowl (left) and self-cleaning centrifugal clarifiers.
(ASSA-Stenman)

Zinc Plating (Alkaline)

The newer alkaline zinc plating baths deposit zinc faster with better uniformity and yield a bright coating, provided solution quality is maintained. Coarse filters must be used (50—100 μm) because of the slimy nature of the sludge formed, with periodic carbon treatment to remove organic impurities. Continuous filtration is recommended with solution agitation and strict bath temperature control, but batch filtering is also used. In this case the sludge is allowed to settle before the solution is drawn off for filtering; and cleaned from the tank before refilling. Precoat filters employing diatomaceous earth should not be used with alkali zinc plating solutions since any silicates present may dissolve in the solution.

Copper Plating

High-throw acid copper sulphate plating baths require continuous filtration (at 15 μm) at high flow rates to ensure uniform deposits, together with periodic carbon treatment to remove organic impurities. Systems consisting of pump and filter combinations are recommended with a separate carbon chamber for periodic purification when necessary. Slurry tank, related piping and valves are useful if the baths have to be batch carbon treated and when being made up before the brightener is added. The slurry tank provides for easier pump priming and addition of chemicals. A carbon canister purification chamber can be adapted to any filter with bypass valve and piping to control the flow through the carbon.

Plastics such as polypropylene, PVC or CPVC are the most suitable materials for pump and filter construction.

Dip Plating Solutions

Chemical solutions for direct copper and nickel plating are normally filtered after make-up and pH adjustment and periodically batch filtered at suitable intervals. Carbon treatment may also be required periodically to remove organic impurities, but for this the solution must be cooled to a non-active temperature. Non-metallic filter elements and filter construction must be employed, a suitable filter rating being 15 μm. Baths operate at temperatures up to 205°F. The filtration of electroless nickel solution removes nickel phosphite, which is a by-product of the plating process. Since its solubility is lower in hot solution than cold, hot filtration is more effective. If allowed to accumulate, it adversely affects bath stability and deposit appearance. Cloudiness or precipitation in a used bath is generally due to nickel phosphite.

If continuous filtration is employed and the filter is located upstream of the heat exchanger used to heat the solution, flow through the heat exchanger will gradually decrease as the filter collects contaminants.

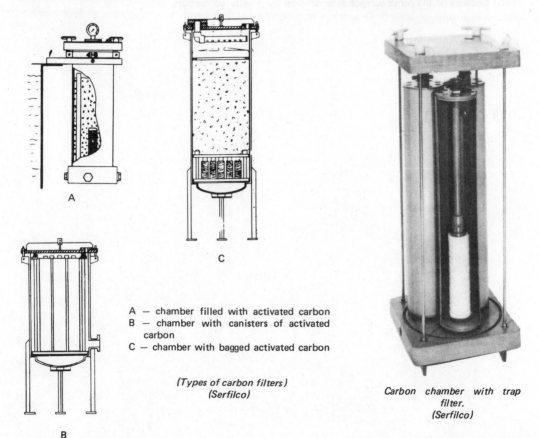

A — chamber filled with activated carbon
B — chamber with canisters of activated carbon
C — chamber with bagged activated carbon

(Types of carbon filters)
(Serfilco)

Carbon chamber with trap filter.
(Serfilco)

Purification by Carbon Treatment

Activated carbon can be used to purify most plating solutions but should be preceded by filtering (if the system is not continuously filtered) to prevent contaminant particles covering the carbon surface and reducing its effectiveness. There are four basic methods of carbon treatment.

(i)   Carbon cartridge filters to fit standard filter chambers and suitable for use on small volume systems.

(ii) Carbon canisters holding granulated activated carbon for bypass or batch filtering.

(iii) Bulk carbon treatment where granular carbon is loaded into a filter chamber incorporating a separate filter element.

(iv) Carbon precoat filters using powdered carbon.

In cases (ii) and (iii), as a general guide approximately 1 lb of carbon is needed to treat every 100 gallons of plating solution for batch filtering. Flow rates should be relatively slow to allow sufficient contact time for effective absorption. Faster flow rates are possible with carbon precoat filters because of the large surface area offered by powdered carbon.

Trade Effluent Treatment

INDUSTRIAL EFFLUENT is commonly in the form of a sludge which may have a variety of constituents, *eg*

(i)   Colloidal matter (organic activated sludge)

(ii)   Semi-colloidal matter (metallic hydroxides, *etc*)

(iii) Fibrous matter (fibrous sludge)

(iv) Coagulated solids and particles (granular sludge)

(v)   Crystalline products (crystalline sludge)

(vi) Coarse solids (sandy or gritty sludge)

(vii) Mixed, miscellaneous foreign matter and rubbish.

*A Framclean 5 demonstration unit treating trade effluent at
Wincanton Transport's Dagenham depot.
The effluent is contaminated by fuel oil spillages, lubricating
oil and grease drips, road grit, degreasing agents and detergents plus tanker cleanings. These include traces of latex,
vinyl acetate, methyl ethyl ketone, glycol, toluene, sugar
powder, milk, black oil, xylene, methylated spirits, corn
steep liquor, butyl acetate and lubricating oil.*

This Lakos Industrial-Model Separator removes plastic powder from cooling water at a PVC pipe manufacturing facility. The separated powder is bled continuously via manual pinch valves into the large collection dumpster. Excess purged liquid returns to the system via an overflow weir. Collected solids are recovered for re-use.

In most cases it is advantageous to thicken or concentrate the sludge before dewatering treatment. Methods used include chemical treatment, gas flotation, gravity thickening, centrifuging, *etc*. Gravity thickening is usually the most economic process and agglomeration may be assisted by polyelectrolytes. Excessive proportions of such agents can, however, reduce the efficiency of subsequent filters.

Dewatering is then employed to reduce haulage/disposal costs. Until comparatively recently many sludges were only dewatered to a level suitable to make them disposable by incineration. With rising fuel costs alternative methods of disposal are normally more economic, and necessary in any case where the 'dry' sludge is not combustible. Dewatering can substantially reduce the bulk of solids to be disposed of. For example, starting with a sludge that contains 1% solids per 1 000 gallons:-

    Dewatering to 25% solids ratio — volume reduction 88%
    Dewatering to 30% solids ratio — volume reduction 90%
    Dewatering to 40% solids ratio — volume reduction 92.5%
    Dewatering to 50% solids ratio — volume reduction 94%

The significant factor here is how the 'dry' cake packs, as affecting both ease of handling and actual volume to be hauled away. A very dry cake (say 50% solids) is easier to handle than a 'slimy' cake (*eg* 25% solids), but may in fact represent a greater skip volume because it does not pack so well. The actual volume reduction between the cake with 25% and that with 50% solids is also only 6%, which reduction may require considerably greater filter/separation time and cost.

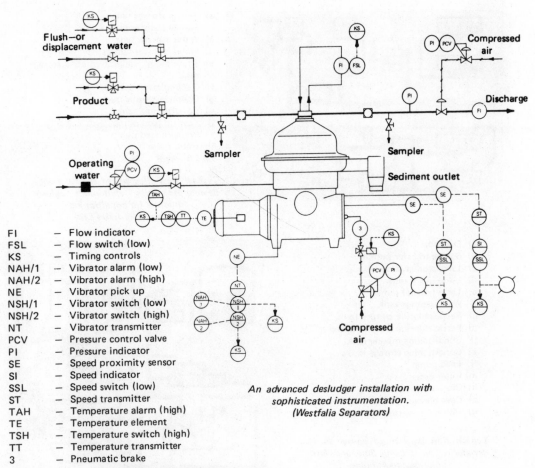

FI   — Flow indicator
FSL   — Flow switch (low)
KS   — Timing controls
NAH/1   — Vibrator alarm (low)
NAH/2   — Vibrator alarm (high)
NE   — Vibrator pick up
NSH/1   — Vibrator switch (low)
NSH/2   — Vibrator switch (high)
NT   — Vibrator transmitter
PCV   — Pressure control valve
PI   — Pressure indicator
SE   — Speed proximity sensor
SI   — Speed indicator
SSL   — Speed switch (low)
ST   — Speed transmitter
TAH   — Temperature alarm (high)
TE   — Temperature element
TSH   — Temperature switch (high)
TT   — Temperature transmitter
3   — Pneumatic brake

*An advanced desludger installation with
sophisticated instrumentation.
(Westfalia Separators)*

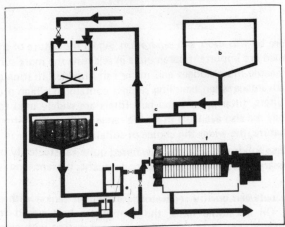

a) Sludge storage/thickening tank
b) Polyelectrolyte storage tank
c) Polyelectrolyte transfer pump
d) Polyelectrolyte dilution tank
e) Sludge/polyelectrolyte feed pump
f) Filter press

*Typical flow diagram of potable sludge
dewatering conditioning with polyelectrolyte
(Edwards & Jones Ltd)*

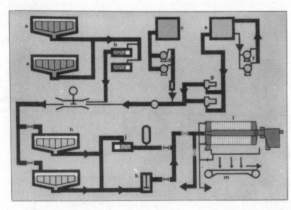

a) Sludge storage tanks
b) Sludge transfer pumps
c) Water storage tank
d) Water transfer pumps
e) Aluminium chlorohydrate storage tank
f) Recirculation pumps
g) Chemical dosing pumps
h) Conditioning tanks
j) Fast fill feed pump
k) Pressure feed pump
l) Filter press
m) Conveyor

Typical flow diagram of sewage sludge dewatering using aluminium chlorohydrate for conditioning (Edwards & Jones Ltd)

a) Digestor
b) Sludge transfer pumps
c) Lime storage silo
d) Lime slurry tank
e) Lime transfer pump
f) Water storage tank
g) Ferric chloride storage tank
h) Ferric chloride transfer pump
j) Conditioning mixing tank
k) Conditioning storage tanks
l) Feed pump
m) Filter press
n) Cloth washing machine
p) Core blowing (compressor/receiver)
q) Filtrate measurement

Typical flow diagram of sewage sludge dewatering plant using lime and ferric chloride conditioning. (Edwards & Jones Ltd)

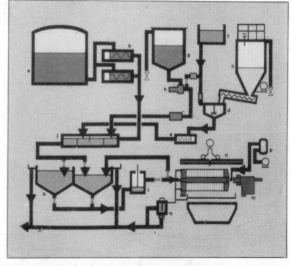

The two basic methods of dewatering are by *filtration* and *separation*. Again the nature of the sludge together with the volume to be handled are important parameters in selecting the more suitable method. Various types of filters can handle most sludges and many can provide filtration at different pressure levels which can be an advantage when handling sludges containing a high proportion of solids. Rotary drum vacuum filters, filter presses and belt filters are widely used for sludge dewatering, amongst other types. They are also available in a wide range of sizes. The firmer the sludge and/or the more fibrous it is in nature, the wider the choice of suitable filters.

Sandy sludges and those containing coarse solids can often be dewatered quite satisfactorily by simple screens. Pressure filters are not necessary unless there are other constituents present tending to produce a binding cake.

With separators, the choice lies broadly between gravity separators (settlement tanks) with or without coalescing units and centrifuges. On a volume basis, the former are best suited for handling large volumes economically; whereas a centrifuge can give greater separation with small

Industrial sludge dewatering plant at Schlitz Brewery, USA.

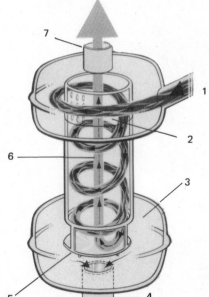

1. Liquid-solids enter here at a tangent and begin a circular flow.
2. Liquids-solids are accelerated through tangential slots into the separation chamber. Solids are centrifugally forced to the inner chamber's perimeter and lose velocity.
3. Separated solids fall gently to the collection chamber.
4. Solids are periodically (as necessary) purged (or bled) from the collection chamber.
5. Deflector plate and spin arrestor maintain a clean solids collection chamber while reversing the liquid's direction of flow.
6. Solids-free liquid spirals up to the centre of the separation chamber.
7. Solids-free liquid outlet

Mode of working of Lakos separator.

volumes but consumes power all the time it is providing through-put. Centrifuges, too, are not generally suitable for handling shear-sensitive sludges as they will then generate a dirty outflow which may need further filtration/separation treatment.

Large scale sludge treatment plants are necessarily tailored to the specific requirements, normally designed for continuous operation and automatic in use. A variety of filters/separators may be employed in the complete system, or integrated into the main unit.

See also chapters on *Centrifuges, Dynamic Separators, Coalescers, Rotary Drum Filters, Filter Presses, Oily Water Treatment,* and *Industrial Water Cleaning.*

SECTION 3

Sub-section (c)

Hydraulic System Filters

EARLIER INDUSTRIAL hydraulic systems operated at pressures of 1 000 lb/in² (70 bar) or less and usually performed satisfactorily with minimal attention to filtering. Often a simple strainer on the pump, or a filter with a cut-off of 25—50 μm provided adequate protection. Some systems, in fact, dispensed with a filter entirely, oil being withdrawn periodically for batch filtering and returned to the system.

Most modern hydraulic systems operate at higher pressures *eg* commonly 2 000—3 000 lb/in² (140—210 bar); with pumps having closer clearances and control valves and servos with even smaller clearances. A combination of higher pressure and reduced clearances calls for the elimination of particles from the system which could cause clogging, requiring protection by finer filters. The general use of smaller reservoirs also gives more rapid circulation of fluid and thus less opportunity for particles to settle out. Higher fluid operating temperatures can mean reduced oil viscosities and less protection against wear, contributing to increased contamination generated within the system. Erosion can be a very real problem in high pressure small bore systems as localized fluid velocities may be as high as 400 mph or more. This can lead to rapid wear on hardened and polished surfaces adjacent to high velocity fluid streams when particles of only 3 to 5 μm are present in the fluid.

In fact, something over 70% of hydraulic system failures are due to contamination or poor fluid condition. Essentially, therefore, filters are necessary in modern hydraulic systems to provide a particular or specified level of contaminant removal. This can vary with the type of system, types of components involved, application and duty cycle.

The basic requirements of a filtration system for hydraulic services are:-

(i)   It should be capable of reducing initial contamination present in the fluid and/or system to the desired level within an acceptable period of time.

(ii)   It must then be capable of maintaining the desired level of contaminant removal over a suitable period (*ie* have sufficient dirt-holding capacity).

(iii)   Filters should preferably incorporate some form of indicating device to show their state in use.

Filters themselves should also have:

(iv)   Adequate element strength and freedom from migration.

(v)   An adequate contaminant retaining capacity.

(vi)   Adequate size for the required maximum flow rate.

(vii) Low back pressure or pressure drop across the filter.

(viii) Low pressure drop relative to flow rate (that is, low pressure drop/flow ratio).

(ix)   Performance maintained over a suitable temperature range (bearing in mind the change in fluid viscosity over that temperature range).

(x)   Component parts suitable for and compatible with the hydraulic fluid concerned.

(xi)   Low weight.

(xii) Compact size.

(xiii) An ability to withstand high pressure surges or high pressure differentials without rupturing or bypassing the medium.

(xiv) Compatibility with standard system components.

(xv)   A design which permits of rapid servicing (for example, easy cleaning or replacement of the element).

(xvi) Economic cost (both initial cost and servicing costs).

Other specific requirements may be mandatory in certain hydraulic systems, such as bypass characteristics to maintain flow in the event of the element becoming clogged; or alternatively visual or audible warning when the filter element requires replacement, or even automatic shutdown to ensure that unfiltered oil is not circulated through the system.

Sources of Contaminants

Contaminants within a typical hydraulic system may be derived from both *external* and *internal* sources. Contaminants from external sources include those introduced during manufacture of components and assembly of the system. These may include casting sand, drawing compounds, weld spatter, machining chips and loose burrs, elastomeric particles from seals and gaskets, assembly compounds, adhesives and even paint particles. Such particles may range in size from 1–500 μm. Additionally airborne dust and dirt, rust and other forms of corrosion may be implanted contaminants with a similar size range.

The environment is also a source of external contaminants during the working of a system, typical entry points for such contaminants being

(i)   air breathers

(ii)   rod seals on hydraulic cylinders (particularly in dirty atmospheres and/or with increasing seal wear).

(iii) access plates and other detachable items.

The system fluid may be a further source of external contamination. New oil as refined and blended is clean (contaminant free), but if stored in a bulk tank or drums is subject to contamination from metal and rubber particles in the filling lines, and possibly metal flakes or scale from the container itself. Water condensation within tanks further contributes to contamination by corrosion products. Typical contaminant size in fluids is 3-10 μm, but much larger particles may be present in bad cases.

Actual contamination arising from delivery and storage varies widely with the industry. The highest standards of cleanliness are achieved in the aircraft industry, using small containers with a quick turnover of stores. The least satisfactory are industrial systems storing bulk fluid under unfavourable environmental conditions for long periods before use. In such cases prefiltering or batch filtering of the stored oil may be advisable before it is introduced into the system. Particular care should also be taken to ensure that top-up fluid is clean, and also the area around the filter absolutely clean before introducing such fluid.

Contaminants from internal sources, *ie* those generated within the working system can be numerous, viz:

- (i)   metal particles produced by
    - (a)   abrasive wear, typically 5–250 μm
    - (b)   galling (adhesive wear) typically 5–750 μm
    - (c)   contamination and erosion, typically 40–250 μm
    - (d)   surface fatigue, typically 5–50 μm
- (ii)   metallic salts produced by
    - (a)   rust and corrosion, typically 5–150 μm
    - (b)   electrolysis, typically 5–150 μm
    - (c)   water contamination, typically sludge
- (iii)   fluid degradation particles (typically 0.2–150 μm), varnish, carbon particles, acids, sludge and microbiological growths.

A further source of internal contaminants is from particles escaping from, or unloaded by, the filter(s) in the system. These may be any of the aforementioned types originally retained by the filter.

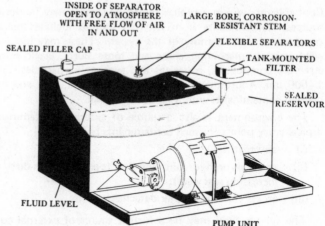

INSIDE OF SEPARATOR
OPEN TO ATMOSPHERE
WITH FREE FLOW OF AIR
IN AND OUT

SEALED FILLER CAP

LARGE BORE, CORROSION-
RESISTANT STEM

FLEXIBLE SEPARATORS

TANK-MOUNTED
FILTER

SEALED
RESERVOIR

FLUID LEVEL

PUMP UNIT

Flexible separator installed in reservoir prevents contaminants entering the reservoir.
(Christie Hydraulics Ltd)

Effect of Contaminants

The majority of contaminants likely to be introduced into a hydraulic system from external and internal sources are abrasive and the resulting wear accounts for about 90% of the failures due to contamination. (The remainder is clogging by sludges). Particles *most* likely to cause wear are those of a clearance size which just pass through clearance spaces between moving parts. Larger particles cannot enter such spaces (although they can contribute to clogging or even cause jamming). Smaller particles can pass through clearance spaces without necessarily abrading the surfaces unless present in large quantities. The degree of protection provided by filtering is thus directly related to the clearance spaces within the system.

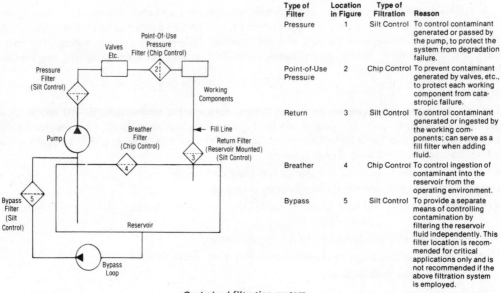

Type of Filter	Location in Figure	Type of Filtration	Reason
Pressure	1	Silt Control	To control contaminant generated or passed by the pump, to protect the system from degradation failure.
Point-of-Use Pressure	2	Chip Control	To prevent contaminant generated by valves, etc., to protect each working component from catastrophic failure.
Return	3	Silt Control	To control contaminant generated or ingested by the working components; can serve as a fill filter when adding fluid.
Breather	4	Chip Control	To control ingestion of contaminant into the reservoir from the operating environment.
Bypass	5	Silt Control	To provide a separate means of controlling contamination by filtering the reservoir fluid independently. This filter location is recommended for critical applications only and is not recommended if the above filtration system is employed.

Optimized filtration system.
(Purolator)

TABLE I — TYPICAL CLEARANCES ON HYDRAULIC SYSTEM COMPONENTS

Component	Item	TYPICAL CLEARANCE μm	mils
Gear pumps	Gear tip to case	0.5–5	0.02–0.2
	Gear to side plate	0.5–5	0.02–0.2
	Fixed side clearance	25–50	1–2
Vane pumps	Vane tip to case	0.5–1	0.02–0.04
	Vane side to case	5–13	0.2–0.5
Piston pumps	Piston to bore	5–40	0.2–1.6
	Valve plate to cylinder	0.5–5	0.02–0.2
Control valves:			
Spool	Spool to bore	5–13	0.2–0.5
Disc		0.5–1	0.02–0.04
Poppet		13–40	0.5–1.5
Servo valves:			
Spool		1–4	0.04–0.16
Flapper		18–63	0.7–2.5
Orifice		100–450	4–18
Cylinders	Piston to bore	50–250	2–10
	Rod bearings	1.5–10	0.06–0.4
Motors	See Pumps		
Actuator bearings	Plain/Sliding bearings	1.5–10	0.06–0.4
	Rolling bearings	1.5–10	0.06–0.4

Specifically, particles larger than 25 μm are called *chips,* and particles between 3 and 25 μm *silt.* Reference may then be made to filters providing *silt control* (3—5 μm absolute rating); *partial silt control* (10—15 μm absolute rating); and *chip control* (25—40 μm absolute rating). Basically, therefore, chip control guards against catastrophic failure; and silt control against degradation failure.

Protection Levels

Typical clearances employed on hydraulic system components range from 15—40 μm for low pressure components down to about 5 μm for high pressure components (or even less for miniature valves) — see also Table I. Most components, too, will have critical areas which are particularly subject to clearance problems. Examples are:-

Gear pumps — tooth to housing and gear to side plate clearances.

Vane pumps — vane tip and motor to side plate clearance.

Axial piston pumps — cylinder block to valve plate, piston to cylinder and slot to swashplate clearances.

Spool valves — eccentricity (resulting in varying clearance).

Throttle valves — orifice shape (a groove type orifice is less prone to silting).

Poppet valves — valve seat (erosion).

Accepting 25 μm as a general level of protection required for low pressure industrial hydraulic systems, and in the absence of specific requirements from the component manufacturers, the following filter ratings are recommended for different systems:

	filter rating
Low pressure systems with generous clearances	25—40 μm
Low pressure heavy-duty systems	15—25 μm
Typical medium pressure industrial systems	12—15 μm
Mobile hydraulic systems	12—15 μm
General machine tool and other high quality systems	10—12 μm
High performance machine tool and other high pressure systems where reliability is critical	3—5 μm
Critical high pressure systems and controls using miniature components	1—2 μm

Hydraulic Filter Types

Examples of different types of filter elements used in hydraulic filters are given in Table IIA. Paper (cellulosic media) and wire mesh are widely favoured but can only provide partial silt control. Sintered porous metal, asbestos fibre and glass microfibre media are capable of providing full silt control. The latter type (glass microfibre) is a recent development, now used as a medium for both chip control and silt control filters. It offers good pore size distribution, greater open area than cellulose or wire mesh media because of the smaller fibre diameter, and better dirt holding capacity. Its chief disadvantage is that it is low in strength although this can be enhanced with resin treatment. It is normal practice to support glass microfibre elements on both the upstream and downstream sides. Asbestos fibres can have an even smaller diameter than glass microfibres, making them even more effective for silt control filtering. The material is, however, regarded as hazardous to health and also subject to migration.

TABLE IIA – TYPES OF ELEMENT CONSTRUCTION

Element	Approximate Filtration Range micron = μm	Remarks
Felt	25–50 microns	Subject to element migration unless resin-impregnated.
Paper	Down to 10 microns or better	Low permeability, low element strength. Subject to element migration.
Fabric	Down to 20 microns	Higher permeability than papers. Higher strength with rigid back-up mesh, etc.
Wire gauze	Down to 35 microns	Suitable for suction strainers, tank strainers, etc.
Wire wound	Down to 25 microns	Good mechanical strength.
Wire cloth	Down to 10 microns	Expensive, but well suited to high pressure systems with high strength and freedom from migration.
Edge type (ribbon element)	40–70 microns	Low resistance to flow with reasonable strength (self-supporting).
Edge type (paper disc)	10 down to 1 micron or better	Degrees of filtration variable with compression. High resistance to flow. Clogs readily.
Edge type (metal)	Down to 25 microns	Very strong self-supporting element; suitable for high temperatures, ie full system pressures.
Sintered woven wire cloth	10–20 microns usual	High strength, suitable for high temperatures. Complete freedom from element migration. High cost. Low dirt capacity.
Glass microfibre	Down to 3 microns or better	Modern preferences for silt control filters – superior performance to cellulosic fibres and wire meshes.
Asbestos fibre	Down to 3 microns or better	Effective as silt control filters, but decreasing application because of possible carcinogenic rating.
Sintered porous metal	Down to 2½ microns	Good mechanical strength, self-supporting and suitable for high pressures and temperatures. Low dirt capacity. Element migration not entirely eliminated under severe conditions.
Sintered porous metal with woven wire reinforcement	Down to 2½ microns	Very high strength. Suitable for full line pressures.
Sintered PTFE	5 to 25 microns	High cost, subject to element migration. Strength improved by reinforcement.
Sintered polythene	30 microns	Low resistance to flow and freedom from element migration. Not suitable for temperatures above 60°C (140°F).
Sintered metal felts	Down to 5 microns or better	High cost, but freedom from element migration. Difficult to clean (elements usually replaced).
Membrane filters	Down to sub-micron sizes	Low mechanical strength and poor dirt capacity. Main use is for extreme cleaning of test rigs, etc, or oil reclaiming.
Magnetic filters	Ferrous particles only	Little or no resistance to flow.
Filter mats (cellulose etc)	Down to 0.5 microns	Used in batch filters or prefilters.
Filter cloths	Down to 10 microns or better	May be used in batch filters or air breathers.

TABLE IIB – PERFORMANCE OF MESH STRAINERS

Mesh	Wire Diameter			Size of Opening		Approximate Open Area
	swg	inches	mm	inches	mm	%
60	35	0.0089	0.213	0.0083	0.211	25
	36	0.0076	0.194	0.0091	0.231	30
	37	0.0068	0.172	0.0099	0.251	35
	38	0.0060	0.152	0.0107	0.272	41
	39	0.0052	0.133	0.0115	0.292	47
80	38	0.0060	0.152	0.0065	0.165	27
	39	0.0052	0.133	0.0073	0.185	34
	40	0.0048	0.122	0.0077	0.196	38
100	40	0.0048	0.122	0.0052	0.132	27
	41	0.0044	0.112	0.0056	0.142	31
	42	0.0040	0.101	0.0060	0.152	36

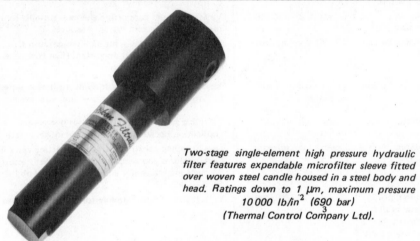

Two-stage single-element high pressure hydraulic filter features expendable microfilter sleeve fitted over woven steel candle housed in a steel body and head. Ratings down to 1 μm, maximum pressure 10 000 lb/in^{-2} (690 bar)
(Thermal Control Company Ltd).

Element strength and construction can affect the choice of media. Elements of very low mechanical strength are precluded from high pressure applications. Even if backed by a rigid screen, or otherwise rigidly reinforced, there is still the possibility of element migration, or that of localized failure under pressure surges.

It should be appreciated that even in a high pressure system with steady flow the pressure to which the filter element is subjected is only that of the differential pressure or pressure drop across the element. The element strength required is, therefore, only that of the maximum pressure drop rating (with a suitable safety factor) although the filter body will have to withstand the full system pressure. Pressure surges occurring in the system may (momentarily) increase the differential pressure across the element by a substantial amount, but not to the amount of the surge pressure (unless the filter is completely clogged), this figure being applied only to the filter body. In all cases, the actual physical pressure applied to the filter element can only be the differential pressure realized across the element – hence the fact that comparatively low strength materials can be used

TABLE III — FILTER ELEMENT TYPES AND CHARACTERISTICS

	Minimum Particle Size Retained (µm)		Pore Size Control	Flow Capacity	Dirt Holding Capacity	Resistance to Migration	Mechanical Strength	Consistency	Cost
	Nom	Absolute							
Wire gauze		60–100	Fair	High	Poor	Very good	Very good	Very good	Low
Shaped wire		60–80	Fair	High	Fair	Very good	Very good	Very good	Moderate
Metal disc (stack)		60–100	Fair	High	Fair	Very good	Very good	Very good	Moderate
Felt (pad)	30–40		Poor	Moderate	Good	Poor	Poor	Fair	Low
Felt (pleated)	25–35		Poor	Moderate	Good	Poor	Low	Fair	Low
Paper (pleated)	10–20	25–35	Fair	Very low	Fair	Poor	Poor	Fair	Low
Impregnated (papers)	10–15	10–35	Fair	Very low	Fair	Poor	Poor	Fair	Low
Paper ribbon	50–100		Fair	Moderate	Good	Poor	Fair	Good	Moderate to low
Paper disc	5	20–25	Fair	Low	Good	Fair	Low	Fair	Moderate to low
Woven wire mesh	5	10	Very good	Moderate	Poor	Very good	High	Good	High
Woven wire cloth	5	10	Very good	Fair	Poor	Very good	High	Very good	Very high
Wire cloth and paper		10–25	Good	Low	Poor	Good	Fair	Good	High
Glass microfibre	1,2,3	1,2,3	Moderate	High	High	Poor	Low	Very good	Low
Sintered metal	2,5 or 10	2,5 or 10	Very good	Moderate	Fair	Very good	Very good	Very good	Moderate to low

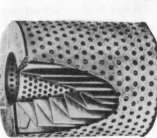

Typical pleated paper filter (left) and wire clad filter (right)

for high pressure filters. On the other hand certain types of filter elements are capable of with-standing extremely high differential pressures of the same order as line pressures and in this case can be referred to as true high pressure elements.

Cleanable vs Disposable Filter Elements

In general low cost filter media are regarded as disposable (replaced with a new element) as the cost of re-cleaning may be as high or higher than the replacement element. Certain media may be difficult or almost impossible to clean anyway, or be susceptible to damage if re-cleaned. The more robust media — *eg* wire mesh and sintered porous metal elements — are more economically re-cleaned, when they may be used a number of times. Three to seven cycles of cleaning and re-use are typical, but depends on the service conditions and cleaning facilities available. The most suitable cleaning system for such types is an ultra-sonic bath.

Filter Location

Choice of position or positions for the filter(s) in a hydraulic system is largely a matter for the individual designer to decide. On older systems a single filter was often fitted on the pump suction side, or inside the tank or reservoir. This had the advantage that the filter did not have to carry the full system pressure and was isolated from any surge pressures. However, the filter was, of necessity, fairly coarse and of large area in order not to restrict flow to the pump, and if it did become clogged, could cause the pump to cavitate unless the flow was bypassed straight to the pump. This logical method of preventing pump cavitation meant that both the pump and system were fed with unfiltered fluid under such conditions. The one merit of such a system is that suction-type filters can be less robustly constructed and are thus less costly than pressure-type filters. On many modern systems, however, the only filtering on the suction side of the pump is provided by a strainer in the tank or reservoir (Fig 1). These are so designed that adequate suction flow will be maintained under all conditions by attention to strainer and tank inlet and outlet pipes, so that cavitation conditions are avoided. This provides filter protection for the pump inlet.

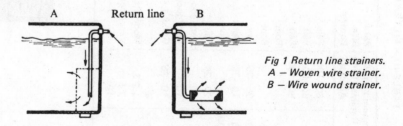

Fig 1 Return line strainers.
A — Woven wire strainer.
B — Wire wound strainer.

Such inlet filters, of course, do not remove any pump-generated contamination which is fed directly into the system on the pressure side. Equally, they are not necessary in systems with closed reservoirs, with silt-control filtration on the return line, or where fluid is introduced into the system upstream of the return line filter.

Pressure Line Filtering

A pressure line filter is located on the delivery side of the pump and is thus exposed to full system pressure. It will protect the following system from pump-generated or pump-passed contaminants, but not from any contaminants generated downstream of the filter.

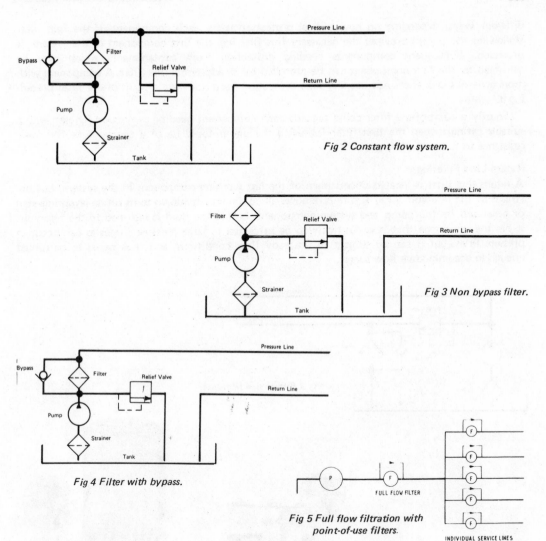

Fig 2 Constant flow system.

Fig 3 Non bypass filter.

Fig 4 Filter with bypass.

Fig 5 Full flow filtration with point-of-use filters.

Three possible filter configurations are shown in Figs 2—4. Locating the filter before the relief valve gives constant flow through the filter (Fig 2). Located downstream of the relief valve the flow through the filter will depend on system demand; and in off-load periods will have leakage flow or full flow depending on whether the control valve is of blocked-centre or open-centre type, respectively (Fig 3). Such positioning thus makes it more difficult to estimate the varying flow rates to which the filter may be subjected and so the former system is normally preferred. In this case a bypass across the filter is essential to eliminate excessive pressure build-up against the pump should the filter become clogged (Fig 4).

Additional protection for the system can then be provided by further filters preceding critical components, or point-of-use filters (see Fig 5). Filter requirements can be selected in a number of different ways, depending on how critical protection is for each component. If the first filter (following the pump) provides the necessary fine filtering, the first component in the system is protected. Subsequent components *needing* protection from contaminants which may be generated by the first component can be preceded by an additional fine filter. A component with more generous clearances not needing such protection need not have a point-of-use filter preceding it.

Equally a point-of-use filter could precede *each* component needing protection (chosen with a suitable rating); when the first filter following the pump could be of a coarser type for lower resistance to full pump flow.

Return Line Filtering

A return line filter is located downstream of the last working component in the system, but upstream of the reservoir – Fig 6. It thus removes all contaminants (down to its rating level) ingested or generated by the pump and system components before the fluid is returned to the reservoir. It has the advantage that it is not likely to be subjected to large pressure surges as can occur in pressure lines, but it can be subject to unsteady flow conditions, and thus needs to be robust enough to accommodate flow surges.

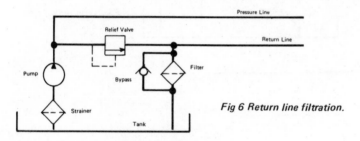

Fig 6 Return line filtration.

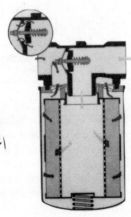

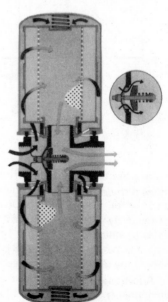

UCC 'Maxi Flow' return line filter, nominal rating 10 μm.

Sperry Vickers 'Revolver' off-line filter available with alternative elements for fine (3 μm) medium (12 μm) and coarse filtering (25 μm and 35 μm).

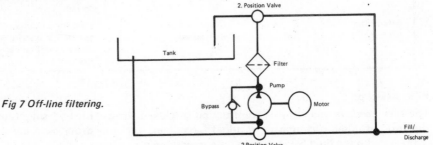

Fig 7 Off-line filtering.

Bypass or Off-Line Filter

A bypass filter is located in a separate loop between the pump and reservoir, this loop operating independently of the main system. Its purpose is to provide a means of cleaning the fluid contained in the reservoir only (Fig 7).

Its particular use is for overall fluid cleaning at suitable maintenance intervals. It can, if necessary, be operated when the main system is in use. It does not, of course, dispense with the need for filter(s) in the main system since it only cleans the amount of fluid present in the reservoir.

Batch Filtering

Batch filtering is similar to bypass filtering in that fluid is drawn from the reservoir and passed through a filter before being returned for further use. This is carried out by an independent unit which may be used to batch-filter any number of separate systems.

Table IV summarizes the different types of filters and filter locations.

TABLE IV — FILTER TYPES AND LOCATION — HYDRAULIC SYSTEMS

Position or Type	Degree of Filtration	Remarks
Suction line	100—150 μm	Must have low flow resistance to prevent pump cavitation.
Main pressure line	Down to 15 μm as required	High strength elements and high pressure case required. Can be bypassed for cold starts.
Individual pressure lines (Point-of-use-filters)	Down to 5 μm if required, but under 25 μm	Gives maximum protection to individual components. Normally specified for chip control only to avoid high pressure drops.
Return line	Down to 3 μm	High strength case not required. Usually specified for silt control.
Breathers	Down to 25 μm if required	Fitted to reservoir or tank to eliminate ingestion of airborne contaminants.
Bypass filter (Separate loop)	Down to 25 μm	Can be employed during a run-in period to assist in removal of ingested external contaminants; also for routine oil cleaning.
Magnetic plug	Ferrous particles only	Can be fitted in reservoir, particularly useful during run-in period.
Batch filter (External)	Down to 5 μm if required	Used for cleaning and reclaiming old oil in a system. May also be used to prefilter raw oil from storage.

Filter Selection

The filter *medium* and element construction employed for specific hydraulic filters is chosen on the basis of filter performance required, acceptable pressure drop, mechanical strength, compatibility with the fluid being used and other working parameters.

Compatibility with the system fluid must relate to the system temperatures involved to ensure that no degradation of the element or its seals occurs during its normal service life. Degradation can occur through:

(i)   Absorption of fluid into the filter medium or binder causing swelling (increased pressure drop and choking); or migration of particles downstream.

(ii)   Hardening or embrittlement of the filter element which can cause cracking and breakdown of the material.

(iii)   Disintegration of the element.

In general asbestos, glass microfibres and wire mesh are fully compatible with all hydraulic fluids (provided the complete filter does not include parts in aluminium, cadmium, magnesium or zinc which are attacked by water-in-oil fluids). Cellulosic media tend to swell in water and are not generally suitable for water-in-oil and water-glycol fluids. Filters with active media cannot be employed as these are capable of removing additives commonly used in hydraulic oils.

Compatibility with other system components needs little comment, other than that the filter should be readily fitted and coupled to existing units and the fact that filters of the required size are available to fit standard line sizes, *etc.* It is also desirable that the form of the filter is such that it is readily accessible for removal of the bowl or body and element for cleaning or element replacement.

Pressure Drop

Pressure drop is related to the form and type of element chosen (*ie* element permeability), but in practice is more dependent on the design and size of the complete filter, rather than media characteristics alone.

For any given type and size of filter, pressure drop characteristics can be evaluated from manufacturer's data which are directly applicable to new elements. The corresponding 'K' factor can be found by substitution in the basic formula

$$P = K \nu Q$$

Typically, filters for high pressure hydraulics are designed with a 'K' factor yielding not more than 15 lb/in^2 (1 bar) pressure drop at maximum rated flow with a specific fluid. Lacking other data, performance can be estimated fairly accurately for other flow rates, or for other fluids, from the basic formula. Similarly, approximations for the performance of other sizes of the same design of filter can be derived from the previous formulas. The variations of the 'K' factor with time, or contaminant build up, cannot, however, be determined other than by practical tests.

The basic formula also indicates that the pressure drop will vary with fluid viscosity, *(ie* fluid working temperature). Performance figures quoted for a given viscosity can be corrected for other viscosities (working temperatures) by the same formula $P = K\nu Q$

Flow Rate

In selecting a filter the maximum flow rate and maximum acceptable pressure drop for the system must be known as these will affect the element size required. Minimum requirement is that the filter should be sized to handle the maximum flow rate possible from the pump.

Filter weight is generally a less significant factor, although here it can be noted that filters with re-cleanable elements are usually heavier and bulkier than their disposable element counterparts. Excessive size (or weight) could, however, inhibit the use of a line filter at a point where it would be most effective. Also with the more expensive types of element, a reduction in size represents a direct reduction in cost. Equally the availability of small, compact filters for in-line duties favours their use for individual component protection, where they can be more effective than a single system filter.

The subject of high pressure surges needs further comment. Certain media, whilst possessing excellent filtering properties, have low strength when wetted and can burst under high differential pressures, or become displaced, allowing the fluid to bypass the element. Multiple construction can usually guard against such failures, but permanent damage to a filter element can result. The solution is not always a matter of filter design, or type. Thus if peak pressures of 10 000 lb/in^2 (700 bar) are realized in a 2 000 lb/in^2 (14 bar) system, which is not uncommon, the employment of a filter with a pressure rating of five times the normal maximum differential pressure is not necessarily a logical, or practical answer. A better solution in such cases may be to investigate the system design as a whole, relocating the filter in a more favourable position and possibly applying surge damping to the system.

Cost is an indeterminate factor. In general, the finer the degree of protection provided the higher the cost of the filter, but the overall savings in terms of reduction in wear and increased reliability of service can be very real. Because filters are such unobtrusive components their importance is often under-rated and one should err on the side of over-protection rather than under protection (or purely nominal protection), unless this is quite inconsistent with the system economics or performance requirements. For example, the finer the degree of filtration required the shorter is likely to be the time between element cleaning, unless an extra large size of filter is fitted. Where system maintenance receives scant attention, a bypass may be fitted to the 'fine' filter, with the distinct possibility that the system will continue to be operated for a considerable period with the filter ineffective. The advantages of employing fine filtering initially are then destroyed.

Protection Devices

Filter housings commonly incorporate protective devices — *eg* shut-off valves, check valves, reserve flow valves and bypassing facility.

Shut-off valves are usually incorporated in the filter head, automatically sealing the inlet and outlet lines when the filter bowl is removed (*eg* to replace an element). They also have the advantage of minimizing air entrainment during replacement of a filter element. It should be noted that shut-off valves (where fitted) are normally effective only at low system pressures (*ie* not full system pressure unless specifically stated). (Fig 8).

Check valves may be fitted to inlet and outlet ports to prevent reverse flow occurring through the filter.

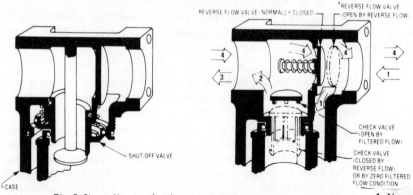

Fig 8 Shut-off valve (left) and check and reverse flow valve
(right).

1. Normal in flow
2. Filtered flow
3. Normal out flow
4. Reverse flow (not filtered)

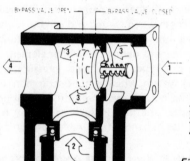

1. Flow in
2. Filtered flow
3. Bypass flow
4. Flow out

Fig 9 Bypass valve.

Reverse-flow valves may be fitted to provide a bypass loop in the event of reverse flow conditions and thus eliminate any back pressure on the element. With some elements reverse flow can result in damage.

Bypass housings incorporate a bypass valve which opens at a predetermined differential pressure across the filter element (Fig 9). Flow is then partially through the filter element and partially through the bypass. In the event of the filter becoming fully clogged, flow is maintained through the bypass. Significant parameters are the opening or 'cracking' pressure of the bypass valve; its resealing pressure (typically 60–75% of the 'cracking' pressure); and the maximum obtainable pressure drop through the bypass at rated flow.

A filter with a bypass housing only provides complete protection (filtration) when the bypass is closed, as in normal use. A non-bypass housing is essential when all the fluid must be filtered all the time. In this case the onset of clogging causing an increase in differential pressure to a predetermined level, can trigger a visual and/or audible alarm via a pressure switch or similar device.

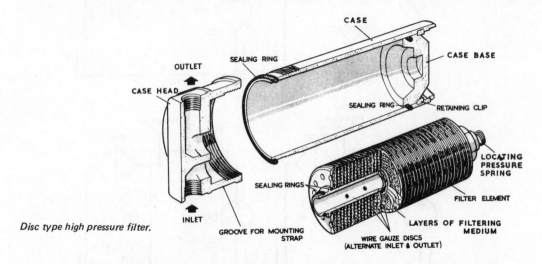

Disc type high pressure filter.

TABLE V – ACCEPTABLE CONTAMINANT LEVELS IN HYDRAULIC SYSTEMS

Type of System	Maximum particle count		Contamination class to CETOP EP70H	
	5 m	15 m	5 m	15 m
Low pressure, general industrial hydraulics	10^6	64×10^3	21	17
Low pressure, heavy duty hydraulics	25×10^4	16×10^3	19	15
Medium pressure industrial hydraulics	13×10^4	8×10^3	18	14
Mobile hydraulics	13×10^4	8×10^3	18	14
High pressure industrial hydraulics	32×10^3	4×10^3	16	13
High pressure, high performance industrial hydraulics and machine tools	16×10^3	10^3	15	11
Aircraft hydraulics	16×10^3	10^3	15	11

Contaminant Levels

Modern practice favours the regular sampling and determination of contaminant levels in hydraulic systems. Contaminant levels are then expressed in terms of counts of particles of 5 μm and 15 μm size, or CETOP contamination classes — see chapter on *Contaminant Levels.* Suggested acceptable contaminant levels are given in Table V.

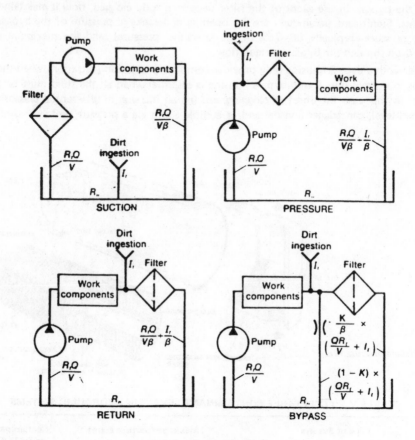

*Fig 10 Computer models for hydraulic
filters.
(Parker-Hannifin Ltd).*

System Models for Computer Solutions

A filter model is developed by choosing a point in the system and writing an equation for the contaminant particles entering and leaving that point. (See also Fig 10).

It will be appreciated that different locations of the filter(s) require different system models. Thus a suction-line filter removes contaminants before they enter the pump. Since the reservoir collects all generated and ingested contaminants, it can be considered as the contaminant ingestion point for the circuit.

A pressure-line filter removes contaminant either between the pump and the other components or between any of the components. The ingestion point is thus either between the pump and filter or at the reservoir.

A bypass circuit allows a large portion of the total pump flow to bypass the filter. In such a circuit, the filter handles only the amount of flow necessary to maintain the contamination level required by the system components. This lower flow specification allows the use of a smaller, less costly filter, but can still provide maximum component life. In the bypass circuit, the ingestion point can be after the work components but before the bypass line, or at the reservoir.

Suction-line Filter Model

For the suction-line filter, the reservoir is chosen as the point of reference. The equation for the number of particles in the reservoir at any time (R_t) is

$$R_t = R_o + \frac{R_x Qt}{V\beta_x} + I_i t \frac{R_x Qt}{V}$$

where R_o = initial number of particles: $R_x Qt/V\beta_x$ = number of particles of given size entering through the return line: I_i = number of particles entering through ingestion (including wear particles): and $R_x Qt/V$ = number of particles leaving through the suction line; β_x = filter rating.

Since the terms depend on the number of contaminant particles in the reservoir at any time, the time interval must be small to approximate the true relationship for the number of particles versus time. Therefore, the equation becomes:

$$R_t = R_o + \frac{R_x Q\Delta t}{V\beta_x} + I_i\Delta t - \frac{R_x Q\Delta t}{V} \tag{1}$$

where Δt is a small increment of time over which the change in the number of particles is viewed. The smaller Δt the more accurate the results. As Δt approaches zero, it becomes dt, and the equation can be rewritten as

$$\frac{R_t - R_o}{dt} = \frac{R_x Q}{V\beta_x} + I_i - \frac{R_x Q}{V} \tag{2}$$

Equation (1) is in the form for digital computer solution, while Equation (2) can be solved with differential equations.

For computer solution, a programme must be written to start at $t = 0$ and calculate the number of particles in the reservoir for a given time increment, flow rate, reservoir volume, β ratio, and ingestion rate. At $t = 0$, there is no ingestion or flow rate: therefore, $R_t = R_o$. Then, using $R_t = R$, at $t = 0$, calculate R_t at $t = 1$, and so forth until the time of interest is reached, at which point R_t equals the number of particles in the reservoir for a given contaminant size range.

The mathematical solution to Equation (2) is

$$R_t = R_x \exp\left(-\frac{EQt}{V}\right) + \frac{I_i V}{EQ}\left[1 - \exp\left(-\frac{EQt}{V}\right)\right] \tag{3}$$

The number of particles in the reservoir at any time for the suction filter circuit can be solved by substituting the system parameters into Equation (3) or by using a computer programme.

Similarly, models can be developed for pressure and return-line filters. Models for these two systems are identical, and the number of particles in the system can be calculated from:

$$R_t = R_x \exp\left(-\frac{QKEt}{V}\right) + \frac{(I_i - KI_iE)\,V}{QEK}\left[1 - \exp\left(-\frac{QKEt}{V}\right)\right] \tag{4}$$

where

$E = I - 1/\beta$

K = proportion of pump flow through filter

V = reservoir volume (ml)

Q = pump flow ml/min

Fig 11 provides a quick solution to this equation.

The filter model for the bypass system is developed by adding the particles entering the reservoir and subtracting those leaving the reservoir and is given by

$$R_t = R_x + \left(1-K\right)\left(\frac{QR_x}{V} + I_i\right)\Delta t + \frac{K}{\beta_x}\left(\frac{QR_x}{V} + I_i\right)\Delta t - \frac{QR_x t}{V}$$

This equation can be rearranged, simplified and put in differential form to yield

$$R_t = R_0 \exp\left(-\frac{QKEt}{V}\right) + \frac{V-EKV}{QKE}\left[1 - \exp\left[\left(-\frac{QKEt}{V}\right)\right]\right] \tag{5}$$

For a digital solution, this equation can be rearranged and simplified to

$$R_{t+i} = R_t + (1-K)\left(\frac{QR_t}{V} + I_i\right)\Delta t + \frac{K}{\beta_x}\left(\frac{QR_t}{V} + I_i\right)\Delta t - \frac{QR_t \Delta t}{V}$$

Using the Equations

As indicated by the β ratio, no filter removes 100% of all ingested particles. Rather, the system eventually reaches an equilibrium where contaminant concentration remains constant. If this concentration is below the sensitivity level of the most sensitive component, system life will be satisfactory.

Tolerable contaminant concentration is usually specified in terms of SAE oil classifications, as shown in the graph. Thus, before a filter can be selected, required oil cleanliness and maximum particle size must be specified, based on the wear and clog resistance of the most sensitive component. Then, maximum contaminant concentration can be found from the graph.

Once contaminant concentration, reservoir volume, flow rate, and particle ingestion rate are specified, the equations can be used to manipulate filter β ratio and location to optimize system

Return-Line Filter Nomogram

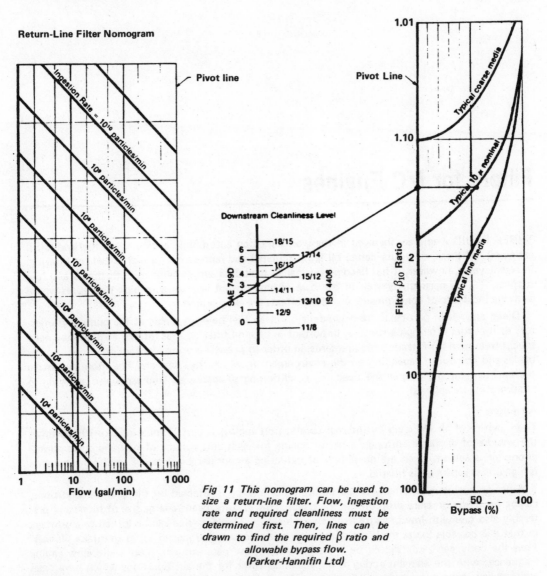

Fig 11 This nomogram can be used to size a return-line filter. Flow, ingestion rate and required cleanliness must be determined first. Then, lines can be drawn to find the required β ratio and allowable bypass flow.
(Parker-Hannifin Ltd)

reliability and cost. In general, the procedure involves calculating the required β ratio for the different filter locations. In addition, for the bypass filter, the percentage of bypass can be altered to optimize β ratio and contaminant concentration.

Filter cost generally increases with increasing size and increasing β ratio, with size having more effect. Since suction and pressure-line filters must handle higher-pressure flows, these installations may require larger, more expensive filters. Return-line and bypass filters, on the other hand, operate at lower pressure and are, therefore, usually less expensive.

See also *Filter Selection Guides.*

Filters for I/C Engines

THREE FLUID media are involved in the working of an automobile engine — air, fuel and lubricating oil. Of these, only lubricating oil is recirculated and represents a primary need for filtering. In recent years, however, it has become normal to include a simple filter in both the air and fuel supplies. This is particularly true in the case of high output engines with high flow rates where both the incidence of contaminants and their effects are exaggerated.

Diesel engines in particular are dependent on clean fuel being available at the pump and injectors so that fuel filtering becomes as important as lube oil filtering. Gas turbine engines may need special treatment for filtration requirements, in order to prevent erosion and fouling of compressor blades and corrosion, depending on the environment in which they operate. The more aggressive the environment the greater the need for conditioning of intake air (the same also applying to reciprocating i/c engines).

Air Filters

The quantity of air inducted by internal combustion engines is vast. Something like 10 000 times the volume of air passes through a petrol engine for each unit volume of fuel and since atmospheric air is seldom clean the possibility of inducting a considerable mass of solid contaminants is high unless intake air is filtered.

Since an engine is essentially an air pump, its efficiency is affected by the suction conditions, calling for a low pressure drop on the inlet side. This in turn means a large size of filter; and preferably also one with low pressure drop characteristics. The large size can be turned to advantage in that it is possible to use the body of the filter as a resonant chamber to act as an intake silencer. Thus the body can — or should be — designed as a low pass acoustic filter well below engine frequency; with the element acting as a mechanical filter for the air. Solutions which have been adopted vary from one extreme to the other — from efficient acoustic filters with poor or indifferent mechanical filtering, to efficient mechanical filters with little or no silencing effect. Equally on vehicle engines, size may be too restricted (affecting engine performance or carburettor calibration); or unnecessarily large (thus requiring a bulky and possibly heavy structure to be rigidly supported above the engine).

Originally the oil-wetted filter was widely favoured for air intake filters. Effective filtration with such types, however, depends on a uniform degree of wetting of the wire mesh with oil, which is seldom achieved in practice. The oil bath air filter is better in this respect, provided the oil level is maintained, but again efficiency tends to be inconsistent.

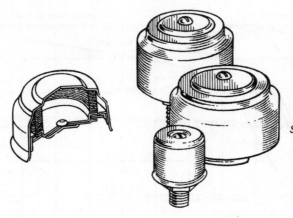

Simple air filters or breathers.
(Tecalemit)

AAF 'Cycoil' oil-bath intake filter and silencer.

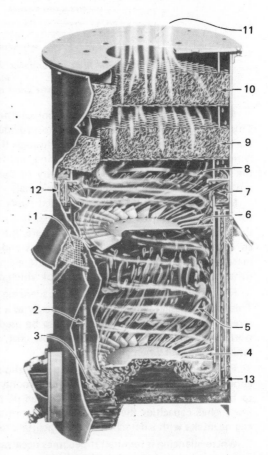

Dirty air enters under the rain shield and passes through removable bug screen (1), then passes downward through the space (2) between the inner and outer cylinders. At (3) it impinges against oil, depositing the heavier dust particles immediately, picks up oil and then passes upward through vanes (4) which impact a whirling motion to the air and oil mixture. In chamber (5) the whirling air and oil are thoroughly mixed and the centrifugal action developed throws a large portion of the dust against the oil-coated walls of the inner cylinder. The air-oil mixture then passes through vanes (6) which impart a still faster whirl, throwing the oil with the dust it has collected outward by centrifugal action. At the top of the cylinder (7) is an enlarged chamber into which most of the oil and dirt are thrown from the air stream. The pre-cleaned air then passes upward through orifice (8) and through the double filter cells (9) and (10) leaving the cleaner at (11) to pass into the engine or compressor. The air which reaches the filter cells contains a mist of oil which is collected by the cells and drains out around the outer edges. This continuous flow of oil keeps the filter cells thoroughly washed so that any dust collected on them is immediately carried away.

The oil which is thrown out at (7) and the oil which drains from the filter pads passes downward to the oil reservoir through pipes (12) and (13). There the dirt settles out and the oil recirculates.

Maintenance consists of periodically draining the dirty oil, removing the inspection plate to scrape out accumulated sludge, and refilling with clean oil. If properly maintained, it should never be necessary to remove the filter cells for cleaning, but the top is made removable and the filter cells may be lifted out, inspected, or cleaned in case unusual conditions make this necessary.

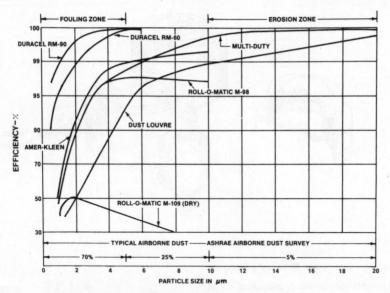

Typical filter performance versus fouling for gas turbine air
intakes.
(AAF filter types referred to)

A variation on these types is the polyurethane foam cartridge housed in a simple container. This cartridge is impregnated with oil to provide mechanical filtering, the oil held in the pores of the foam trapping dust as air passes through the filter. Whilst more consistent than the original wire mesh type, the efficiency of filtering, and to a lesser extent, the actual pressure drop through the filter, still depends on the uniformity of the oil application. If the cartridge is allowed to dry out the practical filtering effect can be virtually nil.

Most modern air filters favour pleated paper elements of a similar type and form to those used for oil filters, with the element employed in the form of an annular cartridge, but with flow from the outside to the inside. Contaminants are thus collected on the outer surface of the pleats. Such an element can be restrained by end rings and further stabilized by inner and outer perforated metal tubes or wire screens. The complete element or cartridge is then simply mounted inside a suitable container, the shape and form of which may vary considerably.

For simple air filter duties, without silencing, the cartridge may itself form the complete filter. This sort of design would be used primarily as a crankcase breather filter, or a filter on a hydraulic reservoir breather. It may, however, also be used as an intake filter on very small internal combustion engines because of its simplicity, low cost, and low pressure drop. The complete filter is then replaced as a unit when clogged.

For general air intake filtering duties, without silencing, up to flow rates of the order of 200 cubic feet per minute, a cowl type is commonly preferred. With this type it is usual for the cover to be held by a screw or nut so that it can be removed to replace the cartridge when necessary. For higher capacities the body or casing normally becomes a permanent fitting mounted to the engine intake with a detachable lid to facilitate removal of the cartridge.

Where silencing is required it becomes necessary to increase the volume of the unit, typically by increasing the diameter of the filter element or annulus without necessarily increasing the depth of corrugation (or even reducing this depth because of the greater surface area); and also to add extra volume outside the cartridge, if necessary.

There are, of course, numerous variations on these themes. Some engine manufacturers may adopt standard filters, others employ special designs. Ducting may also be incorporated to provide feed air through the filter from the most suitable point, as well as to increase the effective volume of the intake 'resonant chamber'. It is sufficient to repeat that the majority of modern intake filters are of the pleated paper element type with replaceable cartridge. Unlike oil filters using a similar element, paper elements can be cleaned, utilizing a back flow of compressed air. Some may even be specified as suitable for cleaning by back-washing with a suitable solvent. Normal practice, however, is to replace the cartridge rather than clean an air filter element.

'Foilgard' oil filter for heavy duty equipment employs a patented element of blended virgin wood and cotton fibres formed into individual discs.

Air Filter Sizing

The size of air filter required can be based on the air consumption requirements of the engine which, theoretically, are given by the following formula:-

$$\text{ft}^3/\text{min air required} = \frac{2\pi D^2 \, L \, N \, n}{4 \times 1728}$$

This quantity is derived as twice the swept volume of one cylinder multiplied by engine speed multiplied by number of intake strokes occurring together,

where D = bore, inches
        L = stroke, inches
        N = rev/min
        n 1
        n = number of inlet strokes occurring together

For practical calculation this formula can be simplified to

$$\text{Filter capacity (ft}^3/\text{min)} = \frac{D^2 \, L \, N}{K}$$ where bore and stroke dimension are in inches

$$\text{Filter capacity (m}^3/\text{min)} = \frac{d^2 \, l \, N}{1000 \, k}$$ where bore (d) and stroke (l) dimensions are in centimetres

Appropriate values of the respective constants K and k are given in Table I.

TABLE I – CONSTANTS FOR AIR FILTER SIZING

	Type of Engine or Compressor	K	*k
1	Cylinder four-stroke or two-stroke	1100	18000
2	Cylinder four-stroke or two-stroke	1100	18000
3	Cylinder four-stroke or two-stroke	1100	18000
4	Cylinder four-stroke or two-stroke	1100	18000
3	Cylinder two-stroke	733	12000
5	Cylinder four-stroke	733	12000
6	Cylinder four-stroke	733	12000
4	Cylinder two-stroke	550	9000
7	Cylinder four-stroke	550	9000
8	Cylinder four-stroke	550	9000
12	Cylinder four-stroke	366	6000
16	Cylinder four-stroke	275	4500
1	Cylinder single acting single stage compressor	1100	18000
2	Cylinder single acting single stage compressor	1100	18000
3	Cylinder single acting single stage compressor	733	12000
4	Cylinder single acting single stage compressor	550	9000
6	Cylinder single acting single stage compressor	366	6000
1	Cylinder double acting single stage compressor	1100	18000
2	Cylinder double acting single stage compressor	550	9000
3	Cylinder double acting single stage compressor	366	6000
2	Cylinder single acting two stage compressor	1100	18000
4	Cylinder single acting two stage compressor	1100	18000
6	Cylinder single acting two stage compressor	733	12000
2	Cylinder double acting two stage compressor	1100	18000
4	Cylinder double acting two stage compressor	550	9000
6	Cylinder double acting two stage compressor	366	6000

*Where dimensions are in millimetres multiply constant k by 1000

Alternatively the following formula can be used:

Ft^3/min Displacement Formula :
$$\frac{D^2 \times L \times rev/min \times N}{K_1 \times K_2}$$

where D = bore in inches

L = stroke in inches

rev/min = revolutions per minute

N = (A) number of cylinders – engine

(B) number of low pressure cylinders – compressor

K_1 = 2200 for (A) two cycle engines with scavenging blower

(B) four cycle engines naturally aspirated of 4 or more cylinders

1760 for (A) pump scavenged engines

(B) air compressors – single cylinder – single acting

(C) air compressors – single cylinder – double acting

(D) air compressors – two or more low pressure cylinders – double acting

(E) four cycle engines – one, two or three cylinders

K_2 = 1 for two cycle engines

2 for four cycle engines

1 for single acting compressor

½ for double acting compressor

Oil Filters

The function of the oil filter is to deal with contaminants which may be contained in the lubricating oil and prevent them from reaching sensitive engine parts, without restricting normal oil flow to the various points requiring lubricating. The oil pump is normally mounted within the engine sump with the filter connected to give either full flow or bypass circuits. The former passes all the oil output from the pump through the filter and is normal in modern practice, although the bypass sytem is still used on some designs.

Internal sources of contamination include wear products from the rubbing surfaces of the engine, blow-by gases leaking past the rings of the pistons, and degradation of the oil itself. Modern crankcase lubricants are capable of dispersing many of the contaminants which originally caused sludge and varnish deposits to occur, as well as containing additives which greatly extend oil life (that is, prevent oxidation, chemical breakdown, or other forms of degradation).

Wear products are normally highly abrasive, but produced mainly during the first 10 to 20 hours of the engine's life. Satisfactory protection is provided by both an oil change after a nominal running-in period, as specified by the engine manufacturer, and the system filter. In specialized cases running-in may be completed on a dynamometer rig.

Blow-by gases comprise exhaust gases and unburnt fuel mixture leaking into the crankcase with each complete cycle of the piston. They are in the main removed through the crankcase breather, but can react with an oil which is not in good condition, or other contaminants. Piston rings can never provide a complete gas seal, so blow-by gases are always present in the crankcase. It is also significant that the presence of foreign matter in the piston ring areas can seriously decrease their efficiency, resulting not only in loss of engine performance but giving a higher proportion of blow-by gases below the pistons.

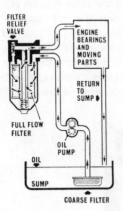

Fig 1 Full flow system.

Winslow heavy duty full flow oil filter.
(Powell Duffryn)

Full Flow Filtering

A typical full flow system is shown in Fig 1, where the filter is in line between the pump and bearings or points at which the oil is distributed. The main limitation is that the oil pressure in the bearings depends partially on the restriction due to the filter, plus the fact that the filter must be large enough to handle the volume of oil flow involved. This may be as high as 5 gal/min (23 lit/min) on the larger automobile engines.

Pressure drop through the filter will be affected by the condition of the filter, and also the viscosity of the oil. Thus with cold oil pressure drop may be excessive and to safeguard against this such filters normally incorporate a valve which opens under excess pressure to bypass the filter element. This is normally set to open when the pressure drop across the element reaches a figure of about 15 lb/in² (1 bar). The bypass valve closes immediately the oil has warmed up and its viscosity falls to reduce the pressure drop through the filter below 15 lb/in² (1 bar). If the excessive pressure drop is due to another cause, such as a clogged element, the bypass valve will remain open as long as that cause remains. Under such circumstances, of course, the filter remains out of the circuit.

A further refinement which may be incorporated in full flow filters is an anti-drainback valve. The sole purpose of this is to prevent oil draining back through the filter into the oil pump and thence the sump when the engine is stopped, thus retaining the filter full of oil. On restarting oil is then immediately circulated from the filter to the bearings. If the filter could drain when the engine is stopped, no oil would flow to the bearings until the engine has run for a sufficient time on restarting for the oil pump first to fill the filter.

An alternative solution is to mount the filter at such a position that with the engine stopped it cannot drain back and empty itself through the pump. Since the filter is normally mounted externally and higher than the sump for ease of replacement of the element or cartridge, the attitude of the filter alone may not be sufficient to guard against 'siphon' draining, when an anti-drainback valve can be used to advantage.

Bypass Filtering

A bypass system is shown in Fig 2. Here the oil pump feeds the main gallery direct but this line is tapped and taken to the filter with a return line from the filter to the sump. Oil is fed at the same pressure to the bearings and filter, but the actual quantity reaching the filter is controlled by a restrictor (normally incorporated in the filter itself). This ensures that the bearings receive the main oil supply, with only a proportion of the oil delivered by the pump passing through the filter. This part flow filter requires no relief valve for it automatically isolates itself in the event of becoming clogged. Nor does it need an anti-drainback valve since initial flow from the pump to the bearings is not dependent on the filter being filled with oil. In some cases, however, an anti-drainback valve may be incorporated in the filter to ensure faster initial circulation to the bearings.

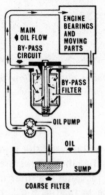

Pleated paper filter element with bypass (Purolator)

Fig 2 Bypass system.

In the case of bypass filter systems it is generally recommended that the rate of flow through the filter should be at least one tenth of the flow rate of the engine and that the quantity of oil treated by the bypass filter should be at least five times that of the total oil volume in the circulating system.

The bypass system has the advantage that the same size of filter will have a higher efficiency than a full flow filter since the flow rate is lower. However, the protection offered is incomplete and the oil has to circulate a number of times before there is the probability that the total volume has passed through the filter. This is still a probability rather than a certainty and particles can readily bypass the filter line and be fed directly to the bearings. It offers a solution where volume flow is high and would need a large size of full flow filter, or high flow rates with lowered efficiency through a smaller full flow filter. Practical evidence, however, favours the full flow filter as the logical choice for modern automobile engines of all types and sizes.

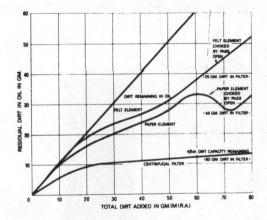

Fig 3 Comparison between the performance of paper element, felt element and centrifugal filters.

Centrifugal-type oil filters are also employed as bypass filters, particularly on larger engines and stationary engines. Their performance is generally superior to paper or felt element filters, particularly as regards their filtering capacity at high levels of contamination — see Fig 3. They are, however, appreciably more expensive than simple filters and are thus not normally employed for general vehicle applications; also they are not normally regarded as suitable for full flow filters.

Additional protection for the oil circuit is also normally provided at the oil pump intake, usually in the form of a simple strainer. This will prevent larger particles from entering the pump and thus the recirculatory system. Properly located, and with a suitable design of sump, this will also prevent the pump from picking up water which may have contaminated the oil. This water will normally, but not necessarily, separate out at the bottom of the sump. In the presence of contaminants, however, it may form an emulsion with the oil.

Some protection may also be provided at the oil filter, although this is not common. Again a simple strainer is usually sufficient or a wad of steel wool. Since oils are now commonly dispensed from sealed cans and thus enter the engine with manufacturer's purity, filtering of top-up or filling oil is not usually considered necessary. Obvious precautions, such as wiping clean the neck of the filter and not pouring new oil from a dirty container or through a dirty funnel must be observed. Other sources of external contamination are dirt or dust entering the dipstick hole when the dipstick is removed and replaced; or through the crankcase breather. When operating in dust-laden atmospheres the open end of the breather may need to be fitted with its own filter. In other cases sufficient protection is afforded by terminating the open end of the breather inside the air intake filter.

Almost all full flow oil filters are of the surface media type since this provides minimum restriction to oil flow. The filter comprises two parts; a filter housing and a filter element or cartridge. In some designs the housing and cartridge are combined in a single unit which can be unscrewed and replaced with a new unit when a filter change is called for. The latter has come into more widespread use during recent years.

Various materials are used for disposable oil filter elements — paper, felt, bulk fibre, wound yarn spools, *etc*. The impregnated paper element of pleated form is the most popular type as this can provide a cut-off of the required order and also has the necessary strength to withstand the differential pressures which may be involved. This element is arranged annularly in a circular 'can' with perforated inner and outer tubes to produce a cartridge. Similar construction applies in the case of a replaceable unit where the cartridge is permanently fixed inside the outer casing.

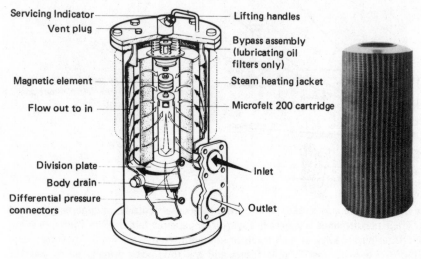

Vokes Cartridge type microfelt filter

Typical Vokes disposable felt type element cartridge. The pleated cylinder is supported by perforated-metal sleeves.

Felt elements are particularly favoured for large capacity diesel engine oil filters because of their property of filtering in depth with large dirt-holding capacity and low pressure drop. Synthetic fibre felt is superior to natural fibre felt in density and uniformity, resistance to engine acids and complete resistance to water. It is also a stronger material. All pleated felt elements are, however, normally supported either by special spacers or wire mesh to withstand pressure.

Oil Filter Rating

The degree of filtration required for satisfactory protection has tended to become more stringent with modern engine designs and production techniques yielding closer tolerances. Whereas a filter cut-off of 30 μm or higher was considered adequate a decade ago the present standard is to provide filtration of particle sizes of 20 μm or less (for example, 10–15 μm or 10–20 μm), with high efficiency (over 99%).

Oil Filter Size

The size of oil filter required is determined by the flow capacity and acceptable pressure drop. Increasing the flow rate through a particular size of filter will increase the pressure drop. A suitable size is normally established on obtaining the necessary flow rate with a pressure drop of the order of 3 to 5 lb/in^2 (0.2 to 0.3 bar) at the actual working viscosity of the fluid. If necessary two or three more filter units can be mounted in separate casings on a common head to operate in parallel, rather than resorting to a single large filter of the same capacity.

Maximum working pressure for lubricating oil filters is usually of the order of 100 lb/in^2 (7 bar). This figure may be approached when the oil is very cold, but normal working pressure is usually substantially lower.

TABLE II – NORMAL OIL FILTER ELEMENT LIFE

Application	Normal Use	Arduous Conditions	Poor Operating Conditions and Unfavourable Ambient Surroundings
Automobile engines	500–1000 hours or 10 000 miles	Up to 500 hours or 5 000 miles	100–250 hours
Marine engines	1000 hours	500 hours	500 hours
Large stationary engines	1000 hours	500 hours	—
Turbines, etc	2000 hours upwards	Up to 2000 hours	—
Portable power units	1000 hours	500 hours	200–500 hours

Oil Filter Life

Life of the modern lubricating oil filter element is of the order of 500 to 1000 hours, although this will depend on the working conditions — Table II. It is impossible to give specific figures since life will depend on engine design, quality and type of lubricating oil, and operating conditions, as well as frequency of oil changes and the actual time elapsed between oil changes. Engine manufacturers normally give specific recommendations which are commonly held to be conservative or 'safe'. Under certain operating conditions, however, it may be highly desirable to effect a filter change at much closer intervals. Equally, if a filter change is specified in terms of engine hours or mileage only, the oil filter should be changed at least once a year regardless of whether the recommended hours or miles have been realized. This is particularly necessary in the case of marine engines derived from automobile engines where less than 500 hours engine running time is common-place during a single year.

All full flow filters incorporate a bypass device or relief valve. This is located in the housing in the case of a throw-away filter. With a replaceable cartridge type of filter the bypass may be mounted in the filter housing, filter centre bolt, or even in the engine block.

Fig 4 shows the action of a bypass device. Under normal conditions full flow filtering is provided. As the filter becomes partially clogged and resistance to oil flow builds up the element is forced away from its top seating against the spring in the bottom of the casing. This sliding displacement of the cartridge down the centre bolt opens a passage for through flow of oil so that a percentage of the flow bypasses the actual element. Under normal operating conditions with a typical automobile engine (and without a filter change) this is likely to occur after some 5 000 to 10 000 miles of driving. From that point on, until replaced, the oil is being treated as a bypass or part flow system, although the actual proportion of oil flowing through the filter element may remain quite high.

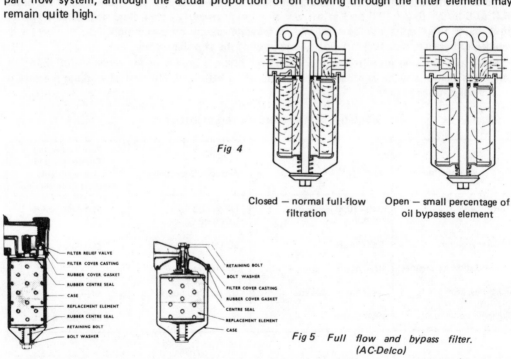

Fig 4

Closed — normal full-flow filtration

Open — small percentage of oil bypasses element

FILTER RELIEF VALVE
FILTER COVER CASTING
RUBBER COVER GASKET
RUBBER CENTRE SEAL
CASE
REPLACEMENT ELEMENT
RUBBER CENTRE SEAL
RETAINING BOLT
BOLT WASHER

RETAINING BOLT
BOLT WASHER
FILTER COVER CASTING
RUBBER COVER GASKET
CENTRE SEAL
REPLACEMENT ELEMENT
CASE

Fig 5   Full flow and bypass filter. (AC-Delco)

Full Flow plus Bypass Filtering

In particular applications, notably stationary diesel engines, marine engines, diesel locomotive engines, and other heavy-duty internal combustion engines, the lubricating system may be fitted with a full flow filter to removal all large impurities, together with a finer bypass filter — eg see Fig Fig 5. The duty of the latter is to remove fine carbonaceous matter which would otherwise tend to build up in and clog the main filter.

Edge-type filters are favoured for such bypass filters, because of their ability to remove very fine particles. If the lubricating oil involved is of a detergent type, however, carbonaceous particles present are even more finely dispersed. Whilst an edge-type filter will remove these particles it will only do so at the expense of increasing back pressure due to the impermeable nature of the ultra-fine solids held back by the filter element. An alternative type of filter for the bypass is thus usually necessary in such cases.

'Open' system intake filters designed specifically
for marine gas turbines.
(Separation Systems Ltd)

AC-Delco fuel filter.

Fuel Filters (Petrol Engines)

Contaminants in the fuel can clog or partially clog jets and drilled or cored passages in the carburettor, upsetting their metering performance to cause loss of power, poor starting characteristics. or even damaged exhaust valves through overheating produced by an excessively weak mixture. Quite small particles may lodge on the seat of the needle valve, causing the carburettor to flood. Abrasive particles may abrade the accelerator pump seal or score valves or valve seats. There is the further consideration that abrasive particles carried through the carburettor and into the combustion chambers may result in scoring of cylinder walls or loss of efficiency of piston rings.

Provided normal precautions are taken when filling the tank, few contaminants should be introduced at this stage. The possible exception is water which is always likely to be present in small proportions in pump petrol. The main cause of fuel contamination is corrosion or deterioration of the inner surfaces of the tank itself, or the redistribution of foreign matter already in the tank.

Coarser particles can be retained in the tank by a coarse mesh strainer fitted in the tank at the outlet point. Water will settle in the bottom of the tank and would not normally be drawn up if the outlet pipe is positioned correctly; and even if it is a coarse strainer is reasonably effective in arresting it.

Not all tanks have strainers and the only protection provided is usually a mesh strainer or simple filter on the entry side of the fuel pump together with a settling or sediment bowl on the pump inlet. The filter may be in line, or even omitted. Further protection is usually provided at the carburettor entry with another simple strainer.

This system generally works quite well, provided the sediment bowl is cleaned at suitable intervals. It may or may not show an accumulation of water in the bottom of the bowl, but sediment will usually appear after a reasonable period of running. If water does appear in the bowl and there is a separate strainer between the pump and tank, then it can be suspected that the tank is fairly heavily contaminated with water. Rather than leave the settling bowl to deal with this the contents of the bottom of the tank should be siphoned or pumped out, making sure that suction is from the lowermost point of the tank. This should continue until only pure petrol is being withdrawn, showing that all the water has been removed.

The modern trend is to screen the fuel delivery at the point of entry to the fuel pump but dispense with the sediment bowl. Instead an in-line filter is mounted between the pump and the carburettor. A pleated paper element is employed in a more or less standard design of full flow filter, except that no bypass device is incorporated. Also the size of filter needs to be fairly generous as relatively high flow rates may be involved with large capacity engines operating at maximum speed (when fuel delivery requirements are most critical). To assist in assessing the condition of the filter the body is often made in transparent plastic (such as, transparent nylon or glass). The contaminants to be looked for are both dirt and water.

The paper element must, of course, be resistant to both petrol and water. Working pressure is very low, so little support is needed for the element. Typically, flow is arranged from the outside to the inside, with the element simply located in a housing. This is normally connected to the fuel line at each end by short lengths of hose.

As with other types of modern paper element filters, in-line fuel filters are made with separable housings and replaceable cartridges, or integral throwaway units. Metal housings are normally employed where the size of the filter or the application is such that it requires clamping brackets or special fittings. Plastic housings may be used for smaller or lighter units.

With a gravity flow fuel system a larger size of filter would normally be selected to ensure negligible pressure drop. This will also provide a slightly higher filter efficiency, which is generally an advantage with such systems.

The in-line fuel filter between pump and carburettor is by no means a standard on modern automobile and similar types of engines. It is, however, becoming increasingly favoured for large engines or those with specialized or critical applications. In such cases alternatives to pleated paper elements may be employed, as dictated by a particular specification or operating requirements.

Fuel Filters (Diesel Engines)

In the case of diesel engines in-line fuel filtering is essential immediately prior to the injection pump. An additional filter may be fitted in the fuel line from the tank. One or both these filters is fitted with a fuel bowl for water separation and a visual indication of fuel condition.

The form of filter used is similar to that of a conventional oil filter with pleated paper or felt element, but without a relief valve. The body may be fitted with a point for draining off water and sediment, or made readily detachable for the same purpose. Automatic fuel spill valves or air release valves may be fitted, if required, and needle type air vents may be fitted to eliminate air locks.

See also chapter on *Machine Intake Air Filters.*

Oil Reclaimation

OIL IS no longer a cheap commodity so cleaning oil and reclaiming oil from systems where it has become contaminated is an important modern process. It usually becomes cost effective to install an oil treatment plant where annual oil consumption exceeds about 2 200 gallons (10 000 litres); or in systems with a reservoir capacity in excess of 165 gallons (750 litres).

The actual treatment required varies widely from plant to plant, depending on the amount and nature of the impurities present. Several stages of pretreatment may be necessary before final cleaning and classification, *eg* screening and/or gravity sedimentation in a settling tank to remove coarse impurities.

For actual oil cleaning the choice normally lies between filters and centrifuges. Filters have the advantage of being straightforward low cost units with the ability to remove all suspended solids down to a specified particle size. They do, however, have only limited ability to handle high sludge concentrations or viscous fluids, and to remove water. Centrifuges have the advantage of being able to handle larger volumes continuously with high separation and ability to treat even viscous oils with a sludge content up to 10% by volume. Also, there are various types available for different duties. These subdivide into *purifiers, clarifiers* and *concentrators;* and also into solids-retaining and self-cleaning types.

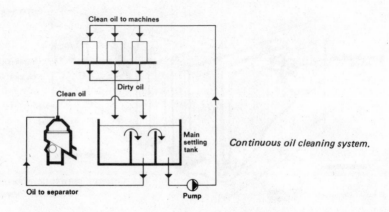

Continuous oil cleaning system.

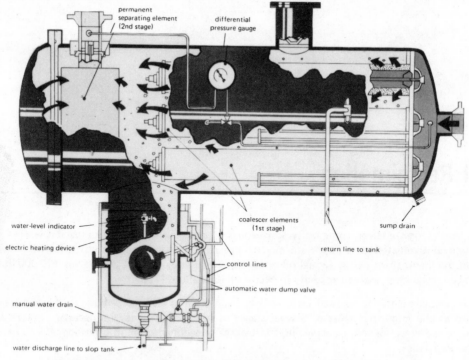

Faudi filter/water separator. The first stage is designed to break the fuel-water emulsion and simultaneously remove solids by microfiltration. The water, coalesced into large droplets, flows into the water sump.

The second stage serves for separating the finest drops of water still in suspension in the fuel. The water level in the sump can be checked by a sight glass. The water sump can be drained either manually or by an automatic drain valve. The degree of contamination of the unit is indicated by a differential pressure gauge.

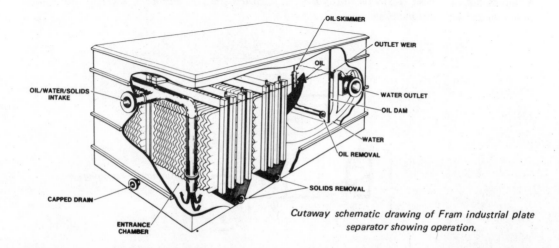

Cutaway schematic drawing of Fram industrial plate separator showing operation.

Centrifugal Purifiers

A centrifugal oil purifier has a bowl designed for separation of both water and oil. The two basic types are shown in Fig 1. Water supplied to the bowl at the start of the run forms a rotation ring with a vertical cylindrical surface inside the edge of the top disc. When the liquid seal has been established in this way, oil is fed to the bowl and separation commences.

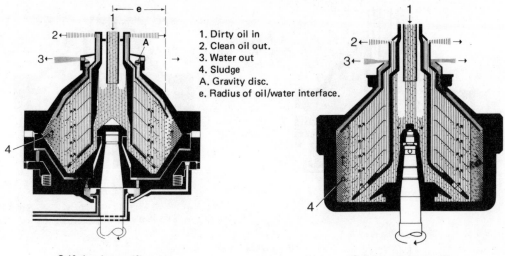

1. Dirty oil in
2. Clean oil out.
3. Water out.
4. Sludge
A. Gravity disc.
e. Radius of oil/water interface.

Self-cleaning purifier.   *Solids-retaining purifier.*

Neck of purifier bowl equipped with paring discs for oil and water. The stationary impellers convert energy of rotation into a pressure head.
1. Feed
2. Oil
3. Water
A. Gravity disc.

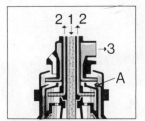

Fig 1 (Alfa-Laval)

The feed rises into the disc stack through aligned holes in the distributor and intermediate discs, whose function is to shorten the free settling path of water droplets and sludge particles. Sludge is deposited on the bowl wall, while water passes between the bowl hood and top disc to overflow from the neck of the bowl. The clean oil leaves the bowl by the upper outlet.

For optimum separation results the interface (e-line) between oil and water in the bowl should lie outside the disc stack, but inside the edge of the top disc (to prevent oil from escaping through the water outlet). The position of the e-line is regulated according to oil density by the diameter of the interchangeable gravity disc at the water outlet.

Centrifugal Clarifiers (Fig 2)

The centrifugal clarifier has no separate water outlet and is designed to separate solids from oil. Feed is from the edge into the zone of maximum centrifugal force with sludge separating outwards.

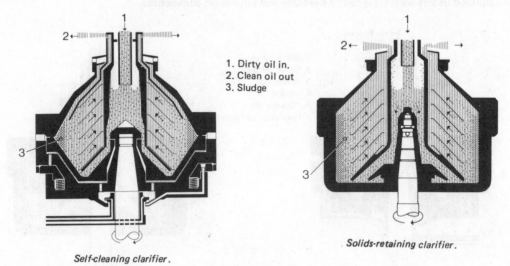

1. Dirty oil in.
2. Clean oil out
3. Sludge

Self-cleaning clarifier.

Solids-retaining clarifier.

Fig 2 (Alfa-Laval)

Fram coalescing plate separator. Plate packs are aligned vertically or horizontally according to the type of oil and solids contamination to be removed.

Centrifugal Concentrators (Fig 3)

The concentration bowl works in the reverse mode to a purifier. With distribution holes and inter-face closer to the axis of rotation, it is designed to remove traces of a lighter liquid (oil) from a denser one (water). Typical concentrator duties include:-

(i)   Separation of tramp oil from emulsion-type coolants.

(ii)   Reclamation of oil from waste water.

(iii)   Purification of synthetic hydraulic fluids which are denser than water.

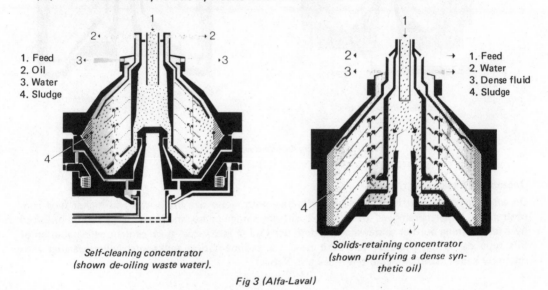

1. Feed
2. Oil
3. Water
4. Sludge

1. Feed
2. Water
3. Dense fluid
4. Sludge

*Self-cleaning concentrator
(shown de-oiling waste water).*

*Solids-retaining concentrator
(shown purifying a dense synthetic oil)*

Fig 3 (Alfa-Laval)

Clean oil to machines

Dirty oil

Cooled water

Hot water

Cold water

Clean tank

Foul oil tank

Plate heat exchanger

Heated water

Pump unit

Oil purifiers

*Hydraulic oil purification system in an auto engine
factory, with two centrifugal purifiers connected in
parallel and regenerative plate heat exchanger for
preheating and cooling the oil.
(Alfa-Laval)*

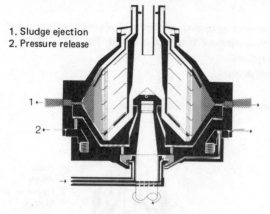

1. Sludge ejection
2. Pressure release

Self-cleaning separator:
centrifugal unloading

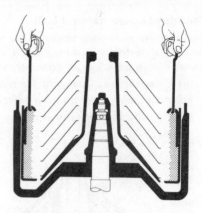

Solids-retaining separator:
manual unloading.

Fig 4 (Alfa-Laval)

Decanter or Peeler Centrifuges (Fig 4)

Decanter or *peeler* centrifuges are more effective with larger size impurities and higher feed concentrations. Water is removed from the oil with the sludge phase, and if necessary can be followed by a self-cleaning purifier to dewater the desludged oil phase. A two-stage centrifuge installation of this type can often dispense with the need for sedimentation tanks even when dealing with relatively heavily contaminated oils — see also Table I.

TABLE I — COMPARISON OF CENTRIFUGE OIL CLEANERS

Type	Maximum particle size	Minimum particle size	Maximum feed concentration	Method of sludge unloading	Water removal from oil
Purifier (solids retaining)	500 μm	0.5 μm	10%	manual	as separate phase
Purifier (self-cleaning)	500 μm	0.5 μm	10%	intermittent (hydraulic)	as separate phase
Clarifier (solids retaining)	500 μm	0.5 μm	10%	manual	no
Clarifier (self-cleaning)	500 μm	0.5 μm	10%	intermittent (hydraulic)	no
Decanter	20 mm	2 μm	40%	continuous (mechanical)	with sludge phase
Peeler	10 mm	5 μm	60%	batch cycle mechanical/ hydraulic	with sludge phase

Heating

Heating may be employed where bearing oils are involved to reduce viscosity and facilitate pumping and subsequent treatment. Heating may also be used to break down emulsified oils. In certain circumstances, particularly where high oil purity is not involved, heating followed by gravity settlement may be sufficient treatment to recondition an oil.

Mobile Bowser Filtration high vacuum unit for the dehydration, degassification and filtration of transformer oils.

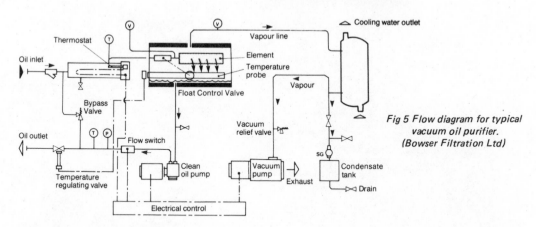

Fig 5 Flow diagram for typical vacuum oil purifier. (Bowser Filtration Ltd)

Distillation

Distillation under vacuum may be used prior to final clarification to remove light fractions from waste oil, in diluent stripping, dehydration and degassification. Such a process is normally carried out under medium vacuum (50 torr). It is also particularly suitable for water, air and solids removal from synthetic oils and hydraulic fluids (*eg* phosphate ester fluids). Higher vacuum processes (1-2 torr) are used for the drying, degassing and filtration of electrical insulating oils.

An example of a vacuum oil purifier system is shown in Fig 5.

See also chapters on *Centrifuges* and *Oily Water Treatment*.

SECTION 4

Filter Selection Guides

FILTER SELECTION is difficult to discuss in general terms since each application may introduce its own particular problems. Usually, too, there will be a number of different types of filter which might be suitable, although specific applications commonly adopt certain types as the virtual standard on the basis of proven satisfactory performance, cost, availability and other commercial considerations.

Intake filters on i/c engines, for example, are of more or less standardized design, mass produced and as a consequence extremely cost effective. Probably the most significant difference here is that a felt element is often prepared for diesels, and a paper element for petrol engines. Similarly in other fields of application. The most suitable type of filter has usually been established by experience, products of individual manufacturers differing mainly in detail design and/or choice of element material — see also Tables I and II.

Filter Rating Required

Filter performance refers to the cut-off achieved by different types of filters. Consideration on such grounds will suggest the most suitable types, although not necessarily the most economic commercial solutions. Again, too, individual assessment of the degree of protection required may vary considerably for a similar application. Thus some machine designers are quite satisfied to adopt protection of the order of 10–20 μm cut-off, whilst others may opt for maximum protection against wear by filtration down to 5 μm absolute. Much depends on the application of the machine and any critical features of its design or operation. Where finer filtering can save 'down time', for example, the additional cost of such filters is more than justified, provided this can be allied to adequate maintenance. The question is not just a matter of filter selection only, but also proper maintenance of filters.

Filter rating alone is no absolute criterion. It must be considered alongside filter efficiency and the capital and operating costs of the filter or seperator concerned. Also there are various methods of determining filter ratings and efficiencies, as explained in the chapter on *Filter Ratings*. The most meaningful figure, now widely adopted, is the beta (β) rating associated with a particle size and efficiency figure.

Table III presents an overall picture in terms of ratings and the range covered by different types of filters and separators. From this it is obvious there will be numerous alternatives to cover a particular rating requirement. It is then necessary to study the characteristics, geometry, *etc* of individual types to assess their suitability for a particular application.

Filter Size

The size of filter needs to be selected with regard to the acceptable pressure drop and life required between cleaning or element replacement. Again this is closely bound up with the type of element and medium employed. In conditions of heavy contamination a filter element with high retention properties may clog too quickly for economic use, calling for a much larger size than normal; or alternatively a different type with better collecting properties so that clogging is delayed. If necessary, the filter may even be given decreasing efficiency properties so that excessive pressure drop build up is avoided, at the cost of some loss of protection — but not necessarily complete loss of protection as would occur with bypass flow initiated at a particular level of clogging.

Overall physical size can also be a significant factor. Where space is at a premium, one particular type of filter or separator may show distinct advantages over another. A decanter centrifuge, for example, is considerably more compact than a filter press for the same capacity and duty. On the other hand a centrifuge needs continuous power to operate it. Thus a true comparison must also consider the cost effectiveness of both types.

Surface versus Depth Filters

Surface type filters generally have relatively low permeability. To achieve a reasonably low pressure drop through the filter the element area must be increased so that the velocity of flow through the element is kept low. Given a projected element area of A and a nominal flow velocity of V at the design maximum capacity (flow rate) of the filter, pleating or otherwise shaping the element so that its surface area is, say, IOA will reduce the flow velocity through the element to V/10. This is the principle adopted with most surface filters; and also with some thicker media such as felts which also filter in depth as well as on the surface. With a thicker medium the increase in surface area possible by pleating or folding is more restricted, so that similar reductions in flow velocity cannot be achieved with the same overall size of element. This is, however, offset by the fact that such media do have higher permeability for comparable cut-off.

Quite obviously by increasing the element area still further the pressure drop can again be reduced. This is typical of panel type air filters where the pressure drop is normally very low — *eg* of the order of 0.1 to 0.15 inches wg when clean.

A very low pressure drop of this order is necessary when dealing with large quantities of air, probably flowing at relatively low to moderate velocities. Appreciable attenuation of the air-flow through the filter could adversely affect the performance of a complete air conditioning system. When handling liquids, on the order hand, pressure drop through the filter is inevitably higher — or tends to be higher — because of the greater viscosity of the fluid. In this case it is more usual for the permissible range of pressure drop to be much more restricted. Thus, typically, with a panel type air filter a tenfold increase in the initial pressure drop may be perfectly acceptable since this may still only be producing a differential pressure of the order of 1 inch wg (less than 0.04 lb/in^2). With a liquid filter, on the other hand, the initial pressure drop may be 5 or 10 lb/in^2, or even more, when a twofold increase would be a logical end point for useful performance, since with any further increase the flow could be seriously restricted and the high differential pressure damaging to the element.

Compatibility

Other essential requirements from the filter element are complete compatibility with the fluid and system. Compatibility with the fluid itself means freedom from degradation or chemical attack, or a 'chemically compatible element'. In the majority of cases this is not a severe problem as even paper elements may be impregnated or treated to be compatible with a very wide range of fluids.

TABLE I – MEDIA CHARACTERISTICS SUMMARIZED

Media	Filter Action	Normal Minimum Cut-off μm	Advantages	Absolute Cut-off	Disadvantages	Remarks/Typical Application
Paper (untreated)	Surface and absorbent	10–20	Low cost	No	Very low strength	Simple laboratory filters
Paper (treated)	Surface	5–20	Low cost	No	Low strength (improved by pleating) High specific resistance. Only suitable as surface filters. Subject to element migration.	General purpose compact forms of filters for gases and liquids, also limited application in filter presses for facing filter cloths.
Paper discs	Edge (depth)	down to 1	Low cost Adjustable cut-off (by 'stacking' pressure)	Yes	High specific resistance, not cleanable.	Fine filtering of gases and liquids.
Fabrics	Surface	down to 5	Can withstand higher pressures than paper. More suitable for larger sizes of filters	No	Lack rigidity and normally need to be backed up or supported by a screen, mesh, etc.	Fabrics cover a wide range of materials with varying characteristics. Fabric elements may be used for general purpose gas and liquid filters; also for dust collectors, filter cloths, etc.
Felts	Depth	down to 10	Mechanical properties can be closely controlled during manufacture. Available in a wide range of materials, (mostly synthetic)	No	Lack rigidity so need support	Thinner felts alternative to paper for pleated elements. Filter pads for a very wide range of industries.
Woven wire	Surface	down to 6	Performance controlled by weave and mesh. High strength.	Yes	More expensive than cloth or paper.	Widely used in coarse, medium and fine mesh
Mineral wools	Depth	down to 0.1	High permeability, suitable for ultra-fine filtering with micro-diameter fibres and suitable backing — suitable for high temperatures	Yes	Asbestos fibres can represent a health hazard. Flow velocities must be kept low. Not particularly suitable for filtering liquids.	Ultra-fine filtering of air and gases.
Glass fibre	Depth	down to 1 or better	Properties can be controlled and graduated during manufacture. Suitable for high temperatures.			Filter pads or blankets for air filters. Microglass sheets for HEPA filters

Material	Type	Rating / removes	Properties	Cleanable	Limitations	Applications
Diatomaceous earth	Depth		Very effective for fine filtering with low flow resistance	No	Normally suitable for use only as a precoat but can be rendered in sheet form with binder	Precoat filters, particularly suitable for clarifying
Perlite	Depth		Low wet density. Fine filtering capability with low flow resistance	No	As for diatomaceous earth, but normally needs to be used in thicker layers	Precoat filters
Activated charcoal	Adsorbent	Removes vapours, odours, etc.			Granular product, needs containing in a suitable housing.	Final filter for air or water, chemical treatment, etc.
Charcoal cloth	Adsorbent	Removes vapours, odours, etc.	Strong, flexible material with 20 times the adsorbent properties of activated charcoal		High cost	Prefabricated filter elements for colour control, air conditioning, water and chemical treatment, etc.
Fuller's earth (activated clays)	Adsorbent				Granular form — needs a suitable container. Less effective than activated charcoal	Final filters for odour and vapour removal
Anthracite	Depth		High flow rates possible in multi-layer beds with sand		Needs to be treated for maximum hardness	Used in gravity and pressure filters for water treatment and filtering of oils, acids, alkalis, etc.
Sintered metal	Depth	down to 2	Properties can be closely controlled during manufacture. High strength element. Suitable for high temperatures.	Yes	Possibility of element migration. High cost. Not cleanable	Sintered bronze for general duties. Stainless steel or exotic alloys for higher pressures, temperatures and corrosion resistance
Ceramic	Depth	down to 1	Properties can be controlled during manufacture. Suitable for corrosive fluids. Suitable for high temperatures	Yes	High cost. Not cleanable	Particularly suitable for acids, alkalis and other corrosive media
Membranes	Surface	down to 0.005	Available in a wide range of materials	Yes	Require vacuum or pressure source. Low flow rates. Clogged by fibrous or slimy contaminants.	Ultra-fine filtering and clarification in specialized applications

TABLE II – REPRESENTATIVE RANGE OF CONTAMINANT REMOVAL

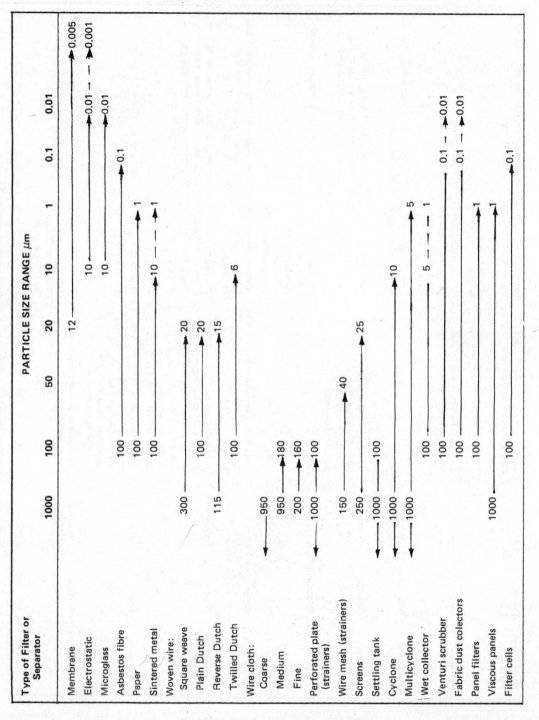

TABLE III – GENERAL GUIDE TO CONTAMINANT SIZES

Contaminant	PARTICLE SIZE μm					
	Under 0.01	0.01–0.1	0.1–1	1–10	10–100	100–1 000
Haemoglobin	X					
Viruses	X	X				
Bacteria			X–X	X		
Yeasts and Fungi			X–X	X		
Pollen				X–X	X	
Plant Spores					X	
Inside Dust	X	X–X	X–X	X–X	X	
Atmospheric Dust				X–X	X–X	
Industrial Dusts				X	X–X	X–X
Continuously Suspended Dusts	X	X–X	X–X			
Oil Mist		X	X–X	X–X		
Tobacco Smoke		X–X	X–X	X		
Industrial Gases			X–X			
Aerosols	X	X–X	X–X	X		
Powdered Insecticides				X–X		
Permanent Atmospheric Pollution	X	X–X	X–X			
Temporary Atmospheric Pollution				X–X	X–X	X–X
Contaminants Harmful to Machines				X	X–X	X–X
Machine Protection						
Normal				X	X–X	X–X
Silt control				X(3–5)		
Partial silt control					X(10–15)	
Chip control					(25–40) X	
Maximum				X–X	X–X	X–X
Air Filtration:						
Primary					X–X	X–X
Secondary				X–X		
Ultra-fine	X		X–X			
Staining Particle Range			X–X	X		

At the same time, however, 'mechanical compatibility' is also necessary to ensure that the element is strong enough for the duty involved, and also free from migration. The latter may or may not be a critical factor. Thus in some systems a certain amount of element migration may be tolerated. In others the fact that element migration could occur would eliminate that particular filter element from the list of possibles.

Whilst 'mechanical compatibility' is largely a matter of system requirements it can also be affected by the nature of the contaminant. Hard, abrasive media forced into soft media may produce physical damage, opening up localized leakage paths through the element. Similarly, a collection of fine abrasive particles on a flexible element may abrade and damage that element. Synthetic fibre filter cloths, for example, are often more prone to damage in this manner than by actual fibre wear or deterioration.

Prefilters

Particularly where fine filtering is required the advisability, or even necessity, of prefiltering should be considered. Thus if the air is heavily contaminated with particles of, say, 100 μm and smaller, and protection of the order of 10 μm or less is required, the filter capable of providing this degree of protection may rapidly become clogged with coarser particles as well. If these are removed by prefiltering through a coarser filter, or even a strainer, the main filter element performance will be maintained for much longer intervals between cleaning or replacement. In fact, with any type of filter which shows virtually 100% efficiency at a particle size substantially lower than the filtering range required, prefiltering is generally worth considering as an economic measure to reduce the dirt load reaching the filter, depending on the level of contamination involved.

Contamination Levels

Contamination level may also affect the type of filter chosen for a particular duty. Thus an oil-bath filter, for example, may be preferred to a dry element type in a particularly dust-laden atmosphere (eg internal combustion engines operating under desert conditions) due to its large dust holding capacity. A typical oil-bath filter, for instance, can accommodate a dust concentration of 40 milligrams per cubic foot of air per hour, operating under severe conditions for 24 hours with substantially constant efficiency and a pressure drop not exceeding 8 inches wg (initial resistance 3.3 inches wg). Larger or heavier dust particles are deposited in the oil bath on entry whilst scrubbing of the air by the large area of oil-wetted surfaces removes the remaining dust. Dust-laden oil then returns to the bath, dust collecting at the bottom displacing oil which is automatically transferred by an overflow pipe to the lower reservoir, from whence it can be reclaimed and re-used when servicing the unit.

Fluid Filters

Basic types of fluid filters are summarized in Table IV, whilst Table VI details typical performance characteristics on a similar basis to that for air filters. It must be emphasized, however, that such a representation can only be taken as a general guide. Particular applications tend to favour a specific type of filter and element, or range of elements. The requirements are also far more diverse than in the case of air since the contaminants may range from sub-micron particles which have to be removed for 'clarification' or polishing, through wear and degradation products in the case of circulatory oil systems, to fibrous and stringy solids in the case of effluents and process liquors, etc. Furthermore, filtering requirements may vary considerably. Thus instead of being a contaminant, the residue collected by the filter may be the valuable part which needs to be removed easily (necessitating the use of a type of filter which builds up a cake). Equally, where the residue collected is contamination, then ease of cleaning or replacement of filter elements may be a necessary feature of the filter design.

TABLE IV — BASIC TYPES OF FLUID FILTERS

Type	Media		Remarks
Surface	(i)	Resin-impregnated paper (usually pleated)	Capable of fine (nominal) filtering. Low permeability.
	(ii)	Fine-woven fabric cloth (pleated or 'star' form.	Lower resistance than paper.
	(iii)	Membranes	Ultra-fine filtering.
	(iv)	Wire mesh and perforated metal.	Coarse filtering and straining.
Depth	(i)	Random fibrous materials.	Low resistance and high dirt capacity. Porosity can be controlled/graduated by manufacture.
	(ii)	Felts	Provide both surface and depth filtering. Low resistance.
	(iii)	Sintered elements	Sintered metals mainly, but ceramics for high temperature filters.
Edge	(i)	Stacked discs	Paper media are capable of extremely fine filtering.
	(ii)	Helical wound ribbon	Metallic media have high strength and rigidity.
Precoat	Diatomaceous earth, perlite, powdered volcanic rock, etc.		Form filter beds deposited on flexible, semi-flexible or rigid elements. Particularly suitable for liquid clarification.
Adsorbent	(i)	Activated clays	Effective for removal of some dissolved contaminants in water, oils, etc. Also used as precoat or filter bed material.
	(ii)	Activated charcoal	Particularly used as drinking water filter.

It is therefore necessary to relate basic filtering requirements to possible types of filters and then study the specific performance of individual designs of filters of suitable type against system requirements. In the case of straightforward applications this generally leaves only a suitable size to be selected. Where other, or more critical, factors are involved, however, close co-operation between potential user and manufacturer may be necessary in order to arrive at an optimum solution, particularly as regards choice of media.

Table II must be read as a very general guide only. The ratings adopted are arbitrary and may differ with the specific requirements or common notations in different industries or fields of application of different type of mechanical filtering elements based on particle removal requirements. It does not indicate suitability as regards cut-off characteristics, chemical compatibility, temperature requirements, *etc*, nor the most suitable form of filter. The latter is normally specific to the application — *eg* in-line filters are normally of cartridge type housed in a pressure-rated container; filters for batch processing may employ plate or leaf elements or cloths; precoat filters are

TABLE V – EXAMPLES OF AIR FILTER TYPES AND PERFORMANCES

Filter Type	Face Velocity ft/min	Average Arrestance	Initial Resistance in w.g.	Recommended Final Resistance in w.g.	Element Servicing
Panel: Glass fibre pad	500	75%	0.10	0.50	Disposable (replace)
Panel — Extruded Surface Pleated	500	25–30%	Depth: 1" 0.40, 2" 0.30, 4" 0.25	1.0, 1.0, 1.0	Disposable (replace)
Cell: Extruded Surface	500	60–65%, 80–85%, 90–95%	0.50, 0.55, 0.60	1.2, 1.2, 1.2	
Viscous Panel (Resin bonded glass pad)	500	80–85%	0.25	0.50	Disposable (replace)
Automatic Roll (Glass fibre media)	500	80%	0.17	0.35 to 0.45 average operating resistance	Roll replaced (typically after 7–9 weeks)

Type	Capacity (ft/min)	Efficiency	Resistance	Average operating resistance	Remarks
Electrostatic	up to 600	400 ft/min — 95% 530 ft/min — 90% 600 ft/min — 85%	0.16 0.24 0.30		
Roll with automatic pre-cleaner	500	30—90%	0.90	1.40	Roll replaced (typically after 12-18 weeks)
Roll with automatic Automatic self-cleaning (for fibrous materials, not abrasive plain dust)	500		0.18	0.75 average operating resistance	Renewable
Automatic Viscous Filter without Bath	500	80%		0.40 average operating resistance	
Extended Surface Bag-type	Up to 500	40—45% 50—55% 60—65% 80—85% 90—95%	0.25 0.30 0.35 0.45 0.55	1.0 1.0 1.0 1.0 1.0	
HEPA	up to 500	99.97% — 99.999%	1.0	2.0—4.0	

TABLE VI – SELECTION GUIDE FOR FLUID FILTERS

	Sub-Micronic	Ultra Fine	Very Fine	Fine	Fine Medium	Medium	Coarse
Element	(under 1)	(1–2.5)	(2.5–5)	(5–10)	(10–20)	(20–40)	(over 50)
Perforated Metal							x
Wire Mesh							x
Wire Gauze						x - x	x
Pleated Paper					x - x	x - x	
Pleated Fabric						x - x	
Wire Wound					x	x - x	
Wire Cloth				x	x - x	x - x	x
Sintered Wire Cloth				x	x - x		
Felt						x - x	
Metallic Felt			x	x - x	x - x		
Edge Type, Paper	x	x - x	x - x	x - x			
Edge Type, Ribbon Element						x	x
Edge Type, Metal					x	x - x	x
Edge Type, Nylon				x - x	x - x	x - x	x
Sintered Metal		x	x - x	x - x	x - x	x - x	
Microglass	x	x - x	x - x				
Mineral Wool			Limited Application for Liquids				
Ceramic	x	x - x	x - x	x - x			
Filter Cloths				x	x - x	x - x	x
Membrane	x	x - x	x - x				
Sintered PTFE				x - x	x - x		
Sintered Polythene						x - x	x

employed for the clarification of liquids; filter presses are employed where collection of the filtrate is the primary requirement; and so on. Individual chapters should be consulted for information on typical filter types employed for specific applications, and their characteristics.

Air Filters

Air filters are described in some detail in the chapters on *Bulk Air Filters* and *Air Filter Services*. Table V summarizes typical performance capabilities of different types of filters which may be employed as a general guide only. Much depends on the degree of protection involved and the volume of air to be treated. Actual requirements can range from normal room protection to the supply of sterile air for critical processes and bio-medical applications.

For positive protection against sub-micronic and small particles up to about 5–10 μm, filters capable of an absolute cut-off are essential. This sets specific limits as regards suitable types. However, for less critical applications a filter with a nominal or mean cut-off in the required range may be satisfactory. Whilst these do not preclude the possibility of larger particles passing through the filter the percentage of such particles passed is not likely to be high and may be negligible.

Data

DENSITY OF GASES (at 60°F and 30 in of Mercury)

Gas	Molecular Formula	Molecular Weight	Specific Gravity Air = 1.0	Weight lb per cu ft	Volume cu ft per lb
Air	—	28.9	1.000	0.07655	13.063
Oxygen	O_2	32.00	1.105	0.08461	11.819
Hydrogen	H_2	2.02	0.070	0.00533	187.723
Nitrogen (atmospheric)	N_2	28.02	0.972	0.07439	13.443
Carbon Monoxide	CO	28.01	0.967	0.07404	13.506
Carbon Dioxide	CO_2	44.01	1.528	0.1170	8.548
Methane	CH_4	16.04	0.554	0.04243	23.565
Acetylene	C_2H_2	26.04	0.911	0.06971	14.344
Ethylene	C_2H_4	28.05	0.974	0.07456	13.412
Ethane	C_2H_6	30.07	1.049	0.08029	12.455
Sulphur Dioxide	SO_2	64.06	2.264	0.1733	5.770
Hydrogen Sulphide	H_2S	34.08	1.190	0.09109	10.979

Approximate Percentage Composition of Air

	By Weight	By Volume
Nitrogen	76.8	79.0
Oxygen	23.2	21.0

MEAN SPECIFIC HEAT OF GASES AT CONSTANT PRESSURE
from 32°F to t F in Btu per lb per F

Temperature F	100	300	500	1000	1500	2000
Air —	0.240	0.241	0.243	0.249	0.257	0.263
Oxygen O_2	0.218	0.222	0.225	0.235	0.243	0.249
Nitrogen N_2	0.248	0.249	0.251	0.256	0.262	0.270
Hydrogen H_2	3.41	3.44	3.45	3.47	3.51	3.55
Water Vapor H_2O	0.444	0.449	0.454	0.472	0.493	0.516
Carbon Monoxide CO	0.248	0.249	0.251	0.258	0.265	0.273
Carbon Dioxide CO_2	0.200	0.213	0.224	0.246	0.262	0.274
Typical Flue Gas of average Bituminous Coal. Based on 20% Excess Air and 5% H_2O	0.243	0.247	0.250	0.260	0.269	0.277

The volume of 1 lb of a gas at any given temperature and pressure may be found from

$$V = \frac{t + 460}{W X P X 35.38}$$

Where V = Volume in cubic feet
t = Temperature F
W = Weight of gas in lb per cubic foot from Table on Page 88.
P = Absolute Pressure in lb per sq in.

CIRCULAR EQUIVALENTS OF RECTANGULAR DUCTS FOR EQUAL FRICTION

Sides	2	2½	3	3½	4	4½	5	5½	6	7	8	9	10	11	12	13	14	15	16	17
4	3.04	3.42	3.77	4.09	4.37	4.63	4.88	5.10												
5	3.37	3.81	4.18	4.55	4.88	5.18	5.45	5.73												
6	3.65	4.17	4.55	4.96	5.32	5.65	5.97	6.27	6.55											
7	3.90	4.43	4.91	5.34	5.72	6.08	6.42	6.75	7.07	7.63										
8	4.12	4.71	5.20	5.67	6.08	6.47	6.85	7.21	7.54	8.17	8.72									
9	4.34	4.97	5.48	5.96	6.42	6.84	7.25	7.62	8.00	8.66	9.25	9.81								
10	4.54	5.21	5.74	6.24	6.74	7.17	7.60	7.99	8.37	9.09	9.76	10.3	10.9							
11	4.72	5.40	5.98	6.51	7.02	7.49	7.93	8.34	8.74	9.50	10.2	10.8	11.4	12.0						
12	4.90	5.58	6.22	6.75	7.29	7.79	8.25	8.69	9.10	9.90	10.6	11.3	11.9	12.5	13.1					
13	5.06	5.76	6.42	6.98	7.56	8.08	8.56	9.02	9.46	10.3	11.0	11.8	12.4	13.0	13.6	14.2				
14	5.21	5.94	6.61	7.21	7.80	8.34	8.85	9.33	9.81	10.7	11.4	12.2	12.8	13.5	14.1	14.7	15.3			
15	5.36	6.11	6.80	7.43	8.02	8.58	9.11	9.62	10.1	11.0	11.8	12.6	13.3	14.0	14.6	15.2	15.8	16.4		
16	5.51	6.28	6.98	7.64	8.24	8.82	9.37	9.90	10.4	11.3	12.2	13.0	13.7	14.4	15.1	15.7	16.3	16.9	17.5	
17	5.64	6.44	7.16	7.83	8.46	9.06	9.62	10.1	10.7	11.6	12.5	13.3	14.1	14.8	15.5	16.2	16.8	17.4	18.0	18.6
18	5.76	6.58	7.33	8.03	8.68	9.30	9.85	10.4	10.9	11.9	12.8	13.7	14.5	15.2	15.9	16.6	17.3	17.9	18.5	19.1

AIR VOLUME IN CFM HANDLED THROUGH BRANCH PIPES

Diameter of pipe	Velocity in pipe in fpm								
	2,000	2,500	3,000	3,500	3,750	4,000	4,500	5,000	5,500
3"	98	123	147	172	184	197	221	246	270
3½"	134	167	200	234	250	267	300	334	367
4"	175	218	262	306	327	350	393	437	480
4½"	221	276	331	387	415	442	497	552	608
5"	273	341	409	473	512	546	614	682	750
5½"	330	413	495	578	618	660	742	824	908
6"	393	491	589	688	736	786	884	982	1,080
7"	534	668	802	936	1,002	1,070	1,204	1,338	1,472
8"	699	874	1,048	1,220	1,309	1,396	1,571	1,745	1,920
9"	882	1,105	1,325	1,546	1,652	1,766	1,988	2,210	2,430
10"	1,092	1,364	1,637	1,910	2,046	2,182	2,456	2,730	3,000
11"	1,320	1,650	1,980	2,310	2,475	2,640	2,970	3,300	3,630
12"	1,570	1,965	2,355	2,750	2,946	3,140	3,535	3,915	4,320
13"	1,840	2,305	2,765	3,225	3,457	3,685	4,150	4,610	5,057
14"	2,140	2,670	3,207	3,740	4,009	4,276	4,810	5,345	5,880
15"	2,454	3,068	3,618	4,290	4,602	4,910	5,520	6,135	6,740
16"	2,795	3,491	4,190	4,885	5,236	5,587	6,280	6,983	7,685
17"	3,153	3,940	4,730	5,520	5,911	6,305	7,100	7,881	8,665
18"	3,534	4,418	5,300	6,185	6,627	7,068	7,950	8,835	9,720
19"	3,938	4,923	5,907	6,890	7,384	7,876	8,865	9,845	10,825
20"	4,364	5,455	6,546	7,400	8,182	8,728	9,515	10,910	11,625
22"	5,280	6,600	7,920	9,235	9,899	10,560	11,875	13,200	14,520
24"	6,283	7,854	9,425	11,000	11,781	12,566	14,125	15,708	17,275
26"	7,374	9,218	11,061	12,900	13,827	14,748	16,580	18,435	20,250
27"	7,952	9,940	11,918	13,906	14,910	15,904	17,892	19,880	21,868
28"	8,552	10,690	12,828	14,950	16,035	17,104	19,215	21,380	23,485
30"	9,818	12,272	14,727	17,190	18,408	19,636	22,090	24,544	27,000
32"	11,170	13,962	16,755	19,550	20,944	22,340	25,175	27,924	30,700
33"	11,880	14,850	17,820	20,970	22,274	23,760	26,730	29,700	32,670
34"	12,610	15,762	18,915	22,050	23,644	25,220	28,350	31,524	34,650
36"	14,136	17,670	21,204	24,725	26,507	28,272	31,800	35,340	38,850
45"	22,090	27,612	33,135	38,657	41,400	44,180	49,702	55,225	60,748

DUCT SIZING CHART

CFM	Equiv. dia. inches	Side of Rectangular Duct inches																	
		4	5	6	7	8	9	10	11	12	13	14	15	16	17	18	19	20	21
50	5.4	6	5																
100	6.4	9	7	6															
150	7.3	12	9	7															
200	8.1	15	11	9	8														
250	8.6	17	13	10	9	8													
300	9.1	20	15	12	10	9													
350	9.5	22	16	13	11	10													
400	10.0	24	18	14	12	11	9												
450	10.4	27	20	15	13	11	10												
500	10.7	30	22	17	14	12	11												
550	11.1		24	18	15	13	12	10											
600	11.5		26	20	16	14	13	11											
650	12.0		28	22	18	16	14	12	11										
700	12.5		28	22	18	16	14	12	11										
800	13.0		34	26	21	18	16	14	13	12									
900	13.5			29	23	20	17	15	14	13									
1000	14.1			32	25	21	19	17	15	14									
1100	14.5			34	27	23	20	18	16	15									
1200	15.1			36	29	24	22	20	18	16	14								
1300	15.3			39	32	26	23	21	19	17	15	14							
1400	15.9			42	34	28	25	22	20	18	16	15							
1500	16.3			45	36	30	26	23	21	19	17	16	15						
1600	16.7			48	39	32	28	25	22	20	18	17	16						
1700	17.2				42	34	30	26	23	21	19	18	17						
1800	17.5				44	36	32	28	24	22	20	18	17	16					
1900	18.0				46	38	24	29	26	23	21	19	18	17					
2000	18.3				48	40	36	30	27	24	22	20	19	18					
2200	19.0				52	43	38	32	29	26	23	21	20	19	18				
2400	19.6				58	47	41	35	31	28	25	23	22	20	19	18			
2600	20.1					51	43	37	33	30	27	25	23	21	20	19			
2800	20.5					55	46	39	34	31	28	26	24	22	21	20	19		
3000	21.1					58	48	41	36	33	30	27	25	23	22	21	20		
3200	21.5					61	51	44	38	35	32	29	26	25	23	22	21	20	
3400	22.0					65	54	47	41	37	33	30	28	26	24	23	22	21	
3600	22.6						57	49	43	39	35	32	29	27	25	24	23	21	
3800	23.1						60	52	46	41	36	33	31	29	27	25	24	22	21
4000	23.6						63	55	48	43	38	35	32	30	28	26	25	24	23

SCREENS

MESH APERTURE SIZES AND MICRON (μm) RATINGS

Woven wire mesh linings listed are for standard gauge wire.

Mesh per in.	Wire Gauge SWG	Holes per in²	Aperture ins	Aperture mm	% Free Area	No. of Meshes per cm	No. of Holes per cm²	Micron Rating (μm)
10	23	100	0.076	1.929	58	3.93	15	1929
12	24	144	0.061	1.557	54	4.73	22	1557
16	28	256	0.047	1.211	58	6.30	40	1211
20	28	400	0.035	0.894	50	7.87	62	894
30	32	900	0.022	0.572	46	11.80	139	572
40	34	1600	0.0158	0.4013	40	15.75	248	401
60	37	3600	0.0099	0.2506	35	23.60	560	251
80	39	6400	0.0073	0.1854	34	31.50	995	185
100	41	10000	0.0056	0.1422	31	39.37	1550	142
120	43	14400	0.0047	0.1203	32	47.24	2240	120
150	45	22500	0.0039	0.0997	34	59.00	3481	100
180	47	32400	0.0036	0.0903	42	70.80	5020	90
200	47	40000	0.0030	0.0762	36	78.70	6200	76
250	48	62500	0.0024	0.0610	36	98.40	9680	61
300	48.5	90000	0.0019	0.0483	32	118.00	13924	48

Weave	Micron Rating (μm)	Weave	Micron Rating (μm)
325 x 3200	10.5	28 x 450	50
200 x 2000	13.0	72 x 550	35
185 x 1500	16.0	24 x 250	75
180 x 1440	17.5	24 x 110	100
180 x 1400	17.5	20 x 300	65
180 x 1300	19.0	20 x 200	115
160 x 1100	21.0		
165 x 1440	22.0		
165 x 1100	25.0		

Equivalents   1 Micron = 0.0000393 ins. = 10^{-3} mm
25 Microns = 0.001 ins (approx).

BETA (β) RATINGS FOR FILTERS

THE *BETA RATING* of a filter is established by the ratio of upstream particles to downstream particles of a specified size and is thus expressed as βx, where x is the particle size referred to in micrometres (μm). The higher the beta ratio the greater the number of particles of this size retained by the filter, and hence the greater its efficiency. Effectively, the beta ratio is a direct expression of efficiency, *eg*

for β ratio	efficiency
1	0
2	50%
10	90%
20	95%
50	98%
100	99%
1000	99.9%
10000	99.99%
100000	99.999%

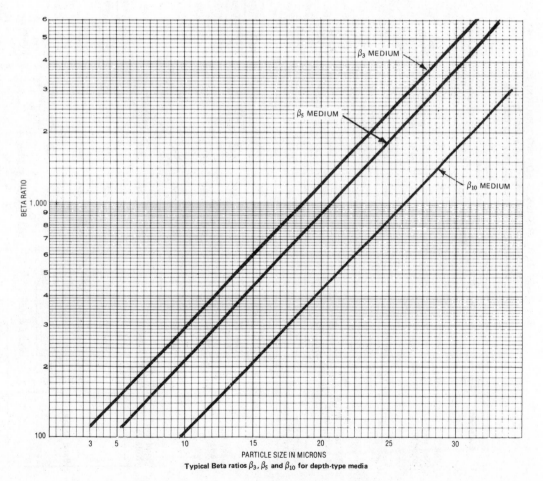

Typical Beta ratios β_3, β_5 and β_{10} for depth-type media

EXHAUST REQUIREMENTS FOR WOODWORKING OPERATIONS (AAF LTD)
Usual branch duct velocity — 4 000 fpm
Minimum main duct velocity — 3 500 fpm

Equipment	Unit of Measurement	Size (Note 1)	Exhaust Volume Bottom	Top	Total
SAWS Self-feed table rip	Dia. In Inches	16 incl. { b.b. / t.b.	440	350	790
		Over 16 { b.b. / t.b.	550	350	900
Swing Saw	Dia. In Inches	20 incl.	—	—	350
		Over 20	—	—	440
Rip, table, mitre & variety saws	Dia. In Inches	16 incl.	—	—	350
		Over 16-24 incl.	—	—	440
		Over 24	—	—	550
Variety Saw with dado head			—	—	550
Gang Rip Saws	Dia. In Inches	24 incl. { b.b. / t.b.	550	350	900
		Over 24-36 incl. { b.b. / t.b.	800	440	1240
		Over 36-48 incl. { b.b. / t.b.	1100	550	1650
		Over 48 { b.b. / t.b.	1400	550	1950
Band Saw (Note 2)	Blade Width In In.	2 Max.	350	350	700
Band Resaws	Blade Width In Inches	2-3 incl. { d.r. / u.r.	350	550	900
		Over 3-4 incl. { d.r. / u.r.	550	800	1350
		Over 4-6 incl. { d.r. / u.r.	550	1100	1650
		Over 6-8 incl. { d.r. / u.r.	550	1400	1950

Equipment	Unit of Measurement	Size (Note 1)	Exhaust Volume Bottom	Top	Right	Left	Total
Vertical Belt Sander	Belt Width In Inches	6 incl. •	—	—			440
		Over 6-9 incl.	—	—			550
		Over 9-14 incl.	—	—			800
		Over 14	—	—			1100
Swing Arm Sander	—	—	—	—			440
JOINTERS	Knife Length In Inches	6 incl.	—	—			350
		Over 6-12 incl.	—	—			440
		Over 12-20 incl.	—	—			550
		Over 20	—	—			800
PLANERS Single Planer	Knife Length In Inches	20 incl.	—	—			785
		Over 20-26 incl.	—	—			1100
		Over 26-32 incl.	—	—			1400
		Over 32-38 incl.	—	—			1765
		Over 38	—	—			2200
Double Planer		20 incl.	550	785			1335
		Over 20-26 incl.	785	1100			1885
		Over 26-32 incl.	1100	1400			2500
		Over 32-38 incl.	1400	1800			3200
		Over 38	1400	2200			3600
MOLDERS, MATCHERS, SIZERS	Knife Length In Inches	7 incl.	440	550	350	350	350
		Over 7-12 incl.	550	800	440	440	440
		Over 12-18 incl.	800	1100	550	550	550
		Over 18-24 incl.	1100	1400	800	800	800
		Over 24	1400	1770	1100	1100	1100

SANDERS					
Disc Sander	Dia. In Inches	12 incl.	—	—	350
		Over 12-18 incl.	—	—	440
		Over 18-26 incl.	—	—	550
		Over 26-32 incl.	—	—	700
		Over 32-38 incl.	—	—	900
		Over 38-48 incl.	—	—	1250
Single Drum Sander	Dia. In Inches	10 incl.	—	—	350
		Over 10	—	—	550
	Surface Sq. In.	Over 400-700 incl.	—	—	785
		Over 700-1400 incl.	—	—	1100
		Over 1400-2400 incl.	—	—	1400
Multiple Drum Sander (Note 3)	Drum Length In Inches	Up to 31	—	—	550
		31 to 49	—	—	785
		49 to 67	—	—	1100
		Over 67	—	—	1400
Horizontal Belt Sander	Belt Width In Inches	6 incl.	440	350	790
		Over 6-9 incl.	550	350	900
		Over 9-14 incl.	800	440	1240
		Over 14	1100	550	1650

FLOOR SWEEP

The volume exhausted for floor sweeps is generally not included in computing total exhaust requirements.

Note 1 — b.b. - bottom branch, t.b. - top branch, u.r. - up run, d.r. - down run.

Note 2 — Connect one branch pipe to hood under table; the second branch at a point near the floor on the up run side of the lower wheel. Enclose the entire lower wheel to form the hood.

Note 3 — All entries under exhaust volume are expressed in cubic feet per min. Multiple Drum Sander exhaust volume is expressed in terms of total exhaust for machine cfm/drum. One hood per drum is minimum. Additional hood at feed side is desirable.

Note 4 — Resistance of each branch is calculated, based on design data, and totaled for the length running from exhaust hood to junction at the next branch. At each junction the SP must be the same in all entering ducts. Difference in SP

Case I: $< 5\%$ neglect - using higher SP.

Case II: $5\% <$ Diff. $< 20\%$ - Increase air flow in run with lower resistance by: Corrected cfm $=$ Design cfm $\sqrt{\dfrac{\text{run with larger SP loss}}{\text{run with smaller SP loss}}}$

Case III: Diff $> 20\%$ - Branch with lower SP should be redesigned.

EXHAUST HOODS — RECOMMENDED DESIGNS

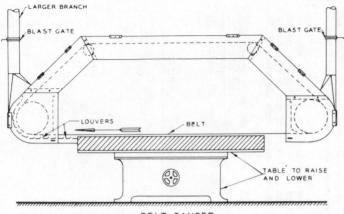

LARGER BRANCH

BLAST GATE

BLAST GATE

LOUVERS

BELT

TABLE TO RAISE AND LOWER

BELT SANDER

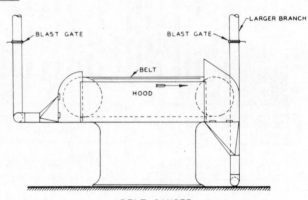

BLAST GATE

BLAST GATE

LARGER BRANCH

BELT

HOOD

BELT SANDER

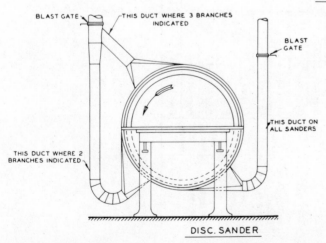

BLAST GATE

THIS DUCT WHERE 3 BRANCHES INDICATED

BLAST GATE

THIS DUCT ON ALL SANDERS

THIS DUCT WHERE 2 BRANCHES INDICATED

DISC. SANDER

FOR VARIOUS EQUIPMENT

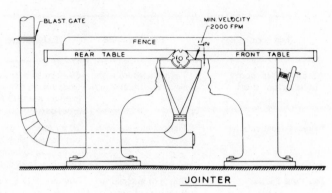

JOINTER

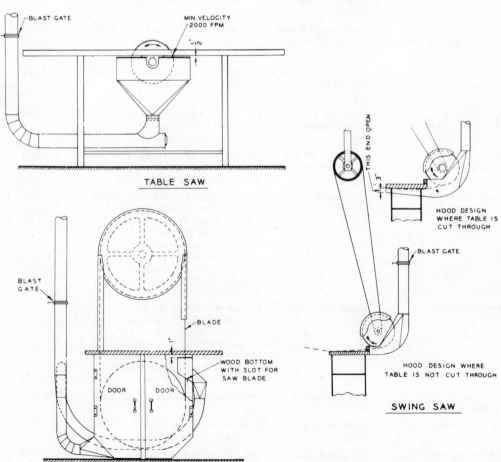

TABLE SAW

SWING SAW

BAND SAW

USUAL EXHAUST VOLUMES AND CONVEYING VELOCITIES FOR DUST PRODUCING EQUIPMENT

Dust producing equipment	Exhaust hood	Exhaust requiements	Conveying velocities in fpm	
			Branch	Main
Abrasive blast rooms (sand, grit or shot)	Tight enclosure with air inlets (usually in roof)	60—100 fpm downdraft (long rooms of tunnel proportions 100 fpm cross-darft)	3 500	3 500
Abrasive blast cabinets	Tight enclosure with access openings	20 air changes per minute but not less than 500 fpm through all openings. Openings to be baffled.	3 500	3 500
Bag Tube Packer	Booth or enclosure (provide spillage hopper)	500 cfm/filling tube; 500 cfm at feed hopper; 950 cfm at spill hopper	3 500	3 500
Barrels (for filling or removing material)	Local hood 180 deg around top of barrel	100 cfm/sq ft barrel top min	3 500	3 500
Shakeout Conveyor	Continuous hood with take-off max of 30 ft apart	350 cfm per ft of belt width with air inlets every 30 ft	3 500	3 500
Belt Wipers (may be required with high speed belts)	Tight fitting hood held against under side of belt	200 cfm per foot of belt width. Not recommended for wet belts as in ore conveying	4 000	4 000
Bins (closed bin top)	Connect to bin top away from feed point	200 fpm through open area at feed points, but not less than 0.5 cfm per cu ft of bin capacity	3 500	3 500
Bucket elevators	Tight casing required	150—200 fpm at all openings. (Exhaust from elevator head) 15 to 18 in gravity vent is also recommended when handling hot, steaming sand. (Equal volumes may be required from foot of elevator to prevent dusting due to spillage from heads).	3 500	3 500
Belt conveyors	Hoods at transfer point	Belt speeds less than 200 fpm— 350 cfm per foot of belt width, but not less than 150 fpm through open area. Belt speeds over 200 fpm—500 cfm per foot of belt width but not less than 200 fpm through open area		
Conveyor to conveyor	Hoods at transfer point	Same as above	3 500	3 500
Chute to conveyor	Hoods at transfer point	Same as above. (Inspection door in chute may be required).	3 500	3 500
Magnetic pulley	Hoods at transfer point	500 cfm per ft of belt width	3 500	3 500

cont...

Dust producing equipment	Exhaust hood	Exhaust requirements	Conveying velocities in fpm	
			Branch	Main
Ceramics Dry Pan Dry Press	Enclosure Local	200 fpm through all openings 500 fpm Automatic feed, 1-5 in. dia branch at die. Manual feed 1-5 in dia branch at supply bin; 1-5 in dia branch at die 500 cfm	3 500 3 500	3 500 3 500
Vibrating feeders — Shakeout hopper to conveyor	Complete enclosure	200 cfm per sq ft of opening (Provide rubber or canvas flexible seals between shakeout hopper sides and end and also feeder sides and end)	3 500	3 500
Fettling, brushing, sagger filling and unload	Downdraft on side hood	100—150 cfm per sq ft of plan area of dust producing operation	3 500	3 500
Floor grate	Side hood	For heavy loads of dry dust and continuous dumping or feeding operations, treat same as shakeout side hoods, see below.	3 500	3 500
	Downdraft	When used occasionally, 200—250 cfm per sq ft of grate area — depending on fineness and dryness of material	3 500	3 500
Grinders Polishing, buffing, etc	Standard wheel hood		4 500	3 500
Grinders Swing frame	Booth	100—150 fpm indraft through opening in booth face for large opening. Never below 100 fpm. Small opening with grinder in front use 200 fpm	3 000	3 000
Grinders Portable and flexible shaft	Downdraft grilles Use side shields where possible	Bench type, 150—250 cfm per sq ft of exhaust grille but not less than 150 cfm per sq ft of plan working area. Floor grille, 200—400 cfm per sq ft of exhaust grille but not less than 100 cfm per sq ft of plan working area	3 500	3 500
Tumbling Mills Hollow trunnion type	Exhaust connection by manufacturer	Use branch diameter same size as exhaust outlet. For round mills branch dia should be 1/6 dia of mill; for square mills, branch dia should be 1 in plus 1/6 side dimension of mill	4 000 5 000	3 500 4 000
Mold Conveyors	Pouring hood	200 to 300 cfm per linear ft of hood with slot velocities of 1 500 fpm. Exhaust take-off every 8 to 10 ft.	2 000	2 000

cont...

Dust producing equipment	Exhaust hood	Exhaust requirements	Conveying velocities in fpm	
			Branch	Main
	Smoke hood — enclosed and semi-enclosed	75 to 100 cfm per linear ft of hood. Enclosed hood can employ exhaust take-offs on approx. 60 ft centres. Semi-enclosed can employ exhaust take-offs every 15 to 20 ft.	2 000	2 000
Mixer	Enclosure	150 minimum fpm through working and inspection openings	3 500	3 500
Pharmaceuticals Coating pans	Air flow into opening of pan	100—150 fpm through opening	3 000	3 000
Shake-outs Foundry	Enclosure	200 fpm through all openings in enclosure, but not less than 200 cfm per sq ft of grate area.	3 500	3 500
	Side hood (use side shields whenever possible)	700—1000 fpm through openings		
Apron conveyor for light flask work	None	Ventilate conveyor equivalent to 75 to 100 cfm per sq ft of gross grate area, assuming all grates open at any one time	3 500	3 500
Belt conveyor for light flask non-ferrous castings	None	Same as above	3 500	3 500
Shaker conveyor above floor — snap flask work	Side or overhead hood	Ventilate housing at rate of 125 to 150 cfm per sq ft o gross open area. Assume all doors open at one time. Include area between housing and conveyor sides in volume determination. Usual clearance 1 in or less on each conveyor side.	3 500	3 500
Shaker conveyor below floor — snap flask work	None	Same as above	3 500	3 500
Tunnel Ventilation	Enclosure	When vibrating shakeout hoppers are located in a closed tunnel, ventilate the tunnel at 100 cfm per sq ft of tunnel cross section. Exhaust from transfer points can provide all, or part of, air required. Any additional exhaust required should be taken in rear of shakeout hopper.	3 500	3 500
Screens Vibrating, flat deck	Enclosure	200 fpm indraft through hood openings, but not less than 50 cfm per sq ft of screen area.	3 500	3 500
Cylindrical	Enclosure	100 cfm per sq ft of circular cross-section but not less than 400 fpm indraft through openings in enclosure	3 500	3 500

VOLUME CONVERSIONS – CUBIC FEET TO CUBIC METRES

Cu. Ft.	0	10	20	30	40	50	60	70	80	90
—	—	0·28317	0·56634	0·84951	1·13267	1·41584	1·69901	1·98218	2·26535	2·54852
100	2·83169	3·11485	3·39802	3·68119	3·96436	4·24753	4·53070	4·81387	5·0970	5·3802
200	5·6634	5·9465	6·2297	6·5129	6·7960	7·0792	7·3624	7·6456	7·9287	8·2119
300	8·4951	8·7782	9·0614	9·3446	9·6277	9·9109	10·1941	10·4772	10·7604	11·0436
400	11·3267	11·6099	11·8931	12·1762	12·4594	12·7426	13·0258	13·3089	13·5921	13·8753
500	14·1584	14·4416	14·7248	15·0079	15·2911	15·5743	15·8574	16·1406	16·4238	16·7069
600	16·9901	17·2733	17·5565	17·8396	18·1228	18·4060	18·6891	18·9723	19·2555	19·5386
700	19·8218	20·1050	20·3881	20·6713	20·9545	21·2376	21·5208	21·8040	22·0872	22·3703
800	22·6535	22·9367	23·2198	23·5030	23·7862	24·0693	24·3525	24·6357	24·9188	25·2020
900	25·4852	25·7683	26·0515	26·3347	26·6178	26·9010	27·1842	27·4674	27·7505	28·0337
1,000	28·3169	—	—	—	—	—	—	—	—	—

CUBIC METRES TO CUBIC FEET

Cubic Metres	0	1	2	3	4	5	6	7	8	9
0	—	35·3147	70·629	105·944	141·259	176·573	211·888	247·203	282·517	317·832
10	353·147	388·461	423·776	459·091	494·405	529·72	565·03	600·35	635·66	670·98
20	706·29	741·61	776·92	812·24	847·55	882·87	918·18	953·50	988·81	1024·13
30	1059·44	1094·75	1130·07	1165·38	1200·70	1236·01	1271·33	1306·64	1341·96	1377·27
40	1412·59	1447·90	1483·22	1518·53	1553·84	1589·16	1624·47	1659·79	1695·10	1730·42
50	1765·73	1801·05	1836·36	1871·68	1906·99	1942·31	1977·62	2012·94	2048·25	2083·56
60	2118·88	2154·19	2189·51	2224·82	2260·14	2295·45	2330·77	2366·08	2401·40	2436·71
70	2472·03	2507·34	2546·66	2577·97	2613·28	2648·60	2683·91	2719·23	2754·54	2789·86
80	2825·17	2860·49	2895·80	2931·12	2966·43	3001·75	3037·06	3072·38	3107·69	3143·00
90	3178·32	3213·63	3248·95	3284·26	3319·58	3354·89	3390·21	3425·52	3460·84	3496·15
100	3531·47	—	—	—	—	—	—	—	—	—

BASIC EQUIVALENTS

Imperial Gallons	Pints	Quarts	U.S. Gallons	Cubic Inches	Cubic Feet	Cubic Yards	Litres
1	8	4	1·20095	277·42	·16054	·005946	4·54596
·125	1	·5	·15012	34·68	·02007	·000743	·56825
·25	2	1	·30024	69·355	·04014	·001486	1·13649
·83267	6·66136	3·33068	1	231·0	·13458	·004951	3·785
·003605	·02884	·01442	·004329	1	·000579	·00002143	·016387
6·2288	49·831	24·915	7·48	1728	1	·03704	28·3161
168·178	1,355·424	672·712	201·974	46,656	27	1	·7645
·219975	1·7598	·8799	·2642	61·026	·035316	·001308	1

CUBIC CENTIMETRES PER SECOND TO CUBIC INCHES PER SECOND
(Cubic Centimetres per Second)

c.c. per sec.	0	1	2	3	4	5	6	7	8	9
0	—	0·061024	0·122047	0·183071	0·244095	0·305119	0·366142	0·427166	0·488190	0·54921
10	0·61024	0·67126	0·73228	0·79331	0·85433	0·91536	0·97638	1·03740	1·09843	1·15945
20	1·22047	1·28150	1·34252	1·40355	1·46457	1·52559	1·58662	1·64764	1·70866	1·76969
30	1·83071	1·89174	1·95276	2·01378	2·07481	2·13583	2·19685	2·25788	2·31899	2·37993
40	2·44095	2·50197	2·56300	2·62402	2·68504	2·74607	2·80709	2·86812	2·92914	2·99016
50	3·05119	3·11221	3·17323	3·23426	3·29528	3·35631	3·41733	3·47835	3·53938	3·60040
60	3·66142	3·72245	3·78347	3·84450	3·90552	3·96654	4·02757	4·08859	4·14961	4·21064
70	4·27166	4·33269	4·39371	4·45473	4·51576	4·57678	4·63780	4·69883	4·75985	4·82088
80	4·88190	4·94292	5·0039	5·0650	5·1260	5·1870	5·2480	5·3091	5·3701	5·4311
90	5·4921	5·5532	5·6142	5·6752	5·7362	5·7973	5·8583	5·9193	5·9803	6·0414
100	6·1024	—	—	—	—	—	—	—	—	—

CUBIC CENTIMETRES PER SECOND TO IMPERIAL GALLONS PER MINUTE

c.c. per sec.	0	1	2	3	4	5	6	7	8	9
0	—	·0132	·0264	·0396	·0528	·0660	·0792	·0924	·1046	·1158
10	·1320	·1452	·1584	·1716	·1848	·1980	·2112	·2244	·2376	·2508
20	·2640	·2772	·2904	·3036	·3168	·3300	·3432	·3564	·3696	·3828
30	·3960	·4092	·4224	·4356	·4488	·4620	·4752	·4884	·5016	·5148
40	·5280	·5412	·5544	·5676	·5808	·5940	·6072	·6204	·6336	·6468
50	·6600	·6732	·6864	·6996	·7128	·7260	·7392	·7524	·7656	·7788
60	·7920	·8052	·8184	·8316	·8448	·8580	·8712	·8844	·8976	·9108
70	·9240	·9372	·9504	·9636	·9768	·9900	1·0032	1·0164	1·0296	1·0428
80	1·0460	1·0692	1·0824	1·0956	1·1088	1·1220	1·1352	1·1484	1·1616	1·1748
90	1·1880	1·2012	1·2144	1·2276	1·2408	1·2540	1·2672	1·2804	1·2936	1·3068
100	1·320	—	—	—	—	—	—	—	—	—

CUBIC CENTIMETRES PER SECOND TO U.S. GALLONS PER MINUTE

c.c. per sec.	0	1	2	3	4	5	6	7	8	9
0	—	·0159	·0317	·0476	·0634	·0793	·0951	·1110	·1268	·1427
10	·1585	·1744	·1903	·2061	·2220	·2379	·2537	·2696	·2857	·3013
20	·3170	·3329	·3488	·3646	·3805	·3964	·4122	·4281	·4440	·4597
30	·4755	·4914	·5073	·5231	·5390	·5549	·5707	·5866	·6025	·6182
40	·6340	·6499	·6658	·6816	·6975	·7134	·7292	·7451	·7610	·7768
50	·7925	·8084	·8243	·8401	·8560	·8719	·8577	·9036	·9195	·9353
60	·9510	·9669	·9828	·9986	·9145	·9304	·9462	·9621	·9780	·9938
70	1·1095	1·1254	1·1413	1·1571	1·1730	1·1889	1·2047	1·2206	1·2365	1·2522
80	1·2680	1·2839	1·2998	1·3156	1·3315	1·3474	1·3632	1·3791	1·3940	1·4100
90	1·4265	1·4424	1·4583	1·4741	1·4890	1·5049	1·5208	1·5367	1·5526	1·5685
100	1·585	—	—	—	—	—	—	—	—	—

VELOCITY PRESSURES FOR STANDARD AIR

V	VP	V	VP	V	VP
400	0.01	2,157	0.29	3,024	0.57
566	0.02	2,193	0.30	3,050	0.58
694	0.03	2,230	0.31	3,076	0.59
801	0.04	2,260	0.32	3,102	0.60
896	0.05	2,301	0.33	3,127	0.61
981	0.06	2,335	0.34	3,153	0.62
1,060	0.07	2,369	0.35	3,179	0.63
1,133	0.08	2,403	0.36	3,204	0.64
1,201	0.09	2,436	0.37	3,229	0.65
1,266	0.10	2,469	0.38	3,254	0.66
1,328	0.11	2,501	0.39	3,279	0.67
1,387	0.12	2,533	0.40	3,303	0.68
1,444	0.13	2,563	0.41	3,327	0.69
1,498	0.14	2,595	0.42	3,351	0.70
1,551	0.15	2,626	0.43	3,375	0.71
1,602	0.16	2,656	0.44	3,398	0.72
1,651	0.17	2,687	0.45	3,422	0.73
1,699	0.18	2,716	0.46	3,445	0.74
1,746	0.19	2,746	0.47	3,468	0.75
1,791	0.20	2,775	0.48	3,491	0.76
1,835	0.21	2,804	0.49	3,514	0.77
1,879	0.22	2,832	0.50	3,537	0.78
1,921	0.23	2,860	0.51	3,560	0.79
1,962	0.24	2,888	0.52	3,582	0.80
2,003	0.25	2,916	0.53	3,604	0.81
2,042	0.26	2,943	0.54	3,625	0.82
2,081	0.27	2,970	0.55	3,657	0.83
2,119	0.28	2,997	0.56	3,669	0.84
3,690	0.85	4,423	1.22	5,050	1.59
3,709	0.86	4,442	1.23	5,066	1.60
3,729	0.87	4,460	1.24	5,082	1.61
3,758	0.88	4,478	1.25	5,098	1.62
3,779	0.89	4,495	1.26	5,114	1.63
3,800	0.90	4,513	1.27	5,129	1.64
3,821	0.91	4,531	1.28	5,144	1.65
3,842	0.92	4,549	1.29	5,160	1.66
3,863	0.93	4,566	1.30	5,175	1.67
3,884	0.94	4,583	1.31	5,191	1.68
3,904	0.95	4,601	1.32	5,206	1.69
3,924	0.96	4,619	1.33	5,222	1.70
3,945	0.97	4,636	1.34	5,237	1.71
3,965	0.98	4,653	1.35	5,253	1.72
3,985	0.99	4,671	1.36	5,268	1.73
4,005	1.00	4,688	1.37	5,283	1.74
4,025	1.01	4,705	1.38	5,298	1.75
4,045	1.02	4,722	1.39	5,313	1.76
4,064	1.03	4,739	1.40	5,328	1.77
4,084	1.04	4,756	1.41	5,343	1.78
4,103	1.05	4,773	1.42	5,359	1.79
4,123	1.06	4,790	1.43	5,374	1.80
4,142	1.07	4,806	1.44	5,388	1.81
4,162	1.08	4,823	1.45	5,403	1.82
4,181	1.09	4,840	1.46	5,418	1.83
4,200	1.10	4,856	1.47	5,433	1.84
4,219	1.11	4,873	1.48	5,447	1.85
4,238	1.12	4,889	1.49	5,462	1.86
4,257	1.13	4,905	1.50	5,477	1.87
4,276	1.14	4,921	1.51	5,491	1.88
4,295	1.15	4,938	1.52	5,506	1.89
4,314	1.16	4,954	1.53	5,521	1.90
4,332	1.17	4,970	1.54	5,535	1.91
4,350	1.18	4,986	1.55	5,550	1.92
4,368	1.19	5,002	1.56	5,564	1.93
4,386	1.20	5,018	1.57	5,579	1.94
4,405	1.21	5,034	1.58	5,593	1.95
5,608	1.96	6,113	2.33	8,496	4.50
5,623	1.97	6,128	2.34	8,590	4.60
5,637	1.98	6,140	2.35	8,683	4.70
5,651	1.99	6,153	2.36	8,774	4.80
5,664	2.00	6,166	2.37	8,865	4.90
5,678	2.01	6,179	2.38	8,955	5.00
5,692	2.02	6,192	2.39	9,044	5.10
5,706	2.03	6,205	2.40	9,133	5.20
5,720	2.04	6,217	2.41	9,220	5.30
5,734	2.05	6,230	2.42	9,307	5.40
5,748	2.06	6,243	2.43	9,392	5.50
5,762	2.07	6,256	2.44	9,477	5.60
5,776	2.08	6,269	2.45	9,562	5.70
5,790	2.09	6,282	2.46	9,645	5.80
5,804	2.10	6,294	2.47	9,728	5.90
5,817	2.11	6,307	2.48	9,810	6.00
5,831	2.12	6,320	2.49	9,891	6.10
5,845	2.13	6,332	2.50	9,972	6.20
5,859	2.14	6,458	2.60	10,052	6.30
5,872	2.15	6,581	2.70	10,132	6.40
5,886	2.16	6,702	2.80	10,210	6.50
5,889	2.17	6,820	2.90	10,289	6.60
5,913	2.18	6,937	3.00	10,366	6.70
5,927	2.19	7,051	3.10	10,444	6.80
5,940	2.20	7,164	3.20	10,520	6.90
5,954	2.21	7,275	3.30	10,596	7.00
5,967	2.22	7,385	3.40	10,968	7.50
5,981	2.23	7,492	3.50	11,328	8.00
5,994	2.24	7,599	3.60	11,676	8.50
6,008	2.25	7,704	3.70	12,015	9.00
6,021	2.26	7,807	3.80	12,344	9.50
6,034	2.27	7,909	3.90	12,665	10.00
6,047	2.28	8,010	4.00	13,283	11.00
6,061	2.29	8,109	4.10	13,874	12.00
6,074	2.30	8,208	4.20	14,440	13.00
6,087	2.31	8,305	4.30	14,775	13.61
6,100	2.32	8,401	4.40	14,986	14.00

Dry air at 70°F and 29.92" barometer.

From $V = 4,005 \sqrt{VP}$

V = Velocity fpm

$\sqrt{VP}$ = Velocity pressure, inches of water

VISCOSITY EQUIVALENTS

VISCOSITY SCALES OR UNITS

Gardner Holdt	Barbey	Engler Time	Engler Degrees	Redwood Admiralty	Redwood No.1 Seconds	Saybolt Furol Seconds	Saybolt Universal Seconds (S.U.S.)	Poises at S.G. 1.0	Centistokes
	2800	60	1.18		32		35	.026	2.6
	880	82	1.60		44		50	.074	7.4
	460	120	2.30		65		75	.141	14.1
	320	153	3.00		88	15	100	.202	20.2
	205	230	4.40		128	19	150	.318	31.8
A	148	305	5.90	18	170	23	200	.431	43.1
B	118	375	7.60	23	212	28	250	.543	54.3
B	98	450	8.90	27	254	33	300	.651	65.1
C	72	550	11.8	36	338	42	4000	.876	87.6
D	59	750	14.5	45	423	52	500	1.10	110
E	48	900	17.5	53	518	61	600	1.32	132
F	41	1050	20.6	62	592	71	700	1.54	154
G	36.5	1200	23.0	71	677	81	800	1.76	176
H	32.0	1300	27.0	78	762	91	900	1.98	198
J	29.5	1500	29.0	87	846	1000	1000	2.20	220
M	19.5	2300	42.0	135	1270	150	1500	3.30	330
P	14.5	3000	59.0	175	1695	200	2000	4.40	400
S	11.5	3750	73.0	230	2120	250	2500	5.50	550
U	9.6	4500	87.0	260	2540	300	3000	6.60	660
V	7.4	6000	117	350	3380	400	4000	8.80	880

Label									
W	6.0	7500	145	435	4230	500	5000	11.0	1100
X	5.2	9000	175	530	5080	600	6000	13.2	1320
Y	4.1	10500	205	610	5925	700	7000	15.4	1540
	3.7	12000	230	700	6770	800	8000	17.6	1760
	3.2	13500	260	780	7620	900	9000	19.8	1980
Z-1	2.9	15000	290	870	8460	1000	10000	22.0	2200
Z-3	1.4	30000	590	1760	16920	2000	2000	44.0	4400
Z-5		60000	1170	3600	33850	4000	40000	88.0	8800
Z-6		90000	1750	5300	50800	6000	60000	132.0	13200
Z-6		120000	2300	7000	67700	8000	80000	176.0	17600
		150000	2900	8700	84600	10000	100000	220.0	22000
		300000	5900	17600	169200	20000	200000	440.0	44000
		600000	11700	36000	338500	40000	400000	880.0	88000
		900000	17500	53000	508000	60000	600000	1320	132000
		1200000	23000	70000	677000	80000	800000	1760	176000
		1500000	29000	87000	846000	100000	1000000	2200	220000

PRESSURE CONVERSION FACTORS (LOW PRESSURES)

Atmospheres	Pounds per sq in (lb/in^2)	Ounces per sq in (oz/m^2)	Inches Mercury	Inches Water	Feet Water	Millimetres Mercury	Kilograms per sq cm (kg/cm^2)
1	14.697	235.15	29.921	406.8	33.91	760	1.033
0.068	1	16	2.036	27.68	2.306	51.712	0.070
0.00425	0.0625	1	0.127	1.73	0.144	3.232	0.0044
0.0334	0.491	7.859	1	13.596	1.133	25.40	0.0345
0.00246	0.0361	0.578	0.0735	1	0.083	1.868	0.0025
0.0295	0.433	0.937	0.883	12	1	22.418	0.0305
0.00132	0.0193	0.309	0.0394	0.535	0.044	1	0.0013
0.968	14.223	227.57	28.96	393.7	32.81	735.51	1

PRESSURE CONVERSION FACTORS (HIGH PRESSURE)

lbs/sq ft	lbs/sq in	tons/sq in	tons/sq ft	kilograms/sq cm	kilograms/sq metre
1	0.0069			0.000488	4.882
144	1			0.0703	703.1
2048.21	14.223			1	10 000
0.205	0.00142			0.0001	1
322.260	2240	1	144	157.488	1574880
2240	15.5556	0.0069444	1	1.09366	19036.6

DENSITY AND VISCOSITY OF AIR AT ATMOSPHERIC PRESSURES

Temperature		Specific Weight	Mass Density	Viscosity
°C	°F	lb/cu.ft.	slugs/cu.ft.	Centipoise
-20	-4	0.0873	0.00272	0.01607
-10	14	0.0838	0.00261	0.01658
0	32	0.0807	0.00251	0.01709
10	50	0.0779	0.00242	0.01759
15	59	0.0765	0.00238	0.01783
20	68	0.0753	0.00234	0.01808
30	86	0.0728	0.00226	0.01856
40	104	0.0704	0.00219	0.01904
50	122	0.0682	0.00212	0.01950
60	140	0.0661	0.00205	0.02000

DENSITY AND VISCOSITY OF WATER AT ATMOSPHERIC PRESSURES

Temperature		Absolute Viscosity		Kinematic Viscosity	
°C	°F	Centipoise	slug/ft.sec.	ft.^{2}/sec.	in.^{2}/sec.
0	37	1.793	.0000375	.00001931	.00278
5	41	1.522	—	—	—
10	50	1.309	.0000274	.00001412	.00203
15	59	1.142	—	—	—
20	68	1.008	.0000211	.00001089	.00157
25	77	.893	—	—	—
30	86	.800	.00001675	.000008681	.00125
40	104	.653	.00001368	.000007105	.001025
50	122	.549	.00001150	.000005995	.000864
60	140	.469	.00000950	.000005142	.00074
70	158	.407	.00000850	.000004484	.000645
80	176	.357	.00000747	.000003968	.000572
90	194	.316	.00000661	.000003534	.000508
100	212	.284	.00000592	.000003185	.000458

AREAS OF CIRCLES

Dia.	0.0	0.1	0.2	0.3	0.4	0.5	0.6	0.7	0.8	0.9	Dia.
0	—	·0078	·0314	·0706	·1257	·1963	·2827	·3848	·5026	·6361	0
1	·7854	·9503	1·1309	1·3273	1·5393	1·7671	2·0106	2·2698	2·5446	2·8352	1
2	3·1416	3·4636	3·8013	4·1547	4·5239	4·9087	5·3093	5·7255	6·1575	6·6052	2
3	7·0686	7·5476	8·0424	8·5530	9·0792	9·6211	10·1787	10·752	11·341	11·946	3
4	12·566	13·203	13·854	14·522	15·2053	15·904	16·6190	17·349	18·095	18·857	4
5	19·635	20·428	21·237	22·062	22·902	23·758	24·630	25·518	26·421	27·340	5
6	28·274	29·225	30·191	31·173	32·170	33·183	34·212	35·257	36·317	37·393	6
7	38·484	39·592	40·715	41·854	43·009	44·179	45·365	46·566	47·784	49·017	7
8	50·266	51·530	52·810	54·106	55·418	56·745	58·088	59·447	60·821	62·212	8
9	63·617	65·039	66·476	67·929	69·398	70·882	72·382	73·898	75·430	76·977	9
10	78·540	80·119	81·713	83·323	84·949	86·590	88·248	89·920	91·609	93·313	10
11	95·033	96·769	98·521	100·29	102·07	103·87	105·68	107·51	109·36	111·22	11
12	113·097	114·99	116·90	118·82	120·76	122·72	124·69	126·68	128·68	130·70	12
13	132·73	134·78	136·85	138·93	141·03	143·14	145·27	147·41	149·57	151·75	13
14	153·94	156·15	158·37	160·61	162·86	165·13	167·42	169·72	172·03	174·37	14
15	176·72	179·08	181·46	183·84	186·27	188·69	191·13	193·59	196·07	198·56	15
16	201·06	203·58	206·12	208·67	211·24	213·83	216·42	219·04	221·67	224·32	16
17	226·98	229·66	232·35	235·06	237·79	240·53	243·29	246·06	248·85	251·65	17
18	254·47	257·30	260·16	263·02	265·91	268·80	271·72	274·65	277·59	280·55	18
19	283·53	286·52	289·53	292·55	295·59	298·65	301·72	304·81	307·91	311·03	19
20	314·16	317·31	320·47	323·66	326·85	330·06	333·29	336·54	339·80	343·07	20
21	346·36	349·67	352·99	356·33	359·68	363·05	366·44	369·84	373·25	376·69	21
22	380·13	383·60	387·08	390·57	394·08	397·61	401·15	404·71	408·28	411·87	22
23	415·48	419·10	422·73	426·39	430·05	433·74	437·44	441·15	444·88	448·63	23
24	452·39	456·17	459·96	463·77	467·60	471·44	475·29	479·16	483·05	486·96	24
25	490·87	494·81	498·76	502·73	506·71	510·71	514·72	518·75	522·79	526·85	25
26	530·93	535·02	539·13	543·25	547·39	551·55	555·72	559·90	564·11	568·32	26
27	572·56	576·81	581·07	585·35	589·65	593·96	598·29	602·93	606·99	611·36	27
28	615·75	620·16	624·58	629·02	633·47	637·94	642·43	646·93	651·44	655·97	28
29	660·52	665·08	669·66	674·26	678·87	683·49	688·14	692·79	697·47	702·16	29
30	706·86	711·58	716·32	721·07	725·84	730·62	735·42	740·23	745·06	749·91	30
31	754·77	759·65	764·54	769·45	774·37	779·31	784·27	789·24	794·23	799·23	31
32	804·25	809·28	814·33	819·40	824·48	829·58	834·69	839·82	844·96	850·12	32
33	855·30	860·49	865·70	870·92	876·16	881·42	886·69	891·97	897·27	902·589	33
34	907·92	913·27	918·64	924·01	929·41	934·82	940·25	945·69	951·15	956·625	34
35	962·11	967·62	973·14	978·68	984·23	989·80	995·38	1,001·0	1,006·6	1,012·2	35
36	1,017·9	1,023·5	1,029·2	1,034·9	1,040·6	1,046·4	1,052·1	1,057·8	1,063·6	1,069·4	36
37	1,075·2	1,081·0	1,086·9	1,092·7	1,098·6	1,104·5	1,110·4	1,116·3	1,122·2	1,128·2	37
38	1,134·1	1,140·1	1,146·1	1,152·1	1,158·1	1,164·2	1,170·2	1,176·3	1,182·4	1,188·5	38
39	1,194·6	1,200·7	1,206·9	1,213·0	1,219·2	1,225·4	1,231·6	1,237·9	1,244·1	1,250·4	39
40	1,256·6	1,262·9	1,269·2	1,275·6	1,281·3	1,288·3	1,294·6	1,301·0	1,307·4	1,313·8	40
41	1,320·3	1,326·7	1,333·2	1,339·6	1,346·1	1,352·7	1,359·2	1,365·7	1,372·3	1,378·9	41
42	1,385·5	1,392·1	1,398·7	1,405·3	1,412·0	1,418·6	1,425·3	1,432·0	1,443·8	1,445·5	42
43	1,452·2	1,459·0	1,465·7	1,472·5	1,479·3	1,486·2	1,493·0	1,499·9	1,506·7	1,513·6	43
44	1,520·5	1,527·5	1,534·4	1,541·3	1,548·3	1,555·3	1,562·3	1,569·3	1,576·3	1,583·4	44
45	1,590·4	1,597·5	1,604·6	1,611·7	1,618·8	1,625·0	1,633·1	1,640·3	1,647·5	1,654·7	45
46	1,661·9	1,671·0	1,676·4	1,683·7	1,690·9	1,698·2	1,705·5	1,712·9	1,720·2	1,727·6	46
47	1,735·0	1,744·2	1,749·7	1,757·2	1,764·6	1,772·1	1,779·5	1,787·0	1,794·5	1,802·0	47
48	1,809·6	1,819·0	1,824·7	1,832·3	1,839·8	1,847·5	1,855·1	1,862·7	1,870·4	1,878·1	48
49	1,885·8	1,895·4	1,901·2	1,908·9	1,916·7	1,924·4	1,932·2	1,940·0	1,947·8	1,955·7	49
50	1,963·5	1,973·3	1,979·2	1,987·1	1,995·0	2,003·0	2,010·9	2,018·9	2,026·8	2,034·8	50

GUIDELINES FOR HYDRAULIC FILTER SELECTION (Sperry-Vickers Ltd)

ASSESSMENT AND CLASSIFICATION OF SYSTEM CLEANLINESS LEVEL INTO SEVEN GRADES

Environmental Conditions			Degree of Control
Good	Average	Bad	
3	6	7	Little or no control over contamination ingestion (many exposed cylinders).
2	4	5	Some control over contamination ingestion (few cylinders).
1	2	3	Good control over contamination ingestion (gaitered cylinders).

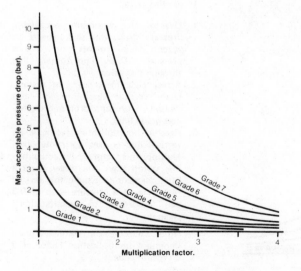

Pressure line filter selection guide

To use this graph:

1. Decide on maximum acceptable pressure drop, this will depend on system requirements or bypass pressure. Draw horizontal line through this value.
2. Assess cleanliness grade in system. Draw vertical line through intersection of pressure drop and cleanliness grade line.
3. Read off multiplication factor where vertical line crosses horizontal axis. Multiply this factor by the actual flow rate at chosen pressure line location. Now select a filter element to handle this revised flow rate at a pressure drop of 1 bar (according to manufacturer's clean rating).

Actual flow x multiplication factor = recommended filter capacity.

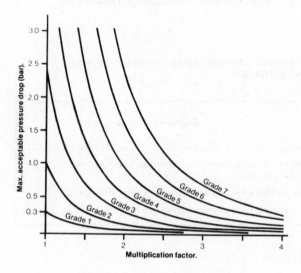

Return line filter selection guide

To use this graph:

1. Decide on maximum acceptable pressure drop, this will depend on system requirements or bypass pressure. Draw horizontal line through this value.
2. Assess cleanliness grade in system. Draw vertical line through intersection of pressure drop and cleanliness grade lines.
3. Read off multiplication factor where vertical line crosses horizontal axis. Multiply this factor by the actual flow rate at chosen return line location. Now select a filter element to handle this revised flow rate at a pressure drop of 0.3 bar (according to manufacturer's clean rating).

Actual flow x multiplication factor = recommended filter capacity.

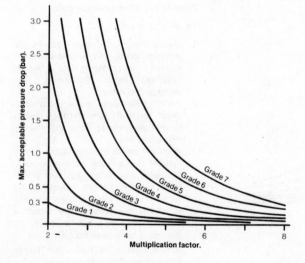

Offline filter selection guide

To use this graph:

1. Decide on maximum acceptable pressure drop, this will depend on system requirements or bypass pressure. Draw horizontal line through this value.
2. Assess cleanliness grade in system. Draw vertical line through intersection of pressure drop and cleanliness grade lines.
3. Read off multiplication factor where vertical line crosses horizontal axis. Multiply this factor by the actual offline pump flow rate. Now select a filter element to handle this revised flow rate at a pressure drop of 0.3 bar (according to manufacturer's clean rating).

Note: To achieve a reasonable life a minimum multiplication factor of 2 is recommended.

Actual flow x multiplication factor = recommended filter capacity.

INDEX

Index